HIDDEN®

Montana

D1435210

HIDDEN ®

Montana

John Gottberg Anderson

Ulysses Press ®
BERKELEY, CALIFORNIA

Published by:
ULYSSES PRESS
P.O. Box 3440
Berkeley, CA 94703-3440

Library of Congress Catalog Card Number 96-60709

ISBN 1-56975-065-3

Printed in Canada by Best Book Manufacturers

10 9 8 7 6 5 4 3 2 1

EDITORIAL DIRECTOR: Leslie Henriques
MANAGING EDITOR: Claire Chun
COPY EDITOR: James Donnelley
EDITORIAL ASSOCIATES: Deema Khorsheed, Nicole O'Hay,
    Aaron Newey, Lily Chou, Kenya Ratcliff
TYPESETTER: David Wells
CARTOGRAPHY: XNR Productions, Madison, WI
    Yellowstone map by Stellar Cartography, Lawrence, KS
COVER DESIGN: Sarah Levin
INDEXER: Sayre Van Young
COVER PHOTOGRAPHY: Front: Larry Ulrich
    Circle and back: Larry Ulrich
    Back: Dewitt Jones
ILLUSTRATOR: Doug McCarthy

Distributed in the United States by Publishers
Group West, in Canada by Raincoast Books,
and in Great Britain and Europe by World
Leisure Marketing

What's Hidden?

At different points throughout this book, you'll find special listings marked with a hidden symbol:

◀ HIDDEN

This means that you have come upon a place off the beaten tourist track, a spot that will carry you a step closer to the local people and natural environment of Montana.

The goal of this guide is to lead you beyond the realm of everyday tourist facilities. While we include traditional sightseeing listings and popular attractions, we also offer alternative sights and adventure activities. Instead of filling this guide with reviews of standard hotels and chain restaurants, we concentrate on one-of-a-kind places and locally owned establishments.

Our authors seek out locales that are popular with residents but usually overlooked by visitors. Some are more hidden than others (and are marked accordingly), but all the listings in this book are intended to help you discover the true nature of Montana and put you on the path of adventure.

Write to us!

If in your travels you discover a spot that captures the spirit of Montana, or if you live in the region and have a favorite place to share, or if you just feel like expressing your views, write to us and we'll pass your note along to the author.

We can't guarantee that the author will add your personal find to the next edition, but if the writer does use the suggestion, we'll acknowledge you in the credits and send you a free autographed copy of the new edition.

ULYSSES PRESS
3286 Adeline Street, Suite 1
Berkeley, CA 94703
E-mail: ulypress@aol.com

Contents

1 EXPLORING MONTANA   1

The Story of Montana   4
Geology   4
History   5
Flora   13
Fauna   14
Where to Go   16
When to Go   18
Seasons   18
Calendar of Events   20
Before You Go   27
Visitors Centers   27
Packing   28
Lodging   29
Dining   30
Driving   31
Traveling with Children   32
Traveling with Pets   33
Women Traveling Alone   33
Gay & Lesbian Travelers   33
Senior Travelers   34
Disabled Travelers   34
Foreign Travelers   35
Outdoor Adventures   36
Camping   36
Boating & Rafting   38
Fishing   39
Winter Sports   40
Guides & Outfitters   40

2 NORTHWEST MONTANA   41

Missoula   42
Bitterroot Valley   51
Flathead Indian Reservation & Lake   57
The Flathead Valley   66
The Northwest Corner   71
Thompson Falls Area   74
Outdoor Adventures   75
Transportation   82

3 GLACIER NATIONAL PARK — **84**

Western Gateways — 85
Glacier National Park — 89
Eastern Gateways — 93
Waterton Lakes National Park — 95
Outdoor Adventures — 97
Transportation — 103

4 NORTH CENTRAL MONTANA — **105**

Great Falls — 106
The Rocky Mountain Front — 113
The Western Hi-Line — 116
Fort Benton Area — 119
Kings Hill — 121
Outdoor Adventures — 123
Transportation — 127

5 SOUTHWEST MONTANA — **129**

Helena Area — 130
Pintler Scenic Route — 140
Butte — 145
Big Hole Valley — 153
Dillon & the Red Rock River Valley — 156
Alder Gulch — 160
Outdoor Adventures — 163
Transportation — 168

6 SOUTH CENTRAL MONTANA — **169**

Bozeman Area — 170
Three Forks Area — 179
West Yellowstone Area — 183
Livingston Area — 186
Big Timber Area — 192
Red Lodge Area — 194
Outdoor Adventures — 199
Transportation — 205

7 YELLOWSTONE NATIONAL PARK — **207**

Outdoor Adventures — 224
Transportation — 230

8 **SOUTHEAST MONTANA**   **232**

Billings Area   233
The Big Horns and Beyond   245
Lower Yellowstone Valley   251
Outdoor Adventures   257
Transportation   259

9 **NORTHEAST MONTANA**   **261**

The Hi-Line   262
The Heartland   267
Outdoor Adventures   272
Transportation   274

Index   276
Lodging Index   285
Dining Index   287
About the Author   292

Maps

Montana	3
Northwest Montana	43
Glacier National Park	87
North Central Montana	107
Southwest Montana	131
Helena	135
Butte	147
South Central Montana	171
Bozeman	175
Yellowstone National Park	209
Southeast Montana	235
Billings	239
Northeast Montana	263

OUTDOOR ADVENTURE SYMBOLS

The following symbols accompany national, state and regional park listings, as well as beach descriptions throughout the text.

▲	Camping			Waterskiing
	Hiking			Windsurfing
	Biking			Canoeing or Kayaking
	Horseback Riding			Boating
	Swimming			Boat Ramps
	Snorkeling or Scuba Diving			Fishing
	Surfing			

ONE

Exploring Montana

Montana is known as "Big Sky" country, and that label is no accident. From the vast prairies that swathe the eastern half of this fourth-largest of the United States, one's view of the heavens seems endless. The handful of rural individualists and urban refugees who make their home here, where the Rocky Mountains flow into Canada, would argue that heaven is everywhere in Montana.

Two of America's greatest national parks frame Montana. On the state's northern edge are the spectacularly chiseled peaks of Glacier National Park, the roof of the Rockies: Glacier's watershed flows in not two but three directions, to the Pacific Ocean, the Gulf of Mexico and Hudson Bay. On Montana's southern border with Wyoming lies the thermal wonderland of Yellowstone National Park, whose geysers and hot springs, canyons and waterfalls, and rich and varied wildlife led most Americans to consider it a myth until little more than a century ago.

In the state's far west, stands of huge and ancient firs and cedars dominate the landscape. The Continental Divide follows the Rocky Mountain backbone in a southeasterly direction from Glacier to Yellowstone, dividing Montana into two unequal halves. Two great rivers, the Missouri and the Yellowstone, drain the eastern prairies where huge dinosaurs once roamed and where Crow, Cheyenne and Blackfeet Indians pursued the world's largest herds of American bison across the plains.

History is everywhere in Montana. The American Indian culture lives on in seven different Indian reservations and numerous state parks and historic sites. Among them is the Little Bighorn Battlefield National Monument; General George Armstrong Custer is popularly cited as having made his "last stand" here, when in fact the demise of Custer's cavalry was the last hurrah for Sioux and Cheyenne warriors in their struggle against white domination. The Meriwether Lewis and William Clark expedition is well chronicled; the explorers twice transited Montana, in 1805 and 1806, opening the way for subsequent settlement. Myriad 19th-century ghost towns still speckle the landscape, remnants of a boom-and-bust mining era when fortunes were made and lost in the same day and vigilante justice ruled many towns.

Montana's urban centers are few and far between. A scant 860,000 people live in this state of just over 147,000 square miles. Billings, Montana's largest city, has fewer than 100,000 residents. People come to Montana to get away from city life, not to find it. As a result, outdoor opportunities abound. Fishing and hunting are religions in the northern Rockies and upper Great Plains, and the less aggressively inclined will find wide-ranging opportunities for boating and whitewater rafting, hiking and horseback riding, skiing and bicycling. Montana is, indeed, a state for all seasons.

Hidden Montana is designed to help you take full advantage of your vacation. It covers popular, "must-see" places, offering advice on how best to enjoy them. It also tells you about many off-the-beaten-path spots, the kind you might find by talking with folks at the local café or with someone who has lived in the area all of his or her life. It describes the state's history, its natural areas and its residents, both human and animal. It suggests places to eat, to stay, to play, to camp. Taking into account varying interests, budgets and tastes, it provides the information you need whether your vacation style involves backpacking, golf, museum browsing, shopping or all of the above.

After providing introductory information, this book starts its statewide tour in Northwest Montana (Chapter Two) and adjacent Glacier National Park (Chapter Three). Straddling the Continental Divide on the Canadian border, Glacier is a vast region of chiseled peaks and broad valleys, of deep blue lakes and racing rivers. South and west of Glacier Park, waves of mountain ranges shelter the likes of enormous Flathead Lake; the National Bison Range, within the Flathead Indian Reservation; the city of Missoula, and the lovely Bitterroot Valley.

Chapter Four (North Central Montana) reaches east from the high Rockies into Charles M. Russell country. The life of this cowboy artist (1864–1926), who made his home in Great Falls, paralleled the emergence of the American West. Visitors search out the museum complex and enormous Missouri River wildlife refuge named in his honor, and visit the historic steamboat port of Fort Benton less than an hour's drive from either.

Chapters Five and Six visit southern Montana. Five delves into the rich gold-rush history of Southwest Montana. Some ghost towns, such as Bannack and Virginia City, survive as historical monuments. Other towns, like Butte, with its open-pit copper mines, and Helena, the state capital whose heart and soul is Last Chance Gulch, are unique combinations of past and present. Six reaches into South Central Montana's "Yellowstone Country," so named for its central river. Burgeoning Bozeman, with its Museum of the Rockies, is the heart of a region that includes historic Livingston and Red Lodge, outstanding ski resorts, the headwaters of the Missouri River and other attractions.

Chapter Seven zooms in on Yellowstone National Park. Although the world's first national park is almost entirely in Wyoming, three of its five gateways are in Montana, and it should be an integral part of any visitor experience here. The expansive park preserves thermal and geological wonders and a remarkable range of wildlife, and is renowned worldwide.

Chapters Eight and Nine cover eastern Montana, and the vast prairies that extend east from the crest of the Rockies. Eight focuses on Southeast Montana, a re-

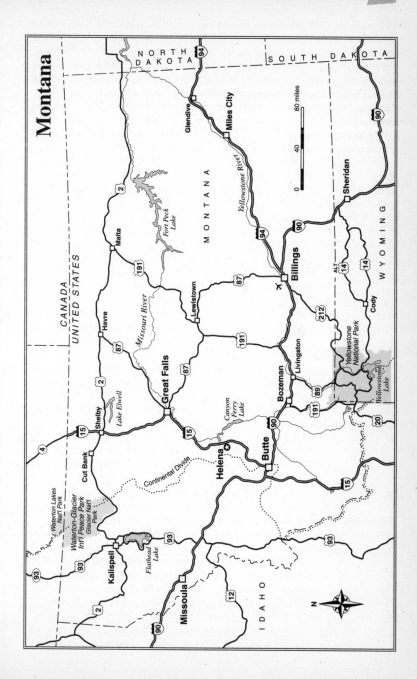

Montana

gion dominated by the lower Yellowstone River. It includes Bighorn Canyon National Recreation Area and Little Bighorn Battlefield National Monument, as well as the large range towns of Billings and Miles City. Nine explores often-overlooked Northeast Montana. Bisected by 134-mile-long Fort Peck Lake on the Missouri River, this region is noted for its history, its recreation, and its amber fields of grain rustling right to the Canadian border.

What you choose to see and do is up to you. One of the joys of exploring this state is its very isolation, and along with that, its decided lack of traffic congestion. Many Montana highways are so wide open that there is no formal daytime speed limit. For some visitors, that means you can scoot from attraction to attraction that much faster, so long as you drive in a "reasonable and prudent manner," as state law requires. For others, it means that while others may race past you like bats out of hell, you can relax and watch the scenery go past: mile after mile after mile of mountain, river and prairie.

▼▼▼▼▼▼▼▼▼▼▼▼▼▼▼▼
The Story of Montana

GEOLOGY

Montana was once a vast and shallow inland sea, its bedrock dating back two and a half billion years and longer. It was only about 100 million years ago, with the formation of the Rocky Mountains, that it began to take on the appearance we recognize today.

The modern Rockies consist mainly of granite, an igneous rock made up of quartz, feldspar and granite, along with traces and veins of metals such as gold, silver, lead and zinc. As molten elements, these minerals blended deep within the earth and welled upward, to the great sea plain and marshy wetlands on the surface.

Very slowly, the two tectonic plates that make up most of the North American continent—the Canadian Shield and the Pacific Plate—drifted toward each other, floating on the molten rock that still bubbled and brewed far under the earth's surface. In a slow collision, the plates crushed against each other and started to buckle and fold, pushing the granite layer upward. This process continues even now, though so slowly that the mountains have only gained a few inches in height during the time humankind has walked the earth.

Dinosaurs, which were abundant in the area when the formation of the Rockies began, would have experienced the buckling phenomenon as occasional earthquakes. Perhaps not coincidentally, the granite mass cracked through the sandstone surface at about the time of the great beasts' extinction, 60 million years ago.

As the north-south block of mountains tilted upward, the softer sedimentary rocks at the surface slid eastward, their waters draining ahead of them. On these often treeless plains, water and wind have been the principal geological forces, sometimes carving fantastic "badland" formations.

The Rocky Mountains as we see them today, however, were shaped by glaciers. A series of ice ages, the last of which ended

10,000 years ago—less than an eyeblink in geological time—covered the high country in accumulations of snow and ice. These glaciers flowed slowly down the mountainsides in solid frozen rivers that gouged deep valleys creating steep mountain faces and marking the courses for the turbulent rivers that would slice canyons hundreds of feet deep. Nowhere is this natural drama so evident as in Glacier National Park, which takes its name from the forces that carved its unforgettable face.

> The Yellowstone area weathers more earthquakes than anywhere in the lower 48 states outside of California.

The lofty mountains attract storm clouds like a magnet, making for rainfall and snowfall many times greater than in the semi-arid prairies to their east. Runoff, from the melting snowpack in spring and the thunderstorms of summer, gives birth to Montana's rivers: notably the great Missouri and Yellowstone, with their myriad forks and tributaries, in the east, but also the Flathead, Bitterroot, Clark Fork and other streams in the west.

The rivers give significance to the Continental Divide, the dotted line on maps that meanders through the wilderness connecting the highest mountain passes. All precipitation that falls east of the Continental Divide flows eventually to the Atlantic Ocean, via either the Gulf of Mexico or, nearer Glacier Park, via Canada's Hudson Bay. West of the Divide, it flows to the Pacific. In some places, the backbone of the continent is marked by nothing more spectacular than a point-of-interest sign at a roadside rest area. In others, as in Glacier Park, crossing the Continental Divide means climbing a switchback road up a wall of granite to the summit of a pass more than a mile above sea level.

Volcanism has had a profound effect in parts of Montana. The earth remains especially restless around the Yellowstone National Park area, which encompasses a giant ancient caldera. Hot springs, geysers, fumaroles and boiling mud appear here in greater concentration than anywhere else on earth. Hot springs throughout the Montana Rockies prove that volcanism remains an active force.

AMERICAN INDIANS American Indians touched the Montana Rockies lightly and with reverence. The Flatheads and Kootenais lived as nomads, huddling around fires in bison-leather tents through thousands of long, brutal winters along the foothills, waiting to follow the spring snowmelt into hidden canyons and ancient forests of the high country. Their population was never large, and these mountain tribes rarely came into conflict—in fact, they rarely encountered one another except on purpose. Intertribal powwows were held at traditional times and places for purposes of trade, social contests, spiritual ceremonies and political diplomacy.

HISTORY

Where warfare did occur, it was mainly among the Plains Indians tribes east of the mountains. The Blackfeet and Crow,

Text continued on page 8.

A Story of Glaciers

Perhaps the most striking features of Montana's varied landscape are the sheer-sided mountains, the deep lakes and the broad valleys typical of Glacier National Park and adjacent regions of the northern Rocky Mountains.

These are a direct result of glaciation during two million years of ice ages, the most recent of which retreated from Montana's high country barely 10,000 years ago. At its peak, this thick layer of snow and ice was several thousand feet deep.

Glaciers are formed under climactic conditions in which winter snowfall exceeds summer snowmelt over an extended period of time. Eventually, the intensive pressure of snow buildup on an alpine icefield causes underlying layers to compress into an almost plastic glacial ice: extremely hard, but able to flow like viscous water. This ice squeezes out between mountain peaks like toothpaste from a tube; gravity keeps the glacier grinding its way downhill at speeds that can reach several miles a day.

So powerful is this unremitting natural force that it acts as a giant conveyor belt. Montana's ancient glaciers flowed in "gelid" rivers, gouging deep valleys, scouring mountain faces, and establishing courses for turbulent rivers that today slice canyons hundreds of feet deep.

Geologists can measure a glacier's advance by the composition of its moraine: the rock, mud and other debris torn from mountain walls and deposited at the glacier's terminus. This marks the point at which the rate of melting equaled the rate of accumulation, and is a reliable indicator of climactic conditions at any particular time in history.

As conditions change, a glacier will advance or retreat; this is true of the 50-some small glaciers remaining in Glacier National Park today. In the century-plus since their discovery by white explorers, they have shrunken periodically, and their future is indeterminate.

The best known of these are Grinnell Glacier, a prominent landmark of the Many Glacier region and accessible by trail from the Many Glacier Lodge, and Jackson Glacier, which flows east off the Continental Divide at Gunsight Pass and is easily visible from the Logan Pass overlook.

Perhaps the most remarkable of the few glaciers still to be found in Montana is the Grasshopper Glacier, high on the Beartooth Plateau above Cooke City near the northeastern entrance to Yellowstone National Park. One of the largest icefields in the continental United States, the glacier takes its name from the millions of grasshoppers—of a now-extinct species—frozen in its sheer 80-foot ice cliff. A 14-mile wilderness trek is required to reach its base, and if winter snow hasn't sufficiently melted, you won't see the insects even then. August is your best bet.

Three or four other glaciers envelop the flanks of 12,799-foot Granite Peak (Montana's highest) and the surrounding Absaroka-Beartooth Wilderness Area, but serious Montana glacier seekers head north to Glacier Park.

Incidentally: when you look at a glacier, the deep blue you see comes from the great compression of glacial ice. It is especially visible in fractures and is intensified on cloudy days. The glacial ice crystals are so dense that they act as prisms, absorbing all colors of sunlight except the blue wavelength, which is reflected back.

Cheyenne and Dakota (Sioux) would send hunting parties into the rich high-country valleys of the mountain people. Before the arrival of the whites, intertribal battles bore little resemblance to the bloodbaths that would come. War parties were generally small and had no firearms, steel or horses. The limited supply of arrows a warrior could carry did not last long in battle, and it was better to save them for hunting if possible, since each handmade arrow represented hours of work.

At least two non-Indian influences—horses and guns—began to change the tribes' way of life long before the first white man set foot in what is now Montana at the beginning of the 19th century. Horses had first come into Indian hands in northern New Mexico in 1680, via the Spanish. By the 1750s, virtually every tribe in the Rockies and Great Plains had bought, captured or stolen enough horses to breed its own herd. Many others were driven off or escaped; these wild steeds spawned the herds of mustangs that even today inhabit remote areas of Montana. Horses let the Indians travel much farther and faster, bringing more frequent contact—friendly or hostile—between tribes.

Guns spread more slowly among American Indians. In the British and French settlements along America's east coast, armies of both colonial powers gave rifles to tribes that helped fight the Seven Years' War (1756–63). Guns meant power to conquer other tribes. Fur traders on what was then the American frontier found that the self-defense needs of the tribes made guns extremely valuable as items of exchange, as well as empowering the tribes to hunt more efficiently (and therefore to trade larger quantities of valuable furs for more guns). As a tribe got guns by trading with whites from the east, it often turned them against rival tribes to the west in order to expand its hunting territory. In this way, firearms often made their way westward ahead of the first white explorers.

The popular notion that all American Indians were infallible defenders of their environments is challenged by what next happened in the northern Great Plains. Utilizing different hunting methods that relied on guns and horses, the Plain tribes slaughtered tens of millions of bison in the four decades ending with the 1880s. This event, among others, resulted in extreme hardship for American Indian tribes who relied on buffalo meat and hides to support their culture.

EXPLORERS AND MOUNTAIN MEN   At the time of the first incursion into Montana by white men, the Indian culture was still strong. The region was a part of the vast Louisiana Purchase, acquired from Spain by France in 1800 and sold to the United States for $15 million in 1803. Some 150 wilderness-bound French trappers and traders penetrated the Rockies shortly thereafter, ignorant of the fact that the territory was now American. But that didn't matter much, since virtually all of these frontiersmen took Indian wives and never returned to civilization.

The first official U.S. foray into what is now Montana was the famous Lewis and Clark expedition. In the spring of 1805, 45 men led by Army Captain Meriwether Lewis and soldier William Clark made their way up the Missouri River and across Montana. They found willing guides in Shoshone interpreter Sacajawea and her French fur-trader husband, who led them all the way to the mouth of the Columbia River on the Pacific coast. In 1806, Lewis and Clark took separate routes back east across Montana, Lewis via the Missouri, Clark via the Yellowstone River, rejoining at the confluence of the two streams near what is now Montana's eastern border. The two leaders' published reports of their remarkable expedition opened the gates to generations of subsequent 19th-century exploration and settlement.

Not all of Lewis' and Clark's men returned home with them. In 1806, for instance, expedition member John Colter left the party to seek his fortune as a trapper and trader on the new frontier. He returned to St. Louis four years later with stories of boiling springs and smoke spewing from the earth: He was the first white man to see the strange landscape that would become Yellowstone National Park. Although most people dismissed Colter's tales as the product of an imagination gone mad in the wilderness, no one ignored the fact that he had also brought back a fortune in beaver pelts.

In 1811, less than a year after Colter's return from the wilderness, John Jacob Astor's American Fur Company sent its first expedition into the Rockies. As large international fur-trading companies established trading posts along the eastern edge of the Rockies, hundreds of freelance adventurers set off to probe deeper into the mountains in search of pelts. These "mountain men"—men like Jim Bridger, Jedediah Smith, David Jackson, Jeremiah "Liver Eatin'" Johnston and Thomas "Broken Hand" Fitzpatrick—explored virtually every valley in the Rockies during the next 30 years, bringing back more than half a million beaver pelts each year. In order to kill animals in such phenomenal numbers, the mountain men not only set their own traps but also traded gunpowder and bullets to the Indians for more furs. By the 1840s, beavers had become nearly extinct in the Rockies. The last of the old-time fur trappers became guides for army expeditions and pioneer wagon trains, or established their own trading posts, where they continued to sell ammunition to the tribes—a practice that soon would become controversial, then illegal.

PIONEERS AND PROSPECTORS   The first wagon train crossed the Continental Divide in 1842. It was made up of 100 frontier families, traveling in Conestoga wagons with a herd of cattle, bound for Oregon. The route they took, which came to be known as the

Oregon Trail, would be used by just about all pioneers en route to the western territories for the next 27 years. But the trail through future Wyoming and Idaho bypassed Montana.

Montana grew around mining booms, cattle ranching and a transcontinental railroad. Only one of the trappers' early trading posts had become a permanent town. Fort Benton, established in 1846, was an important Missouri River port: It was the head of navigation for steamboats from St. Louis for many decades, and was the prime shipping port in Montana until the advent of the railroad.

The first permanent white settlement in Montana was a Jesuit mission established by Belgian Father Pierre-Jean de Smet in the Bitterroot Valley in 1841. Other missions soon followed. But the riches of the earth did far more to attract settlers than did riches from heaven.

Rich placer gold strikes at Bannack in 1862, Virginia City in 1863 and Last Chance Gulch in 1864 led to the creation of the Montana Territory, with its capital (after 1875) at Helena, a small city that grew up around the third gold strike. The first two communities were briefly territorial capitals, but lawlessness made them bad choices. When Henry Plummer, the sheriff of Bannack, was found to be the secret leader of a band of highway robbers and murderers preying on unprotected miners, a vigilante committee took matters into its own hands. Plummer and his gang were hunted down, and the sheriff was hanged. (Today Bannack's population of 3000 has dwindled to about three—it is now a state park—while Virginia City has found new gold in tourism dollars.)

When the sheriff of Bannack was found to be the secret leader of a band of highway robbers, he was hunted down and hanged on the gallows he had built himself.

The Northern Pacific Railroad provided Montana with its first direct rail link with east (Minneapolis) and west (Portland, Oregon) upon its completion in 1883. Cities like Billings, Livingston and Missoula owe their existence to the railroad: Each began as a construction camp before developing into a regional center.

The grasslands of central and eastern Montana were ideal for cattle ranching. With the depletion of the native bison herds to feed railroad crews, boundless grazing land was left empty. The first cattle herds were being driven overland from Texas as early as 1866, but it was the new transportation network that really made Montana's cattle industry economically feasible. Beginning in the mid 1870s, vast ranches that measured in the millions of acres were established in eastern and central Montana under absentee, often British, ownership. These ranches thrived, employing thousands of cowboys and earning their owners bigger profits, in many cases, than the gold and silver mines had ever yielded. (The Grant-Kohrs

Ranch National Historic Site, near Deer Lodge, is testimony to this era.) On some of these ranches, cattle numbered in the millions—on paper, at least. The unfenced rangeland was so big that to actually count all the cattle, let alone round them up and brand them, was impossible.

The demand for more land for railroads, ranches and mines led to conflict between the settlers and the Indians, who fought to protect their traditional hunting grounds. They won a few battles, but inevitably, they lost the war. The last major Sioux and Cheyenne victory was at the Battle of the Little Bighorn in June 1876, when 260 U.S. cavalrymen under the command of General George Armstrong Custer were annihilated. (The site is today a national monument.) The following year, Nez Percé rebel Chief Joseph and his followers, fleeing toward Canada from Oregon and Idaho, were captured a few miles south of the international border. Nez Percé National Historical Park commemorates their flight.

THE DECLINE OF THE OLD WEST   When statehood was granted to Montana in 1889, the frontier already was changing more rapidly than anyone could have predicted. The beginning of the end came with the brutal winter of 1887, when a single blizzard heaped snow higher than the cattle's heads and was followed by weeks of record cold temperatures. When the spring thaw came, few cattle could be found alive: Most had frozen or starved. Some ranch owners lost 90 percent of their herds and went bankrupt, turning their backs on the former ranches.

Newcomers rushed in to seize pieces of the abandoned land. Many started more modest cattle ranches. Others raised sheep—which ruined the rangeland for cattle. Still others, known as "grangers," started dry-land agricultural farms and were hated by both types of ranchers because they fenced open rangeland and built roads. Legal title to land that had been part of bankrupt ranches was vague at best, so violent clashes—known as "range wars"—erupted among cowboys, sheepmen and grangers. The chaos was made worse when some cowboys from the early ranches turned to crime after losing their jobs, forming outlaw bands that lived by armed robbery. Rampant lawlessness continued into the early years of the 20th century. Eventually, when landholders had occupied their ranches and farms long enough to file for legal title under the law of adverse possession, the violence ebbed.

Most mining districts of the Rockies continued to flourish until 1893, when the U.S. Congress ended silver subsidies, bringing about a collapse in the market. The gold-mining industry prospered until 1933, when a similar change in federal law ruined the market. World demand for copper, however, increased. Immense ore deposits at Butte, which came to be known as "the richest hill on earth," created a city of 100,000 people at the turn of the 20th century. Here, too, lawlessness and corruption prevailed as three fabulously wealthy "copper kings"—William A. Clark, Marcus Daly and Frederick A. Heinze—fought for control of the mines and state government. Today Butte's population is only about 33,000, but its open-pit mines remain productive and the town is a living museum of mining prosperity.

MODERN TIMES　Yellowstone became the world's first national park in 1872; the rail junction of Livingston, Montana, founded in 1882, became its first real gateway. Tourists changed here from the main east-west line to a spur line up the Yellowstone River to Gardiner, near Mammoth Hot Springs. This remained the best way into Yellowstone until the 1920s, when many Americans owned automobiles and the first main highways were paved. Ever since, tourism has been central to the Montana economy and has increased steadily.

The homesteading era of 1910–1925 brought thousands of new settlers to Montana, as a new wave of immigrants claimed 320-acre Great Plains farms. Unfortunately, they were not well trained in methods of productively farming semi-arid terrain. At first, the grain-growing land of the north and east produced bumper crops of wheat, but a cycle of drought years that began about 1920 led to bank closures, mortgage foreclosures and general economic disaster. When the Great Depression struck in 1929, Montana had a long head start. Soon the mines and lumber mills were closing as well.

President Franklin Roosevelt's New Deal and other Depression-era programs tied to irrigation and soil conservation helped boost Montana out of the hole. Most important was the construction of the Fort Peck Dam on the Missouri River. Completed in 1940, the dam created a 134-mile-long reservoir that not only helps farms, but also has a major hydroelectric and recreational function. With Fort Peck's boost, Montana agricultural and mining sectors returned to their previous era of productivity.

In the late 20th century, Montana has become a key national producer of petroleum and natural gas. The Kevin-Sunburst Field on the Canadian border near Shelby, the Williston Basin Field on the North Dakota border near Sidney, and the Belle Creek Field near Broadus, in the southeast, are all rich in fossil fuels.

Montana was in the national spotlight in 1996 because of a federal standoff with a right-wing group known as the Freemen, whose enclave is near Jordan. The village in east-central Montana was once called "the lonesomest town in the world" by a New York radio station, but it could hardly be called lonesome now that national media have descended upon it like locusts. The Freemen are one of several groups of extremists who, like other refugees from big-city environments, have found isolation in Montana and Idaho.

Altitude and rainfall are the primary factors when it comes to plant life in Montana. In the arid prairies that blanket the eastern part of the state (except in the major river valleys that draw their water from the mountains to the west) irrigation is essential. The closer the land is to the base of the Rocky Mountains, the drier it is, with natural vegetation that consists mainly of thin layers of grass. This is because the Rockies cast a rain shadow. As weather patterns move from west to east, clouds dump most of their rain or snow on the high, cool mountains, leaving little moisture to fall on the prairies.

The foothills along the eastern edge of the Rockies are even drier than the prairies, since they are not only in the rain shadow but also are steep enough that whatever rain does fall quickly spills away. The foothills are just high enough, however, that cooler temperatures let snow melt more slowly, seeping into the top layer of earth to sustain scrub trees like juniper and numerous flowering shrubs.

The arid prairies blanketing the eastern part of the state are so sparse that it takes 25 to 40 acres to graze a single cow.

Mountain forests change with elevation, forming three distinct bands. On the lower slopes of the mountains, ponderosa pine stand 50 feet tall and more. Spirelike Douglas fir and spruce dominate the higher reaches of the mountains. Between the two bands of evergreen forest, shimmering stands of aspen trees fill the eastern mountainsides and paint them bright yellow in September. On the wetter western slopes, lodgepole pine forests are more frequently found in this transitional zone. Both the aspen and lodgepole pine are what forestry experts call opportunistic species. Stands grow wherever clearings appear in the evergreen woods, because of forest fires, clearcutting or pine beetle infestations. Gradually, over a span of centuries, the taller evergreens will crowd out old aspen and lodgepole stands as new stands appear elsewhere. The distinctive aspen, in particular, is a delicate tree that cannot tolerate high- or low-altitude extremes.

The upper boundary of the deep-green conifer forests is known as timberline, the elevation above which nighttime temperatures drop below freezing year-round and trees cannot grow. Timberline is around 8500 feet in Yellowstone National Park on the southern Montana border, 6000 feet in Glacier National Park on the state's northern border. Above timberline lies the alpine tundra, a delicate world of short grasses and other green plants rooted in permafrost where tiny flowers appear for brief periods each summer.

At the highest elevations, above 10,000 feet, summer freezing prevents even the small plants of the tundra from growing. Clinging to the granite cliffs and boulders grows lichen, a symbiotic combination of two plants that survive in partnership: A type of moss forms a leathery shell that protects an alga, which in turn provides nutrients by photosynthesis to feed the moss. This ingenious arrangement is perhaps the ultimate tribute to life's amazing capacity for adapting to even the harshest environments.

FAUNA   An abundance of wildlife is one of Montana's greatest attractions. You are most likely to get a good look at large animals in Yellowstone and Glacier parks, where long-standing prohibitions against hunting have helped them lose their fear of humans. The wildlife populations are about the same in national forests and wilderness areas, but sightings are much less common because animals generally keep their distance from roads, trails, and human scent.

The eastern foothills and high plains are a favorite habitat of jackrabbits and prairie dogs, coyotes and pronghorn antelope, as well as prairie birds such as hawks, grouse and pheasants.

As the number of coyotes in an area declines, the number of coyote pups born in a litter increases; so although states have paid hundreds of thousands of dollars every year for nearly a century to eliminate these wild canines because ranchers believe they may pose a threat to livestock, coyote populations are on the increase just about everywhere in the west. They are commonly seen not only in open grasslands, but also on the outskirts of urban areas. Intelligent and curious, coyotes can often be spotted observing humans from a distance. They are not generally dangerous to humans, though they may lure and attack small pets.

Pronghorn antelope, once hunted nearly to extinction and until recently listed as a threatened species under the federal Endangered Species Act, are again a common sight on the high plains. They are most common in Montana's southeast. Although these tan-black-and-white deerlike creatures with short legs and large heads are commonly called antelope, they are not related to the true antelope of Africa and Asia—in fact, they are not related to any other living species.

American bison, more often called buffalo (although they are unrelated to Asian buffalo), once roamed throughout the Great Plains and Rocky Mountains. Today they are only found on buf-

WHO'S AFRAID OF THE BIG GRAY WOLF?

Wolves were virtually extinct in this region until 1995, when in a highly controversial move the first gray (timber) wolves were reintroduced to wilderness backcountry in Yellowstone Park, Montana and Idaho. Initial reports are that the several dozen canine relatives are flourishing—much to the chagrin of area ranchers, whose forebears paid bounty hunters for their slaughter.

falo ranches, a growing industry here, and in a few protected areas including Yellowstone National Park and the National Bison Range north of Missoula. When this range was established by President Theodore Roosevelt in 1908, only about 20 wild bison survived from an estimated 50 million a century earlier. Today the 19,000-acre grassland preserve has as many as 500 of the great beasts.

Rattlesnakes are also in the lower mountains and high plains. The good news is that they rarely venture into the higher mountains. Snakes and other reptiles are coldblooded and cannot function in low temperatures, so they are hardly ever found at elevations above about 7000 feet. When hiking at lower elevations, walk loudly and never put your hand or foot where you cannot see it.

Deer, mountain lions and bobcats inhabit the lower mountain ranges, foothills and plateaus. While white-tailed deer and mule deer may be spotted anywhere in the mountains, they prefer to graze in areas where they can browse on undergrowth. Mountain lions hunt deer and prefer areas with high rocks, where they can spot both danger and prey from a distance. Since mountain lions (also known as cougars) are nocturnal and reclusive, it's a stroke of luck to glimpse one darting across the road in your headlights at night. Wild horses graze some remote areas on the west side of the Rockies, including the Bighorn Canyon on Montana's southern border with Wyoming.

Small mammals commonly found in Rocky Mountain forests and meadows include squirrels, chipmunks, raccoons, porcupines and skunks. Large animals include elk and black bears. Because elk prefer high mountain meadows in the warm months, they are rarely seen outside of national parks except by serious hikers who venture deep into the wilderness. Sightings are more common in winter, when the elk descend to lower elevations where grass is easier to reach under the snow. In some areas, usually marked by signs and sometimes offering observation areas, herds of elk may be spotted from the road in winter. The world's largest concentration of elk is in Yellowstone National Park, especially in the Mammoth Hot Springs area. Moose also are found in the Montana Rockies, most frequently in marshy areas at dawn or dusk. These herbivores, the largest members of the deer family (they may weigh over 1000 pounds at full maturity), are hard to spot because of their ability to blend into forest surroundings.

Black bears are elusive, but more common than most hikers realize. In times of drought, when food is scarce, it's not unusual for a bear to raid trash cans along the fringes of civilization. Black bears rarely attack people, but they are unpredictable and can be dangerous because of their size—they typically run 250 to 350 pounds. Most injuries involving bears happen because campers store their food inside tents with them at night. When camping in the forest, it's a better idea to leave all food inside a closed vehicle or suspended from a tree limb.

Grizzly bears, the larger and more aggressive cousins of black bears, live in the backcountry of Glacier and Yellowstone national parks and adjacent wilderness areas, but are extinct in most other parts of Montana. They are listed as a threatened species by the federal government. Attacks on campers and hikers by the 600- to 1000-pound bears are rare but not unheard of.

Beavers once inhabited nearly every stream in Montana and adjacent states. Trapped by the millions for their pelts in the early 19th century, these largest of North American rodents stood at the brink of extinction. More recently, they have too often been considered pests: Beavers build dams in streams, to create ponds around their dome-shaped stick-and-mud lodges. Their dams flood the most desirable areas of mountain valleys. Landowners persisted for many years in poisoning the beavers, or dynamiting their dams and putting up low electric fences to keep them away. Now a protected species, beavers seem to be making a slow comeback. It's not unusual to discover beaver ponds on backcountry streams, and if you watch a pond near sunset, you may get a look at the animals themselves.

Near timberline, Rocky Mountain bighorn sheep are common and easy to spot in alpine meadows. Herds of ewes are protected by a single ram, while other males lead a solitary existence elsewhere until mating season. Then the high crags echo with the crash of horns as young rams challenge their elders for dominance over the female herd. Mountain goats—shaggy, snow-white and solitary—may also be seen in some high mountain areas, especially in Glacier National Park. The small animals most often seen above timberline are golden marmots—large, chubby rodents nicknamed whistlepigs because they communicate with shrill whistles. Smaller rodents called pikas colonize high-altitude rockpiles, where swarms of hundreds of them are sometimes seen.

▼▼▼▼▼▼▼▼▼▼
Where to Go

Montana is too big a place to cover in one two-week trip. Any attempt to visit all the areas described in this book in a single vacation is doomed from the outset. If you try to "see it all," you may find yourself so focused on covering large distances that you sacrifice quiet moments to appreciate the natural beauty you came to see.

Deciding what to see and where to go is a tough choice. The good news is that no matter how many times you visit, Montana will still have plenty of places to discover the next time you come.

Many tourists head straight away to **Northwest Montana**, the state's least arid region on the western slope of the Continental

Divide and (aside from its national parks) the most frequently visited. Its mountains enclose the university city of Missoula; the Bitterroot Valley, flanked on both sides by steep ridges; and the National Bison Range, within the Flathead Indian Reservation. Extending north from Flathead Lake, the largest natural freshwater lake west of the Mississippi River, is the recreational paradise of the Flathead Valley and its central town, Kalispell.

On the northeast rim of this corner of Montana, bordering the Canadian province of Alberta, is **Glacier National Park**, the "roof of the Rockies." Straddling the Continental Divide, its watershed flows in not two but three directions: to the Pacific Ocean, the Gulf of Mexico and Hudson Bay. The park boasts hundreds of miles of trails and thousands of large animals. Its surrounding area includes the Blackfeet Indian Reservation and Canada's Waterton Lakes National Park, together with which Glacier forms the world's only "international peace park."

The Rocky Mountain Front drops dramatically from Glacier National Park to the east, where the prairies slope gently downward to the Missouri River. The regional focus of **North Central Montana** is Great Falls, Montana's second-largest city. The area includes everything from dinosaur digs and ancient "buffalo jumps" to the historic steamboat port of Fort Benton. This is Russell Country, named for turn-of-the-century cowboy artist Charles M. Russell, whose Great Falls studio is now a popular museum of Western art. From Fort Benton, intrepid river runners can launch a fascinating voyage down the wild and scenic Missouri River Breaks.

Southwest Montana is mining country, past and present. Gold rush history lives on here in ghost towns like Bannack, established as the first territorial capital after ore was discovered here in 1862, and Virginia City, which tourism has kept alive and well and far more law-abiding than it was in the 19th century. Butte, whose copper mines once earned it the label "the richest hill on earth," has a stately and historic hillside downtown more reminiscent of old San Francisco than of any other city in the Rockies. Last Chance Gulch remains Helena's main street. The charming state capital is just a short drive from a spectacular Missouri River gorge known as the Gates of the Mountains.

South Central Montana is also known as "Yellowstone Country." Headwaters of the Missouri and Yellowstone rivers, with their sources in Yellowstone National Park (itself only a short drive from the region's major towns), flow northward through Bozeman, Livingston and other towns. Montana State University and its grand Museum of the Rockies are in sophisticated Bozeman, which has become a magnet for out-of-state immigrants. The former coal-mining town of Red Lodge is located right at the foot of the

Absaroka-Beartooth Wilderness and Montana's highest mountains. Other attractions include major ski resorts and the subterranean network of Lewis and Clark Caverns.

Although 2.2-million-acre **Yellowstone National Park** is almost entirely in Wyoming, three of its five gateways are in Montana. The world's first national park (it was established in 1872) is undoubtedly its most famous. A remarkable thermal wonderland of more than 10,000 geysers, hot springs and boiling mud caldrons, plus impressive canyons, waterfalls and high-elevation lakes, Yellowstone sits on the crest of an ancient volcanic crater. It also has perhaps the Rocky Mountains' most varied and accessible wildlife, from elk and moose to bison and grizzly bears.

The prairies of **Southeast Montana** and the lower Yellowstone River Valley were once were the domain of Plains Indians, who hunted bison, deer and pronghorn antelope by the thousands. Eons before them, this area was a veritable Jurassic Park; modern fossil hunters find paradise here. Montana's largest city, the ranching center of Billings, is a gateway to the Crow and North Cheyenne Indian Reservations, the Bighorn Canyon National Recreation Area, and the Little Bighorn Battlefield National Monument, where General Custer met his match in 1876. Nearby is Miles City, which bills itself as "Montana's cowboy capital."

Bisected by 134-mile-long Fort Peck Lake and its surrounding Charles M. Russell National Wildlife Refuge on the Missouri River, **Northeast Montana** offers fine recreational opportunities. And history stays alive through a strong American Indian presence and the Fort Union Trading Post National Historic Site at the confluence of the Missouri and the Yellowstone rivers.

▼▼▼▼▼▼▼▼▼
When to Go

SEASONS

Though it may sound romantic, springtime in Montana is less than appealing. Cold winds, occasional avalanches, brown vegetation and plenty of mud are a few of the reasons why many people in the tourist business shut down their shops and motels in April and take their own vacations to more southerly climes. Just about any other time of year, however, the climate is ideal for one kind of outdoor recreation or another, giving rise to a distinctive summer-and-winter double tourist season.

The traditional summer tourist season, which runs from Memorial Day to Labor Day, is characterized by cool nights, mild days, colorful wildflowers and sudden, brief afternoon rainstorms. In most parts of the Montana Rockies, it's a good idea to start outdoor activities early and carry ponchos or waterproof tarps on all-day hikes, since rain is almost inevitable in the afternoon.

In a common yet peculiar phenomenon, wind currents called "waves" can carry precipitation for long distances from clouds hidden behind the mountains, causing "sun showers." Old-timers say that if it rains while the sun is shining, it will rain again tomorrow. This adage almost always holds true—but then, if it doesn't rain in the sunshine, it's still likely to rain tomorrow. The good news is, summer rains rarely last more than an hour, and skies generally clear well before sunset.

Above timberline, temperatures may fall below freezing at night all summer and typically reach only 40° to 50° Fahrenheit at midday. It is not unusual for Glacier's Going-to-the-Sun Road and other alpine byways to be closed by blizzards even in August, sometimes stranding motorists for an hour or two before snow-plows clear the road.

Early fall—around mid-September—is one of the most delight-ful times to visit the Montana Rockies, as the turning of the aspens paints the mountainsides in yellow with splashes of orange and red, brilliant against a deep green background of evergreen forests. Mountain highways tend to be crowded with carloads of leaf-gawkers on weekends but not on weekdays, while hiking and bik-ing traffic on forest trails is much lighter than during the summer. The weather is generally dry and cool in early fall, making it a great time to take a long wilderness hike or mountain bike excursion. The first light snowfall can be expected in the high country toward the end of September; the first heavy snow typically comes around Halloween. November is hunting season, a good time to stay out of the mountains unless you're armed and dangerous.

The official ski season runs from Thanksgiving Day through March—the period in which all ski areas expect a reliable snow base and within which all ski events and package tours are sched-uled. If you're planning ahead for a major ski vacation, you'll want to schedule it between those dates, too. In reality, snowfall amounts, as well as winter temperatures in the mountains, can vary a lot from year to year, so the actual dates of operation at various resorts can be somewhat unpredictable. These days, the huge artificial snow-making capacity of most ski areas almost always assures a Thanks-

"SNOW EATERS"

East of the Continental Divide, clouds typically build in the early after-noon and then burst into thunder, lightning and sometimes hail. But North Central Montana is more noted for a unique winter weather phenomenon called "snow eaters" by the Blackfeet Indians. Warm "chinook" winds that sometimes sweep down the Rocky Mountain Front in midwinter have been known to raise temperatures by 40 or more degrees (Fahrenheit) in ten minutes or less. Great Falls gets the brunt of these, but their effect is felt as far east as Billings.

giving opening day. While snowmaking usually ceases after March when advance-reservation business slows down, skiing continues until spring temperatures rise enough to erode the snow base. In some years, at some ski areas, late-season skiing may continue well into April. Uncrowded ski trails, discount lift tickets and lots of sunshine make the late season a favorite time for many local ski enthusiasts.

CALENDAR OF EVENTS

JANUARY

Northwest Montana Missoula's **Foresters Ball** is a great excuse for loggers to come in from the cold for a weekend of boisterous fun.

North Central Montana The **Montana Pro Rodeo Circuit Finals** are held in Great Falls the second weekend of the month.

South Central Montana Bozeman's **Montana Winter Fair** is a week-long event that includes livestock shows, sheep-shearing and draft horse–pulling contests, cooking and crafts competitions. The Big Sky resort celebrates its **Winter Carnival** with a variety of sporting events.

FEBRUARY

Northwest Montana The Whitefish **Winter Carnival** and **Grape Expectations Wine and Food Festival** include parades, fireworks and a formal dance, plus torchlight skiing and races on the Big Mountain.

Southwest Montana The 10-day, 500-mile **Race to the Sky Dog Sled Race** from Helena to Holland Lake is exceeded in length (in the United States) only by Alaska's Iditarod. The **Winternational Sports Festival** in Butte and Anaconda features a variety of outdoor and indoor events. Anaconda's **Chocolate Festival** gives town residents a midwinter caffeine and sugar buzz.

Southeast Montana The **Montana Agri-Trade Exposition** in Billings gets farmers and ranchers thinking about the coming year's production.

MARCH

Northwest Montana In Missoula, the **International Wildlife Film Festival** screens videos from around the world for a full week and offers workshops, lectures and seminars.

Glacier National Park As the winter snow melts near Essex, the **Spring Snow Rodeo and Race** gives cross-country skiers one final, late-season fling.

North Central Montana The four-day **C. M. Russell Auction of Original Art** in Great Falls is widely regarded as the nation's largest and finest auction of original Western art of the 19th and 20th centuries.

Southwest Montana As many as 50,000 people are Irish for two days around **St. Patrick's Day** in Butte.

South Central Montana   The Red Lodge **Winter Carnival** climaxes the ski season in this old mining town.

Yellowstone National Park The **World Snowmobile Expo**, which includes power pulls and drag racing, is held in the park's gateway town of West Yellowstone, the "snowmobile capital of the world."

Northwest Montana   Near Whitefish, the exciting Big Mountain celebrates the end of ski season with its annual **Furniture Race:** Participants test chairs and sofas, fitted with skis, on the slopes.

APRIL

Southwest Montana   The **Helena Railroad Fair** is the largest convention of model train enthusiasts in the northern Rockies.

South Central Montana   The **Double Pole, Pad and Pedal** relay race begins at Bridger Bowl with downhill and cross-country ski events, then continues into Bozeman with running and cycling.

Southeast Montana   The 74-mile **Peaks to Prairie** triathlon ends in Billings: Contestants run from the Beartooth Face into Red Lodge, bicycle to Laurel and boat the Yellowstone River to Coulson Park.

Northeast Montana   **Peter Paddlefish Day** in Sidney celebrates the huge prehistoric paddlefish that runs the Yellowstone and Missouri rivers at this time.

Northwest Montana   The three-day **Buffalo Feast and Powwow** at St. Ignatius on the Flathead Indian Reservation features war dances and stick games. Bigfork's **Whitewater Festival** is highlighted by kayak races on Class V rapids and a triathlon. More than 30 Northwest designer beers are available for sampling at the **Garden City Micro Brew Fest** in Missoula.

MAY

Glacier National Park   **Essexpress** is a weekend devoted to railroad history at the Izaak Walton Inn.

Southwest Montana   Dillon's **Rancher Roundup Days** include a combination golf and team-roping event called Rope-N-Stroke.

Southeast Montana   In Billings, an **International Wine Festival** has two days of tastings and auctions to benefit Montana State University; the city also hosts the **All Nations Indian Rodeo Championships** over three days at the end of the month. Miles City's **Bucking Horse Sale** features three days of bucking-bronc riding, thoroughbred and wild-horse racing, street dances and a parade. **Buzzard Day** at Makoshika State Park, near Glendive, includes a variety of outdoor events to celebrate the buzzards' annual return.

Northeast Montana   Memorial Day weekend is notable in Sidney for its **Western Days and Poetry Gathering**. There's a youth rodeo, a pet parade, tractor pull, barbecue and other events.

Northwest Montana   Lovers of Rocky Mountain oysters throng to the **Mission Mountain Testicle Festival** in Charlo to see bull privates cleaned, breaded and deep-fried before serving.

JUNE

North Central Montana   The **Lewis & Clark Festival** in Great Falls includes a re-enactment of the explorers' 1805 passage and encampment on the Missouri River. Fort Benton's **Summer Celebration** includes a parade, concert, art show and fireworks.

Southwest Montana   Helena hosts the **Governor's Cup**, the state's biggest annual road-running event with more than 7000 entries, and the **Montana Traditional Dixieland Jazz Festival**, five nights and four days of Roaring Twenties–style music.

South Central Montana   Montana State University in Bozeman is the site of the **College National Finals Rodeo**, five nights of competition for college scholarships between rodeo riders from around the country. The **Red Lodge Music Festival** attracts 200 teenagers from five states for classical music concerts and recitals.

Yellowstone National Park   The **Upper Yellowstone Roundup** offers a rodeo, parade and community dance in Gardiner, at the park's north entrance.

Southeast Montana   Billings' **Strawberry Festival** and **Festival of Cultures** are popular arts-and-entertainment events. The highlights of **Little Big Horn Days** in Hardin are a full-scale re-enactment of Custer's Last Stand and a "military ball" in 1880s period wardrobe. **Forsyth Rodeo Days** include a parade, dance, trade show and lots of arena action.

Northeast Montana   The **Fort Union Rendezvous** near Sidney is an authentic re-creation of historic trapping and trading days. The **Red Bottom Powwow** in Frazer, on the Fort Peck Indian Reservation, is a traditional Assiniboine fete. **Frontier Days** bring rodeos, parades and the Dirty Shame dance show to Culbertson.

JULY

Northwest Montana   On the Flathead Indian Reservation north of Missoula, the **Arlee Celebration**, a powwow on the Jocko River, features Salish dancing, stick games, horse racing and a rodeo. The **Standing Arrow Powwow**, at Elmo on Flathead Lake, is highlighted by Kootenai dancing. The **Flathead Festival** offers two weeks of classical, jazz, New Age, opera and other musical concerts spread across the Flathead Valley from Bigfork to Whitefish. Missoula hosts an **International Choral Festival** for five days at mid-month, while the **Montana State Fiddlers Contest** is held in Polson in late July. Hamilton has two big events: the **Bitterroot Valley Bluegrass Festival**, with banjo and fiddle workshops and music for the whole family, and the **Bitterroot Valley Good Nations Powwow** featuring American Indian music and arts. **Libby Logger Days** are highlighted by a timber carnival, a parade and widespread entertainment. **Summerfest/Squawfish Days** at Thompson Falls include river races, sports tournaments and various arts and musical events.

Glacier National Park   At Browning on the Blackfeet Indian Reservation, **North American Indian Days** focus on the dancing, singing, drumming and games of this Plains Indian tribe; there's a parade and a rodeo.

North Central Montana   From late July into early August, the Montana State Fair dominates life in Great Falls with top-name entertainment, rodeos and horse races, art and trade shows, and a carnival. The six-day **Central Montana Wagon Train** from the Snowy Mountains ends at Lewistown's annual Fourth of July celebration. Late in the month, Lewistown is at center stage again with its **Central Montana Horse Show, Fair and Rodeo**. The Fort Belknap Indians convene their annual powwow as part of **Milk River Days** in Harlem, also including a parade and crafts exhibits. During **Dinosaur Days** in Choteau, visitors can get special tours of Egg Mountain and The Nature Conservancy's Pine Creek Swamp Preserve.

Southwest Montana   Butte takes six days to celebrate July 4 with parades, concerts, dances and fireworks in its annual **Freedom Festival**, and five more for its **Southwest Montana Fair** two weeks later. Helena's big event is the **Last Chance Stampede and Fair**, a classic four-day Western rodeo with great entertainment. **Western Heritage Days** at the Grant-Kohrs Ranch National Historic Site in Deer Lodge celebrate 19th-century ranch life with roping and branding demonstrations, chuckwagon cookery and performances of cowboy music and poetry. The quiet streets of Bannack State Park, west of Dillon, come to life for **Bannack Days**, featuring pioneer craft demonstrations and activities that include horse-and-buggy rides, black-powder shooting and panning for gold. **Twin Bridges' Floating Flotillas and Fish Fantasies**, a weekend of arts, dances and entertainment, concludes with a floating parade on the Beaverhead River.

South Central Montana   Red Lodge's **Home of Champions Rodeo and Parade**, the **Livingston Roundup Rodeo and Parade** and the **4th of July Rodeo and Parade** in Ennis are weekend-long tributes to Independence Day. Bozeman's **Gallatin Country Fair** runs for five days at mid-month; two weeks later, various restaurants come together for **Taste of Bozeman**, with seating for 2000 on the city's main street. The **Musicians Rendezvous** at a 35-acre park south of Columbus includes concerts, arts exhibits, food booths and a musical-instrument swap and sale. The **Red Lodge Mountain Man Rendezvous** re-creates the fur-trader era of the 1820s and 1830s.

Yellowstone National Park   West Yellowstone celebrates the **Fourth of July** with a parade and fireworks.

Southeast Montana   On the Northern Cheyenne Indian Reservation at Lame Deer, the **Northern Cheyenne Powwow** on the July 4 weekend features parades, dancing, drumming, singing and feasting. There are also big **4th of July celebrations** in Laurel and Roundup and a major rodeo in Harlowton. **Summerfair** in Billings is an arts festival that draws more than 100 artisans from 15 states to benefit the Yellowstone Art Center. **Homesteader Days** in Huntley include such old-style entertainment as a parade, concerts and a big barbecue. In Miles City, the **5th Infantry Encampment** at old Fort Keogh features 19th-century military and lifestyle re-creations in full period dress. The **Eastern Montana "Ski" Festival** at Wibaux is not what you might think: It's an ethnic affair staged for and by the Javorskis and Norskis of this rural community. The festival celebrates the European heritage of this part of the state, especially those whose ancestors immigrated from Eastern Europe and the Scandinavian countries.

Northeast Montana   The granddaddy of all Montana rodeos is the **Wild Horse Stampede** at Wolf Point on the Fort Peck Indian Reservation; evolved from traditional powwows and bucking contests, it features wild-horse races and other events. The **Old Fashioned Fourth Celebrations** at Sidney and Scobey include 19th-century diversions. The **Sand Creek Clydesdale Wagon Train** sweeps through lonely Jordan the following weekend. Glasgow hosts the **Montana Governor's Cup Walleye Tournament**, which brings 200 teams of fishermen to Fort Peck Lake to compete for a $10,000 prize, and the **Northeast Montana County Fair**.

AUGUST

Northwest Montana   The **Western Montana Fair** in Missoula and **Northwest Montana Fair** in Kalispell, scheduled one after the other, highlight the August calendar. Each is five days long and may feature rodeos, horse racing, demolition derbies, country-and-western concerts, parades and fireworks. Musicians stroll Bigfork's main street, and artists display their creations, during the Flathead Lake community's annual **Festival of the Arts**. Ever since Trout Creek, near Thompson Falls on Noxon Reservoir, was proclaimed "Huckleberry Capital of Montana" in 1981, it's held an annual **Huckleberry Festival**, including an arts fair and chili cook-off.

North Central Montana   At the **Great Falls Dixieland Jazz Festival**, 1920s-style bands play for four solid days. Lewistown's **Montana Cowboy Poetry Gathering** is two days of authentic rhymes and recitations, music and dance. The **Great Northern Fair** in Havre includes a rodeo, a demolition derby and a large midway. **Rocky Boy's Annual Powwow** at the reservation south of Havre honors native heritage with dances and crafts.

Southwest Montana   The **Kaleidoscope Festival** in Helena pays tribute to the fine arts, and includes music, sports events and other entertainment. Some 350 American Indian dancers from throughout the American West and Canada perform at the **Montana Big Sky Powwow** in Helena. Anaconda's **Heritage Days** honor former workers at its now-defunct copper smelter with tours, a parade and an ethnic food festival. The **Big Hole National Battlefield Reenactment** recalls one of the major conflicts of the 1877 Nez Percé War.

South Central Montana   The **Sweet Pea Festival of the Arts** in Bozeman attracts big-name national and regional musicians for rock and jazz concerts; there are also sporting events, a parade, arts and crafts and a climactic ball. In Red Lodge, the nine-day **Festival of Nations** pays homage to immigrants from many countries who built the old mining town; highlights include traditional dances, craft demonstrations, an international cooking pavilion and a parade. Angling experts from around the world converge on Livingston for the **International Federation of Fly Fishers Conclave**, largest of its kind in North America. The **Sweet Grass County Cutting Competition** brings dozens of horses and riders to Big Timber to see who's the best at separating a cow from a herd. The **Manhattan Potato Festival** honors the tuber grown by area farmers with a parade and town dance.

Yellowstone National Park   The **Yellowstone Rod Run** at West Yellowstone is a spirited gathering of hot-rod car and truck owners. The nearby **Burnt Hole Historic Reenactment** is a week-long re-creation of a pre-1840 mountain men's camp.

Southeast Montana   Billings' **Big Skyfest** is a four-day extravaganza of races between, and displays of, colorful hot-air balloons. A week later, the **Montana Fair** brings rodeos, livestock exhibitions, concerts and a carnival to Billings. Miles City's **Eastern Montana Fair** is scheduled the last full weekend of the month. Crow Agency, located on the Crow Indian Reservation, becomes the "tepee capital of the world" for five days during the **Crow Fair and Rodeo**, when hundreds of tepees rise from the banks of the Little Bighorn River: events include parades, dancing, singing, feasting and horse races. **Dinosaur Days** in Harlowton include a parade and a community hunt for dinosaur bones. At Huntley's annual **Threshing Bee**, visitors can see antique farming equipment used by early-20th-century homesteaders in operation, and enjoy arts and music.

Northeast Montana   **Wadopana Powwow** is celebrated at Wolf Point on the Fort Peck Indian Reservation. **Winnett Fun Day**, in a village of 200 people an hour's drive east of Lewistown, features motorcycle barrel races, a messy cow contest and a pig mud-wrestling competition. There's not a lot else to do in Winnett.

Northwest Montana   The **Flathead International Balloon Festival** brings dozens of hot-air balloonists to Kalispell for mass public inflations, as well as sky diving and a Saturday barbecue. Libby's **Nordicfest** is a three-day celebration of the logging town's Scandinavian heritage, featuring traditional crafts, food, dancing and sporting events. More than four and a half tons of Rocky Mountain oysters and cowboy beans are served up at the five-day **Clinton Testicle Festival**, just off Route 90 about 25 miles east of Missoula.   **SEPTEMBER**

North Central Montana Great Falls' **Cottonwood Festival** invites visitors to take part in more than 50 old-time activities, from horseshoeing and goldpanning to basket weaving. **Havre Festival Days** include river and bed races, an arts and crafts show, a barbecue and a town dance. Lewistown hosts the **Montana State Chokeberry Festival**, in which a parade, arts exhibit and duck races share time with the tasting and judging of preserves and wine. There are old-fashioned **Threshing Bees** in both Lewistown and Choteau.

Southwest Montana The **Butte Heritage Festival** offers music and entertainment with an ethnic bent, including a closing polka in an old mine. It coincides with the **North American Indian Alliance Powwow**. The **Last Chance Bluegrass Fest** gets Helena stomping its collective feet early in the month.

South Central Montana The **Running of the Sheep** at Reedpoint, about halfway from Bozeman to Billings, is vaguely reminiscent of the famous running of bulls in Pamplona, Spain, as a herd of woolies is driven down the six-block-long Main Street. There's also a parade and contests for the prettiest ewe and ugliest ram. At the **Northern Rockies Llama Classic** in Bozeman, there are clinics in using the South American beast as a pack animal and for its wool, plus a media llama race. Livingston celebrates **Oktoberfest** with beer gardens and oom-pah bands.

Yellowstone National Park **Buffalo Days** in Gardiner includes a parade, street dance and buffalo-meat barbecue.

Southeast Montana **Herbstfest** is a traditional Russian-German harvest festival in Laurel that celebrates with three days of music, dancing, drinking and feasting.

Northeast Montana The **Milk River Wagon Train** is reason for a community parade and festival in Malta. A parade of 80 antique tractors, a barbecue and fiddle music highlight the **Threshing Bee and Antique Show** in Culbertson.

OCTOBER

Northwest Montana Bigfork's **Tamarack Time** is a harvest festival in which individual community members prepare their favorite recipes. The four-day **Glacier Jazz Stampede** in Kalispell presents all kinds of jazz music, from ragtime and big-band to modern improv. Also in Kalispell, the last weekend of October, is **Christmas at the Mansion**, a juried arts-and-crafts show at the Victorian-adorned Conrad Mansion. **Oktoberfest** in Charlo is highlighted by karaoke and yodeling contests.

Glacier National Park Railroad buffs again gather at the Izaak Walton Inn in Essex for the **Alta/Mont Railfan Weekend**.

Southwest Montana Helena combines its **Oktoberfest** celebration with three days of professional rodeo bullriding. Anaconda's **Harvest Fair** is a showcase for local artisans.

South Central Montana As hunting season kicks off, the restaurants of Ennis host **Hunters Feed**, competing for prizes with their wild-game recipes.

Southeast Montana The **Nile Stock Show and Rodeo** in Billings has five rodeo performances in eight days, livestock shows and a trade exhibit with more than 150 presenters.

Northeast Montana In Wolf Point, the region's biggest annual trade show—the **Northeast Montana Exposition**—has everything from crafts exhibits to livestock judging.

Northwest Montana Missoula's three-day **Renaissance Faire** brings back the spirit of the Middle Ages in music and costume, crafts and games. The Flathead Valley kicks off the holiday season with Kalispell's **Christmas City of the North Parade** on Thanksgiving Friday. The following day, Bigfork hosts its annual **Christmas Tree Extravaganza**. **NOVEMBER**

Southwest Montana About 400 bald eagles congregate on the Missouri River near Helena between early November and mid-December to feed on spawning salmon; during this **Bald Eagle Migration**, a visitors center offers hands-on displays and viewing telescopes. Butte holds its **Festival of Trees** the last weekend of the month.

Southeast Montana Billings slips into the holiday spirit with its **Holiday Parade** on Thanksgiving Friday and its **Festival of Trees** the following weekend.

Northeast Montana The **Christmas Parade of Lights** on Thanksgiving Friday launches the holiday season in Sidney.

Northwest Montana **Christmas in Bigfork** is a month-long observance that features colorful lighting displays, caroling, sleigh rides and a variety of special holiday events. Hamilton's **Catch the Magic** is a three-day street fair sponsored by local merchants. **DECEMBER**

North Central Montana During Havre's **Christmas Stroll**, many folks escape the cold in Havre's excavated, Prohibition-era underground city.

South Central Montana Downtown streets close to vehicle traffic and merchants stay open late during **Christmas Strolls** in Bozeman and Livingston.

Southeast Montana Other cities have embraced the **Christmas Stroll** idea, including Billings and Laurel.

For free visitor information packages, including the annual *Montana Vacation Guide*, state highway map and current details on special events, accommodations and camping, contact **Travel Montana**. ~ 1424 9th Avenue, Helena, MT 59620; 406-444-2654, 800-847-4868. In addition, most towns have ▼▼▼▼▼▼▼▼▼ **Before You Go**

VISITORS CENTERS

chambers of commerce or visitor information centers. Tourist information centers are usually not open on weekends. For information on Yellowstone National Park, contact the **Wyoming Division of Tourism**. ~ Route 25 at College Drive, Cheyenne, WY 82002; 307-777-7777. For information on Canada's Waterton Lakes National Park, contact the **Alberta Tourism Partnership**. ~ 705 10045 111th Street, Suite 705, Edmonton, Alberta T5K 2M5, Canada; 403-422-8764.

PACKING

The adage that you should take along twice as much money and half as much stuff as you think you'll need is sound advice as far as it goes. In the more remote reaches of Montana, though, stores selling something more substantial than beef jerky and country-and-western cassettes are few and far between.

Westerners in general, and Montanans in particular, are casual in their dress and expect the same of visitors. Leave your suit and tie at home. Even in summer, you should pack a couple of long-sleeve flannel shirts, jeans and your cowboy boots for evening or ranch wear, but most of the time, you'll be happy in shorts and a T-shirt. In spring and fall, layers of clothing are your best bet, since the weather can change dramatically from day to day and region to region. Winters are downright cold, so pack your very warmest clothing for this time of year!

Other essentials to pack or buy along the way include a good sunscreen and high-quality sunglasses. Cool temperatures often lull newcomers into forgetting that thin high-altitude air filters out far less of the sun's ultraviolet rays; above timberline, exposed skin will sunburn faster than it would on a Florida beach. Umbrellas are oddities: A Montanan keeps chilly afternoon rain from running down the back of his or her neck by wearing a cowboy hat.

If you're planning to camp in the mountains during the summer months, don't forget to pack lots of mosquito repellent.

For outdoor activities, tough-soled hiking boots are more comfortable than running shoes on rocky terrain. Even RV travelers and those who prefer to spend most nights in motels may want to take along a backpacking tent and sleeping bag in case the urge to stay out under star-spangled Western skis becomes irresistible. A canteen, first-aid kid, flashlight and other routine camping gear are also likely to come in handy. Both cross-country and downhill ski rentals are available everywhere you look in the mountains during the winter, though serious skiers may find that the quality and condition of rental skis leave something to be desired. In the summer, mountain bikes may be rented as well. Other outdoor-recreation equipment—kayaks, fishing tackle, golf clubs and gold pans—generally cannot be rented, so you'll want to bring the right gear for your special sporting passion.

A camera, of course, is essential for capturing your travel experience; of equal importance is a good pair of binoculars, which let you explore distant landscapes from scenic overlooks and bring wildlife up close. And don't, for heaven's sake, forget your copy of *Hidden Montana*.

Accommodations in Montana run the gamut from tiny one-room cabins to luxury hotels that blend traditional alpine-lodge ambience with contemporary elegance. Bed and breakfasts can be found in most of the larger or more tourist-oriented towns you'll visit, even in such obscure places as Absarokee and Bigfork. They come in all types, sizes and price ranges. Typical of the genre are lovingly restored Victorian-era mansions comfortably furnished with period decor, usually having fewer than a dozen rooms.

LODGING

The abundance of motels in towns along all major highway routes presents a range of choices, from name-brand motor inns to traditional ma-and-pa establishments that have endured for the half-century since motels were invented. While rather ordinary motels in the vicinity of major tourist destinations can be pricey, lodging in small towns away from major resorts and interstate routes can offer friendliness, quiet and comfort at ridiculously low rates.

At the other end of the price spectrum, peak-season rates at a handful of leading ski resorts can be very costly. To save money, consider staying in more affordable lodging as much as an hour away and commuting to the ski slopes during the day, or plan your vacation during "shoulder seasons," before and after the peak seasons. Even though the summer is a lively time in many ski towns, accommodations are in surplus and room rates often drop to less than half the winter rates.

In some Montana towns, you'll find lavishly restored historic hotels that date back to the mining-boom days of the late 19th century. Many combine affordable rates with plenty of antique decor and authentic personality. Both Glacier and Yellowstone national parks have lodges that offer distinctive accommodations at mid-range rates: the Glacier Park Lodge and Yellowstone's Old Faithful Inn rank high among the Rockies' most memorable historic inns. National park lodges are highly sought after, however, so travelers must make reservations several months in advance.

Guest ranches are located throughout the state. Horseback riding is the common theme of all. Some offer luxury lodging, spa facilities, and a full range of activities that may include fishing, boating and swimming. Others operate as working ranches, providing lodging in comfortably rustic cabins and offering the opportunity to participate in roundups, cattle drives and other ranching activities. Rates at most guest ranches are comparatively expensive, but include all meals and use of recreational facilities. Most guest ranches have minimum-stay requirements ranging from three days to a week.

Whatever your preference and budget, you can probably find something to suit your taste with the help of this book. Remember, rooms can be scarce and prices may rise during peak season: summer in most of the state, winter in ski resorts. Travelers planning to visit a place in peak season should either make advance bookings or arrive early in the day, before the "No Vacancy" signs start lighting up.

Lodging prices listed in this book are high-season rates. If you're looking for off-season bargains, it's good to inquire. *Budget* lodgings generally run less than $50 per night for two people; while satisfactory and clean, they are modest. *Moderate* motels and hotels range from $50 to $90; what they have to offer in the way of luxury will depend on where they are located, but they generally offer larger rooms and more attractive surroundings than budget lodgings. At *deluxe*-priced accommodations, you can expect to spend between $90 and $130 for a homey bed and breakfast or for a double in a hotel or resort. In hotels of this price you'll generally find spacious rooms, a fashionable lobby, a restaurant and often a bar or nightclub. *Ultra-deluxe* facilities, priced above $130, are the finest in the state, offering all the amenities of a deluxe hotel plus plenty of extras.

Room rates vary as much with locale as with quality. Some of the trendier destinations have no rooms at all in the budget price range. In other communities—those where rates are set with truck drivers in mind and those in out-of-the-way small towns—every motel falls into the budget category, even though accommodations may range from $19.95 at rundown, spartan places to $45 or so at the classiest motor inn in town. The price categories listed in this book are relative, designed to show you where to get the most out of your travel budget, however large or small it may be.

DINING

Fine dining in Montana tends to focus on the region's traditional cuisine: beef and trout. Buffalo steaks and wild-game dishes also are popular throughout the state. Most cities have Italian, Mexican and Chinese restaurants, but only in the more sophisticated university towns of Bozeman and Missoula and in scattered resort communities will you find a wide selection of gourmet foods. If your idea of an ideal vacation includes savoring epicurean delights, then by all means seize opportunities whenever they arise. When traveling in Montana, you can go for days between gourmet meals.

Restaurants listed in this book generally offer lunch and dinner unless otherwise noted. Dinner entrées at *budget* restaurants usually cost $8 or less. The ambience is informal, service usually speedy and the crowd often a local one. *Moderate*-priced restaurant entrées range between $8 and $16 at dinner; surroundings are casual but pleasant; the menu offers more variety and the pace is usually slower than at budget restaurants. *Deluxe* establishments tab their entrées from $16 to $24; cuisines may be simple or sophisticated, depending on the location, but the decor is plusher and the service more personalized than at moderate-priced restaurants. *Ultra-deluxe* dining rooms, where entrées begin at $24 and cooking is a fine art, are virtually nonexistent in Montana.

Some restaurants change hands often and are occasionally closed in low seasons. Efforts have been made in this book to include places with established reputations for good eating. Compared to evening dinners, breakfast and lunch menus vary less in price from restaurant to restaurant.

DRIVING

Some first-time visitors to the Rocky Mountains wonder why so few mountain roads have guard rails to separate motorists from thousand-foot dropoffs. The fact is, highway safety studies have found that far fewer accidents occur where there are no guard rails. Statistically, edgy, winding mountain roads are much safer than straight, fast interstate highways. Unpaved roads are another story. While many are wide and well graded, weather conditions or the wear and tear of heavy seasonal use can create unexpected road hazards. Some U.S. Forest Service and Bureau of Land Management roads are designated for four-wheel-drive or high-clearance vehicles only. If you see a sign indicating four-wheel-drive only, believe it. These roads can be very dangerous in a standard passenger car without the high ground clearance and extra traction afforded by four-wheel drive—and there may be no safe place to turn around if you get stuck.

Montana has its share of those straight, fast highways, however, especially in the eastern prairies. This is why, when in 1995 the federal government repealed its mandated speed limits and allowed individual states to determine their own limits, Montana chose to go without a formal numerical daytime speed limit. Instead, the state has a *basic rule* that states: "Vehicles should be driven in a reasonable and prudent manner with regard to the weather, road conditions, traffic patterns, vehicle conditions, and other safety considerations." Violators are subject to speeding tickets. At night, speed limits are 65 miles per hour on interstate highways, 55 on other roads, 35 (day or night) in construction zones.

Some side roads will take you far from civilization, so be sure to have a full radiator and a full tank of gas. Carry spare fuel, water and food. Should you become stuck, local people are usually helpful about offering assistance to stranded vehicles.

Montana gets a lot of snow in the winter months. Mountain passes, not to mention the eastern prairies, frequently become snowpacked. Under these conditions, tire chains are always advised and often required, even on main highways. State patrol officers may make you turn back if your car is not equipped with chains, so make sure you carry them along. At the very least, studded tires—legal in the state from October through May—are recommended. In winter it's wise to travel with a shovel, gravel or cat litter for traction, and blankets or sleeping bags.

A CB radio or car phone isn't a bad idea for extended backcountry driving.

If your car does not seem to run well at high elevations, you should probably have the carburetor adjusted at the next service station. The air at Rocky Mountain altitudes is "thin"—that is, it contains considerably less oxygen in a given volume than air at lower altitudes. The carburetor or fuel-injection unit should be set leaner to achieve an efficient fuel-to-air mixture.

You can get full information on statewide road conditions for Montana at any time of year by calling 800-226-7623; for conditions in Yellowstone National Park, call 307-635-9966.

TRAVELING WITH CHILDREN

Any place that has wild animals, cowboys and Indians, rocks to climb and limitless room to run is bound to be a hit with youngsters. Plenty of family adventures are available in Montana, from manmade attractions to experiences in the wilderness. A few simple guidelines will help make traveling with children a pleasure.

Book reservations in advance, making sure that the places you stay accept children. Many bed and breakfasts do not. If you need a crib or extra cot, arrange for it ahead of time. A travel agent can be of help here, as well as with most other travel plans.

If you are traveling by air, try to reserve bulkhead seats: they have more room. Carry on extras you may need such as diapers, changes of clothing, snacks, toys and small games. When traveling by car, be sure to take along those extras, too. Make sure you have plenty of water and juices to drink; dehydration can be a subtle but serious problem. Larger towns, and some smaller ones, have all-night convenience stores that carry diapers, baby food, snacks and other essentials; national parks also have such stores, though they usually close early.

A first-aid kit is essential for any trip. Along with adhesive bandages, antiseptic cream and something to stop itching, include medicines your pediatrician might recommend to treat allergies, colds, diarrhea or chronic problems your child might have. Mountain sunshine is intense, so take extra care to limit youngsters' exposure for the first few days. Children's skin is usually more tender than adult skin, and severe sunburn can happen before you realize it. A hat is a good idea, along with a reliable sunblock.

Many national parks, monuments and historic sites offer special activities just for children, and some state parks do so as well.

Visitors center film presentations and rangers' campfire slide shows can help inform children about natural history, and head off some questions. Still, kids tend to find a lot more things to wonder about than adults have answers for. To be as prepared as possible, seize every opportunity to learn more, particularly about wildlife, source of consistent curiosity among young minds.

Montana is big dog country. Throughout the Rockies, you may notice more vacationers traveling with their pets than in other parts of the country. Pets are permitted on leashes in virtually all campgrounds. But few bed and breakfasts or guest ranches will accept them, and more run-of-the-mill motels seem to be adopting "No Pets" policies with each passing year.

TRAVELING WITH PETS

Otherwise, the main limitation of traveling with a canine companion is that national parks and monuments prohibit pets on trails or in the backcountry. You are supposed to walk your dog on the roadside, pick up after it, then leave it in the car while you go hiking. Make sure the dog gets adequate shade, ventilation and water. Fortunately, dogs are free to run in national forests; leashes are required only in designated camping and picnic areas.

Wildlife can pose special hazards in the backcountry. At lower elevations in the plains and foothills, campers should not leave a cat or small dog outside at night because coyotes may attack it. In remote forest areas, it's especially important to keep on eye on your dog at all times. Bears are upset by dogs barking at them and may attack even very large dogs. Porcupines, common in pine forests, are tempting to chase and slow enough to catch; if your dog *does* catch one, a mouthful of quills means painfully pulling them out one by one with pliers, or making an emergency visit to a veterinary clinic in the nearest town.

It is a sad commentary on life in the United States, but women traveling along must take precautions. While Montana is reasonably safe compared to more urbanized states, it's entirely unwise to hitchhike and probably best to avoid inexpensive accommodations on the outskirts of towns; the money saved does not outweigh the risk. Bed and breakfasts, youth hostels, and more deluxe hotels and motor inns are generally your safest bet for lodging.

WOMEN TRAVELING ALONE

If you are hassled or threatened in some way, never be afraid to scream for assistance. It's a good idea to carry change for a phone call and to know the number to call in case of emergency.

Montana is a conservative state and not among the more sympathetic to sexual minorities. Nonetheless, you'll find social and support groups in a handful of towns, especially those with larger and more liberal university populations—specifically, at the University

GAY & LESBIAN TRAVELERS

of Montana in Missoula as well as Montana State University in Bozeman.

SENIOR TRAVELERS

Montana is a friendly and hospitable state for senior citizens to visit, especially in the mountains in summer, when cool and sunny weather offers respite from the hot, humid climate of many other parts of the country. Many hotels, restaurants and attractions offer senior discounts that can cut a substantial chunk off vacation costs.

The national park system's Golden Age Passport allows free admission for anyone 62 and older to the numerous national parks, monuments and historic sites in the region; apply in person at any national-park unit that charges an entrance fee. The passports are also good for a 50 percent discount on fees at most national-forest campgrounds. Many private sightseeing companies also offer significant discounts for seniors.

The **American Association of Retired Persons** (AARP) offers membership to anyone age 50 or over. AARP's many benefits include travel discounts with several firms and escorted tours on Gray Line buses. ~ 3200 East Carson Street, Lakewood, CA 90712, 310-496-2277; or 601 E Street NW, Washington, DC 20049, 800-424-3410.

Elderhostel offers all-inclusive packages with educational courses at colleges and universities, some in Montana. ~ 75 Federal Street, Boston, MA 02110; 617-426-7788.

Be extra careful with your health. High altitude is the biggest risk factor. Since some driving routes through Montana cross mountain passes that exceed 10,000 feet in elevation, it's advisable to ask your physician if high altitude is a problem for you. People with heart problems are commonly advised to avoid all physical exertion above 10,000 feet, and those with respiratory conditions such as emphysema may not be able to visit high altitudes at all. In the changeable climate of the Rockies, seniors are more at risk of suffering hypothermia. Tourist destinations may be a long way from any hospital or other health care facility.

In addition to the medications your normally use, it's wise to bring along your prescriptions in case you need replacements. Consider carrying a medical record with you, including your history and current medical status as well as your doctor's name, phone number and address. Make sure that your insurance covers you while you are away from home.

DISABLED TRAVELERS

Montana is striving to make more destinations, especially public areas, fully accessible to persons with disabilities. Parking spaces and restroom facilities for the physically challenged are provided according to both state law and national park regulations. National parks and monuments also post signs that tell which trails are wheelchair accessible. Some national forest recreation areas even have Braille nature trails with marked points of interest appealing to the senses of touch and smell.

Golden Access Passports, good for free admission to all national parks and monuments as well as discounts at most federal public campgrounds, are available at no charge to persons who are blind or have a permanent disability. You may apply in person at any national park unit that charges an entrance fee.

> It's advisable to ask your physician if high altitude is a problem for you.

For more information contact the **Society for the Advancement of Travel for the Handicapped.** ~ 347 Fifth Avenue, Suite 610, New York, NY 10016; 212447-7284. **Mobility International USA** can also help you. ~ P.O. Box 10767, Eugene, OR 97440; 503-343-1284. For valuable tips, contact the **Travel Information Service.** ~ 215-456-9600.

Flying Wheels Travel is a travel agency specifically for disabled people. ~ 143 West Bridge Street, Owatonna, MN 55060; 800-535-6790. You can also contact **Travelin' Talk**, a networking organization. ~ P.O. Box 3534, Clarksville, TN 37043; 615-552-6670.

Passports and Visas Most foreign visitors, other than Canadian citizens, must have a valid passport and tourist visa to enter the United States. Contact your nearest U.S. embassy or consulate well in advance to obtain a visa and to check on any other entry requirements.

FOREIGN TRAVELERS

Customs Requirements Foreign travelers are allowed to import the following: 200 cigarettes (1 carton), 50 cigars or 2 kilograms (4.4 pounds) of smoking tobacco; one liter of alcohol for personal use only (you must be at least 21 years old to bring in alcohol); and US$100 worth of duty-free gifts that can include an additional 100 cigars. You may bring in any amount of currency, although amounts in excess of US$10,000 require a declaration form. Carry any prescription drugs in clearly marked containers; you may have to provide a written prescription or doctor's statement to clear customs. Meat or meat products, seeds, plants, fruit and narcotics are not allowed to be brought into the United States, and there is a long list of other contraband items, from live birds and snakes to switchblade knives, which vacationers hardly ever have with them. For further information, contact the **United States Customs Service.** ~ 1301 Constitution Avenue NW, Washington, DC 20229; 202-566-8195.

Driving If you plan to rent a car, you should obtain an international driver's license before you arrive in the United States. Some rental car companies require both a foreign license and an international license. Virtually all agencies require a lessee to be at least 25 years old and to present a major credit card.

Currency   U.S. money is based on the dollar. Bills generally come in denominations of $1, $5, $10, $20, $50 and $100. Every dollar is divided into 100 cents. Coins are the penny (1 cent), nickel (5 cents), dime (10 cents) and quarter (25 cents). Half-dollar and dollar coins exist but are rarely used. You may not use foreign currency to purchase goods and services in the United States. Consider buying travelers' checks in dollar amounts. You may also use credit cards affiliated with an American company, such as American Express, VISA, Barclay Card and Interbank.

Electricity   Electric outlets use currents of 110 volts, 60 cycles. To use appliances made for other electrical systems, you need a transformer or other adapter. Travelers who use laptop computers for telecommunication should be aware that modem configurations for U.S. telephone systems may differ from their European counterparts. Similarly, the U.S. format for videotapes is different from that in Europe; National Park Service visitor centers and other stores that sell souvenir videos often have them available in European format.

Weights and Measurements   The United States uses the English system of weights and measures. American units and their metric equivalents are as follows: 1 inch = 2.5 centimeters; 1 foot (12 inches) = 0.3 meter; 1 yard (3 feet) = 0.9 meter; 1 mile (5280 feet) = 1.6 kilometers; 1 ounce = 28 grams; 1 pound (16 ounces) = 454 grams or 0.45 kilogram; 1 quart (liquid) = 0.9 liter.

▼▼▼▼▼▼▼▼▼▼▼▼▼▼
Outdoor Adventures

CAMPING

RV or tent camping is a great way to tour Montana's national and state parks and forests during the summer months. Besides saving substantial sums of money, campers enjoy the freedom to watch sunsets from beautiful places, spend nights under spectacular starry skies, and wake up to find themselves in lovely surroundings that few hotels can match.

Most towns have commercial RV parks of some sort, and long-term mobile home parks often rent spaces to RVers by the night. But unless you absolutely need cable television, none of these places can compete with the wide array of public campgrounds available in government-administered sites. Federal campgrounds are typically less developed. You won't find electric, water or sewer hookups in campgrounds at national forests, national monuments or national recreation areas (with the exception of one campground in Bighorn Canyon National Recreation Area). As for national parks, there are more than 300 hookups in Yellowstone and more than 200 in Glacier. The largest campgrounds offer tent-camping loops separate from RV loops, as well as hike-in backcountry camping by permit. A few state park campgrounds in Montana have hookups, notably the various units of Flathead

Lake State Park near Kalispell. You won't find much in the way of sophisticated reservation systems in Montana. In July and August, the largest campgrounds in Yellowstone National Park require reservations through DESTINET (800-365-2267, credit card only); reservations are not accepted at Glacier National Park, nor are they taken for most Yellowstone campgrounds. The general rule in public campgrounds is still first come, first served, even though they fill up practically every night during peak season. For campers, this means traveling in the morning and reaching your intended campground by early afternoon—or, during peak season at Yellowstone, by late morning. In the national parks, campers may find it more convenient to keep a single location for as much as a week and explore surrounding areas on day trips.

> The general rule in public campgrounds is first come, first served. They fill up practically every night during peak season.

For a listing of state parks with camping facilities and reservation information, contact the **Montana Department of Fish, Wildlife & Parks**. ~ 1420 East 6th Avenue, Helena, MT 59620; 406-444-2535. For information on camping in Montana's national forests, call 800-280-2267 or contact the **U.S. Forest Service-Northern Region**. ~ P.O. Box 7669, Missoula, MT 59807, 406-329-3511. For information on camping in national parks and monuments, contact the **National Park Service-Rocky Mountain Regional Headquarters**. ~ P.O. Box 25287, Denver, CO 80225; 303-969-2000.

WILDERNESS AREAS AND PERMITS   The passage of the Wilderness Act of 1993 represented a major expansion of federal wilderness protection. Today more than 4.3 million acres of national forest and Bureau of Land Management (BLM) land in Montana has been designated as wilderness. To be considered for federal wilderness protection, an area must consist of at least five contiguous square miles without a road of any kind. At the time it is declared a wilderness area, the land is limited to uses that existed as of that date. Since most wilderness areas in Montana were created quite recently, since 1978, it is generally the highest peaks, where roads are few and far between, that qualify for wilderness status. Besides protecting ancient forests from timber cutting by newly developed methods like skylining or helicopter airlifting, federal wilderness designation prohibits all mechanized transportation: no Jeeps, motorcycles or all-terrain vehicles, and (after years of heated controversy) no mountain bikes. Wilderness areas usually have well-developed trail networks for hiking, cross-country skiing and pack trips using horses or llamas.

You do not need a permit to hike or camp in most wilderness areas, but plan to stop at a ranger station anyway for trail maps and advice on current conditions and fire regulations. Tent camping is allowed without restriction in wilderness areas and almost all other backcountry areas of national forests, except where posted signs prohibit it. Throughout the national forests in dry season and in certain wilderness areas at all times, regulations may prohibit campfires and sometimes ban cigarette smoking, with stiff enforcement penalties.

For backcountry hiking in Glacier and Yellowstone national parks and most other National Park Service-administered sites, you must first obtain a permit from the ranger at the front desk in the visitors center. The permit procedure is simple and free. It helps park administrators measure the impact of hiking in sensitive ecosystems and distribute use evenly among the major trails.

BOATING & RAFTING

Many of Montana's large natural lakes and manmade reservoirs have large sections administered by federal or state agencies. Flathead Lake, for example, has several state park units on its shores; Bighorn Lake is contained within the Bighorn Canyon National Recreation Area; Fort Peck Lake is entirely encompassed by the Charles M. Russell National Wildlife Refuge. Federal boating safety regulations may vary slightly from state regulations, while Indian reservations have separate rules for boating on tribal lakes. (The southern half of huge Flathead Lake is contained within the reservation of the same name.) More significant than any differences between federal, state and tribal regulations are the local rules in force for specific lakes, which are posted near boat ramps. Ask for applicable boating regulations at a local marina or fishing supply store, or use the addresses and phone numbers listed in "Parks" or other sections of each chapter in this book to contact the headquarters for lakes where you plan to use a boat. The same is true if you're planning a trip on the Missouri or Yellowstone rivers, Montana's two major navigable streams.

Boats—from small motorized skiffs, big, fast bass boats, sometimes even houseboats—can be rented by the half-day, day, week or longer at marinas on many of the larger lakes. At most marinas, you can get a boat on short notice on a weekday, since much of their business comes from weekend recreationists.

Whitewater rafting is a very popular sport in many areas of the Montana Rockies, notably the Flathead River near West Glacier Park, the Smith River south of Great Falls, the Clark Fork and Blackfoot rivers east of Missoula, and a series of rivers flowing north out of Yellowstone Park: the Madison, Gallatin, Boulder, Stillwater and upper Yellowstone. Independent rafters are welcome, but because of the bulky equipment and specialized knowledge of river hazards involved, most adventurous souls stick with group tours offered by the many rafting companies located throughout the state (see "Outdoor Adventures" in the appropriate chapters). State and federal regulations require rafters, as well as people using canoes, kayaks, sailboards or inner tubes, to wear life jackets.

FISHING

Since the splash made by the 1992 Robert Redford movie *A River Runs Through It*, based on the Norman Maclean book of the same title, Montana fishing has received the kind of attention it has always deserved. The state has thousands of miles of streams and hundreds of lakes. The more accessible a shoreline, the more anglers you'll find there, especially in summer. You can beat crowds by hiking a few miles into the backcountry or, to some extent, by fishing on weekdays.

Fish hatcheries stock mountain streams with trout, especially rainbows, the Rockies' most popular game fish. Many coldwater lakes also offer fishing for cutthroat and golden trout, kokanee salmon and mountain whitefish. Catch-and-release flyfishing is the rule in some popular areas, allowing more anglers a chance at bigger fish. Be sure to inquire locally about eating the fish you catch, since some seemingly remote streams and rivers have been contaminated by old mines and mills.

In the warmer lakes and reservoirs of eastern Montana's Great Plains, the most popular game fish is walleye, a large and hard-fighting member of the perch family common in Missouri River reservoirs and other waters. There are also largemouth and small-mouth bass, northern pike, catfish, crappie, and various other species. Most exotic is the paddlefish, an enormous bottomfeeder with a two-foot snout; it hasn't evolved much over 70 million years. Sought for their delicious meat and caviar-like roe, paddlefish, which weigh well over 100 pounds at full maturity, must be snagged with huge treble hooks and stout casting gear. You can chase these fish from May to July in the Missouri and Yellowstone rivers, near their confluence.

For copies of the state's fishing regulations, inquire at a local fishing supply or marina, or contact the **Montana Department of Fish, Wildlife & Parks**. ~ 1420 East 6th Avenue, Helena, MT 59620; 406-444-2535. Montana state fishing licenses are required for fishing in national forests and national recreation areas, but not on Indian reservations, where daily permits are sold by the tribal governments. Yellowstone National Park has a seven-day fishing license, which is sold at any of the park's visitors centers for $5.

An annual nonresident fishing license is costly compared to the resident fee. Short-term licenses (ten days or less) are the best bet for nonresident visitors. Nonresident children normally fish free with a licensed adult. High-lake and stream fishing seasons begin in late spring and run through the fall; most lower-elevation lakes and reservoirs are open year-round for fishing.

**WINTER
SPORTS**

Downhill and cross-country skiing and snowmobiling are all extremely popular in Montana, along with less common cold-weather sports such as dog-sledding. If you're a snowsport lover, you can call Montana's winter "hotline" for current information, updated daily, on weather and snow conditions at downhill ski resorts throughout the state. ~ 406-444-2654, 800-847-4868. You can also call for winter road conditions. ~ 406-444-6339, 800-226-7623.

Montana has 14 downhill ski resorts, the largest of which are The Big Mountain (Whitefish), Big Sky, Bridger Bowl (Bozeman), and Red Lodge. There are more than two dozen groomed cross-country trails in six national forests, extensive backcountry trail systems in Yellowstone and Glacier national parks, and several lodges that cater specifically to Nordic adventurers. Additionally, 23 designated snowmobiling areas in the state connect more than 3500 miles of groomed trails, 600 of them at the self-proclaimed "snowmobile capital of the world": West Yellowstone.

Vehicle "snow parks" in national forests and other recreation areas are closely monitored. Before you can use these to unload your skis or snow machine and head into the backcountry, you must buy a season parking permit, available at most sporting-goods shops. The permit fee is much less than the fine you will be paying if you're caught without one.

**GUIDES
& OUT-
FITTERS**

The best way to assure the reliability of the folks guiding you into the wilderness by horse, raft or cross-country skis is to choose someone who has met the standards of a statewide organization of their peers. For a membership list, contact the **Montana Outfitters and Guides Association.** ~ P.O. Box 1248, Helena, MT 59624; 406-449-3578. For guides and outfitters in Yellowstone Park, contact **TW Recreational Services.** ~ Mammoth Hot Springs, Yellowstone National Park, WY 82190; 307-344-7311.

TWO

Northwest Montana

Northwest Montana is a child of the last Ice Age.

Glacial icecaps and inland seas receded from the Rockies only about 12,000 years ago. Their legacy—a wonderland of steep-sided mountains and broad valleys, of deep blue lakes and racing rivers extending south and west from Glacier National Park—can be enjoyed by all who visit the region today.

Waves of mountain ranges enclose myriad river valleys and lakes, including Flathead Lake, the largest natural freshwater lake west of the Mississippi River.

American Indians, of course, were the first permanent residents of northwest Montana. Nomadic tribes hunted Montana's plains and foraged its valleys for thousands of years before the Flathead settled west of the Continental Divide around A.D. 1500.

French and British trappers may have preceded American explorers Meriwether Lewis and William Clark (1805 and 1806) as the first whites to penetrate the region. In 1841, the first permanent white settlement—a Jesuit mission—was established in the Bitterroot Valley. Gold and silver rushes in the 1850s and 1860s soon led to Montana becoming a territory (in 1864) and a state (in 1889).

Today the economy of northwest Montana depends heavily upon mining and logging, pursuits increasingly supported by a network of hydroelectric dams on the Flathead, Kootenai, Clark Fork and other rivers. But the environmental ethnic is especially strong in this mountainous region. That sentiment is particularly evident among the liberal thinkers in the university town of Missoula and in the tourist-oriented communities near Glacier Park.

The tourist economy is tied closely to outdoor sports and wildlife viewing. Fishing and hunting, hiking and horseback riding, and skiing and river rafting are some of the more popular pastimes. Five national forests and eight designated wilderness areas provide ample opportunities.

Off-track adventurers are guaranteed to see many nonhuman denizens of the forests, mountains and riverbanks—like elk, deer, antelope, bighorn sheep and mountain goats. They may also encounter grizzly bears and mountain lions. Backcountry visitors should consult forest or park rangers to learn appropriate precautions before proceeding into the backcountry.

As elsewhere in Montana, habitation is sparse. There are really only two significant population centers: Missoula, home of the University of Montana and a focus for the state's wood-products industry amid the mountains and valleys of the southwest; and the Flathead Valley, between Flathead Lake and Glacier Park, encompassing Kalispell, Whitefish, Columbia Falls and several other small northwestern towns heavily dependent on year-round tourism.

You can start an exploration of the region from Missoula, at the foot of the Bitterroot Valley, where Montana's first white settlement took place. Route 93 continues north, passing through the Flathead Indian Reservation and skirting the National Bison Range, the Mission Range and Flathead Lake, to Kalispell. West from here, Route 2 extends into the tall timber country around Libby and its nearby Cabinet Mountains Wilderness.

Author Norman Maclean wrote his classic *A River Runs Through It* about life on the Blackfoot River, which runs through the Garnet Range and Lolo National Forest just east of Missoula. The spirit of a people in love with their natural environment, as portrayed in the book and 1992 movie, is typical of the entire region.

▼▼▼▼▼▼▼▼
Missoula

Sitting on the Clark Fork River at the intersection of five river valleys, surrounded by mountains on all sides, the university town of Missoula is unquestionably one of Montana's most attractive communities. It's an intellectually and artistically oriented city, perhaps Montana's most cultured; yet its proximity to outdoor recreation—the Rattlesnake Wilderness Area, which bans motorized travel, begins just a mile from the city limits—makes it a mecca for backpackers, river rafters and fishermen alike.

Missoula (pop. 45,000) got its name from British explorer David Thompson, who mapped the area in 1812 and dubbed it *Ne-missoola-takoo*, meaning "at the cold chilling waters" in the native Salish language. The first settlement here was in 1860, but the town grew quickly as a regional center for mining, logging and the railroad industry.

SIGHTS

Twenty-seven city buildings are today on the National Register of Historic Places, including the old **Northern Pacific Depot**, at the north end of Higgins Avenue, in downtown Missoula's main street. ~ 100 West Railroad Avenue. The station now houses a brewery and restaurant; the biweekly Farmers Market spreads around its portals, and city trolley tours begin at the circle in front. Inquire at the **Missoula Convention & Visitors Bureau** for details on this and other organized tours. ~ 825 East Front Street; 406-543-6623.

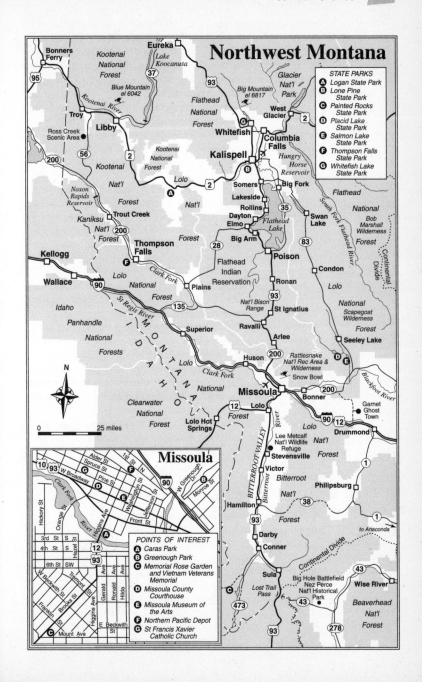

Northwest Montana

STATE PARKS
- **A** Logan State Park
- **B** Lone Pine State Park
- **C** Painted Rocks State Park
- **D** Placid Lake State Park
- **E** Salmon Lake State Park
- **F** Thompson Falls State Park
- **G** Whitefish Lake State Park

Bonners Ferry

Kootenai National Forest

Eureka

Lake Koocanusa

Glacier Nat'l Park

Blue Mountain el 6042

Big Mountain el 6817

West Glacier

Flathead National Forest

Troy

Libby

Whitefish

Columbia Falls

Ross Creek Scenic Area

Kootenai River

Kootenai National Forest

Kalispell

Hungry Horse Reservoir

Noxon Rapids Reservoir

Kootenai Nat'l Forest

Lolo

Somers

Big Fork

Flathead National Forest

Kaniksu Nat'l Forest

Trout Creek

Nat'l Forest

Lakeside

Rollins

Dayton

Elmo

Swan Lake

South Fork Flathead River

Bob Marshall Wilderness

Kellogg

Thompson Falls

Clark Fork

Forest

Big Arm

Flathead Lake

Poison

Condon

Continental Divide

Wallace

Lolo National Forest

Plains

Flathead Indian Reservation

Ronan

Lolo

Scapegoat Wilderness

National Forest

Idaho Panhandle

St Regis River

Nat'l Bison Range

St Ignatius

Superior

Ravalli

Arlee

Seeley Lake

National Forests

Lolo

Huson

Clark Fork

Rattlesnake Nat'l Rec Area & Wilderness

Blackfoot River

Clearwater National Forest

National Forest

Missoula

Snow Bowl

Bonner

Garnet Ghost Town

Lolo Hot Springs

Lolo

Forest

Lolo

Drummond

Lee Metcalf Nat'l Wildlife Refuge

Nat'l Forest

Stevensville

Victor

Bitterroot

Philipsburg

Hamilton

Nat'l

Forest

Darby

Conner

to Anaconda

Sula

Big Hole Battlefield Nez Perce Nat'l Historical Park

Wise River

Lost Trail Pass

Continental Divide

Beaverhead Nat'l Forest

Missoula

POINTS OF INTEREST
- **A** Caras Park
- **B** Greenough Park
- **C** Memorial Rose Garden and Vietnam Veterans Memorial
- **D** Missoula County Courthouse
- **E** Missoula Museum of the Arts
- **F** Northern Pacific Depot
- **G** St Francis Xavier Catholic Church

Alder St

1st St N

W Greenough Dr

Spruce St

Pine St

W Broadway

Washington St

Jefferson St

Monroe St

Clark Fork River

Higgins Ave

Front St

Hickory St

Orange St

3rd St S

4th St S

Hazel St

6th St SW

W Beckwith St

Beckwith St

Tremont St

Brooks St

Gerald Ave

Ronald Ave

Hilda Ave

Franklin St

Higgins Ave

E Beckwith St

Mount Ave

0   25 miles

Just three blocks southeast of the depot is the west end of the **East Pine Street Historic District.** Beginning at Pattee Street and extending five blocks east to Monroe, the thoroughfare boasts fine Queen Anne houses facing a central park strip. Turrets and asymmetrical features intersperse with more neo-classical styles to make this a "must-see" for architecture buffs.

The **Missoula Museum of the Arts,** a half block south of Pine, specializes in art of the western states. A permanent collection includes works by such local luminaries as Kendahl Jan Jubb and Monte Dolack. The museum also offers traveling exhibits, a museum shop and a full slate of community events. Admission. ~ 335 North Pattee Street; 406-728-0447.

Three blocks west is the **Missoula County Courthouse,** a 1910 building with a distinctive copper-domed clock tower that contains a two-ton bell. Painter Edgar Samuel Paxson, best known for his 1899 painting of "Custer's Last Stand," created a series of eight murals depicting different eras of Montana history for the courthouse. Completed in 1914, they surround the upper landing of the main inside staircase. ~ 220 West Broadway; 406-721-5700.

Nearby **St. Francis Xavier Catholic Church** also boasts outstanding artistry in its steeple, its stained-glass windows and its paintings. The church was constructed in 1891; the 66 early-Renaissance–style murals in its sanctuary were the work of Jesuit Brother Joseph Carignano, who created them in just 18 months of 1901 and 1902. ~ 420 West Pine Street.

A short distance southeast of downtown Missoula, the **University of Montana** (UM) spreads across 150 acres and some 50 buildings at the foot of Mount Sentinel, characterized by a giant *M* on its slopes. Chartered in 1893, UM has an enrollment of 10,600 students and is an integral part of life in Missoula. Tours of the tree-lined campus are available; you can also guide yourself around the University Center student union building, modern Washington-

---

✔ CHECK THESE OUT—UNIQUE SIGHTS

- Join a working firefighter on a personal tour of the **Smokejumper Training Center and Aerial Fire Depot** in Missoula, the largest such parachute base in the U.S. *page 45*
- See how the upper crust lived a century ago as you wander through the **Marcus Daly Mansion.** *page 53*
- Cruise through the **National Bison Range,** where more than 500 wild buffalo roam on land set aside by Theodore Roosevelt. *page 57*
- Stroll by the sidewalk cafés and art galleries of **Bigfork,** a blossoming arts community on the northeast shore of Flathead Lake. *page 60*

Grizzly Stadium, the Maureen and Mike Mansfield Library and the Paxson Fine Art Gallery. ~ Campus Drive; 406-243-0211.

Missoula Memorial Rose Garden was established in 1946 to remember World War II casualties. In 1989, the Montana Vietnam Veterans Memorial—a 12-foot-tall bronze sculpture by Deborah Copenhaver—was dedicated in the northeast corner of the park. Forty-four flower beds nurture 326 rose bushes, including a variety of hybrid teas, grandifloras, floribundas and miniatures. ~ 700 block of Brooks Street at Bickford Street.

If you leave the city center area and head west of Reserve Street on South Avenue, you'll come to the **Historical Museum at Fort Missoula**. A complex of 12 historical structures, including an early U.S. Forest Service lookout and a one-room schoolhouse, spreads across 32 acres right in the heart of what was once Fort Missoula (1877–1947). Indoor galleries display thousands of artifacts in permanent and changing exhibits. There's even an area for picnicking. ~ South Avenue West; 406-728-3476.

As Broadway (Business Route 90) extends northwest from downtown Missoula, it passes the **Rocky Mountain Elk Foundation**, which appeals to those who like their animals stuffed. A couple of dozen creatures, including hunters' trophy elk, are exhibited in the taxidermy section. There's also an art gallery with original paintings and bronze sculptures, a theater that presents wildlife films, and a gift shop that sells everything from books and T-shirts to racks of elk antlers. The nonprofit foundation claims to have conserved and restored more than one million acres of natural wildlife habitat across North America. ~ 2291 West Broadway; 406-523-4545.

About seven miles from downtown, next to Johnson Bell International Airport, is the **Smokejumper Training Center and Aerial Fire Depot**. Throughout the summer, U.S. Forest Service smokejumpers, trained to parachute into remote areas to fight wild fires, give guided tours of the largest smokejumper base in the United States and describe their jobs firsthand. Historical photographs and dioramas explain how fires are detected and squelched, sometimes (as in July 1994) at a cost of firefighters' lives. The adjacent Intermountain Sciences Laboratory continues research into new firefighting technologies. Admission. ~ 5765 Route 93 West; 406-329-4934.

◄ *HIDDEN*

DETOURS FROM ROUTE 90 From 1930 to 1953, **Ninemile Remount Depot** was a Forest Service dispatch center that supplied pack animals for firefighting and other backcountry work. The Civilian Conservation Corps built the Cape Cod–style ranger station in the 1930s; today, it is a working ranch open all summer long. Scheduled guided tours are available; you can also take a self-guided tour of the saddle shop, blacksmith shop and corrals.

To reach Ninemile from Route 90, take Exit 82, 22 miles northwest of Missoula, and follow the signs four miles north. ~ Ninemile Road, Huson; 406-626-5201.

Route 90 West enters the Idaho Panhandle at Lookout Pass, 105 miles from Missoula. The interstate follows the Clark Fork and St. Regis rivers along the flank of the Bitterroot Range through Lolo National Forest.

LODGING   The largest of five bed and breakfasts in Missoula is **Goldsmith's Inn**, with seven rooms. A 1911 manse, it was moved to its present site on the Clark Fork and restored in 1989. There's reproduction Victorian antique decor throughout, from the beds to the wallpaper to the handpainted tiles in the baths. (Every room has its own.) Gourmet breakfasts are served at the restaurant next door. ~ 809 East Front Street; 406-721-6732. MODERATE.

More intimate, and certainly more removed from the urban hubbub, is the **Colonial House**, eight miles east of Missoula off Route 90 Exit 113. This three-room B&B, which is surrounded by 25 acres of forests and meadows, delights guests with its family-heirloom antiques. It has a library with a fireplace and television and maintains a smoke-free environment. ~ 13655 Turah Road; 406-258-6787. MODERATE.

Goldsmith's Inn, a bed-and-breakfast, was once home to an early University of Montana president.

For wallet watchers, the **4B's Inn South** is a leading example of a regional chain. The motel has 91 rather sterile-looking guest rooms, all off indoor corridors, with twin or double beds and air-conditioning. There's a large hot tub in a solarium and an adjacent restaurant; the lobby contains all manner of books, magazines and tourism literature. ~ 3803 Brooks Street; 406-251-2665, 800-272-9500. If this one's full, check out **4B's Inn North**. ~ 4953 North Reserve Street; 406-542-7550. BUDGET.

Ruby's Reserve Street Inn, just off Route 90 at the north end of Missoula, is a new entrant in the upscale sweepstakes. Its 128 units are smaller that the Holiday Inn's or Red Lion's (see below), but have similar facilities and are neat and clean. In addition to a swimming pool, hot tub, sauna and workout room available to all guests, the motel has some guest rooms with waterbeds and private hot tubs, as well as larger family units and a children's playground. A complimentary continental breakfast is served. ~ 4825 North Reserve Street; 406-721-0990, 800-221-2057. MODERATE.

Just two blocks from the University of Montana is the **Creekside Inn**, whose 54 rooms all have queen-size beds and cable television. There's also an outdoor pool and an adjacent 24-hour restaurant. Don't expect to get a room here, however, when the UM football team is playing a home game. ~ 630 East Broadway; 406-549-2387, 800-551-2387. MODERATE.

Missoula's foremost property may be the **Holiday Inn Missoula-Parkside**, beside the Higgins Avenue bridge overlooking the Clark Fork River. Every one of the hotel's 200 rooms has either a mountain view or a balcony overhanging its spacious atrium lobby, which resembles a Midwest town square with its brickwork, trees, benches and gaslight lamps. Rooms have queen- or king-sized beds, air-conditioning and desks. Within the inn are a restaurant, lounge (featuring live rock music and casino machines), an indoor swimming pool, hot tub, sauna, workout room and game room. ~ 200 South Pattee Street; 406-721-8550, 800-399-0408, fax 406-721-7427. MODERATE TO DELUXE.

Also highly regarded and also overlooking the Clark Fork is the **Village Red Lion Motor Inn** just east of downtown Missoula. Its 172 rooms are spacious but otherwise pretty standard motel fare—queen beds, desk, air-conditioning, and so forth—but the extras are big city: separate coffee shop and fine-dining restaurant, cocktail lounge with live entertainment, swimming pool . . . the list goes on. ~ 100 Madison Street; 406-728-3100, 800-733-5466, fax 406-728-2530. MODERATE TO DELUXE.

DINING

◄ HIDDEN

Three dozen area restaurants team with local musicians every summer Wednesday from 11:30 a.m. to 1:30 p.m. for **Out to Lunch at Caras Park**. More than 1000 local residents typically attend this Clark Fork riverside gathering each week. Music changes weekly, from big band to acoustic rock to country; admission is free, and the food booths are inexpensive. You can also play on the antique carousel here. A free shuttle bus serves the park from downtown Missoula. ~ Beneath Higgins Avenue Bridge; 406-543-4238. BUDGET.

Avalon Café & Books, in an unmistakable lilac-colored Victorian house near the south shore of the Clark Fork River, offers a diverse choice of vegetarian lunches: spinach lasagna, brie-and-mango crêpes, quiches, pastas, soups, salads and sandwiches. Made-to-order omelettes highlight Sunday brunches, and the everyday espresso drinks come in what may be quart-size cups. Books offer food for thought. ~ 141 South 3rd Street West; 406-542-2474. BUDGET.

A favorite student hangout is **Food for Thought**, located just across the street from the University of Montana campus. Its in-house bakery draws the biggest "aahs" for its fresh-from-the-oven bread, New York cheesecake and espresso fudge brownies, but a full menu is served here from morning 'til way past dark. ~ 540 Daly Avenue; 406-721-6033. BUDGET.

The **Black Dog Café** is Missoula's only 100 percent vegetarian eatery. A pleasant café across Ryman Street from the County Courthouse, it has a full lunch and dinner menu and an outdoor seating area. Closed Sunday. ~ 138 West Broadway; 406-542-1138. BUDGET TO MODERATE.

At **Santorno's Italian Restaurant,** everything is Roma, *bella* Roma. Authentic Old World dinners are served by candlelight on handmade Italian dishes; you can almost imagine the strains of violin music beside your table. Standard pastas, meats, seafood and vegetarian items fill the menu, and there's full bar service. ~ 120 West Front Street; 406-542-1963. MODERATE.

At two Missoula outlets of **The Mustard Seed,** traditional Chinese dishes, from subtle Cantonese to tangy Szechuan, are given a contemporary American treatment in original recipes with fresh ingredients. The restaurants are low-lit, modern and efficient. Wine and beer are served. ~ Southgate Mall, 406-542-7333; and 419 West Front Street, 406-728-7825. MODERATE.

HIDDEN ►

Locals never seem to have any trouble finding the **Alley Cat Grill,** but visitors sometimes do: It's tucked back in an alley off Ryman Street near West Front Street. For an alley hideaway, though, this candlelit dinner house sets a very high standard. The focus is on creative fresh seafood and meat entrées, including fresh steamed clams, grilled swordfish, rack of lamb, and filet mignon in a green peppercorn sauce. Desserts are homemade, and there's a good list of wines, beers and espresso drinks. ~ 125½ Main Street; 406-728-3535. MODERATE TO DELUXE.

One flight above the historic Crystal Theatre, in a former dime-a-dance hall, **The Lily Restaurant** aspires to contemporary elegance. An international menu, ranging from saucy French to spicy Cajun and Thai cuisine, is presented with white tablecloth service beneath high skylit ceilings. An in-house baker prepares elaborate desserts, and the wine and beer list is extensive. Dinner only Tuesday through Saturday. ~ 131 South Higgins Avenue; 406-542-0002. MODERATE TO DELUXE.

SHOPPING

Some 90 vendors take to the streets every Saturday morning and Tuesday evening in summer for the **Missoula Farmers Market.** For a quarter century now, the crops and creations of gardeners and produce growers, bakers and coffee roasters, tinkers and tailors and all manner of artists have been offered for sale in the area fronting the Northern Pacific Depot, now usually overflowing onto Alder Street between North Higgins Avenue and Pattee Street. ~ Circle Square, north end of Higgins Avenue; 406-777-2636.

Just as the street market is an age-old international tradition, the trading post is a trademark of the American West. The **Three Rivers Trading Post** features American Indian crafts as well as many other collectibles and gifts. ~ 1124 Cedar Street; 406-721-2406.

Missoula's largest selection of handicrafts, art and food items made or produced within the state is sold at the **Montana Craft**

Connection. ~ 1605 Stephens Street; 406-549-4486. The **Sutton West Gallery** has rotating monthly exhibits of current work by many of the region's leading contemporary painters, sculptors, potters and jewelers. ~ 121 West Broadway; 406-721-5460. The **Monte Dolack Gallery** offers the work of a nationally known poster artist who lives and works in Missoula. ~ 139 West Front Street; 406-549-3248. Antiques and collectibles are displayed en masse at the **Montana Antique Mall** in the historic Montana Hotel building. ~ 331 West Railroad Street; 406-721-5366.

The Three Rivers Trading Post is a repository of American Indian crafts, including head-beaded buckskin and moccasins, quillwork and carved arrowheads.

The leading local bookstore is **Fact & Fiction**, which often highlights Montana authors with readings and signings. ~ 216 West Main Street; 406-721-2881. **Garden City News** has more than 800 magazines on its racks, as well as a variety of national newspapers and detailed maps. ~ 329 North Higgins Avenue; 406-543-3470. **Re: Sports** markets secondhand outdoor gear and athletic equipment at modest prices. ~ 506 Toole Street; 406-542-2487.

Montana visitors are always delighted to learn that the state has no sales tax, so visits to **Southgate Mall,** the largest shopping center within a 200-mile radius, often seem like Christmas. More than 100 stores are open daily. ~ Brooks Street and South Avenue; 406-721-5140.

As Montana's undeclared "culture capital," Missoula has a wider choice of sophisticated entertainment than anywhere else in the state. **NIGHTLIFE**

For stage aficionados, the **Montana Repertory Theatre,** a topnotch professional company, tours regionally. ~ UM Performing Arts Center; 406-243-4481. The **Missoula Community Theatre** performs year-round; its associated **Missoula Children's Theatre** visits nearly 300 communities a year, making it one of the largest touring children's theaters in America. ~ 221 East Front Street; 406-728-1911.

Music lovers have the **Missoula Symphony Orchestra & Chorale,** whose five-concert subscription series features outstanding guest artists between October and May; its integral ensemble, the **String Orchestra of the Rockies,** performs throughout Montana. ~ Wilma Theatre, 131 South Higgins Avenue; 406-721-3194. Missoula also has a dance troupe, the **Garden City Ballet Company.** ~ 406-721-3675. In addition, the **International Wildlife Film Festival** is presented in Missoula every spring. ~ 406-728-9380. See the daily *Missoulian* or the weekly *Missoula Independent* for schedules, prices and venues.

The **University of Montana Department of Drama/Dance** serves up student theater and dance from September through April in the Masquer and Montana theaters. ~ UM Performing Arts Center; 406-243-4481, box office: 406-243-4581. For information on other campus events, call the UM entertainment hotline. ~ 406-243-2020.

You can find live music of all kinds around the city. For contemporary rock bands on tour, try **Jay's Bar**. Cover. ~ 119 West Main Street; 406-728-9915. For rhythm-and-blues, visit the **Union Club**. ~ 208 East Main Street; 406-728-7980. For jazz, there's the **Old Post Pub**. ~ 103 West Spruce Street; 406-721-7399. Blues and folk-music lovers go to **The Top Hat**. Occasional cover. ~ 134 West Front Street; 406-728-9865.

The **Iron Horse Brew Pub** in the Northern Pacific Depot serves up old-style German pilsners and ambers produced next door at the Bayern Brewing Co. The pub has a full bar, a beer garden and live music; Thursdays are smoke-free. ~ 100 West Railroad Street; 406-728-8866, brewery 406-721-8704. **The Press Box**, across a footbridge from the university's Washington-Grizzly Stadium, is a sports bar featuring three satellite dishes, 16 TVs, 20 casino gaming machines and a restaurant. ~ 835 East Broadway; 406-721-1212.

There's no shortage of casino action. One local favorite is the **Lucky Strike Casino**. On Brooks Street one block from South Avenue, it's open 24 hours and offers poker and keno machines, live poker tables and off-track betting on horse and greyhound races. Low-cost breakfasts, lunches and dinners are served, and there's live entertainment weekends. ~ 1515 Dearborn Street; 406-549-4152.

PARKS

GREENOUGH PARK 🚶🚲🛝 Enjoy this city park by following a one-mile paved path along Rattlesnake Creek, or taking a short drive that parallels it through lush vegetation. Interpretive signs remind visitors of the excellent birdwatching in the park, once part of a Missoula estate. The facilities include picnic areas and restrooms; restaurants and groceries are nearby. ~ From East Broadway, take Madison Street north to Duncan Drive. Turn right on Vine Street and left on Monroe to the park; 406-721-7275.

RATTLESNAKE NATIONAL RECREATION AREA AND WILDERNESS
🚶🚲🐎🛶🛝 These 61,000 acres of rugged mountain country begin just a few miles north of Missoula. Numerous creeks tumble from the high country, where craggy peaks and tiny lakes speckle the alpine landscape. Motorized vehicles and bicycles are permitted in the recreation area—which includes the Montana Snowbowl ski area—but not in the wilderness. Despite its name, rattlesnakes are not a problem. Restrooms are located at some trailheads; restaurants and groceries are in Missoula. ~ Principal

access is off Sawmill Gulch Road, which turns off Rattlesnake Drive about four miles north of downtown Missoula; 406-329-3814.

▲ Tents are permitted anywhere beyond a three-mile radius from the Sawmill Gulch Road trailhead.

LOLO NATIONAL FOREST 🚶🚲🐎🏊🏠🎿⛷️🚤🚣 Based in Missoula, this forest encompasses much of four counties from the Idaho border (east of Sandpoint) to the Continental Divide, excluding Flathead Indian Reservation. It surrounds or borders five wilderness areas and numerous lakes and rivers. Anglers cast for trout, whitefish, kokanee, bass, pike and perch. Facilities include picnic areas and restrooms; restaurants and groceries are in many nearby towns. ~ From Missoula, travel southwest on Route 12, west on Route 90, northwest on Route 200, or northeast via Route 200 to Route 83; 406-329-3750.

▲ There are 416 RV/tent sites and 80 for tents only at 21 campgrounds, none with hookups; no charge to $7 per night; 14-day maximum stay.

WELCOME CREEK WILDERNESS AREA 🚶🐎🏠🚤 This small wilderness, in the northwest corner of Granite County, extends from the crest of the Sapphire Mountains to Rock Creek, about 20 miles southeast of Missoula. Several trails, including those for Welcome Creek and Sawmill Creek, begin from Forest Road 102. ~ To Forest Road 102, take Exit 126 from Route 90 east of Missoula and follow Rock Creek south; 406-329-3814.

▲ Primitive only.

▼▼▼▼▼▼▼▼▼▼▼▼

Bitterroot Valley

The Bitterroot River flows almost due north for 100 miles from the Continental Divide to enter the Clark Fork River just west of Missoula. The valley it has carved, between the Bitterroot and Sapphire Mountains, was the site of the first pioneer settlement in Montana. In 1841, Jesuit Father Pierre De Smet established a Roman Catholic mission at what is now Stevensville. A nearby fort soon followed, and the onrush of settlers wasn't far behind. Today the valley is a thriving grain-growing region with access for visitors to numerous historical locations and outdoor adventures.

Route 93 follows the Bitterroot Valley south from Missoula to Lost Trail Pass, where it enters Idaho.

SIGHTS

Many Missoula workers commute daily from **Lolo**, 11 miles south at the junction of Route 12, which continues to Lewiston, Idaho. **Lolo Hot Springs**, 26 miles west of Lolo, has been a popular getaway for area residents for more than over a century. Built around the site today is The Fort resort, which features an outdoor hot-springs swimming pool and an indoor soaking pool, both open to the public for a fee. ~ Route 12, Lolo Hot Springs; 406-273-2201.

The **Lolo Pass Visitors Information Center**, seven miles farther west on the Montana–Idaho border, is located at 5235 feet at the intersection of ancient Indian trade routes from north, south, east and west. The center, staffed by Clearwater National Forest in summer and closed in winter, contains displays describing the natural and human history of the pass, including Lewis and Clark's passage along the Lolo Trail. ~ Route 12, Lolo Pass; 208-942-3113.

Twenty-eight miles south of Missoula, and just over a mile east of Route 93, is historic **Stevensville**, site of the first permanent white settlement in Montana. Here is Father De Smet's **St. Mary's Mission**, the first Catholic mission in the American Northwest. The grounds of the restored Italianate mission include the chapel and priest's residence, a log-house pharmacy, an American Indian museum, a cemetery, a gift shop, the mission's original apple orchard and a picnic area. Tours are offered daily in summer, other times by appointment. Admission. ~ De Smet Park, West 4th Street, Stevensville; 406-777-5734.

Major John Owen built nearby **Fort Owen** of adobe and logs in 1850, and it soon became a regional trade center. Brochures and interpretive displays lend themselves to self-guided tours of the fort, which is a free state park located one-half mile east of Stevensville junction. ~ Route 269, Stevensville; 406-542-5500.

The life of northern Bitterroot Valley residents through the last half of the 19th century is related at the **Stevensville Historical Museum**. Closed in winter. ~ 217 Main Street; 406-777-3201.

The **Lee Metcalf National Wildlife Refuge** encompasses 2700 acres of wetland along the east bank of the Bitterroot River, two miles north of Stevensville. Named for the late Senator Metcalf, a Stevensville native, the refuge is home to many deer and birds, including osprey, tundra swans and a wide variety of other migratory waterfowl. Dirt roads, interpretive trails and a picnic area are open year-round. ~ Route 203, Stevensville; 406-777-5552.

◆◆

HISTORICAL HOT SPRINGS

American Indians knew Lolo Hot Springs as a meeting place and bathing spot, and as a mineral lick for animals. Lewis and Clark camped here in September 1805 and once again in June 1806. William Clark wrote in his journal that he "found this water nearly boiling hot at the places it spouted from the rocks. . . ." Today you can immerse yourself in the pools and contemplate days of yore at The Fort at Lolo Hot Springs.

Other Bitterroot Valley towns, including Victor, Hamilton and Darby, feature more historical sites. The **Victor Heritage Museum**, housed in an old train station 35 miles from Missoula, features early railroad artifacts in its collection. Closed in winter. ~ Main and Blake streets, Victor; 406-642-3997.

Twelve miles farther, near **Hamilton**, population center of the Bitterroot Valley (pop. 2700), is the valley's preeminent manmade attraction: the **Marcus Daly Mansion**. "Copper King" Daly, an Irish immigrant, and his family used the Georgian revival–style estate as a summer escape from Butte between 1890, when it was built, and 1941, when Mrs. Daly died. The three-story mansion—which contains 42 rooms, 24 bedrooms, 15 baths and seven Italian marble fireplaces in its 24,000-plus square feet—is now owned by the state. Located two miles north of Hamilton on a secondary highway, it is surrounded by 50 planted acres, a tiny fraction of the 22,500-acre Bitter Root Stock Farm that Daly owned. Tours are conducted daily from mid-April to mid-October, by appointment the rest of the year. Admission. ~ Eastside Highway, Hamilton; 406-363-6004.

The ornate brick **Tammany Castle**, a mile south of the mansion, was a stable for race horses; still owned by descendants of the Daly family, it is not open to the public but can be viewed from the highway. ~ Eastside Highway, Hamilton.

Ravalli County Museum preserves pioneer and Indian artifacts in the old 1900 Ravalli County Courthouse. Of note is a display honoring scientists at Hamilton's Rocky Mountain Laboratories who discovered the causes and cures for Rocky Mountain tick fever. Admission. ~ 205 Bedford Street, Hamilton; 406-363-3338.

Little Darby, 17 miles south of Hamilton, boasts the **Darby Pioneer Memorial Museum**, an 1889 log cabin moved from nearby Tin Cup Creek. It now features a re-created trapper's abode and the original Darby phone switchboard. ~ Council Park, Main Street, Darby; 406-821-4503. Also here is the **Darby Historic Ranger Station**, which displays early-20th-century U.S. Forest Service memorabilia and offers current information on Bitterroot National Forest recreation. ~ Main Street, Darby; 406-821-3913.

About four miles south of Darby, consider turning off Route 93 onto Route 473. The road is mostly paved for 28 miles to **Painted Rocks State Park**. ~ West Fork Road, Darby; 542-5500. Five miles south of the state park, look for the **Alta Ranger Station**, ◄ *HIDDEN* the first Forest Service ranger station in the United States. It was built in 1899 by two men using cross-cut saws and axes. Though only traces remain, Alta was then a tent city inhabited by more than 500 gold miners.

Route 93 climbs 31 miles beyond Darby to 7014-foot Lost Trail Pass and the **Lost Trail Powder Mountain** ski area on the

Montana–Idaho border. Route 93 continues south into Idaho. Route 43 turns east, climbing Chief Joseph Pass to the Big Hole Battlefield unit of Nez Perce National Historical Park (see Chapter Four).

LODGING

The Fort at Lolo Hot Springs creates a wilderness feeling while providing a thimbleful of luxury. The main attraction is its natural hot-springs pools. Standard rooms have twin or double beds, desk and chair; deluxe rooms have queen beds, dinettes and sleeper sofas. All have private baths. The resort has a restaurant, a saloon-casino and gift shops. Horses are available for summer rides, snowmobiles for winter excursions. ~ Route 12, Lolo Hot Springs; 406-273-2201. MODERATE.

In the heart of the Bitterroot Valley, **Deffy's Motel** offers a lot for the price. Air-conditioned rooms have queen-size beds, TV and phones (of course), and the motel has a hot-tub for soaking tired driving muscles. A 24-hour restaurant is nearby. ~ 321 South 1st Street, Hamilton; 406-363-1244, 800-363-1305. BUDGET.

The newly renovated **Best Western Hamilton Inn** has 36 spacious rooms, some with kitchenettes. All have desks, queen-size beds and other standard furnishings. The two-story motel has a large outdoor hot tub, and it offers free morning coffee. ~ 409 South 1st Street, Hamilton; 406-363-2142, 800-426-4586, fax 406-363-2142. MODERATE.

HIDDEN ▶

A full range of guest ranches are located at the head of the valley. At the low end is the **Nez Perce Ranch**, three out-of-the-way log cabins (including lofts, each sleeps six) on the Nez Perce Fork of the Bitterroot River. Open June to September, the ranch offers *no* planned activities: You fish, hike and soak in hot springs on your own, and if you want to ride, the owners will line you up with an area outfitter. Prepare meals in your own cabin or drive 10 to

◆◆

✔ CHECK THESE OUT—UNIQUE LODGING

- *Budget:* Cook your own trout breakfast at the isolated **Nez Perce Ranch**, on the banks of the Bitterroot River. *page 54*
- *Moderate:* Share a hot tub or a sunken fireplace at the ecologically self-sufficient **Mandorla Ranch Bed & Breakfast**. *page 61*
- *Moderate to deluxe:* Enjoy the Salish-Kootenai motifs and crafts at Polson's native-owned **KwaTaqNuk Resort at Flathead Bay**. *page 61*
- *Deluxe:* Learn to sail at the **Flathead Lake Lodge** aboard the *Questa*, a 51-foot yacht that won the 1930 Americas Cup for financier J. P. Morgan. *page 61*

Budget: under $50 Moderate: $50–$90 Deluxe: $90–$130 Ultra-deluxe: over $130

40 miles for a restaurant. Clearly, this is designed for the independent, outdoor-oriented vagabond. ~ West Fork Route, Darby; 406-349-2100 (summer), 602-569-6776 (winter). BUDGET.

An Italian-German cowboy? That's Guido Oberdorfer. He and his Swiss wife, Hanny, bought the **West Fork Meadows Ranch** in 1989, and today they combine riding (guests are assigned one horse for their entire stay) and other activities—including mountain biking and rafting—with comfortable lodging and fine dining at his Black Horse Inn (see "Dining"). The ranch, one-half mile past Painted Rock Lake, accommodates 34 guests in seven cabins, a log house and the 6000-square-foot main lodge. ~ Coal Creek Road, Darby; 406-349-2468, 800-800-1437, fax 406-349-2031. MODERATE TO DELUXE.

Nestled against the Selway-Bitterroot Wilderness Area near the foot of lofty Trapper Peak, the **Triple Creek Ranch** combines outdoor programs with luxury accommodations. The adults-only ranch has plush cabins and poolside suites for up to 16 couples and 23 single visitors, each with kitchenettes, stocked refrigerators, complimentary liquor and a private hot tub. Gourmet meals are served in the lodge. Open May through October for a full range of programs, December through February for winter activities. ~ West Fork Road, Darby; 406-821-4664, fax 406-821-4666. ULTRA-DELUXE.

DINING

◄ HIDDEN

Seeming out of place in the central Bitterroot Valley, **The Hamilton** in tiny Victor is a throwback to the traditional pubs of the British Isles. Between games of darts you can enjoy fish-and-chips or fresh fruit cobbler and sip on imported and microbrewed ales and stouts. ~ 104 Main Street, Victor; 406-642-6644. BUDGET.

The Bitterroot's leading restaurant may well be **The Banque Club**, located in an old downtown bank building on two floors. Downstairs, creative Continental cuisine is served in elegant ambience; upstairs, The **Exchange Bar & Grill** offers more casual chowing and drinking at somewhat lower cost. ~ 225 West Main Street, Hamilton; 406-363-1955. MODERATE.

In fact, you can bank on finding a good place to eat in Hamilton, because **Stavers Restaurant** also occupies a turn-of-the-century financial institution. Today, money changes hands for its bistro fare (pastas, chicken, fish, beef and the like); its wines and microbrews; and its great mud pie. ~ 163 South 2nd Street, Hamilton; 406-363-4433. MODERATE.

Bill Clinton has absolutely nothing to do with **Bad Bubba's BBQ**, a Texas-style barbecue joint where you'll get everything from short ribs to catfish to a 32-ounce steak. A favorite here is the half-pound buffalo burgers. ~ 105 North 2nd Street, Hamilton; 406-363-7427. BUDGET.

There may no no better view in the Bitterroot Valley than from **The Grubstake,** located on the slope of Downing Mountain 2000 feet above the valley floor. The unique 16-sided building has a huge central fireplace, a great salad bar and a menu that features steaks, prime rib and Montana mountain trout. Dinner is served at 6:30 nightly. Call for reservations and directions, then plan a half-hour to switchback the eight miles to the restaurant. ~ 1017 Grubstake Road, Hamilton; 406-363-3068. MODERATE.

HIDDEN ▶   Even more out of the way is the **Lost Horse Saloon & Eatery,** in a century-old log cabin by Lolo National Forest. Inside, you eat steak, chicken and burgers; outside, you play horseshoes or volleyball in summer, or sled in winter. From Route 93 eight miles south of Hamilton, turn west three miles on Lost Horse Road, then west another one and one quarter miles on dirt Forest Road 429. ~ 1000 Lost Horse Road, Charlos Heights; 406-363-1460. BUDGET.

Isolated but worth a detour is the **Black Horse Inn,** south of Darby at West Fork Meadows Ranch. Wild game and German cuisine are the featured courses on an adventuresome menu served in a large, rustic dwelling in the upper Bitterroot Valley. A five-course menu special changes nightly. Dinner and Sunday brunch only. ~ Route 473, Darby; 800-800-1437. MODERATE TO DELUXE.

SHOPPING   Art lovers traveling south through the Bitterroot Valley won't want to miss the **Bronze Horse Foundry and Gallery,** the oldest foundry in the Northwest, located about six miles south of Stevensville. The gallery offers collectible sculptures and limited-edition bronze and silver castings. ~ Eastside Highway, Victor; 406-777-3957.

If you're headed for a guest ranch and want to look the part, drop by the **Hamilton Saddlery** for a full range of Stetson hats and Texas boots. You'll also find pack equipment here and silver jewelry. ~ 167 South 2nd Street, Hamilton; 406-363-4190.

PARKS   **BITTERROOT NATIONAL FOREST** 🚶🚴🏇⛷🏕🏊🎣⚓ 🚣🛶🛷🎣 The forest blankets most of the Sapphire Mountains and the lower slopes of the Bitterroots (below the Selway-Bitterroot Wilderness Area) on either side of the Bitterroot Valley. It also shrouds the upper forks of the Bitterroot River. Headquarters are in Hamilton. Facilities include picnic areas and restrooms; restaurants and groceries are in many nearby towns. ~ Most recreational sites are a short distance off Route 93 between Stevensville and Lost Trail Pass; 406-363-3131.

▲ There are 144 RV/tent sites and 16 for tents only at 15 campgrounds, none with hookups); no charge to $8 per night; 14-day maximum stay.

SELWAY-BITTERROOT WILDERNESS AREA 🚶🏇🏕🎣 Some 1.3 million acres in Montana and Idaho are contained in this massive wilderness. Crowned by the crest of the dramatic Bitterroot Range, it extends about 60 miles from 9075-foot Lolo Peak to 10,157-foot Trapper Peak. In Montana, the main attraction to hikers and horseback riders is a series of gorgeous, wildlife-rich creek canyons. Cutthroat trout thrive in alpine lakes and streams. ~ Easiest access to trailheads is from the Twin Lakes campground, reached via Forest Road 429 and Lost Horse Road, which turns west off Route 93 eight miles south of Hamilton; 406-363-7161.

▲ Primitive only.

LAKE COMO RECREATION AREA

Rock Creek rushes from the Bitterroots to feed this three-mile-long reservoir. Facilities include picnic areas and restrooms; restaurants and groceries in Hamilton. Closed September 16 to May 3. ~ Route 93 south from Hamilton 12 miles, then Lake Como Road two miles west; 406-363-3131.

▲ There are 11 RV/tent sites, none with hookups; $8 per night; 14-day maximum stay.

PAINTED ROCKS STATE PARK

Built along the shore of pretty Painted Rocks Lake, deep in the southern Bitterroot Range, this park is open year-round. Picnic areas and restrooms round out the amenities. Restaurants and groceries are in Darby. ~ From Route 93 five miles south of Darby, turn south on paved West Fork Road (Route 473) for 24 miles; 406-542-5500.

▲ There are 25 primitive sites, none with hookups; no charge; 14-day maximum stay.

▼▼▼▼▼▼▼▼▼▼▼▼

Flathead Indian Reservation & Lake

Spanning 1942 square miles of land surrounding the meandering Flathead River and broad Flathead Lake between Missoula and Kalispell, the Flathead Indian Reservation is the home of the Confederated Salish and Kootenai Tribes.

Within this vast and scenic swath of landscape are located the impressive National Bison Range, the charming St. Ignatius Mission, several units of Flathead Lake State Park and other attractions, not the least of which is the foreboding Mission Range that marks the reservation's eastern boundary.

SIGHTS

Most travelers cross the reservation via Route 93 between Missoula and Kalispell. Probably the most intriguing detour along the way—for nature lovers, at least—is the **National Bison Range**. When it was established by President Theodore Roosevelt in 1908, only about 20 wild bison survived from an estimated 50 million a century earlier; most had been wantonly slaughtered during the four decades between 1840 and 1880. Today up to 500 of the great beasts, each of which can weigh a ton or more, roam this reserve's 19,000 acres of natural grassland and scattered woods.

A 19-mile scenic drive begins and ends at the visitors center; it climbs a well-maintained dirt road over Red Sleep Mountain, enabling observation of bison herds (including, in the spring and early summer, many calves). Allow at least 90 minutes. The reserve also harbors herds of elk, mule deer, whitetail deer, bighorn sheep and pronghorn antelope, along with numerous other smaller mammals, ground birds and migratory waterfowl.

To reach the main entrance, turn west off Route 93 on Route 200 at Ravalli, 37 miles north of Missoula; after six miles, turn north again on Route 212, and proceed about four miles to the bison range. Admission. ~ Route 212, Moiese; 406-644-2211

Beyond Ravalli on Route 93, you'll surmount a saddle and find yourself staring into the spectacular **Mission Range** of the Rockies. Sheer, glacier-carved cliffs drop dramatically from the stark, snow-specked, 8000-to-9000-foot climes of Mount Harding, Mountaineer Peak and Daughter of the Sun Mountain, presenting a stunning backdrop for the farms and communities of the Mission Valley below its western flank.

The St. Ignatius Mission was built in 1891 with a million kiln-baked bricks.

Perhaps no view of the Mission Range is more spiritually uplifting than one taking in the **St. Ignatius Mission**. A designated national historic site, the mission was established by the wide-ranging Jesuit Father Pierre De Smet in 1854, 13 years after he founded St. Mary's Mission at modern Stevensville. Flathead and other tribes erected the current church in 1891 from lumber and kiln-baked bricks. Brother Joseph Carignano, whose work also adorns St. Francis Xavier Church in Missoula, painted the mission's 58 wall and ceiling murals. Nineteenth-century artifacts and American Indian crafts are exhibited in the original log chapel and priest's residence, located next to the current church. ~ Off Route 93, St. Ignatius; 406-745-2768.

Beyond St. Ignatius, you're deep in the heart of the **Flathead Indian Reservation** on which more than half of the 6700 enrolled tribal members live. Powwows are held in July at opposite ends of the reserve in the villages of Arlee and Elmo. The southeast and northwest corners of the reservation are primitive areas open to tribal members only. Most of the eastern flank of the reservation, from Flathead Lake to the Jocko River, comprises the **Mission Mountains Tribal Wilderness Area,** with public trailheads providing access to high-country lakes and peaks. ~ P.O. Box 278, Pablo, MT 59855; 406-675-2700.

A mile north of Pablo, where tribal headquarters are located, the new **Sqélix'w-Aqsmakni'k Cultural Center,** "The People's Center," includes an exhibit gallery of Salish, Pend d'Oreille and

Kootenai tribal life. Guided interpretive tours and educational programs are also offered, and there is an excellent gift shop. ~ Route 93, Pablo; 406-675-0160. Ten miles southwest of Ravalli at the foot of Hewolf Mountain, the **Agnes Vanderburg Cultural** ◄ HIDDEN **Camp**, open summers, offers free instruction in Salish and Pend d'Oreille language, crafts and customs to tribal and non-tribal members alike. ~ South Valley Creek Road, Ravalli; 406-745-4572.

On either side of Pablo are the **Ninepipe National Wildlife Refuge** and the **Pablo National Wildlife Refuge,** which together contain more than 4500 acres of pond-and-wetland habitat for waterfowl and for the day use of curious visitors. ~ Dellwo Road and Minersinger Trail, Pablo; 406-644-2211.

FLATHEAD LAKE   At the town of Polson, seven miles north of Pablo and just over halfway from Missoula to Kalispell, Route 93 meets **Flathead Lake,** the largest natural freshwater lake west of the Mississippi River. Twenty-eight miles long and 15 miles at its widest, the lake boasts 185 miles of shoreline. A driving loop of the lake is 86 miles by paved highway.

Polson, the largest town on the lakeshore with 3300 people, has a thriving resort business heavily oriented toward boating and fishing. Fishermen come from all over North America to test the deep waters of Flathead Lake, gouged by the last glaciers. It is likewise popular with other boating enthusiasts, from motorboaters to sailboaters. A good way to explore is aboard the 41-foot tour boat *Port Polson Princess.* ~ Polson; 406-883-2448.

Polson has two interesting museums. The **Polson-Flathead Historical Museum** focuses on Polson's pioneer heritage as the Flathead's earliest settlement and includes a saddle that once belonged to notorious "Calamity Jane" Canary. ~ 802 Main Street, Polson; 406-883-3049.

The **Miracle of America Museum,** a mile south, features U.S. military history and World Wars I and II poster art, as well as logging artifacts, the Montana Fiddlers Hall of Fame and a 65-foot boat said to have belonged to mythical lumberjack Paul Bunyan. Admission. ~ 58176 Route 93, Polson; 406-883-6804.

Bunyan is said to have gouged the sheer walls of the Flathead River Gorge, which drains the lake. Water, regulated by the **Kerr Dam,** flows through the channel at a rate of a half-million gallons a second. At 204 feet, the concrete dam is more than 50 feet higher than Niagara Falls. ~ Kerr Dam Road, Polson; 406-883-4450.

Around the lakeshore northeast and northwest of Polson are six separate units of **Flathead Lake State Park** (see "Parks" section below).

The hamlet of Dayton, 23 miles northwest of Polson with a view toward Wild Horse Island, is the site of Montana's only winery: **Mission Mountain Winery**. Because the winter climate is too harsh for viticulture, most grapes are imported from Washington's Columbia Valley, then blended here. The cabernet sauvignon and Johannesburg riesling are surprisingly good; other vintages include chardonnay, white riesling and ruby red champagne. The tasting room is open daily, from May to October. ~ Route 93, Dayton; 406-849-5524.

North from Dayton along Route 93, around the western lake-shore, you'll spot numerous residences overlooking Flathead Lake, often spectacularly situated in beautiful communities like Rollins and Lakeside. On the way, the highway passes the West Shore Unit of Flathead Lake State Park. West Shore's rock formations attract hikers and photographers.

At Somers, Route 93 breaks away from Flathead Lake and con-tinues to Kalispell, only eight miles farther north. Lower Valley Road (Route 82) continues east, along the north end of the lake and across the Flathead River, to Route 35. The town of **Bigfork** is two miles south of this junction.

Located where the Swan River enters Flathead Lake, Bigfork blossoms with the spring flowers that line its main street and hang outside its sidewalk cafés and restaurants. The village is rapidly gaining a statewide reputation as a center for the fine and performing arts. The **Bigfork Art & Cultural Center**, for in-stance, exhibits the paintings, sculptures and crafts of local arti-sans. ~ 525 Electric Avenue, Bigfork; 406-837-6927. Across the street, the new, million-dollar **Bigfork Summer Playhouse** pre-sents popular live theater. ~ 526 Electric Avenue, Bigfork; 406-837-4886.

Boat tours are a great way to see Flathead Lake. One option: the 51-foot racing sloop *Questa*, which won the 1930 Americas Cup for financier J. P. Morgan. ~ Flathead Lake Lodge, Bigfork; 406-837-4391, 800-332-7148.

From Bigfork, Route 35 returns to Polson down the east shore of the lake, a distance of 32 miles. The orchards along this shore were once famous for their plump, sweet cherries, but a 1989 cold snap destroyed the industry. Determined growers have replanted; some are experimenting with other fruits.

The **Swan Lake Road** (Route 83), which tucks itself behind the Mission Range and takes the 124-mile back-door route to Missoula, begins near Bigfork. It follows the Swan River south nearly to its source, crosses a saddle and proceeds down the Clear-water River to its confluence with the Blackfoot. The principal re-sort communities along this route are **Swan Lake**, at the southern end of the 12-mile-long lake of the same name, and **Seeley Lake**. Near Seeley Lake are state parks at **Salmon Lake**, five miles south, and **Placid Lake**, six miles southwest.

LODGING

◀ HIDDEN

Mandorla Ranch Bed & Breakfast, at the foot of the Mission Range on the Flathead Indian Reservation, couldn't ask for a more beautiful setting. Five guest rooms, three with private baths, share a log home with oak antiques, American Indian motifs, original Western art and mounted game. A deluxe suite even has a fireplace and private entrance to a hot-tub solarium. A 25-foot sunken fireplace and sofa sit beneath the cathedral ceiling of the "great room," and there's a TV room and library adjacent. The 35-acre ranch is home to a host of animals, including horses, and there are riding trails directly behind it. Designed in 1980 to be ecologically self-sufficient, it is four miles east of Route 93 via Eagle Pass Road. ~ 6873 Allard Road, St. Ignatius; 406-745-4500. MODERATE.

On Flathead Lake, you can't do better than the **KwaTaqNuk Resort at Flathead Bay**, where you can get lakefront accommodation and a hefty helping of American Indian culture with it. The 112 high-ceilinged rooms have Salish-Kootenai motifs and all the standard amenities, including private baths. The Best Western–associated resort offers a restaurant, a lounge and casino, a gift shop and an art gallery, two swimming pools (one indoor) and a whirlpool; it also features a native crafts pavilion and offers boating and water-sports rentals from its marina. ~ 303 Route 93 East, Polson; 406-883-3636, 800-882-6363, fax 406-883-5392. MODERATE TO DELUXE.

Swan Hill Bed and Breakfast, a large and luxurious redwood country home on ten acres overlooking Flathead Lake, features an indoor pool with a skylit cathedral ceiling. The four guest rooms have Queen Anne, wicker or whitewashed pine furnishings; three have private baths. A full breakfast is served on an outdoor deck that is frequently visited by deer in the evening. ~ 460 Kings Point Road, Polson; 406-883-5292, 800-537-9489. MODERATE.

Only a mile from Bigfork, the **Flathead Lake Lodge** is a 2000-acre ranch with a dual emphasis: riding and water sports. For horse lovers, there's morning and evening instruction and trail rides. "Our family's been involved in rodeo for years, so we even teach team roping," owner Doug Averill said. In the afternoon, attention shifts to the lake, where guests learn to sail and team aboard J. P. Morgan's Americas Cup prototype, the 51-foot *Questa*, in match racing with other yachts. Lodging is in three lodges and 20 two- and three-bedroom log cottages. Full family-style meals are served in the central lodge. Open May to October, with a one-week minimum stay during peak season. ~ P.O. Box 248, Bigfork, MT 59911; 406-837-4391, fax 406-837-6977. DELUXE.

Low-cost accommodations are hard to come by in this region, especially during the peak summer tourist season, so the two-story **Timbers Motel** is a pleasant surprise. Located at the south end of town, this inn has 40 pleasantly furnished units, all with full baths and in-room coffee; facilities include an outdoor swimming pool, whirlpool and sauna. ~ 8540 Route 35, Bigfork; 406-837-6200, 800-321-4546. BUDGET.

A lovely bed and breakfast is **Burggraf's Countrylane B&B**, on Swan Lake nine miles southeast of Bigfork. With seven lakefront acres and a selection of fishing boats and canoes for guests, it's a rural getaway. There are five rooms, each with private bath; a honeymoon suite has a jacuzzi tub and walk-in shower. A full breakfast is served. No smoking, pets or children under 12. ~ Rainbow Drive on Swan Lake, Bigfork; 406-837-2468. MODERATE.

DINING

It would be hard to find a setting more peaceful than at the **Allentown Restaurant**, which sits at the edge of the Ninepipe National Wildlife Refuge at the foot of the striking Mission Range. Dinner entrées here focus on steaks, seafood and pasta; soups and sandwiches are popular at lunch. Big picture windows offer a fine view of the refuge's ducks and other waterfowl. ~ 41000 Route 93, Charlo; 406-644-2588. MODERATE.

The **China Garden** is one of Montana's better Asian restaurants—at least if you like Americanized dishes like chop suey and egg foo yung. They're accompanied by a pleasant view across Flathead Lake. ~ Routes 93 and 35, Polson; 406-883-4048. BUDGET TO MODERATE.

One of the Flathead's best places for fine dining in a beautiful setting is the **Montana Grill on Flathead Lake**. A large, modern log cabin facing a small lakefront park, just west of the point where the highway from Kalispell hits Flathead Lake's north shore, it draws raves for its mesquite broiler and its summer Sunday brunches. Steaks, chicken, seafood (including lake fish, of course) and pasta are the bill of fare. ~ 5480 Route 93 South, Somers; 406-857-3889. MODERATE TO DELUXE.

◆◆◆

✔ CHECK THESE OUT—UNIQUE DINING

- *Budget:* Sip a cup of 10¢ coffee at **Sykes' Grocery, Market & Restaurant** in Kalispell, where they've served three meals a day since 1905. *page 68*
- *Moderate to deluxe:* Sneak down an alleyway in order to savor the fresh seafood at Missoula's **Alley Cat Grill**. *page 48*
- *Moderate to deluxe:* Waltz upstairs from the Crystal Theatre to **The Lily Restaurant**, in a former dime-a-dance hall in Missoula. *page 48*
- *Deluxe:* Eat your fill of gourmet wild game at **Tracy's Restaurant at Meadow Lake**, in a country-club community near Columbia Falls. *page 69*

Budget: under $8 Moderate: $8–$16 Deluxe: $16–$24 Ultra-deluxe: over $24

There's more dining by the lake at the **Bridge Street Gallery &
Wine Café**. Contemporary American and imaginative ethnic cuisine are served in a gallery of international art or on an outside
deck surrounded by herb and flower boxes. The café also has one
of the area's best wine lists, by the bottle or the glass. Closed
January through March. ~ 408 Bridge Street, Bigfork; 406-837-
5825. MODERATE TO DELUXE.

The **Bigfork Inn** offers a country-style Swiss-chalet atmosphere
and outdoor dining just down the block from the Bigfork Summer
Playhouse, so it's a hit with theatergoers. Fresh seafood, chicken
and steaks are the year-round dinner fare, along with hearty sandwiches at lunch (served summers only). ~ 604 Electric Avenue,
Bigfork; 406-837-6680. BUDGET TO MODERATE.

At the **Swan River Cafe**, you can get European and American
dishes geared to the diner who prefers his or her cuisine on the
lighter side. The recently remodeled building has a pleasant veranda that overlooks Bigfork Bay on Flathead Lake. Closed January and February. ~ 360 Grand Avenue, Bigfork; 406-837-2220.
MODERATE.

Col. Doug Allard's Flathead Indian Museum and Trading Post is
worth a stop if only to sample some of the huckleberry products
made here, including jams, syrups, ice cream and milkshakes.
Adjoining the expansive souvenir shop is a museum display of
beaded Flathead tribal clothing from the early 1900s. Beadwork
replicas are sold, as are a wide range of souvenirs and regional art.
~ Route 93, St. Ignatius; 406-745-2951.

SHOPPING

The **Four Winds Historic Village and Trading Post** is a private
venture featuring several 19th-century buildings from around the
Mission Valley that were reassembled at this site. Among them is an
1885 train depot that now houses owner Preston Miller's antique
toy and train collections (toured by appointment only). The active
trading post, which re-creates a store of a similar era, is almost a
museum in its own right. You'll find everything from Nez Perce
cornhusk bags, porcupine-quill headdresses and cedar-bark baskets to beaded moccasins, T-shirts and cassette tapes of traditional
music. ~ Route 93, three miles north of St. Ignatius; 406-745-4336.

◄ HIDDEN

On the south side of Flathead Lake, **Three Dog Down** has been
rated "best in the world" by *Glamour* magazine for its sheepskin
bedding, pillows and comforters. ~ 61543 Route 93, Polson; 406-
883-3696.

The region's biggest antique market, with 6000 square feet of
display space, is **The Osprey Nest Antiques** at the north end of
Flathead Lake. ~ Milepost 101, Route 93, Somers; 406-857-3714.

The Great Montana Mercantile and Trading Post has a fine selection of local and regional crafts and products. ~ 469 Electric

Avenue, Bigfork; 406-837-3001. You'll also find paintings, sculptures and weavings by many contemporary Montana artisans at the 25-year-old **Kootenai Galleries**, open May to September and by appointment. ~ 573 Electric Avenue, Bigfork; 406-837-4848. There are numerous other galleries in this artists' community, especially along this three-block stretch of Electric Avenue.

HIDDEN ▶

Quilters, take note: It may be out of the way, but **Quilts and Cloth** is just the shop you've been looking for. Buy locally made quilts or the supplies with which to make them; if you've got an idea in your mind but lack the skills to produce it yourself, order a handcrafted quilt to your own design and specifications. ~ Route 83, Seeley Lake; 406-677-2730.

NIGHTLIFE

The **Port Polson Players** present two plays, one each in July and August, at the Mission Valley Performing Arts Center in Boettcher Park. ~ P.O. Box 1152, Polson, MT 59860; 406-882-9212.

The **Bigfork Summer Playhouse** is the area's most acclaimed theater company, offering productions of a variety of popular shows, every summer night except Sundays. ~ 526 Electric Avenue, Bigfork; 406-837-4886.

Bigfork locals tipple at the **Tall Pine Lounge**, where there's live music on weekends. ~ Lakehills Shopping Center, Bigfork; 406-837-6714. Or they sip finer vintages at the **Bridge Street Gallery & Wine Café**. ~ 408 Bridge Street, Bigfork; 406-837-5825.

PARKS

MISSION MOUNTAINS WILDERNESS AREA 🏃🏇🏠⤵ The majestic peaks and high alpine lakes of the Mission Range are preserved within this wilderness, which extends north-south for about 30 miles (beginning opposite the southern end of Flathead Lake) and tilts eastward toward the Swan River Valley. Panoramic views and wildlife are memorable. Some alpine lakes are home to the rare golden trout, worth a trip in itself for many anglers. The wilderness is abutted on the west by the Mission Mountains Tribal Wilderness. Restaurants and groceries are in Seeley Lake and other towns. ~ Easiest access is from the east, off Route 83 north of Seeley Lake. There are trailheads at the ends of Forest Roads 79 (Lindbergh Lake Road) and 561, both a short distance south of Condon; 406-329-3750.

▲ Primitive only.

FLATHEAD LAKE STATE PARK 🏃🚴🏇🏠⤴〰🚣🛶 🛥🛥⤵ Comprising six separate units around the circumference of Flathead Lake—two on the west shore, three on the east, plus Wild Horse Island—this park offers water-sports access to the huge lake. Gouged by glaciers more than 10,000 years ago, the lake has a surface area of 188 square miles and a maximum depth of 339 feet. Anglers consider its lake trout legendary. Traveling clockwise around the lake from Polson, the park units are: *Big Arm* (Elmo; 406-849-5255), with boat rentals and access to Wild Horse Island; *Wild Horse Island* (Elmo; 406-849-5255), a 2163-acre wilderness in the lake's west arm that is indeed home to a handful of wild horses, as well as bighorn sheep and bald eagles, restricted to day use only; *West Shore* (Lakeside; 406-844-3901), known for its intriguing rock formations; *Wayfarers* (Bigfork; 406-837-4196), a day-use area at Bigfork; *Yellow Bay* (south of Bigfork; 406-982-3291), in the heart of the cherry-orchard country; and *Finley Point* (near Polson; 406-887-2715), with a marina set on a forested peninsula at the south end of the lake. Facilities include picnic areas and restrooms; restaurants and groceries are in several towns, including Bigfork and Polson. Day-use fee, $3. ~ On Route 93 on the lake's west side, Big Arm is two miles east of Elmo and West Shore is four miles south of Lakeside; take a boat from Big Arm to Wild Horse Island. On Route 35 along the east shore, Wayfarers is at Bigfork; Yellow Bay is 13 miles south of Bigfork; Finley Point is six miles northeast of Polson, then three miles north via Finley Point Road; 406-752-5501.

▲ There are 120 RV/tent sites at five campgrounds, including 16 hookups at Finley Point; $8 to $9 per night; seven-day maximum stay. For reservations call 406-755-7275.

LAKE MARY RONAN STATE PARK Shrouded in a forest of Douglas fir and Western larch west of Flathead Lake, this pleasant lakefront park is a favorite of birdwatchers, huckleberry pickers and mushroom hunters. The heartshaped, two-mile-wide lake is also frequented by trout, bass and kokanee fishermen. Picnic areas, restrooms; groceries in Dayton. Day-use fee, $3. ~ Seven miles northwest from Route 93 at Dayton via Lake Mary Ronan Highway; 406-752-5501.

▲ There are 27 primitive sites, none with hookups. No charge for Montana residents, $7 to $8 per night for nonresidents; 14-day maximum stay.

JEWEL BASIN HIKING AREA This unique, specially designed recreation area is northeast of Bigfork in the northern Swan Range. Neither horses nor mountain bikes are permitted on the 38 miles of trails that wind through its 15,349 acres of mountains and lakes, streams and wildflower-rich meadows west of Hungry Horse Reservoir. ~ From Route 83 northeast of Bigfork, take Echo Park Road north three miles to Jewel Basin Road, then proceed about five miles further to trailheads off Forest Road 5392; 406-755-5401.

◄ HIDDEN

▲ Primitive only.

PLACID LAKE AND SALMON LAKE STATE PARKS Located four miles apart, very near Seeley Lake in the Clearwater Valley, these parks are popular with water-sports enthusiasts. Canoeing in particular is excellent in this area. Snowfall keeps both closed from December through April. Facilities include picnic areas and restrooms; restaurants and groceries are in Seeley Lake. ~ Salmon Lake is five miles south of Seeley Lake on Route 83. Placid Lake is three miles south of Seeley Lake via Route 83 and three miles west on Placid Lake Road; 406-542-5500.

▲ There are 40 RV/tent sites at Placid Lake, 25 RV/tent sites at Salmon Lake, none with hookups; $7 to $9 per night; 14-day maximum stay.

▼▼▼▼▼▼▼▼▼▼▼▼▼▼
The Flathead Valley

Stretching about 40 miles north from the top end of Flathead Lake, flanked on the east by the lofty peaks of Glacier National Park and on the west by the evergreen-shrouded Salish Mountains, the Flathead Valley nestles around the meandering Flathead River. A bustling tourist region with lumber and fruit-growing industries (especially cherries), it has not one but three regional centers, all situated within 15 miles of one another: Kalispell, Whitefish and Columbia Falls.

SIGHTS

As the largest town for more than 100 miles in any direction, **Kalispell** is a good place to begin an exploration of the region. The town of 13,000 people is 32 miles from West Glacier and only eight miles north of Flathead Lake.

Founding father Charles Conrad made a fortune as a Missouri River trader after his family lost its Virginia plantation during the Civil War. In 1895 he built a new estate, now known as **The Conrad Mansion**. The three-story, 26-room Norman-style home, set amid three acres of gardens, still contains most of its original Victorian decor: oak woodwork in the Great Hall, sleigh-style beds, imported marble in the bathrooms. Period-attired guides offer one-hour tours daily from mid-May to mid-October. Admission. ~ Woodland Avenue at 4th Street East, Kalispell; 406-755-2166.

Worth a look is Kalispell's art museum, the **Hockaday Center for the Arts**. The work of regional and national artists is exhibited in three galleries; there's also a permanent collection of Western art and a sales gallery. ~ 2nd Avenue and 3rd Street East, Kalispell; 406-755-5268.

Whitefish, 15 miles north of Kalispell via Route 93, is a lure for younger adults who like to play hard day and night. The town—located on the main east-west Amtrak line—is a recreation center. It is situated on the south shore of seven-mile-long **Whitefish Lake**, and is just eight miles from **The Big Mountain**, a long-established ski destination. The resort opens a chairlift (admission) in summer to a mid-mountain viewing station and restaurant. ~ Big Mountain Road, Whitefish; 406-862-3511.

Aluminum and timber are the economic mainstays in **Columbia Falls**, but the town's position as western gateway to Glacier Park, only 15 miles east, is almost equally as important. Attractions here range from the sublime to the ridiculous. On the one hand, there's quaint **St. Richard's Catholic Church**, which dates from 1891. ~ 1210 9th Street West, Columbia Falls; 406-892-5142. On the other hand, you might opt to pass an afternoon at the **Big Sky Waterslide & Miniature Greens**, a water park with nine slides. Admission. ~ Route 2 East, Columbia Falls; 406-892-5025.

LODGING

The Flathead Valley is bed-and-breakfast country: There are at least 40, and the number is growing. A favorite in Kalispell is the **Switzer House Inn**, a 1910 Queen Anne Revival home between downtown and Woodland Park. Three of the four bedrooms, all decorated in English-country style, have queen-sized beds; the other has twins. There's also a library/TV room. Full breakfasts feature homemade granola and fruit compotes. ~ 205 5th Avenue East, Kalispell; 406-257-5837, 800-257-5837. MODERATE.

One block away, the **Stillwater Inn** has four guest rooms in a circa-1900 Victorian. A broad stairway leads from the entrance area to the rooms; two share a bath, and the other two have private facilities. A full breakfast is served each morning, and mountain bikes are available for guests' use. ~ 206 4th Avenue East, Kalispell; 406-755-7080. MODERATE.

You can get off the Route 93 motel strip and stay downtown at the **Kalispell Grand Hotel**. The refurbished 1909 hotel has two restaurants, a casino and a lounge (featuring live bands on weekend nights). Guest rooms, on the second and third floors, are comfortably spacious with modern baths and good-sized beds. A complimentary continental breakfast is served. This probably isn't the place for disabled guests because there is no elevator. ~ 100 Main Street, Kalispell; 406-755-8100, fax 406-752-8012. MODERATE.

Kalispell's leading lodging is offered at the **Best Western Outlaw Inn**, which comes with all the bells and whistles: indoor swimming pools, jacuzzis, a sauna, tennis and racquetball courts, a fine-dining restaurant, a lounge with live music and a casino. The 225 guest rooms are sufficiently spacious but otherwise standard motel rooms. ~ 1701 Route 93 South, Kalispell; 406-755-6100, fax 406-756-8994. MODERATE TO DELUXE.

In Whitefish, the **Mountain Holiday Motel** offers bang for your buck. The property offers indoor and outdoor swimming pools, a hot tub, a sauna and guest laundry. The 34 rooms are neat and comfortable, with private patios and some refrigerators. Coffee is always on in the lobby. ~ 6595 Route 93 South, Whitefish; 406-862-2548, 800-543-8064, fax 406-862-3103. BUDGET TO MODERATE.

Up on The Big Mountain you'll find the **Hibernation House,** an old-style economy ski lodge in the village at the foot of the chairlifts. Each of the 42 basic rooms has a queen-size bed, a set of bunks, a phone and a private bath with shower. Shared facilities include a TV lounge, laundry and hot tub. A full breakfast is included. ~ 3812 Big Mountain Road, Whitefish; 406-862-1982, fax 406-862-1467. BUDGET TO MODERATE.

The **Bad Rock Country B&B** stands out in the Columbia Falls area. Old West antiques and majestic mountain views typify the seven guest rooms (all with private baths) in this elegant country house, set on 30 acres near the west entrance to Glacier Park. Four rooms in new log cabins have fireplaces and patios. Guests enjoy gourmet breakfasts and hot-tub relaxation. ~ 480 Bad Rock Drive, Columbia Falls; 406-892-2829. DELUXE.

For a full listing of accommodations or assistance in finding a room, contact the **Flathead Convention & Visitors Association.** ~ 15 Depot Loop, Kalispell; 406-756-9091.

DINING

HIDDEN ▶

You may not find cheaper meals anywhere than at **Sykes' Grocery, Market & Restaurant.** In business since 1905, Sykes' serves three meals a day, seven days a week. Coffee is still just a dime a cup, quarter-pound burgers cost $1.50, pork chop dinners run $3.50. Besides a deli and ice-cream counter, Sykes' sells fresh produce and camping gear, and operates a pharmacy, all in the same shop. ~ 202 2nd Avenue West, Kalispell; 406-257-4304. BUDGET.

The **Bulldog Pub & Steakhouse** is at the head of the pack for Old World ambience and hearty steaks. Shrimp, chicken and prime rib are good, too. Enter off a parking lot around the corner from Kalispell City Hall; expect an intriguing weapons collection mounted on the walls, smoky air and loud blues. ~ 208 1st Avenue East, Kalispell; 406-752-7522. MODERATE.

For a good family-style café, check out the **Lighterside Restaurant.** You'll find homemade breads and desserts, a salad bar with more than 30 choices, and a menu that focuses on all-American cuisine. ~ 221 Main Street, Kalispell; 406-752-3668. BUDGET TO MODERATE.

Located midway between Kalispell and Whitefish, **Fenders Restaurant & Lounge** is built around a classic automobile theme. Antique vehicles, like a '57 Ford and a '55 Chevy, have been remodeled into restaurant booths, and other period memorabilia decorate the walls. The menu is heavy on steak and seafood, as well as barbecued ribs and Cajun-style chicken. ~ 4090 Route 93 North, Kalispell; 406-752-3000. MODERATE.

Hankering for Southwestern-style Mexican food? The **Glacier Grande Rio Grande Cafe** will relieve that craving. Look for blue-corn enchiladas, mile-high tostadas and the Flathead's best margaritas. ~ 10 Central Avenue, Whitefish; 406-862-9400. MODERATE.

A longtime local hangout is **The Place**, known for its steaks and chicken dishes, its barbecued ribs and its savory pizzas. It's across the viaduct from downtown, on the road to The Big Mountain. ~ 845 Wisconsin Avenue, Whitefish; 406-862-4500. BUDGET TO MODERATE.

Drawing raves on the east side of the Flathead Valley is **Tracy's Restaurant at Meadow Lake**. Located within a resort condominium community by an 18-hole championship golf course, Tracy's offers creative "new American" preparations of wild game, as well as seafood and prime rib. ~ 1415 Tamarack Lane, Columbia Falls; 406-892-7601. DELUXE.

SHOPPING

If you're looking for Montana-made crafts and products, visit **Mostly Montana** in the 40-store Gateway West Mall. ~ Route 2 West, Kalispell; 406-752-6662. Another option, **The Melon Basket**, can be found in the 50-store Kalispell Center Mall. ~ 20 North Main Street, Kalispell; 406-752-8778. There's also **Montana Expressions**, which carries an assortment of locally made furniture, accessories and textile art. ~ 17 Main Street, Kalispell; 406-756-8555.

The place to go for collectibles is the **Kalispell Antiques Market**, which represents 30 different dealers. ~ 1st and Main streets, Kalispell; 406-257-2800.

Art lovers must visit **The Gallery** for its exhibits of local artists' works: oils, watercolors, bronzes, prints, pottery and woodcarving. ~ 6080 Route 93 South, Whitefish; 406-862-5569. There's a more avant-garde collection of art, furniture and gifts at the **Bohemian Grange Hall**, behind a coffee-roasting establishment. ~ 5810 Route 93 South, Whitefish; 406-862-7633.

The area's best bookstore is **Bookworks**, a locally owned shop that emphasizes volumes of regional interest, especially nature and the outdoors. ~ 110 Central Avenue, Whitefish; 406-862-4980.

Silvertip covers all ends of the sporting-goods spectrum, including camping, hiking and water sports. ~ 33 Baker Avenue, Whitefish; 406-862-2600.

NIGHTLIFE

The performing arts are lively in the Flathead. The **Whitefish Theatre Company**, a community troupe, offers everything from musicals to dramas in a year-round season, including summer

SONGFUL SUMMERS

The year's big cultural event is the **Flathead Festival**, extending through the final three weeks of July. Nationally known jazz, country, rock, classical, chamber and American Indian artists perform at venues throughout the valley. ~ P.O. Box 1780, Whitefish, MT 59937; 406-862-1780.

Shakespeare. ~ P.O. Box 1463, Whitefish, MT 59937; 406-862-5371. The **Glacier Orchestra & Chorale** presents 11 concerts in an October to May season, often with guest conductors and performers. ~ 140 1st Avenue East, Kalispell; 406-257-3241.

On an everyday basis, locals frequent **Moose's** for darts and lively conversation on a sawdust floor. ~ 173 North Main Street, Kalispell; 406-755-2337. The lively **Blue Moon**, at the Whitefish-Kalispell junction, rages with country-western music and dancing. ~ 6105 Route 2, Columbia Falls; 406-892-9925.

For loud rock music and general rowdiness, you can't top a two-block stretch of Central Avenue in downtown Whitefish. Try the **Great Northern** for a rocking good time . ~ 27 Central Avenue; 406-862-2816. Hang at **Casey's** for a night out on the town. ~ 101 Central Avenue; 406-862-8150. **The Palace** will have plenty to keep you busy. ~ 125 Central Avenue; 406-862-2428. Lap down some beers at **Bulldog Saloon**. ~ 144 Central Avenue; 406-862-5601. Another great spot is the **Great Northern Brewery**, which is located in Whitefish's old Cadillac Hotel building. ~ 2 Central Avenue; 406-863-1000.

Popular among the valley's poker-and-keno crowd is the **Gold Nugget Casino**. ~ 740 West Idaho Street, Kalispell; 406-756-8100.

PARKS

WOODLAND PARK A lagoon runs through the heart of this Kalispell municipal park, providing a serene setting for a variety of activities, from strenuous sports to strolls through a rose garden. Swans, geese and ducks inhabit the lagoon; peacocks and pheasants wander an aviary. The park has an Olympic-size municipal swimming and diving pool; other facilities include ball fields, horseshoe pits and a fitness course. In winter, there's ice-skating and sledding. Picnic areas and restrooms round out the amenities. ~ Follow 2nd Street East from downtown Kalispell to Woodland Park Drive; 406-752-6600, ext. 274.

LONE PINE STATE PARK Located just outside Kalispell, 182-acre Lone Pine occupies a glacial knoll overlooking the Flathead Valley. With its interpretive programs and films, pine-and-fir forest, wildflowers and bird life, it's an educational resource for valley schools. Facilities include a visitors center, an archery range, picnic areas, restrooms and handicapped-accessible hiking trails. Day-use fee, $3. ~ Four miles southwest of Kalispell on Foys Lake Road, then one mile north on Lone Pine Road; 406-755-2706.

WHITEFISH LAKE STATE PARK Providing water-sports access to beautiful, seven-mile-long Whitefish Lake, this state park is one of Montana's most popular. A well-kept beach has a children's area. Visiting anglers can rent boats to pursue northern pike, lake whitefish and trout.

Facilities include picnic areas, restrooms and snack bar. Day-use fee, $3. ~ One-half mile west of downtown Whitefish on Route 93, turn north a mile on West Lakeshore Drive; 406-862-3991 or 406-752-5501 (winter).

▲ There are 25 RV/tent sites without hookups; $7 to $9 per night; seven-day maximum stay.

FLATHEAD NATIONAL FOREST 🚶🚴🏇 🐎🏊🏠⛵🚣🛶 🚤🛥 Covering more than two million mountainous acres south and west of Glacier National Park, this forest encompasses Hungry Horse Reservoir, the Jewel Basin Hiking Area, The Big Mountain ski resort and many other important recreational sites. There are picnic areas and restrooms; restaurants and groceries are in the Flathead Valley. ~ Most highways and secondary roads that lead out from the Flathead Valley penetrate the forest. The greatest concentration of sites are off the East Side and West Side roads that flank Hungry Horse Reservoir, joining near the Spotted Bear Ranger Station; 406-755-5401.

▲ There are 243 RV/tent sites, nine for tents only, in 12 campgrounds, none with hookups; $4 to $7 per night; 14-day maximum stay.

▼▼▼▼▼▼▼▼▼▼▼▼▼▼▼▼

The Northwest Corner

The region west of Kalispell is a land of dense, Pacific Northwest–like forests of towering pines and firs, jagged peaks rich in timber and silver ore, and mountain streams harnessed for hydroelectric power. Route 2 is the artery of this district; the main centers are Libby, on the Kootenai River, and Eureka, near the Canadian border.

If you discover an unusual percentage of tall, blue-eyed blonds among Libby's 3000 residents, blame it on a Norwegian lumber mill operator named J. Neils. In the late 1800s, he wrote friends and relatives in Minnesota, seeking people to work for him. Several hundred Scandinavian loggers migrated west with their families. Today their contributions are recalled every September in the Nordicfest celebration.

SIGHTS

Libby is located 89 miles from Kalispell and 83 miles from Sandpoint, Idaho. It is the home of **Libby Dam**, 17 miles east on the Kootenai River. Built in 1975 for hydroelectricity and flood control, the dam is 420 feet high, 310 feet wide at its base and more than a half-mile long at its crest. Guided tours of the dam's powerhouse are offered each hour from 10 a.m. to 4 p.m., daily from Memorial Day to Labor Day. ~ Route 37 North, Libby; 406-293-5577.

The Libby Dam has created serpentine, 90-mile-long, 370-foot-deep **Lake Koocanusa**, which extends north into Canada's British

Columbia province. Along its shores are several recreation areas and campgrounds; you may also see bald eagles and osprey fishing, and bighorn sheep on steep slopes.

Lake Koocanusa's name comes from combining "Kootenai" and "Canada" with "USA."

Back in Libby, the **Heritage Museum** features area history, wildlife and economy, though perhaps most interesting is the 12-sided log cabin in which it's housed. The grounds also include a miner's cabin and a loggers' cookhouse. Open summers only. ~ 1367 Route 2 East, Libby; 406-293-7521.

West of Libby 18 miles is **Troy**, where the Asarco Corp. operates the largest silver mine in the United States: It removes four million ounces of the precious ore annually. The **Troy Museum**, housed in an old railroad depot, displays artifacts recalling Troy's heyday as a late-19th-century logging and mining. Open summers only. ~ Route 2, Troy; 406-295-4216.

The **Ross Creek Cedar Grove Scenic Area** is 25 miles south of Troy near Bull Lake; it boasts an interpretive trail, less than a mile long, that leads among giant old-growth western red cedar trees, some 175 feet tall and estimated at more than 500 years old. ~ Route 56; 406-295-4693.

Equidistant (67 miles) from both Libby and Kalispell, eight miles south of the Canadian border on Route 93, the Christmas tree-farming center of **Eureka** is at the heart of Kootenai National Forest. In the little town, the **Tobacco Valley Historic Village** relates area history museum-style. ~ Main Street, Eureka; 406-296-2514. To the northeast, the **Ten Lakes Scenic Area** invites visitors to follow a mountain road to lakes renowned for their hiking and fishing. ~ Grave Creek Road, Eureka; 406-882-4451.

LODGING

The **Kootenai Country Inn B&B**, three miles north of Libby on Route 37, is surrounded by 40 riverfront acres. It has two guest rooms in a private cottage with common living quarters, three more in the main house. There's also a hot-tub gazebo; rafts can be rented for floating the Kootenai River. ~ 264 Mack Road, Libby; 406-293-7878, fax 406-293-9518. MODERATE.

In the heart of Libby, **The Caboose Motel** has 28 comfortable, air-conditioned rooms with queen-size beds. The property includes an adjacent restaurant and lounge. ~ 714 West 9th Street at Route 2, Libby; 406-293-6201, fax 406-293-3621. BUDGET.

Canada-bound travelers might stop for a couple of nights at **Huckleberry Hannah's**, a bed and breakfast just four miles south of the border in the Tobacco River Valley near Eureka. The old country home has five guest rooms, each with a private bath; it is enveloped in 50 wooded acres beside trout-filled Sophie Lake. Call for directions! ~ 3100 Sophie Lake Road, Eureka; 406-889-3381. BUDGET TO MODERATE.

Expect to fight for a seat at **Beck's Montana Cafe** on Thursday
nights. That's when prime rib is the featured menu item at this
longtime favorite, located at the western edge of Libby. Roasted
chicken and the salad bar are popular every night; on Sundays,
there's a full hot buffet. ~ 2425 Route 2 West, Libby; 406-293-
6687. MODERATE.

DINING

You could have guessed that **White Knight Pub & Seafood** has
excellent fish and chips . . . but it has much more. Homemade clam
chowder is great, and there's an extensive choice of other seafood
as well as standard pub meals. ~ 419 Mineral Avenue, Libby;
406-293-5332. MODERATE.

Here's honesty in advertising. This corner of Montana is clearly
off the beaten track, as **The Boondocks** so eloquently admits.
Three blocks north of the main highway through Troy, it serves
three meals daily, including Mexican food and sourdough pizza.
This is also the place to catch all the local gossip. ~ 407 North 2nd
Street, Troy; 406-295-5780. BUDGET.

The **Kootenai Gallery of Fine Art** displays the works of noted
Montana painter Marjorie D. Caldwell and other artists of the
Western genre. ~ 580 Greers Ferry, Libby; 406-293-9320.

SHOPPING

This is timber country, and where there's wood, there are people carving it. Afternoon tours are welcomed at the **Cedar Creek
Store**'s sizeable woodworking shop. ~ 4381 Route 2 West, Libby;
406-293-3531. If you're in Eureka, make arrangements to visit the
Dave Clarke Studio. Clarke is a chainsaw sculptor who makes fast
work of raw logs, turning them into precision images of people and
animals. ~ Eureka; 406-296-3261.

The **Pastime** was built in 1916 as a pool hall, and you still can see
its original woodwork behind the bar. There's live music weekends.
~ 216 Mineral Avenue, Libby; 406-293-9925. For even more rus-
ticity, drive seven miles north from Libby to the **Red Dog Saloon**,
surrounded by Kootenai National Forest. ~ 6788 Pipe Creek Road,
Libby; 406-293-8347. Gamblers prefer the **Treasure Mountain
Casino**. ~ Route 2 West, Libby; 406-293-8764.

NIGHTLIFE

KOOTENAI NATIONAL FOREST 🚶🚴🏇🛶🎣🏕️⛷️🚤 ⛴️
It's almost a given that this 2.2-million-acre national
forest contains more board feet of lumber than any other in
Montana. Within its boundaries are 90-mile-long Lake Koocanusa
and the Cabinet Mountains Wilderness. Picnic areas and restrooms
are among the facilities. Restaurants and groceries are in Libby,
Eureka and other towns. ~ Route 37, which follows the Lake
Koocanusa shoreline, connects Route 2 at Libby with Route 93 at
Eureka; 406-293-8861.

PARKS

▲ There are 531 RV/tent sites, none with hookups, and 18 sites for tents only at 15 campgrounds; no charge to $7 per night; 14-day maximum stay.

CABINET MOUNTAINS WILDERNESS AREA 🚶 🏇 ⛺ 🛶 Comprising 94,000 acres west of Libby along the spiny crest of the Cabinet Mountains, this wilderness extends 33 miles, climaxed by 8712-foot Snowshoe Peak. Trails lead to alpine lakes and streams. Vegetation is denser here than in most other mountain districts of Montana. Denizens include deer, elk, bighorn sheep, mountain goats and an occasional grizzly bear. ~ Many trails begin from logging roads branching off Route 2. Or take Flower Lake Road, just south of Libby, to several other trailheads; 406-293-8861.

▲ Primitive only.

LOGAN STATE PARK 🚶 🚴 ⛺ 🛶 🎣 🚤 ⛵ 🛶 Once called Thompson Chain of Lakes State Park, this park near the source of the Thompson River is the focal point of a necklace of small lakes and ponds. The park is on the north shore of Middle Thompson Lake, largest of the group. Fishing and birdwatching are the main attractions. Facilities include picnic areas and restrooms; restaurants and groceries are in Libby and Kalispell. ~ Off Route 2, 39 miles southeast of Libby; 406-293-7190.

▲ There are 50 RV/tent sites, none with hookups; $7 to $9 per night; seven-day maximum stay.

▼▼▼▼▼▼▼▼▼▼▼▼▼▼
Thompson Falls Area
The meandering, and sometimes thundering, Clark Fork River is the focal point of this region, best explored on Route 200 west of Missoula. It includes Thompson Falls, an outdoor recreational gateway about 100 miles northwest of Missoula, and long, skinny Noxon Rapids Reservoir.

SIGHTS
Thompson Falls' **Old Jail Museum** was built in 1907 as a prison and sheriff's residence; it offers an interesting depiction of early settlement and law enforcement. Open May to September or by appointment. ~ Madison Street and Maiden Lane; 406-827-3496.

The surrounding pine-forested mountains of Lolo National Forest are home to bighorn sheep; there's a viewing station on the highway eight miles east of Thompson Falls.

The head of 27-mile-long **Noxon Rapids Reservoir** is about six miles northwest of Thompson Falls along Route 200. The reservoir was created by the earth-filled Noxon Rapids Dam on the Clark Fork River. Another dam forms Cabinet Gorge Reservoir on the state's western border, just east of Idaho's majestic Lake Pend Oreille.

LODGING

The **Bighorn Lodge,** located on the Bull River above Cabinet Gorge Reservoir, is a country inn with four guest rooms (all with private baths) and a big deck with fine mountain views. There's hiking, riding, canoeing and fishing in the surrounding national forest. A full breakfast is served. ~ 2 Bighorn Lane, Noxon; 406-847-5597, fax 406-847-5502. MODERATE.

◄ HIDDEN

The physically challenged need not let their disability keep them from enjoying a guest ranch, not when there's a place like the **Blue Spruce Lodge.** Located in the foothills of the Bitterroots near Noxon Rapids Reservoir, the lodge and most activities are totally accessible: Its owner, Russ Milleson, who has been confined to a wheelchair since 1974, says, "Life is short, and nature is perhaps our greatest healer." The lodge accommodates 16 people. Activities include trail riding, fishing and whitewater rafting. ~ 451 Marten Creek Road, Trout Creek; 406-827-4762, 800-831-4797. MODERATE.

DINING

By reservation, you can get gourmet wild game and Continental cuisine at **Lonesome Dome.** As a walk-in, you can still get solid Italian fare and good cappuccinos. ~ 709 Main Street, Thompson Falls; 406-827-4337. BUDGET TO MODERATE.

The usual fare in this corner of the state is traditional home cooking, and no one does it better than **Granny's Home Cooking.** Granny serves three meals daily; try her salad bar, hand pressed burgers and homemade pies. ~ 921 Main Street, Thompson Falls; 406-827-3747. BUDGET.

PARKS

THOMPSON FALLS STATE PARK 🏃 ⛵ 🚣 🚤 🛥 ⛴ Nature walks and birdwatching along the Clark Fork River, and boating and fishing access to Noxon Rapids Reservoir, are the highlights of this park, open from May through September. There are picnic areas and restrooms. Day-use fee, $3. ~ Two miles northwest of the town of Thompson Falls off Route 200; 406-827-3732 (summer), 406-752-5501 (winter).

▲ There are 20 primitive sites; $5 per night for residents, $7 to $8 for non-residents; 14-day maximum stay.

▼▼▼▼▼▼▼▼▼▼▼▼▼
Outdoor Adventures

FISHING

Robert Redford's 1992 movie *A River Runs Through It* may have brought Montana flyfishing to the awareness of a nation of anglers, but the richness of the fishing life has never been a secret to anyone who lives in the state. That's especially true in northwest Montana. The streams and lakes flowing from the Rockies' western slopes offer trout, walleye and many other species worthy of *any* fish story.

Huge populations of trout—rainbow, brook, cutthroat and brown, in particular—inhabit the creeks and rivers that flow from the Continental Divide. In the Missoula and Flathead Valley areas, this is the predominant fish. Mountain whitefish and bull trout are also widely found in rivers and lakes, and many lakes have yellow perch.

Other species may not be as widely distributed. Huge Flathead Lake and nearby Whitefish Lake are known for their lake trout and lake whitefish. Whitefish Lake also has northern pike, as do several lakes in the Seeley-Swan region. You'll find kokanee salmon, a favorite of gourmets, in lakes Koocanusa and Mary Ronan, among others. Noxon Rapids Reservoir, on the Clark Fork near the Idaho border, boasts ten different species of fish, more than anywhere else on the west side of the Continental Divide.

Many fishing equipment companies also operate guided tours to area rivers and lakes as an adjunct service. Contact **Grizzly Hackle Fishing Company**. ~ 215 West Front Street, Missoula; 406-721-8996. In Polson, call **Tom's Tackle**. ~ 108 1st Street East, Polson; 406-883-6209. **Streamside Anglers** are flyfishing specialists. ~ 317 South Orange Street; Missoula, 406-728-1085. **Lakestream Flyshop** is another option. ~ 15 Central Avenue, Whitefish; 406-862-1298. One leading company is **Wilderness Outfitters**. ~ 3800 Rattlesnake Drive, Missoula; 406-549-2820. In Columbia Falls, call **Glacier Fishing Charters**. ~ 375 Jensen Road, Columbia Falls; 406-892-2377.

BOATING

On Flathead Lake, numerous marinas will rent boats of all sizes for fishing or pleasure boating. One such establishment is **Flathead Surf & Ski**. ~ 303 Route 93, Polson; 406-883-3900. You can also contact the **Big Arm Resort and Marina**. ~ Route 93, Elmo; 406-849-5622. **Bigfork Marina & Boat Center** rents all kinds of boats. ~ 100 Parkway Avenue, Bigfork; 406-837-5556.

Also in the Flathead Valley, rentals for boating activities on Whitefish Lake are available from **Big Sky Boat Rentals**. ~ 220 Minnesota Avenue, Whitefish; 406-862-9191. Also in Whitefish is **Club Cabana Water Sports Rentals**. ~ 1390 Wisconsin Avenue, Whitefish; 406-862-3253.

RIVER RUNNING

The River Wild, Meryl Streep's 1994 adventure movie about whitewater rafting, was filmed in Montana. And while few would challenge a Class VI rapid of the type Streep and co-star Kevin Bacon tackled, there are floating opportunities of all kinds available throughout northwest Montana. That goes for kayakers and canoeists as well as rafters.

In the Missoula area, popular trips are through Hell Gate Canyon and Alberton Gorge on the Clark Fork River, and down the Blackfoot. **Pangaea Expeditions** is among the outfitters who run

Fly-fishing
Haven

The prospect of laying a hand-tied lure on a placid stretch of river and reeling in a giant trout has a romance shared by few outdoor recreations. And few places are better suited to the sport of fly fishing than western Montana.

Here, after all, runs the Blackfoot River, scene of Norman Maclean's classic novel, *A River Runs Through It*, whose film success popularized fly fishing for a whole new generation of anglers. The Clark Fork and the Bitterroot and Swan rivers rank among the best trout streams in North America, along with the Big Hole, the Madison and others in the southern part of the state.

The roots of fly fishing date back at least two thousand years. Macedonians were known to have used artificial flies in upland lakes and streams. The first known sport fishing manual, published in England in 1496, described a dozen hand-tied flies (six of them still in use today). But fly fishing as it's known in the 1990s did not become possible until now when the horsehair line was reinvented. The modern flycasting line—typically nylon with a plastic covering, tapered to a monofilament leader—provides the weight for casting the virtually weightless fly; it can float atop the water or sink below the surface.

A flexible fiberglass or graphite rod, usually about eight feet long, is whipped in a motion that sends the line and lure to a precise location in the water. This is the true test of the skilled angler: the ability to "read" the water, to where fish are most likely to strike, and to place the fly to drift over that exact spot.

Artificial flies may be made from silk, fur, feathers or other materials, but they usually resemble a natural food source for the fish: insects (such as mayflies, caddis flies and midges), freshwater shrimp or snails, for instance.

The angler's challenge is to simulate the insect's natural behavior and outwit the fish—either by "wet-fly" fishing with the lure underwater, or "dry-fly" fishing on the surface of the water. Dry-fly anglers try to cast a slack line, allowing their lure to remain naturally on the surface as long as possible before it is caught in the current.

Lodges throughout western and southern Montana provide fly-fishing guides and instruction. For visitors with money to burn and a powerful passion to catch trophy-size cutthroat, rainbow and German brown trout, it's hard to top the facilities operated by **Big Hole River Outfitters**. From June to October, experienced guides take visitors out for dry-fly fishing. ~ Wise River; 406-832-3252.

One other spot in Montana is something of a mecca for fly fishers. **Dan Bailey's Fly Shop**, in the south-central part of the state, was established in 1938. Today it is one of the largest wholesalers of fishing tackle on earth, producing more than a half-million trout flies annually. Each August, Livingston hosts the International Federation of Fly Fishers Conclave, largest of its kind on the continent. ~ 209 West Park Street, Livingston; 406-222-1673.

these streams. ~ P.O. Box 5753, Missoula, MT 59801; 406-721-7719.

Northwest Montana's most popular area for rafting is on the various forks of the Flathead River, on the west side of Glacier National Park. If you're not an experienced rafter, the best and safest way to go is with an outfitter.

For rentals of river equipment, check out **The Trailhead**. ~ Higgins Avenue and Pine Street, Missoula; 406-543-6966.

KAYAKING & CANOEING Kayakers enjoy the same rivers as rafters. But if you prefer lake water to whitewater, **Glacier Sea Kayaking** allows you to explore Flathead Lake's coastline and islands by day or by moonlight. ~ Route 93, Rollins; 406-862-9010.

The region's best canoeing is in the Seeley-Swan area and at the Thompson Chain of Lakes. On Route 83, the **Clearwater Canoe Trail** has a put-in four miles north of Seeley; canoeists can glide down the Clearwater River for an hour or two to the north end of Seeley Lake, then take a footpath back along the stream.

An hour's drive west of Kalispell at **Logan State Park**, the ten-mile Thompson Chain of Lakes beside Route 2 demands only a few very short portages.

The **Blackfoot River Kayak School**, east of Missoula, rents kayaks on a daily and weekly basis. ~ 11780 Route 200 East, Bonner; 406-258-5254.

DOWNHILL SKIING Montana's largest destination ski resort, and one of its oldest, is **The Big Mountain**, overlooking Whitefish Lake about 12 miles (as the eagle flies) west of Glacier National Park. Established in the 1960s, The Big Mountain is just that: It has more than 3000 acres of skiing terrain and some 60 runs, served by seven chairlifts and two surface lifts. The vertical drop is 2300 feet from a summit elevation of 7000 feet. Here there are gentle groomed slopes for beginning skiers, steep and deep powder for experts. Base facilities include lodge and condominium accommodations, restaurants and bars, and ski shops with full rentals. ~ Big Mountain Road, Whitefish; 406-862-3511.

Day-use ski areas (with no on-site lodging) in northwest Montana include:

Montana Snowbowl, 12 miles northwest of Missoula. Advanced skiers appreciate the steep-sided bowls, but there are also beginners' slopes. Two chairlifts and two surface tows serve 30 runs; vertical drop is 2600 feet from a summit elevation of 7600 feet. ~ 1700 Snowbowl Road, Missoula; 406-549-9777.

Marshall Ski Area, seven miles east of Missoula. It is heavily geared toward beginning and intermediate skiers. One chairlift and two surface lifts serve seven runs and a 1500-foot vertical. It also offers night skiing. ~ 5250 Marshall Canyon Road, Missoula; 406-258-6619.

Lost Trail Powder Mountain, straddling the Montana-Idaho border above the Bitterroot Valley, 91 miles south of Missoula. The snow arrives here early in the season and stays late. Two chairlifts and two rope tows serve 18 runs in the Bitterroot National Forest. There's a 1200-foot vertical drop from a top elevation of 7800 feet. ~ Route 93, Conner; 406-821-3211.

Turner Mountain, in the Purcell Mountains west of Lake Koocanusa in northwesternmost Montana. A single tow climbs to the top of the 5952-foot peak; more than half of the 14 runs that descend 2117 feet of vertical to the base area are deemed expert. ~ Route 508, Libby; 406-293-4317.

**CROSS-
COUNTRY
SKIING**

The Big Mountain boasts an excellent 15-kilometer track for cross-country skiers; in fact, it's a training center for U.S. Olympic bi-athletes and Nordic racers. ~ Big Mountain Road, Whitefish; 406-862-3511.

Nightingale Nordic is a complete Nordic resort 25 miles southwest of Missoula. ~ Graves Creek Road, Lolo; 406-273-2415. **Holland Lake Lodge** has a 25-kilometer trail system and full lodging and rental packages in the Swan River Valley. ~ Route 83, Condon; 800-648-8859.

At **Chief Joseph Pass,** near Lost Trail Pass, a 24-kilometer network of rated trails, groomed weekly, has been developed by the Bitterroot Cross Country Ski Club. ~ Route 43, Conner.

GOLF

When the snow disappears, the golf courses flourish. Among the leading public courses in northwest Montana is the **Buffalo Hill Municipal Golf Club,** a 27-hole championship course with views from The Big Mountain to Flathead Lake. ~ North end of Main Street, Kalispell; 406-755-5902. The **Larchmont Municipal Golf**

✔ CHECK THESE OUT—UNIQUE OUTDOOR ADVENTURES

- Go for a moonlight kayak around Wild Horse Island in Flathead Lake, the largest natural freshwater lake west of the Mississippi River. *page 78*
- Tackle the champagne powder atop The Big Mountain, Montana's largest destination ski resort. *page 78*
- Join the Missoula-based Adventure Cycling Association, a leading bike-touring organization, on a two-wheeled spin. *page 80*
- Trek 35 miles of trails among 25 alpine lakes in the Jewel Basin Hiking Area. *page 82*

Course is an 18-hole course that hosts the Montana Open golf tournament. ~ 3200 Old Fort Road, Missoula; 406-721-4416.

In the Glacier Park area, the **Flathead Valley Golf Association** will make advance tee-time reservations for visiting golfers at any of the area's nine 18-hole courses. ~ 15 Depot Loop, Kalispell; 800-392-9795. It seems as though every community of any size throughout the region has its own municipal nine-hole course. Inquire locally.

TENNIS

Local parks and recreation offices are happy to share the locations and open hours of municipal courts. Call for information in Missoula at 406-721-7275. In Kalispell, contact 406-752-6600, ext 274. Missoula's **McCormick Park** is a good place to swing a racket. ~ Cregg Lane at the Orange Street Bridge. Or you can try Kalispell's **Northridge Park**. ~ Northridge Drive.

RIDING STABLES

For trail rides of a few hours to all day, check out **East Fork Outfitters** at the Camp Creek Inn. ~ 7674 Route 93 South, Sula; 406-821-3508. Or you can try **L-Diamond-E Ranch Outfitters**, which will take you by horse to sapphire mines. ~ Rock Creek Road, Clinton; 406-825-6295.

Big Sky Rides, near Lone Pine State Park, specializes in family adventure with gentle trail rides and week-long horsemanship camps for kids. ~ 750 Foys Lake Road, Kalispell; 406-755-7433.

PACK TRIPS & LLAMA TREKS

While many horse-packing outfitters serve hunters in particular, others prefer riders who simply enjoy the outdoors. They'll take you anywhere, even through the most remote reaches of wilderness. Try **Rocky Mountain Adventures**. ~ 756 Little Sleeping Child Road, Hamilton; 406-363-0200. Or you can check out **Babcock Creek Outfitters**. ~ 280 Twin Lakes Road, Whitefish; 406-862-7813.

Guided llama pack trips—you walk, but the llama carries your load—are offered in the Missoula area by **Tranquility Base Llamas**. ~ Route 263, Frenchtown; 406-626-4207. In the Bitterroot Valley there's **Allaman's Montana Adventure Trips**. ~ West Fork Road, Darby; 406-821-3763. In the Glacier Park area try the **Great Northern Llama Co**. ~ 600 Blackmer Lane, Columbia Falls; 406-755-9044.

BIKING

Missoula has been called "one of the top ten bicycling cities in the United States" by *Bicycling* magazine. The sentiment clearly carries north into the Flathead Valley area.

So important is bicycling to northwest Montana that the **Adventure Cycling Association** (ACA), formerly known as Bike-Centennial and regarded as America's leading bike-touring organization, has established its national headquarters there. The ACA publishes touring maps and supports a national network of touring routes. ~ 150 East Pine Street, Missoula; 406-721-1776.

Local bicycle shops have information on planned activities and mountain-biking routes. Favorite locations for the latter include the **Rattlesnake National Recreation Area** near Missoula and **The Big Mountain Ski and Summer Resort** outside of Whitefish. Another popular area is **Kreis Pond**, with 35 miles of designated mountain-bike trails near the Ninemile Ranger Station and Remount Depot, 27 miles northwest of Missoula. ~ Lolo National Forest, Huson; 406-626-5201.

National forest roads and trails are generally open to mountain biking, but wheeled vehicles—motorized or not—are not allowed in designated wilderness areas.

Bike Rentals   Leading bike shops for rentals and repairs include **New Era Bicycles**. ~ 741 South Higgins Avenue, Missoula; 406-728-2080. In Columbia Falls, try **All Season Sport & Cycle**. ~ 615 Nucleus Avenue, Columbia Falls; 406-892-2755.

HIKING

Northern Montana is one of the greatest places on earth for hiking, backpacking and mountaineering. Quite aside from Glacier National Park, there are thousands of miles more throughout the national forests and wilderness areas of the region. All distances listed are one way unless otherwise noted.

MISSOULA   Crazy Canyon Trail (3.4 miles), in the Pattee Canyon Recreation Area near Missoula's southeastern city limits, presents a moderate climb to the top of 5158-foot Mount Sentinel, overlooking Missoula from the south side of the Clark Fork River. You can descend from here via the **Hellgate Canyon Trail** (2.1 miles) to the banks of the Clark Fork, or via the **"M" Trail** (1.8 miles) to the University of Montana campus.

Stuart Peak Trail (12 miles) is a strenuous ascent through the Rattlesnake National Recreation Area and Wilderness. Beginning at the Sawmill Gulch Road trailhead, it traverses Spring Gulch and then rises above the timberline for great views from the upper slopes of 7960-foot Stuart Peak. The loop trail returns past Twin Lakes and Lake Creek. The elevation gain is more than 3800 feet from the trailhead.

BITTERROOT VALLEY   Lake Como Trail (7 miles) circles a reservoir popular among water-sports enthusiasts, 14 miles south of Hamilton at the foot of the Bitterroot Mountains. With virtually no elevation gain, it's an easy walk. A trailhead is at Lake Como Recreation Area; from the trail's end, a one-mile walk along the road beside the dam will return you to your start.

The best way to hike the **South Lost Horse Creek Trail** (13 miles) is from the top down. The trailhead is on the Idaho border at the west end of 18-mile-long Lost Horse Road (Forest Road 429), nine miles south of Hamilton off Route 93. From Bear Creek, cross a 6100-foot Bitterroot Mountain pass to Fish Lake, then descend 1700 feet down the steep-sided canyon of South Lost Horse Creek. Moderate.

FLATHEAD INDIAN RESERVATION AND LAKE Numerous trails penetrate the Mission Mountains Wilderness Area. One of the shortest and most spectacular is the **Turquoise Lake Trail** (4.6 miles), which climbs to a sparkling glacial lake nestling beneath a sheer cliff at the 5800-foot-level of Daughter of the Sun Mountain. The moderately strenuous trail begins at the end of 12-mile-long Forest Road 561 southwest of Condon, halfway between Swan Lake and Seeley Lake.

The **Jewel Basin Hiking Area** has been set aside by the U.S. Forest Service and Flathead National Forest for foot travel only. Located 15 miles from Kalispell and about five miles from Bigfork, it has 35 miles of trails. Access is from West Side Road (Hungry Horse Reservoir) or from Jewel Basin Road, off Foothill Road (northeast of Bigfork). There's fishing and camping at 25 alpine lakes, wildlife and seasonal floral displays.

FLATHEAD VALLEY The **Danny On Memorial Trail** (5.6 miles) climbs The Big Mountain, seven miles north of Whitefish, from the lodge at the foot of the slopes. Named for a noted botanist and photographer of the region, the trail passes through beautiful meadows with views across the Flathead Valley. For a shorter (3.8-mile) one-way downhill hike, take the chairlift up the mountain.

Guided day and weekend hikes through the northern Montana backcountry are organized by the **Montana Wilderness Association**. Each trip is limited to a few hikers, though, so advance reservations are necessary. ~ 43 Woodland Park Drive, Kalispell; 406-755-6304.

Equipment If you didn't come properly equipped for backpacking, you can buy boots, packs, tents, sleeping bags and warm clothing at many places throughout the region. Full rentals of all outdoor gear are available from **Rent A Sport**. ~ 1748 South Avenue West, Missoula; 406-549-8225.

▼▼▼▼▼▼▼▼▼▼
Transportation

CAR

Route 90, the main east–west interstate highway through Montana, connects Missoula with Seattle and Coeur d'Alene, Idaho, to the west; with Butte, Bozeman and Billings to the east. The primary north–south artery is **Route 93**; from the Idaho border at Lost Trail Pass, it runs north through the Bitterroot Valley to Missoula, where it crosses Route 90. It then continues north to the Canadian border via Flathead Lake, Kalispell and Eureka. **Route 2**, which runs east from Sandpoint,

Idaho, through Libby and Kalispell to Glacier National Park and beyond, is the other important route in northwest Montana.

For road reports, call 800-332-6171 statewide; or call Missoula at 406-728-8553 or Kalispell at 406-755-4949.

Missoula's **Johnson Bell International Airport** is served by Continental, Delta and Northwest, as well as regional carrier Horizon. ~ Route 93 West, Missoula; 406-728-4381. Kalispell's **Glacier Park International Airport** is served by Delta and Horizon. ~ 4170 Route 2 East, Kalispell; 406-257-5994.

AIR

Greyhound Bus Lines runs east–west through Montana from Seattle to Missoula, Billings and points east. ~ 800-231-2222. **Intermountain Transportation** provides regional bus service. ~ 403 Second Street East, Whitefish; 406-862-6700.

Major stations for Greyhound are in Missoula ~ 1660 West Broadway; 406-549-2339. There's also a station in Kalispell. ~ 1301 Route 93 South; 406-755-4011.

BUS

Amtrak's Seattle–Chicago "Empire Builder" cuts across northern Montana, stopping at Whitefish en route from Idaho to North Dakota. ~ North Central Avenue, Whitefish; 406-862-2268, 800-872-7245.

TRAIN

Missoula has 10 agencies and the Flathead Valley has 12 in Kalispell and Whitefish. At Missoula's Johnson Bell International Airports, you'll find **Avis Rent A Car** (800-331-1212), **Budget Rent A Car** (800-527-0700), **Hertz Rent A Car** (800-654-3131) and **National Interrent** (800-227-7368).

At Glacier Park International Airport east of Kalispell are **Avis Rent A Car** (800-331-1212) and **National Interrent** (800-227-7368).

CAR RENTALS

Missoula's **Mountain Line** is an extensive citywide bus system with reasonable fares. ~ 406-721-3333.

PUBLIC TRANSIT

Transportation in the Missoula area is provided by **Yellow Cab**. ~ 406-543-6644. In the Flathead Valley, **Kalispell Taxi & Airport Shuttle** offers 24-hour service. ~ 406-752-4022.

TAXIS

THREE

Glacier National Park

Spectacular Glacier National Park, is the crown jewel of the Montana Rockies. Embracing some 1600 square miles of mountain scenery where the Continental Divide meets the Canadian border, the park is known for its chiseled peaks (several of which exceed 10,000 feet), some 250 deep turquoise lakes, and more than 730 miles of hiking and horseback trails: the most of any national park in America. Glacier's watershed flows in not two but three directions: to the Pacific Ocean, the Gulf of Mexico and Hudson Bay.

Glacier Park takes its name not from the snowfields that cap its highest peaks, but from the dramatic geological activity that created its stunning landscapes. Ending about 10,000 years ago, the series of ice ages that cloaked much of North America saved their finest artistry for this mountainous region. As rivers of ice forced their way down mountainsides, they sculpted sheer cliff walls, gouged valleys and lakes, and laid the future foundation for alpine meadows and streaming waterfalls and cascades. The panorama is best seen from Going-to-the-Sun Road, the lone highway to cross the park. This engineering marvel has been termed "the most beautiful 50 miles in the world."

Beasts are far more at home here than man. Elk, deer, mountain goats and bighorn sheep range widely throughout Glacier, and several hundred grizzly bears make their homes in the park. Bird life includes the white-tailed ptarmigan and numerous raptors, while more than 1,000 species of plants have been identified in the park, including many colorful wildflowers best seen in the early summer months.

Archeological findings indicate that American Indians knew this terrain as long ago as 11,000 years. In the modern era, Blackfeet and other Plains tribes—who migrated to the east side of the mountains in pursuit of bison about A.D. 1600—have used the park area for hunting and spiritual purposes. Even today, the Blackfeet, whose reservation borders the park to the east, revere Glacier as a sacred place.

Hudson's Bay Company fur trappers were the first white men to penetrate the region; miners and ranchers followed. But Glacier's very ruggedness saved it from exploitation. It was brought to the attention of the American public by the Great Northern Railroad, which joined in competition with other transcontinental railways (Northern Pacific in Yellowstone, Canadian Pacific in Banff) in routing its track around the park and promoting Glacier as the "Switzerland of America."

Glacier National Park was formally created in 1910, and the Great Northern undertook the building of hotels and chalets to match the Swiss image. Many of them remain today, magnificent tributes to a bygone era. Going-to-the-Sun Road was begun in 1916 and completed in 1932 to coincide with the creation of the world's first "international peace park": Glacier and Alberta's adjacent Waterton Lakes National Park were given this designation by acts of both the U.S. Congress and Canadian Parliament, with a push from regional chapters of Rotary International. Today, more than two million visitors a year swarm through the two parks.

Alberta's Waterton Lakes National Park, smaller by far than Glacier (covering just over 200 square miles), nevertheless features similarly striking mountain terrain and offers many of the same activities and services. Several trails cross the frontier between the two parks; the primary road access is the Chief Mountain International Highway, at the extreme northeast edge of Glacier Park.

If you're approaching Glacier from Kalispell and the west, you'll take Route 2 to West Glacier, then detour onto Going-to-the-Sun Road. If you're proceeding north from Great Falls to Glacier, you can take Going-to-the-Sun Road west off Route 89 in the Blackfeet Indian Reservation on the east side of the park.

▼▼▼▼▼▼▼▼▼▼▼▼▼

Western Gateways

East of Columbia Falls, itself at the edge of the Flathead Valley only 15 miles from West Glacier, Route 2 knifes through a string of small communities: Hungry Horse, Martin City, Coram. These Flathead Riverside villages, each at an elevation slightly higher than the last, lead the traveler to Glacier National Park's west entrance. While the settlements themselves may be charming, they come with baggage: the sort of unabashedly commercial "attractions" that are the bane of too many national park gateways.

SIGHTS

There is, for instance, the **House of Mystery**, said to be situated on a vortex. Admission. ~ Route 2, Hungry Horse; 406-892-1210. The **Great Bear Adventure** is a drive-through park for *ursus* lovers who prefer the safety of their own cars. Admission. ~ Route 2, Coram; 406-387-4099. At the **North American Wildlife Museum** you needn't remain in your car—the creatures are stuffed. Admission. ~ Route 2, Coram; 406-387-4018. And the **Glacier Maze** has bumper boats, miniature golf and two levels of puzzling passageways. Admission. ~ Route 2, Coram; 406-387-5902.

Better you should inhale the view from **Hungry Horse Dam**. The reservoir formed by this 564-foot dam, four miles off Route 2, extends snakelike for 33 miles between the rugged Swan and Flathead ranges of the Rockies. A visitors center describes the dam's construction on the South Fork of the Flathead River. ~ West Side Road, Hungry Horse; 406-387-5241.

The South, Middle and North forks of the Flathead form the **Flathead National Wild and Scenic River** system, the nation's longest. Between them the three forks stretch 219 miles across spectacular wilderness and near-wilderness. The North and Middle forks define the western boundary of Glacier National Park. Whitewater rafters, kayakers and fly-fishermen are regular visitors. ~ West Glacier; 406-755-5401.

At **West Glacier**, where many of the Flathead River rafting companies are headquartered, is the west entrance to the national park. Nontourists who want to avoid the twisty-turviness of Going-to-the-Sun Road can stay on Route 2, crossing the Continental Divide at mile-high Marias Pass and reaching East Glacier Park, 55 miles away, in less than 90 minutes.

This southern highway follows the original (and still highly operational) Great Northern route up the Middle Fork of the Flathead. One essential stop is at the old rail camp of Essex, whose **Izaak Walton Inn** is a veritable museum of railroad memorabilia. ~ Route 2, Essex; 406-888-5700.

The isolated community of **Polebridge**, about 32 miles north of West Glacier and 41 miles from Columbia Falls, offers access to Glacier Park's northwest frontier across the Flathead River's North Fork. Rough gravel roads lead to this village, boxed in on either side by high mountains. There are cabins, a hostel and a mercantile here, but no electricity: Everything runs on kerosene or propane.

LODGING

Two pleasant motels will appeal to wallet watchers and travelers with pets. The **Hungry Horse Motel** has 20 rooms and a swimming pool. ~ 8808 Route 2 East, Hungry Horse; 406-387-5443. BUDGET. TO MODERATE.

The **Middle Fork Motel**, nestled in a pine grove, has nine rooms, including kitchenettes and nonsmoking rooms. ~ 9533 Route 2 East, Martin City; 406-387-5900. BUDGET TO MODERATE.

Opposite the Amtrak station in West Glacier is the **Glacier Highland Motel**, especially appealing to winter visitors with snowmobile rentals and a jacuzzi tub. The Highland has 33 rooms, a restaurant and a swimming pool. ~ Route 2 East, West Glacier; 406-888-5427, 800-766-0811, fax 406-888-5764. MODERATE.

Great Northern Chalets has 12 log homes that each accommodate four to six guests. Every chalet has a fireplace and kitchen, and the resort includes an indoor pool and spa, a sauna and sun room, and a restaurant. There are nonsmoking and handicapped-accessible rooms. Guests are invited to join rafting, fishing and horseback trips in summer, cross-country skiing and snowmobile excursions in winter. ~ West Glacier; 406-387-5340, 800-735-7897, fax 800-387-9007. DELUXE.

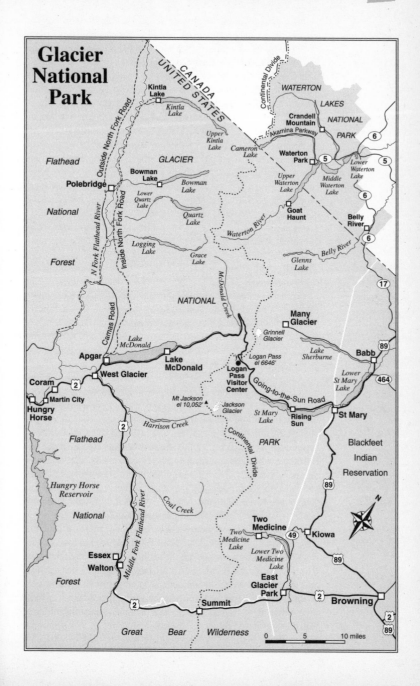

Glacier National Park

The **Izaak Walton Inn** is just across the Middle Fork of the Flathead from the national park. Diesel helper engines that idle in a railyard 100 feet from the inn's front door and hilltop cabooses that shelter overnight hikers and nordic skiers on the edge of the adjacent Great Bear Wilderness are testimony to its railroad heritage: The Izaak Walton was built in 1939 to lodge Great Northern Railroad service crews. Today it is a National Historic Register property surrounded by trestles and tunnels. The rustic lobby, simple wood-paneled rooms and country-style restaurant hold a museum's worth of memorabilia. ~ Route 2, Essex; 406-888-5700. DELUXE.

The **North Fork Hostel** might be booked months ahead in summer. But if you can reserve a bunk at this rustic house, you'll have ready access to recreation around Bowman, Kintla and several other long glacial lakes. Mountain bikes and some backpacking equipment are available for rent. Hostelers share a kitchen, washrooms and other facilities. ~ North Fork Road, Polebridge; 406-756-4780. BUDGET.

DINING

This corner of Montana is famous for its huckleberries, and there may be no better place to sample these wild delicacies than at **The Huckleberry Patch**. Try them in pancakes, muffins, cookies, milkshakes and more. The restaurant serves three home-cooked meals daily, and an adjoining mercantile store markets a very wide selection of T-shirts and other reasonably priced gifts and native artifacts. It also offers a wildlife display. ~ 8866 Route 2, Hungry Horse; 406-387-5670. BUDGET TO MODERATE.

Area locals prefer to hang out at the **Silver Basin Inn**. Hearty beef dinners and homemade desserts top the fare at this café, formerly known as Mike & Aggie's Hide-a-Way. ~ 9050 Route 2 East, Hungry Horse; 406-387-5600. BUDGET.

Nearer the west entrance, the **Glacier Highland Motel Restaurant** serves up staunchly Montana cuisine: big omelettes for breakfast, oversized sandwiches for lunch, chicken and steak for dinner. ~ Route 2, West Glacier; 406-888-5427. MODERATE.

PARKS

GREAT BEAR WILDERNESS AREA 🏃🐎🛶 Wedged between Glacier National Park and the Bob Marshall Wilderness Area ("The Bob"), the Great Bear Wilderness is indeed one of the principal remaining strongholds of the grizzly bear. It encompasses the sources and upper reaches of the Middle Fork of the Flathead River, with alpine lakes and peaks ranging above 8000 feet. ~ Most trails that penetrate this wilderness begin either off Route 2 on the south side of Glacier Park, principally in the Essex area, or from the Spotted Bear Ranger Station near the head of Hungry Horse Reservoir; 406-755-5401.

▲ Primitive only.

From its magnificent sculpted peaks to its
abundant pristine lakes, Glacier National Park
is a natural wonderland, one that no traveler

Glacier National Park

can afford to miss. It's also a hiker's and biker's paradise with un-
limited trails to choose from, and anglers will find its lakes stocked
with trout.

SIGHTS

Entering the park at West Glacier, stop at **Glacier Park Headquarters** for maps and information. ~ West Glacier; 406-888-5441.
Nearby is the splendid new **Travel Alberta Visitors Center**. A
replica *Tyrannosaurus rex* skeleton greets you at the door, and elsewhere there are impressive displays and detailed information for
motorists who plan to continue north of the international border,
perhaps to Waterton Lakes National Park, after their visit to
Glacier. ~ West Glacier; 406-888-5743.

  Apgar Village, located two miles from West Glacier where the
McDonald River flows out of **Lake McDonald**, has a visitors center as well as a lodge and motel, a campground, a restaurant and
deli, a general store, three gift shops and boat and bicycle rentals.
Apgar Village is at the junction of the park's two principal roads:
the 40-mile **Inside North Fork Road**, which goes to Bowman and
Kintla lakes and other sites in the park's rarely visited western
boundary region, and Going-to-the-Sun Road. ~ 406-888-5484.

  For its first ten miles, this 52-mile highway traces the southeastern shore of Lake McDonald, the park's longest and deepest
(472 feet) body of water, through forests of larch and lodgepole
pines. At the head of the lake is the full-service **Lake McDonald
Lodge,** complete with general store and gas station; narrated
one-hour lake cruises (admission) begin here four times daily. ~
406-888-5727.

  Going-to-the-Sun Road is normally kept open year-round as far
as Lake McDonald, which is at 3153-foot elevation. (Larger trail-

GLACIER NATIONAL PARK EXPERIENCES
- Sample Montana's most famous wild berries in pancakes, cookies and
  milkshakes at **The Huckleberry Patch** in Hungry Horse. *page 88*
- Mount a horse or board a boat at **Many Glacier** to view the Grinnell
  Glacier and some of the park's most spectacular peaks. *page 90*
- Stay at the venerable **Glacier Park Lodge** and marvel at the massive
  tree trunks that support its four-story atrium. *page 93*
- Put on your cross-country skis and follow 35 kilometers of set
  tracks from the historic **Izaak Walton Inn.** *page 100*

ers and recreational vehicles—those longer than 20 feet and wider than 7½ feet—may be restricted from traveling the road.) The lodge, like the road beyond this point, usually opens in early June and is closed by the end of September. But cross-country skiers frequently begin winter explorations of Glacier Park from this point.

Though there are many small glaciers on its higher peaks, Glacier Park was named for the geologic glaciation that carved its features, rather than for its rivers of ice.

As the road begins to climb beyond Lake McDonald, the mountains' western slopes come into view. The increased precipitation on this side of the mountains has yielded occasional groves of old-growth cedar and hemlock.

About eight miles from Lake McDonald, Going-to-the-Sun Road makes a 90-degree turn to the northwest and begins a rapid climb (with but a single hairpin switchback) to subalpine meadows and 6646-foot **Logan Pass**. It traverses the precipitous **Garden Wall**, passes the **Weeping Wall** (where springs pour from the side of the cliff) and affords unparalleled panoramas of mountains, glaciers, waterfalls and the McDonald River valley.

Surrounded by snow drifts as late as August, Logan Pass sits on the Continental Divide. Its visitors center offers a variety of interpretive programs, guided hikes and other activities, many of them focusing on the natural history of the high country.

Descending the east side of the Divide, the road offers several views south toward 10,052-foot Mount Jackson and **Jackson Glacier**, a source of the St. Mary River.

The descent ends at **St. Mary Lake**, another long, narrow body of water. The **St. Mary River** flows north from here, making its way to Hudson Bay in northern Ontario. At **Rising Sun**, about midway along the lake's northwestern shore, there's a campground, motor inn and restaurant; 90-minute, naturalist-led boat tours of St. Mary Lake (admission) begin here. ~ 406-732-4430.

Another visitors center with activities and interpretive programs is located at **St. Mary**, where Going-to-the-Sun Road terminates at its junction with Route 89 outside the park entrance. Here also you'll find a campground and other lodging, restaurants, a garage and a general store. A historic ranger station, built in 1913 at the Red Eagle Lake trailhead, has been refurbished to its original appearance; it is not often open, unfortunately, but visitors can peer into its windows! ~ 406-732-4431.

Two of Glacier Park's most scenic locations—Many Glacier and Two Medicine—aren't accessible from Going-to-the-Sun Road; instead, there are separate approaches to each from the east side of the park.

To get to **Many Glacier**, head north on Route 89 from St. Mary, as if you were proceeding to Canada's Waterton Lakes. After nine miles, turn left at Babb junction; then follow Many Glacier Road about 12 miles west, along the Swiftcurrent River and Lake Sherburne, to the **Many Glacier Hotel**. Surrounded by some of the park's most starkly magnificent summits—one of whose cliffs drops an amazing 4200 feet, farther than any in California's world-renowned Yosemite National Park—the hotel sits on turquoise **Swiftcurrent Lake**, one of a series of small lakes fed by Grinnell Glacier. Boat tours across Swiftcurrent and Josephine lakes, boat rentals and guided horse trips are available at Many Glacier. There are also guided naturalist walks; wildlife watching, especially for bears, is excellent here.

Two Medicine is the name given to three lakes, a river and a park community in the southeastern section of Glacier. It's reached by traveling 20 miles south from St. Mary on Route 89, another nine miles west and south toward East Glacier on Route 49, and then nine miles west past Lower Two Medicine Lake on Two Medicine Road. A historic chalet near the shore of Two Medicine Lake has a general store and snack bar (but no lodging), and there are lake cruises (the *Sinopah* schedules four trips a day on the two-mile-long lake; admission) and boat rentals as well as a campground. Some of Glacier's finest hiking is among the colorful foliage and through the twisting valleys of this corner of the park.

LODGING

The **Lake McDonald Lodge**, built in 1913, is one of several impressive historic lodges in or adjacent to the national park. Set on the west side of the park, at the north end of Lake McDonald in a grove of giant cedars, the lodge has 100 guest units—individual cabins and double rooms in the main lodge and motel annex—all with private bathrooms. Its huge lobby contains a big stone fireplace and collection of big-game trophies. Facilities include a fine-dining restaurant, a coffee shop, a lounge and a camp store. Open early June to late September. ~ Going-to-the-Sun Road, Glacier National Park; 406-888-9920. MODERATE TO DELUXE.

The **Many Glacier Hotel** offers unquestionably the most awesome view of any lodge in the park: across Swiftcurrent Lake toward spectacular Grinnell Glacier, which tumbles down the east face of the Continental Divide from 9500 feet. The hotel has 200 guest rooms—small, basic, but with private baths—and a spacious lobby and dining area. Request a lakeside room. Open early June to mid-September. ~ Many Glacier Road, Glacier National Park; 406-732-4411. MODERATE TO DELUXE.

Glacier Park, Inc., Lodging is the operator of six National Park inns, with a common reservation line travelers can call for rates and information on all of them. In addition to the Lake McDonald Lodge and the Many Glacier Hotel, the company also operates a number of motels. ~ 602-207-6000.

Village Inn Motel has 36 rooms at the south end of Lake McDonald. ~ Camas Road, Apgar Village, Glacier National Park; 406-888-5632. MODERATE.

Rising Sun Motor Inn on the northern shore of St. Mary Lake has 72 cabins and rooms. ~ Going-to-the-Sun Road, Glacier National Park; 406-732-5523. BUDGET TO MODERATE.

Swiftcurrent Motor Inn has 88 motel rooms and rustic cabins. ~ Many Glacier Road, Glacier National Park; 406-732-5531. BUDGET TO MODERATE.

DINING

Eddie's Restaurant is a good choice on the west side of the park. Families enjoy a wide-ranging menu—everything from burgers, spaghetti and fresh salads to steak and seafood entrées—in a casual atmosphere near Lake McDonald. Three meals a day are served. Open late May to mid-September. ~ Camas Road, Apgar Village; 406-888-5361. MODERATE.

Other meals are available in park lodges or, especially on the east side of the park, in gateway communities like East Glacier Park and St. Mary.

SHOPPING

Every lodge and store in the park has a souvenir outlet. The best of the bunch—and the one with the longest season, open from the second week of May through October—may be the **Montana House of Gifts**, a regional craft shop at Apgar Village, on the west side of the park. ~ Going-to-the-Sun Road, Apgar Village; 406-8885393.

PARKS

GLACIER NATIONAL PARK 🚶 🚴 🚶 🏇 ⛺ ⛰ 🎣 🛶 🚤 🛥
◢ Rugged mountains and deep glacial lakes, as well as the longest system of hiking trails in any national park, are the highlights of this wildlife-rich, 1600-square-mile preserve that crowns the Continental Divide. The 52-mile Going-to-the-Sun Road connects its green western boundary with the striking Rocky Mountain Front that marks its eastern flank. Picnic areas, restrooms, amphitheaters and visitors centers round out the amenities. Lodges and restaurants are located at several sites, and groceries are in Apgar and West Glacier, St. Mary and East Glacier Park. ~ Enter from the west at West Glacier, 32 miles northeast of Kalispell on Route 2; from the east at St. Mary, 155 miles northwest of Great Falls on Route 89; 406-888-5441.

▲ There are 1001 RV/tent sites in ten campgrounds, including 215 sites with RV hookups in nine campgrounds; $8 to $10 per night. (As of early 1997, some of these may be forced to close until additional federal funding is available for the National Park Service.) Seven-day maximum stay. No reservations. Opening dates vary from early May to mid-June, closing dates from early September to mid-October. Primitive camping is permitted at Apgar Village and St. Mary through the winter.

The entire eastern edge of Glacier National Park is ▼▼▼▼▼▼▼▼▼▼▼▼▼▼
bounded by the Blackfeet Indian Reservation, which **Eastern Gateways**
is half as large as the park itself. This land of sharp
geological contrast, one and a half million acres in extent, contains
all of the park's eastern gateways.

St. Mary, located where Going-to-the-Sun Road meets Route 89, **SIGHTS**
is one of about ten communities on the reservation. **East Glacier Park**, at the southeastern corner of the national park, 31 miles from St. Mary, is another. It is most notable for its historic **Glacier Park Lodge**. ~ Route 49, East Glacier Park; 406-226-5551. The adjacent community of East Glacier Park that has grown up nearby has an Old West facade and a keen orientation toward outdoor recreation, mainly in the Two Medicine Lake region to its west.

The shield-shaped **Blackfeet Indian Reservation** stretches from the dramatic Rocky Mountain Front across sone 50 miles of prairies to the town of Cut Bank, and a similar distance south from the Canadian border. It is the home of the Blackfoot tribe, Montana's largest. Of its 9000 members, 7000 live on the reservation. ~ P.O. Box 850, Browning, MT 59417; 406-338-7276.

Browning is the seat of tribal government and the site of the North American Indian Days celebration in mid-July. Located 13 miles northeast of East Glacier Park, it is the focus of most visitor interest in the reservation.

The **Museum of the Plains Indian** is one of Montana's finest small museums. Its galleries include an interpretive collection of traditional clothing and artifacts of the Blackfoot and other northern Great Plains tribes, contemporary paintings and sculptures by tribal artists, an audio-visual presentation and changing exhibits. The museum shop is a good place to find authentic arts and crafts. Half-day and full-day tours of the reservation's **historic sites** (406- ◄ *HIDDEN* 338-7406, 800-215-2395) begin at the museum. ~ Route 89 opposite Route 2 junction, Browning; 406-338-2230.

Nearby, the **Bob Scriver Museum of Montana Wildlife & Hall of Bronze** presents the work of one of Montana's best-known wildlife sculptors. A gallery sells his bronzes and the work of other artists; also interesting are Scriver's adjacent studio, foundry and workshop, which the public can tour during summers. Admission. ~ Routes 2 and 89, Browning; 406-338-5425.

The **Glacier Park Lodge** is a tourist attraction in its own right. The **LODGING** huge structure, built of fir and cedar logs at the end of World War I, has a four-story atrium, supported by tree trunks, and a brilliant wildflower garden in front of its entrance. All 155 guest rooms are clean and well maintained. Facilities include a restaurant, coffee shop and lounge and game room as well as a swimming pool, a nine-hole golf course and horse stables. Closed mid-September to early June. ~ Route 49, East Glacier Park; 406-226-5551. DELUXE.

Nearby, for the budget backpacker, there's **Brownie's Grocery and AYH Hostel**. This two-story log hostel has 31 beds in male and female dormitories and a couple of private rooms. A community kitchen, showers, laundry and equipment storage are available. Closed from mid-October to the beginning of May. ~ 1020 Route 49, East Glacier Park; 406-226-4426. BUDGET.

"No vegetarians: We eat *beef!*" proclaims the **Bear Creek Guest Ranch**. Established in 1933 a quarter-mile outside the national park boundary, the ranch provides accommodation in rustic private cabins and lodge rooms, as well as full board (bed and breakfast only in fall and winter). A visit to Bear Creek is highlighted by its riding program, including pack trips into the Bob Marshall Wilderness and rodeo clinics on roping and barrel racing. ~ P.O. Box 151, East Glacier Park, MT 59434; 406-226-4489, 800-445-7379. DELUXE.

Two of the more affordable East Glacier motels are open from May to September, are handicapped-accessible and welcome pets. The **Mountain Pine Motel** has 26 rooms, some with kitchens, on lovely pine-shaded grounds. ~ Route 49, East Glacier Park; 406-226-4403. BUDGET TO MODERATE. **Jacobson's Scenic View Cottages** include 12 units and a playground for kids; the cottages have TVs but no phones. ~ 1204 Route 49 North, East Glacier Park; 406-226-4422. BUDGET TO MODERATE.

The 70 rooms at the **St. Mary Lodge and Resort** could use an overhaul, but they'll do in a pinch, if other park accommodations are booked. There's a restaurant and lounge. ~ Route 89 at Going-to-the-Sun Road, St. Mary; 406-732-4431, 800-452-7275, fax 406-732-9265. MODERATE.

If you want to stay near the Museum of the Plains Indian on the Blackfeet Indian Reservation, try the **War Bonnet Lodge**. The modern motel has 40 units, a restaurant and lounge. ~ Routes 2 and 89, Browning; 406-338-7610. MODERATE.

DINING

The **Goat Lick Dining Room** is the place to bring big appetites on the east side of the park. Rocky Mountain trout, steaks and finger-lickin' favorites like barbecued chicken and ribs are served up in a room with the ambience of the Old West. Don't forget your bib. Closed mid-September to early June. ~ Glacier Park Lodge, Route 49, East Glacier Park; 406-226-5551. MODERATE.

Nearby, the **Glacier Village Restaurant** offers hearty sit-down pancake-and-egg breakfasts and cafeteria service for lunch and dinner. Closed mid-September to early June. ~ Route 2 East at Route 49, East Glacier Park; 406-226-4464. BUDGET TO MODERATE.

For those who can't go long without Mexican food, **Serrano's** offers generous portions of enchiladas and tacos. The restaurant, open evenings only, occupies a historic log home. Closed mid-October to May 1. ~ 29 Dawson Avenue, East Glacier Park; 406-226-9392. MODERATE.

West of Browning near the Kiowa junction, the rustic **Old Nine Mile Inn** is a classic roadhouse that serves hefty helpings in a casual atmosphere daily from 7:30 a.m. to 8:30 p.m. There's a children's menu here as well. ~ Route 89, Browning; 406-338-7911. MODERATE.

SHOPPING Don't miss the excellent gift shop at the **Museum of the Plains Indian,** offering authentic Plains Indian arts and crafts. ~ Route 89 opposite Route 2 junction, Browning; 406-338-2230.

▼▼▼▼▼▼▼▼▼▼▼▼

Waterton Lakes National Park

The three interlocked Waterton Lakes and scenic Cameron Lake are the main attractions of Alberta's Waterton Lakes National Park. Make your headquarters in the Waterton Park townsite, 21 miles northwest of the nearest U.S.–Canada border crossing (at Chief Mountain). Situated on a small promontory that extends into Upper Waterton Lake, it is framed to the north and west by lofty peaks and steep cliffs. In summer, the town bustles with tourist vehicles and wandering wildlife; in winter, when the Chief Mountain International Highway is closed, it's just the animals, cross-country skiers and a handful of hardy year-round residents.

SIGHTS The **Park Visitors Center**, which is open daily from mid-May to mid-September, features interpretive displays and presents audiovisual shows; guided walks and special-interest programs are offered on a regular basis. ~ Park Entrance Road at Prince of Wales Road. A second interpretive center, located at Cameron Lake, is open seasonally as well. For information year-round, contact the **Park Headquarters.** ~ 403-859-2224.

The townsite has a small **Heritage Centre** museum and art gallery open summers and by appointment. ~ 403-859-2624.

One of the most popular activities in the park is taking the narrated two-hour voyage through windy Upper Waterton Lake with **Waterton Inter-Nation Shoreline Cruises.** The 200-passenger boats run all the way to Goat Haunt, in Glacier Park at the southern end of the lake, where they make a 20-minute stop throughout July and August. In May, June and September, the vessels have a more limited schedule with no stops. Admission. ~ 403-859-2362.

Numerous short scenic drives lead to other attractions. The **Akamina Parkway** winds through the narrow Cameron Valley, where Alberta's first producing oil well was drilled over a century ago, for ten miles west to Cameron Lake. The nine-mile **Red Rock Parkway** to Red Rock Canyon follows the much wider Blakiston Valley, passing exhibits on Waterton geology, prehistory and history en route. Just north of the park's northeastern entrance on Alberta Route 6, a small herd of bison can be observed from an overlook at the **Buffalo Paddocks**.

LODGING

Waterton Park's hotel and six motels are all solidly booked well in advance for the peak summer months. Unless you're camping, reserve months ahead or plan to drive at least 27 miles (from Cardston, the next closest town with lodging) to reach the park. For assistance, contact the **Waterton Chamber of Commerce**. ~ Waterton Park, AB T0K 2M0, Canada; 403-859-2203. Or try the **Alberta Tourism Office**. ~ 800-661-8888.

The national park's landmark is the stately and majestic **Prince of Wales Hotel**, built in 1927 on a grassy knoll just north of the townsite. Its Bavarian-style architecture is only one lure of this 89-room hotel; another is its unforgettable view of the length of Upper Waterton Lake all the way into Montana. The hotel has a fully licensed restaurant and lounge, and a British-style high tea is served every afternoon in Valerie's Tea Room. Elevators rise only to the fourth floor, which means guests staying in the fifth- and sixth-story rafters will have to do some stair climbing. Open mid-May to late September only; in off-season, contact Station 0928, Phoenix, AZ 85077; 602-207-6000. ~ Prince of Wales Road, Waterton Park; 403-859-2231 or 403-226-5551. DELUXE.

In July and August, hikers can take the Waterton Inter-Nation cruise one way to Goat Haunt, then enjoy a ten-mile return trek along the shoreline.

My favorite among the in-town motels is the **Kilmorey Lodge**. With 23 rooms and suites on the shore of Emerald Bay, this country inn has drawn national accolades for its personalized service and its housekeeping. Furnishings are antique, and there are eiderdown comforters on all the beds. Most units are nonsmoking; children 16 and under stay free with parents. The Lamp Post Dining Room is Waterton's best restaurant, and the lodge has a separate lounge and coffee shop. The Kilmorey is a rarity in Waterton in that it's open year-round. ~ 117 Evergreen Avenue; 403-859-2334, fax 403-859-2342. MODERATE TO DELUXE.

Another upscale accommodation is the 23-room **Aspen Village Inn**. Closed in winter. ~ P.O. Box 100, Waterton Park; 403-859-2255, fax 403-859-2033. MODERATE TO DELUXE. There's also the 70-room lakeside **Bayshore Inn**. ~ 111 Waterton Avenue; 403-238-4847, fax 403-859-2291. MODERATE TO DELUXE. For rustic mountain lodging, stay at the 13-unit **Crandell Mountain Lodge**. ~

P.O. Box 114, Waterton Park; phone/fax 403-859-2288. MODER-
ATE TO DELUXE.

The clean and comfortable **El-Cortez Motel** has 35 rooms with
TVs and free coffee; kitchenettes and family-size units cost extra.
Closed mid-October through April. ~ Mountview Road; 403-859-
2366. BUDGET TO MODERATE.

Near Cameron Falls is the **Northland Lodge**, with eight rooms,
two of them budget-priced and sharing a bath. Guests here can
watch TV in a central lounge with a fireplace. Closed mid-October
through April. ~ Evergreen Avenue; 403-859-2353. BUDGET TO
MODERATE.

DINING

The best restaurant in Waterton National Park is **The Lamp Post
Dining Room**. Three gourmet meals a day are served in a casual atmosphere at this lakeside country lodge, open year-round. The
restaurant is fully licensed, and service is superb. ~ Kilmorey Lodge,
117 Evergreen Avenue; 403-859-2334. MODERATE TO DELUXE.

At **Valerie's Tea Room** you can get a formal English-style high
tea every afternoon, complete with scones, jam and cream. ~ Prince
of Wales Hotel, Prince of Wales Road; 403-859-2231. MODERATE.

PARKS

WATERTON LAKES NATIONAL PARK

Much of the same rugged mountain scenery of Glacier
National Park extends across the Canadian border to this park,
whose centerpiece is the three interlocked Waterton Lakes. Wildlife, including bears and mountain goats, is equally impressive here.
There are 160 miles of hiking and horse trails in the park, which
covers more than 200 square miles. Facilities include picnic areas,
restrooms, amphitheaters and visitors centers; lodges, restaurants
and groceries are in Waterton Park townsite. ~ By road from the
east side of Glacier National Park, take Route 89 north 13 miles
from St. Mary, then Route 17 (the Chief Mountain International
Highway) 14 miles to the U.S.–Canada border. Waterton Park
townsite is another 20 miles northwest; 403-859-2224.

▲ There are 367 RV/tent sites, and 24 for tents only, at three
campgrounds, including 95 with hookups in the Waterton Townsite Campground; $10 to $16 (Canadian) per night, not including hookup charge; 13-day maximum stay. No reservations.
Campgrounds open early May to late September. Primitive camping permitted at the Pass Creek Picnic Area during fall, winter
and spring.

▼▼▼▼▼▼▼▼▼▼▼▼▼
Outdoor Adventures

FISHING

You don't need a license to fish in Glacier
National Park; this makes fishing an especially
popular activity among visitors. Be sure to pick
up a pamphlet describing park regulations, however, from any
ranger station or visitors center.

Glacier naturalists ceased stocking the park's lakes and rivers a number of years ago when they found that the introduced fish were curtailing the reproduction of native species. Today's rainbow, brook, cutthroat and bull trout, as well as mountain whitefish, may be difficult to catch, but anglers consider them worth the effort. You'll have best luck from a boat over the large lakes' deepest holes, or casting from the shore of smaller alpine lakes.

If you prefer to fish with an outfitter, try **Glacier Fishing Charters.** ~ 375 Jensen Road, Columbia Falls; 406-892-2377.

Licenses are required in Waterton Lakes National Park. They may be purchased from the national park information center in Waterton townsite.

BOATING   In Glacier National Park, the **Glacier Park Boat Company** rents a variety of vessels—including rowboats, canoes and boats with six-horsepower motors—on several lakes. Scenic launch tours are also offered. ~ 406-752-5488. In summer, contact the various rental outlets directly. On Lake McDonald contact **Apgar Village.** ~ 406-888-5609. Also try the **Lake McDonald Lodge.** ~ 406-888-5727. On Swiftcurrent and Josephine lakes, the **Many Glacier Hotel** has boat rentals for your enjoyment. ~ 406-732-4480. On Two Medicine Lake check out the rentals at the **Two Medicine Lake Boat Dock.** ~ 406-226-4467.

In Waterton Lakes National Park, you'll find rentals at the Emerald Bay Marina on Upper Waterton Lake (in Waterton Park township), and boat ramps on both the Upper and Middle lakes. Sailing and wind surfing, as well as scuba diving, are popular on windy Upper Waterton Lake, but less stable craft are discouraged.

RIVER RUNNING   The Middle and North forks of the Flathead River, which define the western boundary of Glacier National Park and converge near the community of West Glacier, are very popular whitewater rivers. The **Montana Raft Company** may be the most experienced of several outfitters that run these rivers. ~ Route 2, West Glacier; 406-888-5466. Another river runner is the **Glacier Raft Company.** ~ Box 218, West Glacier; 406-888-5454. For an unforgettable adventure, contact **Great Northern Whitewater.** ~ Box 278, West Glacier; 800-535-0303 in Montana, 800-735-7897 out-of-state. Another good company is **Wild River Adventures.** ~ Box 272, West Glacier; 406-387-9453.

In Waterton Lakes National Park, rafting is popular on the Belly River; it flows northward out of Glacier Park near Chief Mountain. Inquire about outfitters at park headquarters.

Kayaking and canoeing can be hazardous in larger lakes of both parks, especially McDonald, St. Mary and Upper Waterton, which often funnel heavy western winds toward the drier eastern

Beware
the Bear

Of all the great mammals of the Rocky Mountains, none is as feared or as respected as the grizzly bear. Once numbering at about 50,000 in the lower 48 states, ranging from the Mississippi River west to the Pacific Ocean, this great bear was reduced by white settlement to fewer than 1000 on 2 percent of its former range. Today, most grizzlies—protected as a threatened species under the federal Endangered Species Act—inhabit the national parks and wilderness areas running down the spine of the Rockies from the Canadian border through Yellowstone National Park.

In western Montana, Glacier National Park and the adjacent Great Bear Wilderness are two of its strongholds. Biologists estimate there are several hundred resident grizzlies.

Ursus arctos horribilis is the second largest omnivore (that is, meat and plant eater) in North America, superseded only by the polar bear. Males can weigh more than 1000 pounds, females 600. Though nocturnal, an adult can be aggressive if intruders disturb it . . . or its cubs.

The grizzly is easily distinguished from the more docile American black bear (*Ursus americanus*) by its broad head; a well-defined shoulder muscle, which helps it dig for rodents, insects and roots; and its frequently silver-tipped, or "grizzled," fur coat. Grizzlies don't climb trees as well as black bears, but they can outrun horses in a sprint.

Only occasionally do backcountry visitors see grizzlies today. Even in Yellowstone Park, once renowned for its begging roadside bears, they have been removed to the wilderness. Wildlife watchers who want to observe grizzlies should look during the dawn and dusk hours around the fringes of woodlands and meadows, near water . . . from a distance.

To avoid grizzly encounters, travel in numbers, make plenty of noise (by talking, singing or even wearing bells) and avoid hiking at night. Clean cooking gear immediately after use, and store food in airtight containers away from your campsite. Don't bury your garbage; pack it out.

If confronted by a grizzly while hiking, do *not* turn your back and run. Move slowly away, avoiding eye contact. If the grizzly charges, stand your ground: Bears often feign a charge or run past you. As a last resort, curl into a ball and play dead, covering your neck and head with your hands and arms. If a grizzly invades your camp, find a tree or boulder to climb as high as you can. If you are attacked, fight back with any weapon, including your fists. Playing dead will *not* work here.

Grizzlies kill humans only infrequently; more often they die at the hands of man. But like the wise Scout, it's best to be prepared.

prairies. Stay close to shore if you're paddling here. Wilderness lakes such as Bowman and Kintla, in the far northwest of Glacier Park, are especially popular among canoeists. Both craft can be rented at McDonald, Two Medicine and Swiftcurrent lakes in Glacier National Park (see "Boating"), and at Cameron Lake in Waterton Lakes National Park.

CROSS-COUNTRY SKIING

Near Glacier Park, the **Izaak Walton Inn** has extensive backcountry packages. The Inn maintains some 35 kilometers (22 miles) of groomed trails, as well as a telemark hill and two backcountry bowls. Ski rentals are available here. A trail-use fee is charged to skiers who do not stay at the inn (see "Lodging"). ~ Route 2, Essex; 406-888-5700.

For those with their own equipment, there are numerous popular Nordic ski trails in and around Glacier National Park, in the Lake McDonald, Polebridge, St. Mary and East Glacier areas.

Waterton Park has no organized nordic facility, but many of its 160 miles of hiking trails are employed by cross-country skiers in winter. A 10.5-kilometer (6.5-mile) trail along the shore of Cameron Lake is groomed weekly.

The nearest downhill ski resort is the Big Mountain at Whitefish in the Flathead Valley (see Chapter Two).

GOLF

The 18-hole **Waterton Lakes Golf Course**, built in 1936, is renowned for its scenic beauty. For non-duffers, it also has a panoramic restaurant. Closed from mid-October to March. ~ 403-859-2114.

RIDING STABLES

In Glacier National Park, **Mule Shoe Outfitters** operate small corrals at Many Glacier and Lake McDonald for guided rides through the park. Beginning July 1 and continuing through Labor Day, they range from two hours to all day. First-timers are welcome. ~ Many Glacier, 406-732-4203; Lake McDonald, 406-888-5121.

In Waterton Lakes National Park, **Alpine Stables**, just east of the Waterton Park townsite, offers short and long rides to lakes and to prairies during the summer season. ~ 403-859-2462.

PACK TRIPS & LLAMA TREKS

The 900-odd miles of backcountry trails in the combined national parks, not to mention the expansive adjacent wilderness areas and national forests, are open to horses as well as hikers. Outfitters can take you anywhere with advance notice. You might try **Glacier Wilderness Guides**. ~ Box 535, West Glacier; 406-888-5466. There's also **Spotted Bear Outfitters**. ~ Box 293, West Glacier; 406-888-5588. In East Glacier Park, try **Bear Creek Outfitters**. ~ Box 151, East Glacier Park; 406-226-4489. Or try **Great Divide Guiding & Outfitters**. ~ P.O. Box 315, East Glacier Park;

406-226-4487. In Waterton Park, contact **Alpine Stables**. ~ 403-859-2462.

For llama treks, consult the **Great Northern Llama Co.** ~ 600 Blackmer Lane, Columbia Falls; 406-755-9044.

Bike touring is encouraged through **Glacier National Park,** and several tour operators lead groups across the Continental Divide on Going-to-the-Sun Road. But because of the increased danger of accidents during the peak travel season—mid-June to Labor Day—bicyclists are restricted from hazardous sections of the narrow, winding highway between 11 a.m. and 4 p.m. Bicycles are not permitted on park trails or off-road.

BIKING

National forest roads and trails are generally open to mountain biking, but wheeled vehicles—motorized or not—are not allowed in designated wilderness areas.

Bike Rentals   For rentals and repairs on the west side of Glacier Park, visit **All Season Sport & Cycle**. ~ 615 Nucleus Avenue, Columbia Falls; 406-892-2755. You can also rent bicycles in Glacier National Park at the **Village Inn Motel**. ~ Camas Road, Apgar; 406-888-5632.

Glacier National Park itself has 730 miles of trails, more than any other national park. Waterton Park has another 160 miles. And there are hundreds of miles more throughout the adjoining national forests and wilderness areas. (All distances listed for hiking trails are one way unless otherwise noted.) Be sure to obtain a backcountry permit from a national-park visitors center!

HIKING

The best available guide to hiking this region is *Glacier National Park and Waterton Lakes National Park: A Complete Recreation Guide* by Vicky Spring (Seattle: The Mountaineers, 1994).

Guided day and weekend hikes through the northern Montana backcountry are organized by the **Montana Wilderness Association**. Each trip is limited to a few hikers, though, so advance reservations are necessary. ~ 43 Woodland Park Drive, Kalispell; 406-755-6304.

GLACIER NATIONAL PARK   The **Avalanche Lake Trail** (2 miles) begins at the Avalanche Creek campground, four miles from Lake McDonald. Its first section—the broad and paved 300-yard **Trail of the Cedars**—is a wheelchair-accessible route that loops through an old-growth forest of western red cedars. Then it rambles up the churning gorge of Avalanche Creek to the lake itself, fed by a series of waterfalls that tumble down 2000-foot cliffs on its far side.

The **Garden Wall** (11.8 miles) features a traverse from the Logan Pass Visitors Center to the Granite Park Chalet, then a rapid descent to "The Loop," a 150-degree switchback on Going-to-the-Sun Road. The trail negotiates the precipitous slope of the ice-sculpted Garden Wall, often more appropriate for mountain goats than people.

The **Hidden Lake Nature Trail** (3 miles) is among the park's most popular. Starting from the Logan Pass Visitors Center, it begins with a one-and-a-half-mile long boardwalk across a fragile alpine meadow, a natural amphitheater of wildflowers called the Hanging Gardens of Logan Pass. You can return to the visitors center from a scenic overlook, where the boardwalk ends, or continue another mile and a half on a rough trail that drops rapidly to Hidden Lake.

If you've never been close to a glacier before, you can get a close-up look at Grinnell Glacier Trail's crevasses, bergschrunds and nunataks.

The **Grinnell Glacier Trail** (5.5 miles) leaves from the Many Glacier Hotel, climbing slowly past Lake Josephine, then rapidly (about 1500 feet) to Upper Grinnell Lake and the glacier. The scenery is spectacular.

The **Two Medicine Lake Circuit** (7.2 miles) loops around the most southerly of Glacier's large lakes. Most of this relatively easy hike, which includes crossing a swaying suspension bridge, is through woodlands. An additional 1.7-mile, gently rising side trip will bring you to pretty Upper Two Medicine Lake.

The **Boulder Pass Trail** (31 miles) is one of the park's most challenging. It can be done either eastbound from Kintla Lake (near Polebridge) or westbound from Goat Haunt at the south end of Upper Waterton Lake. In either case, you'll have a climb of well over 3000 feet to the summit of 7470-foot Boulder Pass on the Continental Divide. Alpine meadows, rocky summits and a wealth of wildlife are the highlights of this hike.

The official park hiking and backpacking concessionaire, **Glacier Wilderness Guides** has been hiking the backcountry for 15 years. Trips range from one to six days. Experienced guides carry all the group equipment and most of the food; participants handle only their personal gear and some food. Among the trails explored: **Belly River** (12 miles), **Cut Bank Creek** (14 miles), **Stoney Indian Pass** (56 miles), **Two Medicine** (7 miles) and **Waterton Lake–Bowman Lake** (26 miles). ~ Route 2, West Glacier; 406-888-5466.

WATERTON LAKES NATIONAL PARK　Short but strenuous is the **Bears Hump Trail** (1.5 miles round trip), which climbs 650 feet from the national park information center, opposite the Prince of Wales Hotel, to one of the best viewpoints in the park.

The **Bertha Lake Trail** (4.3 miles) begins at the Waterton Lake townsite and climbs 1500 feet up a series of steep switchbacks to the lovely lake, wedged in a deep subalpine valley. En route, just 1.8 miles from the trailhead, Bertha Falls cascade over a cliff face.

The **Twin Lakes Loop Trail** (15.5 miles) is usually regarded as a weekend backpack. Hikers slowly ascend the forested Bauerman Valley from the end of Red Rock Parkway before stopping overnight at Upper Twin Lake, one of two small alpine tarns. Bighorn sheep and mountain goats are often seen here. The return trail climbs through Blue Grouse Basin, then descends the valleys of Lone and Blakiston creeks back to Red Rock Canyon.

Able hiking companions are the **Canadian Wilderness Nature Guides** trained naturalists who take anywhere from one to 20 outdoors lovers (of any age or ability) on walks emphasizing Waterton's fauna, flora and geology. ~ 403-859-2252.

▼▼▼▼▼▼▼▼▼▼
Transportation

Route 2, which runs eastbound through Kalispell and West Glacier, then skirts the south side of Glacier National Park en route to East Glacier Park, Browning and points east, is the most important access route to the national park. In Browning, this highway crosses northbound Route 89 from Great Falls. This route transits St. Mary and extends to the Canadian border.

CAR

The 52-mile **Going-to-the-Sun Road** links West Glacier and St. Mary through the heart of Glacier National Park. Because the road is steep and narrow, no vehicles or car trailers longer than 20 feet, or wider than seven and a half feet including mirrors, are permitted over Logan Pass. (In the wake of National Park Service funding cuts, this route may someday be restricted to park shuttles only. No decision has been made at this writing.)

Principal access to Waterton Lakes National Park is the **Chief Mountain International Highway,** which branches west off Route 89, 13 miles north of St. Mary.

Kalispell's **Glacier Park International Airport** is served by Delta and Horizon. ~ 4170 Route 2 East, Kalispell; 406-257-5994.

AIR

Regional bus service is available through **Intermountain Transportation,** which connects to Greyhound routes in Missoula and other cities. ~ 403 2nd Street East, Whitefish; 406-862-6700.

BUS

Amtrak's "Empire Builder" stops daily in each direction, at Browning, East Glacier Park, Essex, West Glacier and Whitefish, en route from Chicago to Seattle. ~ 800-872-7245.

TRAIN

No rental companies maintain agencies in the national parks. The nearest rentals are available at the Glacier Park International Airport between Kalispell and Columbia Falls (see Chapter Two).

CAR RENTALS

Glacier National Park provides scheduled transportation between its various lodges and railway stations on historic **Red Buses.**

PUBLIC TRANSIT

There's also a daily service from the Glacier Park Lodge (at East Glacier Park) to the Prince of Wales Hotel (at Waterton Park). ~ 406-226-5551.

Also within Glacier Park, **Rocky Mountains Transportation** runs a shuttle service several times daily, with numerous stops, on Going-to-the-Sun Road between West Glacier and St. Mary. ~ 406-862-2539.

FOUR

North Central Montana

Montana's north-central region encompasses many of the extremes of the Montana experience. Extending from the Bob Marshall Wilderness Area east across the Missouri River to the wide-open rangeland "where the buffalo roam, where the deer and the antelope play," this is an area that is both as old and as new as you'll find in the state.

Stand atop the Continental Divide west of Great Falls, where the Rocky Mountain Front drops dramatically to the northern Great Plains, and you may get some idea of the region's geographical magnitude. This broad, slow-flowing stream provides water for the arid farmland, habitat for waterfowl and other wildlife, recreation for the sportsman and sportswoman.

Two centuries ago, tens of millions of American bison, in herds of thousands, cavorted through these mountains and prairies. Hunted to near-extinction in the 19th century, they nearly met the same fate as their reptilian Jurassic predecessors, whose bones and other fossil remains have been found en masse along the Rockies' eastern slope. More skeletons of *Tyrannosaurus rex,* believed to have been the largest dinosaur ever to walk the earth, have been found in Montana than in all other discovery areas put together.

Blackfoot Indians, horsemen and hunters who relied heavily on bison to provide food and hides for clothing and shelter, once dominated this region. Around the turn of the 19th century, the first whites penetrated the upper Missouri: first French Canadian trappers, and soon thereafter the trailblazing Lewis and Clark expedition. The American explorers followed the Missouri upstream in 1805, taking two weeks to portage around the Great Falls. In the mid-19th century, Fort Benton became the single most important port on the Missouri, with steamboats traveling upstream all the way from New Orleans to deliver and receive goods.

Today, north-central Montana's economy focuses on Great Falls. With 55,000 people, this trade and industrial center on the Missouri River is a haven for outdoor sports lovers and the site of a major Air Force base. Havre, with a population of 10,200, is the only other town in the region with more than 3000 people.

▼▼▼▼▼▼▼▼▼▼
Great Falls

Great Falls is Montana's heartland. Not a "mountain town," not a "cowboy town," the state's second-largest city is near enough to the Rocky Mountain crest to be a recreational gateway, near enough to eastern Montana's semiarid ranch country to be an agricultural center. It's a place in between, straddling history as it does the Missouri River, mindful of its roots as a 19th-century trade hub but also a thoroughly modern center of national air defense and a hydroelectric power industry.

Great Falls is best known, in fact, as "The Electric City." The series of dams on the Missouri just below the community provide power to a huge area, and the river's water supports a thriving wheat and barley industry in the rolling hills north of here.

When Lewis and Clark first ventured into this stretch of the Missouri in 1805, they discovered a different river from the one visitors see today. Over a ten-mile stretch there were five cataracts, which they called the "Great Falls of the Missouri": "A sublimely grand spectacle," Lewis wrote in his journal. He quickly noted that "the river was one continued sene of rappids and cascades which I readily perceive could not be encountered with our canoes." The party was forced to portage their equipment around the falls; the 18-mile ordeal took 15 days to complete.

SIGHTS

Today, as a result of five hydro projects, the falls are not the spectacles that Lewis observed. The feature usually called the Great Falls—the farthest downstream (ten miles from downtown) and, at 80 feet, the largest of the five falls—is now contained by Ryan Dam, built in 1915. **Broadwater Overlook Park** features a heroic bronze sculpture by Montana artist Bob Scriver that commemorates the portage and has a visitors center with interpretive displays. ~ 10th Avenue South and 2nd Street; 406-761-4434.

Undoubtedly the best place to experience the river locally is **Giant Springs/Heritage State Park**, three miles east of the city off River Drive. "The largest fountain I ever saw" is how Lewis described the springs, which bubble from the earth at a rate of nearly eight million gallons per hour and flow 201 feet to the Missouri. (The spring is one of the world's largest; the *Guinness Book of World Records* lists the outflow, named the Roe River, as the world's shortest river.) The day-use park also features a visitors center and rainbow trout hatchery that offers self-guided and interpretive tours. Downriver a mile by car or trail are blufftop lookouts over scenic Rainbow Falls. ~ 4600 Giant Springs Road; 406-454-5840.

Great Falls was also the home of C. M. Russell (1864–1926), the nation's most acclaimed frontier artist. (See "Charles M. Russell: The Cowboy Artist" in this chapter.) The **Charles M. Russell Museum Complex** includes his home, his original log-cabin studio

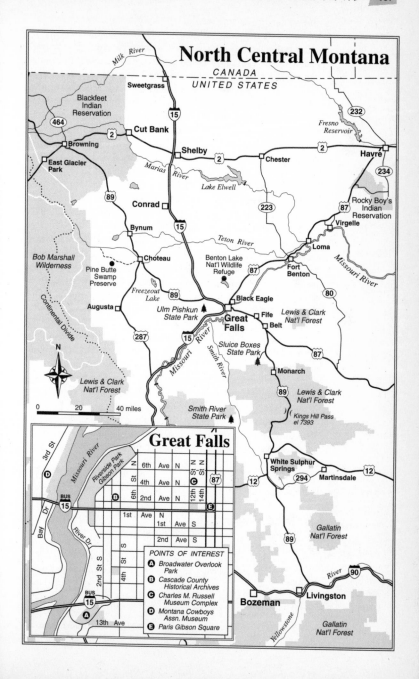

North Central Montana

CANADA
UNITED STATES

Milk River
Sweetgrass
Blackfeet Indian Reservation
464
Cut Bank
Browning
East Glacier Park
Shelby
Marias River
Chester
Havre
Fresno Reservoir
232
234
Rocky Boy's Indian Reservation
89
Conrad
Bynum
Lake Elwell
223
87
Virgelle
Loma
Bob Marshall Wilderness
Pine Butte Swamp Preserve
Choteau
Teton River
Benton Lake Nat'l Wildlife Refuge
87
Fort Benton
Missouri River
Freezeout Lake
89
Augusta
Ulm Pishkun State Park
Black Eagle
Great Falls
Fife
Belt
Lewis & Clark Nat'l Forest
80
287
15
Missouri River
Smith River
Sluice Boxes State Park
Monarch
87
Continental Divide
N
Lewis & Clark Nat'l Forest
89
Lewis & Clark Nat'l Forest
0   20   40 miles
Smith River State Park
Kings Hill Pass el 7393

Great Falls

3rd St
Missouri River
Riverside Park
Gibson Park
6th Ave N
N
St
N
St
87
BUS 15
Bay Dr
River Dr
6th St
4th Ave N
2nd Ave N
12th St
14th St
1st Ave N
1st Ave S
2nd Ave S
2nd St S
4th St
BUS 15
13th Ave

White Sulphur Springs
12
294
Martinsdale
12
Gallatin Nat'l Forest
89
Bozeman
Livingston
90
Yellowstone River
Gallatin Nat'l Forest

POINTS OF INTEREST
Ⓐ Broadwater Overlook Park
Ⓑ Cascade County Historical Archives
Ⓒ Charles M. Russell Museum Complex
Ⓓ Montana Cowboys Assn. Museum
Ⓔ Paris Gibson Square

and an outstanding art museum. The world's most extensive collection of Russell's original works is here: oils, watercolors, pen-and-ink sketches, metal and wood sculptures, even some accompanying poetry. All of it focuses on the cowboys, American Indians and wildlife of the northern prairies and Rocky Mountain slopes. Also displayed are works by Russell's contemporaries and other artists of the American West, as well as the John Browning Firearms Collection. There is an excellent gift shop. Admission. ~ 400 13th Street North; 406-727-8787.

Another center for the arts is **Paris Gibson Square**, an imposing stone building constructed in 1895. Its galleries include the Center for Contemporary Arts, a fine-art shop and a café. ~ 1400 1st Avenue North; 406-727-8255.

And the **Montana Cowboys Association Museum** has a log-cabin display of Old West memorabilia at the fairgrounds. ~ 311 3rd Street Northwest; 406-761-9299.

West of the Russell Museum and Paris Gibson Square is Great Falls' most architecturally interesting neighborhood, the **Northside Residential Historic District**, dating from 1885. Thirty-nine homes on 3rd and 4th Avenues North, between Park Drive and 10th Street, are described in a one-hour walking tour that begins at the **Cascade County Historical Archives**. ~ 301 2nd Avenue North; 406-452-3462.

It's not something most visitors are immediately aware of, but the Great Falls area is Ground Zero. That is to say, some 200 long-range nuclear missiles are buried in silos just beneath the surface of the innocent-looking plains that surround the city. The 341st Strategic Missile Wing, based at **Malmstrom Air Force Base**, has command of the site. ~ 2nd Avenue North, east of 57th Street. Visitors with an interest in this sort of thing can learn more at the **Base Museum and Air Park**, just inside the main gate, where a Minuteman missile, numerous historic aircraft and other military

NORTH CENTRAL MONTANA EXPERIENCES

- Tour the Prohibition-era tunnels of **Havre Beneath the Streets** to see old shops and speakeasies, even a brothel and a Chinese opium den. *page 117*
- Travel by jetboat or horseback to **Klicks' K Bar L Ranch**, a 13-cabin guest ranch that has been in the same family since 1927. *page 115*
- Consume a "campfire" steak at **Eddie's Supper Club** in Great Falls while enjoying the strains of a twin piano bar. *page 110*
- Take a commercial boat tour from Fort Benton down the **Upper Missouri National Wild and Scenic River**, or rent a canoe and do it yourself. *pages 124*

vehicles are displayed. Hours vary seasonally; it's best to call ahead. ~ 406-731-2705.

If warheads are violent modern history, **Ulm Pishkun State Park** represents some violent history of the ancient world. Thousands of years ago, American Indians drove herds of bison up this mile-long *pishkun*, or buffalo jump, from which the beasts plunged to their deaths. Arrowheads, knives, hide scrapers, hammers and other tools have been discovered at this site, believed to be the largest of its kind in the United States. To reach it, take Route 15 south ten miles from Great Falls to Ulm (Exit 270); then follow signs four miles north. Admission. ~ Ulm-Vaughn Road at Goetz Road; 406-454-3441.

LODGING

The four-story **Great Falls Inn** only opened in February 1994, but it has already convinced many that it can deliver quality for price. Its 45 spacious rooms have queen-size beds and wood furnishings; 16 are equipped with refrigerators and microwaves. A continental breakfast comes with the room price. There's a laundry on the third floor and a fireplace in the lobby. ~ 1400 28th Street South; 406-453-6000. BUDGET.

Perhaps the best of a handful of options for B&B lovers is the European-flavored **Triple Crown Motor Inn**. It's located in the heart of downtown Great Falls. All 49 rooms are air-conditioned, with cable television (and HBO). Guests get a complimentary cocktail on arrival and free coffee and doughnuts each morning. Children 12 and under stay free with adults. ~ 621 Central Avenue; phone/fax 406-727-8300, 800-722-8300. BUDGET.

Located at the north end of the city, the two-story **Sovekammer Bed & Breakfast** inn, decorated with Danish antiques, offers private baths with each of its four rooms. There are no room phones, but TV is available on request. Smoking is not permitted. ~ 1109 3rd Avenue North; 406-453-6620. MODERATE.

The **Best Western Heritage Inn** is at the head of the class in Great Falls. Its central atrium/courtyard, designed in a loose French Quarter–style, has an indoor swimming pool, hot tubs, saunas, a video arcade and a sidewalk café. Just off the courtyard is a family-style restaurant and a bustling casino/lounge, complete with a crocodile at the player piano. The two-story motor inn— near the south freeway entrance to Great Falls—has 240 spacious and modern rooms with queen beds and writing desks. ~ 1700 Fox Farm Road; 406-761-1900, 800-548-0361, fax 406-761-0136. MODERATE.

Wright Nite Inns Wagon Wheel Motel aims to please the romantic. Many of its 130 rooms have honeymoon themes—there's a Love Boat stateroom, an Arabian sultan's suite, a jungle, a barn, and more, with heart-shaped bubble baths, no less. A stretch limo will deliver you; once there, your room phone urges you to dial "your romantic horoscope." Even unromantic travelers will enjoy the indoor pool, jacuzzi and sauna. ~ 2620 10th Avenue South; 406-761-1300, 800-800-6483. MODERATE.

DINING

At **Mama Cassie's Italian Ristorante**, the emphasis is on pasta. But Mama also dishes out generous portions of chicken cacciatore, Italian submarines and New York cheesecake. This is a homey sort of place open for three meals a day. ~ 319 1st Avenue North; 406-454-3354. BUDGET.

For Mexican food, **El Comedor** is a pleasant, off-the-main-drag establishment operated by a family from south of the border. There's nothing too gourmet here—you'll get the standard enchiladas, burritos and tostadas amid a decor of sombreros, serapes and piñatas—but it works when you're in the mood for something spicy. ~ 1120 25th Street South; 406-761-5500. BUDGET.

The best place to get your morning coffee is **Morning Light**. The beans are roasted on the premises, and a selection of daily luncheon sandwiches, from veggie to chicken salad to roast beef, greets late risers or lunchtime diners. ~ 900 2nd Avenue North; 406-453-8443. BUDGET.

Eddie's Supper Club is a long-established local favorite. Eddie's pioneered the "campfire" steak; some argue that it's the best steak in Montana. Breakfast, lunch and dinner are served in the coffee shop, furnished with formica-topped tables, and the low-lit, vinyl-upholstered dining room. The lounge boasts a twin piano bar. ~ 3725 2nd Avenue North; 406-453-1616. BUDGET TO MODERATE.

Jake's Restaurant offers seafood specialties in an atmosphere of casual elegance. Surf-and-turf entrées are also popular. The adjoining Good Times Bar has an à la carte menu of its own. ~ 1500 10th Avenue South; 406-727-1033. MODERATE.

HIDDEN ►

Families enjoy **Borrie's** on the north side of the Missouri River opposite downtown Great Falls. Established in 1939, the hard-to-find restaurant serves up traditional Italian (lasagna, ravioli, spaghetti) and American (steaks, seafood, chicken) fare with an ebullient ambience. Dinner only. ~ 1800 Smelter Avenue, Black Eagle; 406-761-0300. MODERATE.

The kids want spaghetti, the wife wants prime rib, but you feel like a plate of chow mein? No problem. **3D International**, owned and operated by the Grassechi family for five decades, has it all. Located like Borrie's across the 10th Street Bridge, this art deco–style restaurant may also have the city's best salad bar. ~ 1825 Smelter Avenue, Black Eagle; 406-453-6561. MODERATE.

SHOPPING

Perhaps the best place to claim memories of Great Falls is the shop at the **Charles M. Russell Museum Complex**. The museum shop

Charles M. Russell: The Cowboy Artist

Perhaps no artist more exemplified the American West than Charles Marion Russell, a hard-drinking, tough-talking, whimsical whisper of a man who learned to punch cows and ride with the Indians, but who attracted a circle of friends that included presidents and movie stars.

Born in St. Louis, Missouri, in 1864, Russell was never cut out for his parents' high-society lifestyle. When Charles was 16, his father shipped him off to Montana to what was hoped would be a "school of hard knocks" for the rebellious youth . . . but the lad thrived on it.

Initially a failure as a sheepherder, Russell was befriended by a mountain man, Jake Hoover, who taught him how to survive in the Wild West. The pair shared a tiny sod-roofed cabin in the Little Belt Mountains until Russell got a job as a night wrangler at a cattle ranch. That left his days open to paint, draw and sculpt.

One of the reasons that Russell's works stand out from those of other Western artists is that he lived what he put on canvas. Even though his vivid depictions of the West began to earn him a profit, he continued to wrangle cattle for another decade. He also spent a full winter with the Blackfeet, learning their spoken language as well as a sign language that any Plains Indian tribe could understand.

Eventually, Russell found it expedient for his artistic career to move from the prairie. He relocated to Great Falls in 1897, married, and three years later built a home in a fashionable neighborhood near downtown. In 1903, he constructed a separate log studio—"a cabin just like I used to live in," he said.

For the rest of his life, until his death in 1926, this was Russell's sanctuary, a place where he surrounded himself with his personal collections of cowboy and Native American lifestyles, and where he produced every last work he painted or sculpted. Both the house and the studio are now a part of the C. M. Russell Museum Complex, donated by Russell's widow, Nancy, to the city of Great Falls.

Russell's works—more than 4500 oils and watercolors, pen-and-ink drawings, clay and wax sculptures and illustrated letters (he was a renowned storyteller)—symbolize the adventure and the freedom of the West as he knew and loved it. For many easterners, the work of "America's Cowboy Artist" was their principal link to the romance of the Old West.

Russell was a lifelong defender of the pre-20th-century West, and he decried the rapid changes he saw during his lifetime.

"I liked it better when it belonged to God," he said.

specializes in reproductions of Western art but has a good selection of books and various quality souvenirs. And every year in mid-March, art lovers from around the world converge on Great Falls for the C. M. Russell Auction of Original Western Art, usually held at the Best Western Heritage Inn. Since it began in 1969, the annual auction has raised more than $2 million to support the museum. ~ 400 13th Street North; 406-727-8787.

For Montana-made merchandise, visit **Fantastik Baskets**. Its wares include pottery and other crafts, food baskets and elk- and buffalo-hide accessories. ~ 2110 10th Avenue South; 406-727-9760.

Great Falls' Farmers Market takes place throughout the summer, 5 to 6:30 p.m. on Wednesday and 8 a.m. to noon on Saturday. Fruit, vegetables, baked goods and craft items are sold at **Whittier Park** on the south side of the Civic Center. ~ Central Avenue and 1st Street.

One of Great Falls' main shopping centers is the **Holiday Village Mall**. ~ 1200 10th Avenue South; 406-727-2088. There's also **Westgate Mall**, which is anchored by a department store. ~ 1807 3rd Avenue Northwest; 406-761-2464.

NIGHTLIFE   As befits a city of 55,000, Great Falls has an active music scene. It's headed by the **Great Falls Symphony**, which plays an October-to-May classical season and a late-June pops concert at the Gibson Park bandshell (Park Drive). Besides a 65-member orchestra, the symphony includes a string quartet, a wind quintet and a 70-voice choir. ~ Civic Center; 406-453-4102.

Between October and April, the **Great Falls Community Concert Series** stages six musical events with guest artists. Performances may range from Broadway show tunes to ethnic choirs; diverse musicians may include renowned classical artists and popular ensembles. ~ Civic Center; 406-453-9854.

From mid-June to mid-August, the **Great Falls Municipal Band**—which has been playing every year since 1895—performs free Wednesday-night concerts at the Gibson Park bandshell.

For drinks and dancing, **Philly's** in the Holiday Inn Great Falls has as many regulars as any lounge in town. ~ 400 10th Avenue South; 406-727-7200. **Club Cigar** wins kudos for its historic downtown atmosphere. ~ 208 Central Avenue; 406-727-8011. **The Max**, in the Best Western Heritage Inn, is clearly Great Falls' number-one casino. ~ 1700 Fox Farm Road; 406-761-1900.

PARKS   **GIANT SPRINGS/HERITAGE STATE PARK** 🧍🚴🛶⚓ One of the world's largest freshwater springs (7.9 million gallons per hour) bubbles into the world's shortest river (the Roe River, 201 feet) by the banks of the Missouri River. The springs were discovered by

Lewis and Clark in 1805. An adjacent fish hatchery is open for public viewing. There are picnic areas, restrooms, a visitors center and concession stand; restaurants and groceries are in Great Falls. Day-use fee, $3. ~ Three miles east from downtown Great Falls via River Drive; turn left onto Giant Springs Road; 406-454-5840.

ULM PISHKUN STATE PARK 🏃 The largest buffalo jump yet identified in the United States, this was a site where ancient American Indians drove herds of bison off a cliff. A variety of primitive tools have been uncovered. Picnic tables, restrooms, and interpretive displays round out the amenities. ~ Ten miles south from Great Falls on Route 15 to Ulm (Exit 270), then four miles north; 406-454-5840.

BENTON LAKE NATIONAL WILDLIFE REFUGE 🏃🚲 Nine-mile-long, gravel-surfaced Prairie Marsh Drive loops through the marshy lakes and wetlands of this 12,300-acre reserve, where more than 175 species of birds and land animals have been observed. Pick up a brochure at the visitors center; its numbers correspond to 10 interpretive stops along the road. Restrooms and a visitors center are among the facilities. Closed November to March. ~ Take Bootlegger Trail north 14 miles from Great Falls to the refuge's visitors center.

▼▼▼▼▼▼▼▼▼▼
The Rocky Mountain Front

Route 89 north, connecting Great Falls with Glacier National Park's eastern portals, draws ever closer to the dramatic Rocky Mountain Front, where the range's craggy peaks drop suddenly to the prairies, unbuffered by the waves of lower mountains found to the west.

SIGHTS

The largest town in these environs is **Choteau,** a center for outdoor recreation and dinosaur digging, with a population of about 1800. Choteau (pronounced "SHO-toe") is the gateway to the nation's best-known wilderness area, several wildlife refuges and a paleontological reserve.

Displays of fossils and artifacts in the town's **Old Trail Museum** interpret some of these regional attractions. Attached to the museum, located at the north edge of town, is a block of frontier-style craft shops, as well as an ice-cream parlor and the log-cabin studio of artist Jesse Gleason. Admission. ~ Route 89, Choteau; 406-466-5332.

Several roads head west from Choteau into **Lewis and Clark National Forest** and the fringe of the **Bob Marshall Wilderness.** "The Bob," as it is known to wilderness lovers, preserves more than a million acres of rugged mountains, rivers and lakes. Neither motorized vehicles nor bicycles are permitted in this land of grizzly bears and mountain lions. ~ 406-466-5341.

At the foot of the Rocky Mountain Front, the Teton River flows through a wetland that is a spring feeding ground for grizzlies and home to the largest population of bighorn sheep in the United States. The Nature Conservancy purchased and set aside 18,000 acres as the **Pine Butte Swamp Preserve**, 17 miles west of Choteau, to protect the flora and fauna of this unique region. Tours from the interpretive center here are offered by appointment only. ~ Bellview Road; 406-466-5526.

HIDDEN ► The conservancy also owns the adjoining **Egg Mountain** fossil field. This site on the Willow Creek Anticline, 12 miles west of Choteau, is where the first dinosaur eggs were discovered in North America. Beginning the last week of June and running through the third week of August, free one-hour guided tours of the site are offered at 2 p.m. daily, led by a member of the paleontology field program from Montana State University's Museum of the Rockies. ~ Bellview Road; 406-994-6618.

The Nature Conservancy's Egg Mountain fossil field is where the first dinosaur eggs (42 of them, in 14 nests) were discovered in North America.

There are federal wildlife management areas near Choteau at Pishkun Reservoir, Willow Creek Reservoir, Ear Mountain, Sun River, Blackleaf Creek and elsewhere. The most accessible—because the highway to Great Falls runs right through its heart—is the **Freezout Lake Wildlife Management Area**. A birdwatcher's checklist of 187 species spotted here is available from reserve headquarters. Winter visitors may want to drive through the rural village of Augusta, 26 miles southwest of Choteau, then ten miles west to the **Sun River Game Range**, where herds of elk and deer find a welcome cold-weather sanctuary. ~ Route 89, Fairfield; 406-454-3441.

LODGING   Of a handful of small motels in Choteau, the best may be the two-story **Hensley 287 Motel**. The motel has 15 rooms, three of them two-bedroom suites and six of them kitchen units, on Route 287 southwest of downtown. All rooms have queen-size beds and cable television. ~ 20 7th Avenue Southwest, Choteau; 406-466-5775. BUDGET.

The **Country Lane Bed & Breakfast** is a peaceful and pleasant rural getaway, and not without touches of true luxury. Set back off the highway a mile and a half north of Choteau, it offers king- and queen-size beds and a heated indoor swimming pool, as well as a gift shop and a full gourmet breakfast each morning. ~ Route 89 North, Choteau; 406-466-2816. MODERATE.

There are numerous guest ranches along the Rocky Mountain Front. An especially good one, not far from the Bob Marshall Wilderness, is the **Seven Lazy P Ranch**. Located 30 miles west of Choteau on the North Fork of the Teton River, it focuses on horse pack trips into The Bob and seasonal fishing and hunting. Guests stay in six rustic cabins, five with private baths; most socializing is around the large stone fireplace in the main lodge. Meals are hearty and ranch-style. Three-day minimum stay, American plan. ~ Canyon Road, Choteau; 406-466-2044. MODERATE.

Thirty-five miles west of Augusta on Gibson Lake, at the edge of "The Bob," is **Klicks' K Bar L Ranch**. This rustic ranch, in the Klick family since 1927, cannot be reached by road: You arrive either by horseback or via jetboat across the lake. Thirteen cabins share toilet/shower facilities, as well as a natural hot-springs pool. Activities include riding and catch-and-release fly fishing. ~ Box 287, Augusta, MT 59410; 406-467-2771 summer or fall, 406-264-5806 winter or spring. MODERATE.

DINING

Three meals a day, seven days a week, the **Log Cabin Family Restaurant** dishes up ample portions of good American food: pancakes, burgers, fried chicken. There's a children's menu, too. ~ 102 Main Street, Choteau; 406-466-2888. MODERATE.

The **Outpost Deli** provides a more casual alternative for less hearty appetites. Deli sandwiches and soups are the popular choices here, as well as ice cream on hot summer days. ~ 819 7th Avenue Northwest, Choteau; 406-466-5330. BUDGET.

◄ *HIDDEN*

Well off the beaten track some 22 miles north of Choteau is **The Rose Room**, a supper club that is well known to area residents but which sees few visitors. Call for reservations, then try the locally produced beef or the deep-fried shrimp. ~ Route 219, Pendroy; 406-469-2205. MODERATE.

NIGHTLIFE

◄ *HIDDEN*

Katy's Wildlife Sanctuary is a very rustic local bar in a village some 14 miles north of Choteau. The only wildlife you'll find within its doors, however, is of the two-legged variety. It's a fun place to catch some true Montana flavor. ~ Route 89, Bynum.

PARKS

LEWIS AND CLARK NATIONAL FOREST 🧍🚴🐎 🎿🏕️🚤 ⛷️🚣 The eastern edge of the Rocky Mountain Front, below the Bob Marshall Wilderness, and a handful of small mountain ranges southeast of Great Falls—the Little Belt, Big Snowy, Highwood and Castle mountains—are encompassed by this national forest. Facilities include picnic tables and restrooms. ~ Reach the Rocky Mountain Front section of the forest via various secondary roads that lead west off Routes 89 and 287 from Choteau and Augusta. Route 89 (Kings Hill Scenic Byway) cuts through the Little Belt Mountains section of the forest between Great Falls and White Sulphur Springs; 406-791-7700.

▲ There are 241 RV/tent sites and 29 for tents only at 15 campgrounds, none with hookups; no charge to $6 per night; 14-day maximum stay.

BOB MARSHALL WILDERNESS AREA 🚶 🏇 🛶 🔦 The second-largest wilderness in the lower 48 states, "The Bob" and its adjoining preserves (the Great Bear and Scapegoat wilderness areas) occupy more than one and a half million very wild, rugged and mountainous acres on the Continental Divide. Some 1800 miles of trails crisscross the region. ~ From the east, main access to "The Bob" is via Canyon Road (off Route 89 near Choteau), which follows the Teton River nearly to its headwaters; Sun River Road (off Route 287 in Augusta), which ends at Gibson Reservoir; and Augusta Ranger Station Road (also from Augusta), which extends up Wood Creek. There are major trailheads at the terminus of each. You can also approach the wilderness from the west (off Route 83) or from the north (at Spotted Bear Ranger Station southeast of Hungry Horse; 406-791-7700.

🔺 Primitive only.

▼▼▼▼▼▼▼▼▼▼▼▼▼▼
The Western Hi-Line

Route 2, running east about 400 miles along the Canadian border from the Blackfeet Indian Reservation to Williston, North Dakota, and paralleled by the Great Northern Railway line, is known to Montanans as "the Hi-Line." The western section of this route runs from Cut Bank to Havre. Cattle ranching and grain production, notably wheat, sustain the economy of this northernmost tier of the state, which extends more than one-eighth of the way across the United States.

SIGHTS

At the eastern edge of the Blackfeet Indian Reservation, still within the shadow of the high peaks of Glacier National Park, is **Cut Bank**, a major grain-storage center that marks the western corner of Montana's Golden Triangle. This region, which stretches from Great Falls (100 miles southeast of Cut Bank) to Canada, from the Rocky Mountain Front to the Missouri River, is literally one of the breadbaskets of the nation. Farms between Havre and Cut Bank produce more than half of the wheat and barley grown in Montana, one of the top five states in those commodities. You may see huge combine harvesters in the fields in late August and September.

Routes 2 and 15 intersect at the grain and railroad town of **Shelby**, 23 miles east of Cut Bank. Shelby's **Marias Museum of History and Art** recalls such snippets of past glory as the 1923 world heavyweight championship fight here between Jack Dempsey and Tommy Gibbons. In all, the ten-room museum displays 10,000 items, including several re-created early-20th-century rooms. The free museum is open daily except Sunday in summer, but from September to May is open Tuesday afternoons only. ~ 206 12th Avenue, Shelby; 406-434-2551.

Shelby is just 35 miles south (via Route 15) of the Canadian border at Sweetgrass, the busiest international port of entry between Blaine, Washington (connecting Seattle and Vancouver) and Pembina, North Dakota (connecting Minneapolis and Winnipeg). Between Shelby and the border, the Kevin-Sunburst Oil Field is Montana's largest: It has pumped some 80 million barrels of oil since its discovery in 1922.

Along the eastern edge of the field runs the **Whoop-Up Trail**, which connected the steamship port of Fort Benton with Fort Whoop-Up, on Canada's Old Man River, beginning in 1868. An important transportation link, it was partially restored by Boy Scouts in the 1960s; where the deeply rutted "bulltrain" trail crosses the Marias River southeast of Shelby, a historical marker notes the site of old Fort Conrad. Other points of interest include tepee rings left by nomadic Indian tribes.

In the little town of **Chester**, almost midway from Shelby to Havre, you'll find the **Liberty County Museum**. Housed in a former Methodist church, the museum is a repository of fascinating items and photographs from northern Montana's late-19th-century homesteading era. Closed in winter except by appointment. ~ 210 2nd Street East, Chester; 406-759-5256.

The area's leading recreational center is **Lake Elwell**, on the Marias River southwest of Chester. A marina near the Tiber Dam, open mid-May to mid-September, is a center for boating, fishing and camping, as well as autumn bird hunting.

Havre, the largest town on the Hi-Line (and the home of Montana State University–Northern), benefits economically from both the 100 miles of grain fields to its west and the 300 miles of ranch country to its east. The city hopes to attract history buffs with **Havre Beneath the Streets**, a four-year project (completed in 1994) that restored long-disused tunnels and underground corridors beneath the community. Developed around 1900 in the early

◄ HIDDEN

◆◆◆

HUTTERITE HAMLETS

Several **Hutterite colonies** are located in the region north of Great Falls and east of Glacier Park. People of German descent, the Hutterites follow a simple lifestyle similar in many ways to the Amish of the eastern United States. The men are always clad in black suits and hats, the women in colorful homemade skirts and kerchiefs on their heads. Communities include Rimrock (near Sunburst), Hillside (near Sweetgrass), Eagle Creek (near Galata), Rockport (near DuPuyer) and Miller (near Bynum). To visit one of their communities, inquire at the **Shelby Chamber of Commerce**. ~ 187 Main Street, Shelby; 406-434-2775.

days of the Great Northern Railway and last put to serious use by Prohibition-era bootleggers, they now welcome visitors. Public tours include a saloon, drugstore, meat market, bakery, barber shop, laundry, tack shop, hardware store and even a brothel and Chinese opium den. Admission. ~ 100 3rd Avenue, Havre; 406-265-8888.

Havre got its start in 1879 when **Fort Assiniboine** was constructed; it was then the largest military fort west of the Mississippi River. ~ Route 87, six miles southwest of the current town site. Guided tours of the fort are offered through the **H. Earl Clack Memorial Museum**, which features archaeological and area history displays. Closed in winter. Admission. ~ Route 2 at the Hill County Fairgrounds, Havre; 406-265-9913.

The museum also organizes one-hour guided tours of the **Wahkpa Chug'n** archaeology site, a prehistoric campsite and bison kill ground on the banks of the Milk River, believed to have been used as long as 2000 years ago. ~ Behind Holiday Village Shopping Center, Route 2 West; 406-265-6417.

Twenty miles south of Havre is the **Rocky Boy's Indian Reservation**. Located in the foothills of the Bears Paw Mountains, the reservation is home to about 2500 Chippewas and Crees. ~ Box Elder; 406-395-4282.

LODGING   How could you go wrong with a motel that matter-of-factly lists its location as "next to a 27-foot-tall Talking Penguin"? That Chilly Willy–looking fellow standing outside **Glacier Gateway Inn** trumpets the town's distinction as the "coldest spot in the nation," which it has been on occasion. The motel is not so ostentatious; its 18 rooms have queen-size beds and air-conditioning (the latter presumedly for summers). There's also an exercise room. Breakfasts are complimentary. ~ 1121 East Railroad Street, Cut Bank; 406-873-5544. BUDGET.

In Shelby, the **O'Haire Manor Motel** has 40 rooms in a two-story establishment with a modern fitness room and hot tub. All rooms have cable TV and phones, and there's a coin laundry as well. ~ 204 2nd Street South, Shelby; 406-434-5555, 800-541-5809. BUDGET.

TownHouse Inns of Havre boasts the most full-service accommodation on Montana's northern plains. A modern café overlooks an atrium swimming pool and spa; there's also a fitness room and sauna. The casino claims to be "Havre's most liberal." Wood furnishings are a nice touch in the otherwise-ordinary rooms. ~ 629½ West 1st Street, Havre; 406-265-2728. MODERATE.

El Toro Inn is a good alternative for wallet watchers. With 41 rooms off two floors of inside corridors, this is a cozy motel with cable TV and a guest laundry. Microwave ovens and refrigerators are available on request, and children 11 and younger stay free with adults. ~ 521 West 1st Street, Havre; 406-265-5414. BUDGET.

Kathy's Kitchen delights with home-style cooking just off Route 15. Don't miss Kathy's pies, said to be the best on the Hi-Line. ~ 156 Main Street, Shelby; 406-434-2503. BUDGET.

DINING

    Boxcars appeals to the northern palate with its menu of barbecued ribs, fried chicken and the like. The restaurant, done up in the decor of an old railroad station, also serves a hearty Sunday buffet. A lounge and casino adjoin. ~ 619 West 1st Street, Havre; 406-265-2233. BUDGET.

    Beef lovers get great deals on steaks at the **Black Angus Supper Club**. Nightly dinner specials start at $6.95, and full cuts of prime rib au jus, including salad bar, cost not too many dollars more. A variety of seafood is also available. BUDGET TO MODERATE. The adjoining **4B's Restaurant** is open 24 hours for family-style fare. ~ 604 West 1st Street, Havre; 406-265-9721. BUDGET.

The back bar at the **Palace Bar** was built in St. Louis in 1883 and carried up the Missouri River on a steamboat. Towering and ornate, it is worth a visit just to see it. ~ 228 1st Street, Havre; 406-265-7584.

NIGHTLIFE

BEAVER CREEK COUNTY PARK 🚶‍♂️🚴🏇🏕️⛵ Extending for 16 miles along Beaver Creek Road south of Havre, this is the nation's largest county park, covering approximately 10,000 acres. There's fishing in two lakes and many fine scenic views. Facilities include picnic tables and restrooms. ~ Take Route 234 (Beaver Creek Road) south from Havre toward Rocky Boy's Indian Reservation; 406-395-4565.

PARKS

    ▲ There are 100 RV/tent sites plus eight for tents only, none with hookups. No charge.

Historic Fort Benton, 42 miles northeast of Great Falls via Route 87, has been called "the birthplace of Montana." Established as a Missouri River trading post for buffalo robes by the American Fur Company in 1846, it was named for Missouri senator Thomas Hart Benton. Its importance mushroomed in 1860, when steamboats began docking here after journeying from St. Louis or New Orleans; no port in the world was farther (3485 miles) from an ocean.

▼▼▼▼▼▼▼▼▼▼▼▼
Fort Benton Area

For the next 27 years, until the Northern Pacific Railroad arrived in 1887, effectively ending river trade, Fort Benton was the most important city in Montana. The **Riverfront Steamboat Levee**, now a national historic landmark, became the rowdiest four blocks in

SIGHTS

the West after gold was discovered in the nearby hills in 1862. Saloons and brothels were open 24 hours a day, and gunfights were more common than royal flushes. ~ Front Street between 14th and 18th streets; 406-622-5494. The restored **I.G. Baker House** once was the headquarters for the most powerful trading company in the territory. ~ Front Street between 16th and 17th streets. **St. Paul's Episcopal Church** was built in Norman-Gothic style by stonemasons in 1880. ~ Choteau and 14th streets.

Many of the buildings facing the Riverfront Steamboat Levee date from the steamboat era, including the Grand Union Hotel, Stockman's National Bank, the mercantile T. C. Power & Co. and the city's first firehouse.

The only building still standing on the site of **Old Fort Benton** is an adobe blockhouse, believed to be the oldest standing building in Montana. Interpretive signs describe the layout of the rest of the fort, some ruins of which remain. ~ Old Fort Park, Front Street. Artifacts from the fort and the town's heyday are on display next to the fort in the **Museum of the Upper Missouri**. Open summers only. Admission. ~ Front and 19th streets; 406-622-5494.

Opposite the museum, on the riverbank, stands the **Lewis and Clark State Memorial,** a bronze sculpture of the two explorers with their native guide, Sacajawea, by Bob Scriver. About four blocks north, the **Museum of the Northern Great Plains** is Montana's state agricultural museum, with exhibits that trace a century of farm history as well as a veritable outdoor park of antique machinery. It's open summers only. Admission. ~ 1205 20th Street; 406-622-5316.

Fort Benton's position on the Missouri River has not been forgotten in modern times: It is the departure point for commercial boat tours and float trips down the **Upper Missouri National Wild and Scenic River**. Contact the Bureau of Land Management for information. ~ P.O. Box 1160, Lewistown, MT 59457; 406-538-7461.

From Fort Benton to the James Kipp Recreation Area northeast of Lewistown, the broad, slow-flowing Missouri winds through the scenic White Cliffs, Citadel Rock State Monument, Hole-in-the-Wall and other geological curiosities, offering sightings of abandoned homesteads and a great deal of wildlife. The **Upper Missouri River Visitors Center** has full information for prospective river travelers. Closed in winter. ~ 1718 Front Street, Fort Benton; 406-622-5185.

Tiny **Loma**, 14 miles northeast of Fort Benton up Route 87 where the Marias River enters the Missouri, is of note for two small but excellent museums. The **House of a Thousand Dolls** displays numerous playthings dating back to the 1830s. Admission. ~ 406-739-4338. The **Earth Science Museum** exhibits mineral finds, fossils and railroad memorabilia. Admission. ~ 406-739-4357. The little town also features a picturesque trail along the banks of the Missouri, with interpretive signs describing the steamboat era.

There's a shuttle service for floaters and canoeists 28 miles northeast of Fort Benton at Virgelle, a primary put-in point for floats of the Missouri River Breaks. After Virgelle, the Missouri turns east while Route 87 proceeds north.

Southeast of Fort Benton via Route 80 is the village of **Geraldine**, a gateway to the BLM-administered **Square Butte Natural Area**, noted for its geology and its raptor colony. ~ 406-538-7461. Also nearby is the **Highwood Mountains** national forest region, popular among hikers and campers.

There are two small motels in Fort Benton. Neither is anything spectacular, but both are adequate. **Fort Motel** is located on Route 87. ~ 1809 St. Charles Street, Fort Benton; 406-622-3312. BUDGET. **Pioneer Lodge** is situated next to the old T. C. Power & Co. store facing the levee. ~ 1700 Front Street, Fort Benton; 406-622-5441. BUDGET.

LODGING

The Banque Club occupies the premises of the former Stockman's National Bank on the levee opposite the Grand Union Hotel. The days of the open range may be gone, but the cuts of homegrown Montana beef served up at this supper club perpetuate the memory. ~ 1318 Front Street, Fort Benton; 406-622-5272. MODERATE.

DINING

The Kings Hill area south of Great Falls, an alternate and more direct route from the city to Yellowstone National Park, is known for its rural pleasures and scenic vistas in the Little Belt Mountains. The interesting old spa and mining town of white sulfur springs are en route.

▼▼▼▼▼▼▼▼▼
Kings Hill

For 23 miles east from Great Falls, Route 89 runs together with Routes 87 and 200 across rolling farmland. An interesting detour en route is **Mehmke's Steam Engine Museum**. This is the world's largest privately owned collection of steam engines, all of them still operational. A sizeable variety of other antique farm machinery is also on display. It's a mechanic's dream . . . or nightmare. ~ Route 87/89/200, Fife; 406-452-6571.

SIGHTS

Near Belt, Route 89 turns south off Route 87/200 as the **Kings Hill National Scenic Byway**, crossing the Little Belt Mountains to White Sulphur Springs. ~ 406-547-3361.

This 71-mile Lewis and Clark National Forest highway follows Belt Creek past **Sluice Boxes State Park**, located at an abandoned railroad grade. ~ Evans-Riceville Road, Belt; 406-454-3441. The highway rolls on through the historic mining and ranching communities of Neihart and Monarch to 7393-foot Kings Hill Pass. On the south side of the pass is the **Showdown Ski Area**, Montana's oldest. ~ Route 89, Neihart; 406-236-5522.

On the east side of the Big Belt Mountains, about 28 miles south of Showdown, is the town of **White Sulphur Springs**. The hot springs from which the community takes its name have been compared to Germany's famed Baden-Baden spa. They have high levels of chloride, sulfate, sodium, potassium and bicarbonate, as well as calcium, silica and magnesium. Known for centuries by American Indians, today the 135° springs are enclosed by (and cooled at) the **Spa Hot Springs Motel**. Two pools are open year-round to the public. Admission. ~ 202 West Main Street, White Sulphur Springs; 406-547-3366.

> To American Indians, the healing mineral waters of White Sulphur Springs were known as "wampum waters."

The casual visitor to White Sulphur Springs is more likely to spot the cut-granite Victorian mansion, looming high on a hill over the town, than the springs themselves. This is **The Castle**, built in 1892 as a private home and now housing the **Meagher County Museum**. Open summers, the museum displays period furnishings and memorabilia of regional history; an adjacent carriage house exhibits antique buggies. Admission. ~ 310 2nd Avenue Northeast, White Sulphur Springs; 406-547-3370.

The White Sulphur Springs area was once awash in mineral wealth. An 1864 gold strike in Confederate Gulch yielded $16 million worth of ore in a half-dozen years, but few ruins remain at the site of Diamond City, the hub of the boom. However, several abandoned buildings still stand at ghostly **Castle Town**. Some 35 miles southeast of White Sulphur Springs in the Castle Mountains, this silver, lead and zinc town supported five mines and three smelters in the 1880s and 1890s. The last structures were deserted in the 1920s.

A few original log buildings also survive at **Fort Logan**, 18 miles northwest of White Sulphur Springs via Route 360. Listed on the National Register of Historic Places, the 1870 army post was constructed to protect miners from hostile Indians. A blockhouse, a stable and officers quarters remain at the site, now a ranch headquarters. Five miles beyond Fort Logan is **Camp Baker**, launch point for rafting and float-fishing trips down the Smith River.

LODGING

Right on the Kings Hill Byway, ten miles south of Showdown, the **Montana Mountain Lodge** offers five rooms with private baths. In winter, cross-country skiers and snowmobilers can head out on extensive trail systems that begin at the front door. The lodge provides a hot tub, of course, and snowmobile rentals; a full breakfast is included, and dinner is available. ~ 1780 Route 89 North, White Sulphur Springs; 406-547-3773, 800-631-4713. MODERATE.

American Indians called them "wampum waters." Today, two year-round pools at the **Spa Hot Springs Motel** contain the healing mineral waters of White Sulphur Springs. The motel's 21 rooms aren't fancy, but they have private baths and offer free access to the pools (nonguests must pay an admission fee). ~ 202 West Main Street, White Sulphur Springs; 406-547-3366. BUDGET.

The **Bonanza Creek Country** guest ranch, 40 miles east of White Sulphur Springs off Route 12, keeps an intimate feeling by restricting itself to just 16 guests at any one time. There's a variety of lodging: an 1880s duplex, a Plains Indian tepee, a cowboy's cabin, even a sheepwagon. Horseback riding, mountain biking and fishing are favored activities here. ~ Lennep Route, Martinsdale; 800-476-6045, fax 406-572-3306. MODERATE TO DELUXE.

DINING

The **Girdle Mountain Summer House** serves gourmet prix-fixe dinners—by advance reservation only—in an unlikely village 21 miles east of Great Falls. Bring your own wine or other beverage. ~ Route 87/89, Belt; 406-277-3367. MODERATE.

◄ *HIDDEN*

The **Lazy Doe** is locally famous for its beef, its salads, and especially its occasional fresh crab and lobster feeds. ~ Route 87, Monarch; 406-236-9949. MODERATE.

PARKS

SLUICE BOXES STATE PARK 🚶🚴🏊⛺🎣 Deep in the gold-rush country of the Little Belt Mountains, this park incorporates a trail that leads along an abandoned railroad grade to impressive geological features. Picnic tables and restrooms are available. Day-use fee, $3. ~ Take Route 89 five miles south from Belt off Route 200; the park is at the junction of Evans-Riceville Road; 406-454-3441.

SMITH RIVER STATE PARK 🚣🛶🎣 At this unique state park, a 61-mile stretch of the remote Smith River canyon is set aside for rafters and fishermen on float trips. River enthusiasts put in at Camp Baker, 23 miles northwest of White Sulphur Springs, and take out at Eden Bridge, about 20 miles south of Great Falls. Rafters pay a $15 application fee, plus a per-person fee, to use the river route. Facilities include picnic tables, toilets and hand-launch access. ~ To the put-in, take Route 360 northwest from White Sulphur Springs 16 miles toward Fort Logan, then follow signs north seven miles on Smith River Road to Camp Baker; 406-454-3441.

▲ There are 22 primitive camps for boaters and rafters.

Outdoor Adventures

North central Montana spans the extremes of cold-water and warm-water fishing in the northern Rockies. At higher elevations, the Teton River and other streams flowing from the Rocky Mountain Front are excellent for several species of trout. The Milk and Marias rivers carry trout, catfish and perch. Warm-water species like bass,

FISHING

walleye, northern pike, catfish and perch do well in the Missouri River, especially below Fort Benton.

For tackle and information try **Mountain Bait & Tackle**. ~ 414 9th Street South, Great Falls; 406-453-2551. Another good bet is **Wolverton's Fly Shop**. ~ 210 5th Street South, Great Falls; 406-454-0254.

Inquire at any shop about guided expeditions, or contact **Montana River Outfitters**. ~ 1401 5th Avenue South, Great Falls; 406-761-1677.

BOATING

The Upper Missouri National Wild and Scenic River is a major draw for river lovers who don't need whitewater to enjoy the scenery. For 149 miles downstream from Fort Benton this broad, slow-flowing stream meanders past striking geological features and abandoned homesteads.

Ask about commercial boat tours, or get information about renting a vessel and navigating downstream, at the **Upper Missouri River Visitors Center**. ~ 1718 Front Street, Fort Benton; 406-622-5185. You can also obtain information at the wild and scenic river headquarters north of Lewistown. ~ Route 191; 406-538-7461. Among the leading commercial operators is **Missouri River Outfitters**. ~ P.O. Box 762, Fort Benton, MT 59442; 406-622-3295.

Elsewhere in the region, the Tiber Marina on Lake Elwell, southwest of Chester, offers boat rentals, and such lakes as Gibson Reservoir (west of Choteau) and Lake Frances (at Valier) have boat launches and other facilities.

RIVER RAFTING & CANOEING

Most of the rivers of eastern Montana are too slow for whitewater rafting, and many of them are quite muddy. An exceptions is the Smith River south of Great Falls, a 61-mile stretch administered by Montana State Parks. **Lewis & Clark Expeditions** runs the Smith. ~ 4085 Cheff Lane, Ronan; 406-644-2446.

For independent Missouri River floaters, **Virgelle Mercantile**, at the Virgelle river-ferry landing on the Missouri about 30 miles northeast of Fort Benton off Route 87, rents rafts and canoes and operates a shuttle service. ~ Big Sandy; 406-378-3110. **Montana River Outfitters** also rents rafts and offers guided voyages. ~ 25th Avenue Northeast and Old Havre Highway, Great Falls; 406-761-1677.

Canoeists are served with both rentals and guided trips by the **Flowing Rivers Guide Service**. ~ 1809 Darlene Street, Billings; 406-252-5859. In Loma, contact the **Missouri River Canoe Company**. ~ HC 67 Box 50, Loma, MT 59460; 406-378-3110.

DOWNHILL SKIING

None of the ski areas in eastern Montana has on-site lodging, but there are several excellent day resorts.

Showdown Ski Area, on the Kings Hill Scenic Byway 60 miles south of Great Falls, is Montana's oldest ski area. The resort in the Little Belt Mountains has two chairlifts and two tows serving 34 runs and 1400 feet of vertical from an 8200-foot summit. ~ Route 89, Neihart; 406-236-5522.

Rocky Mountain Hi is in Lewis and Clark National Forest on the fringe of the Bob Marshall Wilderness, 28 miles west of Choteau. The area boasts 25 trails served by a chairlift and a rope tow; vertical drop is 1000 feet from a 7400-foot summit. ~ South Fork Teton River Road, Conrad; 406-278-5308.

Bear Paw Ski Bowl draws its clientele from the Havre area. It has one chairlift, one tow and nine runs on a 900-foot vertical drop from a summit elevation of 5280 feet. ~ Rocky Boy's Indian Reservation, Box Elder; 406-265-8404.

CROSS-COUNTRY SKIING

The Kings Hill Winter Sports Complex has 18 kilometers of groomed trails for all abilities in Lewis and Clark National Forest. ~ Route 89, Neihart; 406-236-5522.

Ski Rentals Scheels All Sports carries downhill and cross-country rentals. ~ 3 Holiday Village Mall, 1200 10th Avenue South, Great Falls; 406-453-7666. Bighorn Wilderness specializes in Nordic skis. ~ 600 Central Avenue, Great Falls; 406-453-2841.

GOLF

Among the leading 18-hole public courses is the R.O. Speck Golf Course. ~ River Road, Great Falls; 406-761-1078. Tee off at the Marias Valley Golf & Country Club. ~ Route 417 South, Shelby; 406-434-5940. You may also try the Beaver Creek Golf Course. ~ Route 2 West, Havre; 406-265-7861.

TENNIS

In Great Falls, Montana Park has a number of courts. ~ 18th Street Southwest and Fox Farm Road. Contact Great Falls Recreation & Park Activities for more information. ~ 2 South Park Drive; 406-771-1265.

RIDING STABLES

For standard trail riding, Miller Outfitters offers a stable of Tennessee walking horses. ~ 663 Vaughn South Frontage Road, Great Falls; 406-761-5184. Bonanza Creek Country, a guest ranch east of White Sulphur Springs, offers rides into the Crazy and Little Belt mountains. ~ Lennep Route, Martinsdale; 800-476-6045.

PACK TRIPS

For trips into the Bob Marshall Wilderness and adjacent wildernesses, a reputable outfitter is A Lazy H Outfitters. ~ P.O. Box 729, Choteau, MT 59422; 406-466-5564. There's also the JJJ Wilderness Ranch. ~ P.O. Box 310, Augusta, MT 59410; 406-562-3653.

BIKING

National Forest roads and trails are generally open to mountain biking, but wheeled vehicles—motorized or not—are not allowed in designated wilderness areas. Local bicycle shops have information on planned activities and mountain-biking routes.

Among the most popular areas for mountain bikers is Kings Hill, with 212 miles of trails from the Showdown Ski Area. The 12-mile **Kings Hill Loop Trail**, at about 7500 feet elevation, is a favorite of many. ~ Route 89, Neihart; 406-547-3361. In the **Highwood Mountains**, where there are 16 miles of trails, novices like the two-and-a-half-mile **Thain Creek Loop Trail** at 4600 feet elevation. ~ Highwood Road, Highwood; 406-791-7700.

Great Falls' **River Road**, which follows the Missouri River downstream for five miles from downtown's 10th Avenue Bridge to Giant Springs/Heritage State Park, is paralleled by the **River's Edge Trail**, an immensely popular urban bike route.

Bike Rentals   **Central Bike** offers rentals, repairs, and information. ~ 705 Central Avenue, Great Falls; 406-453-8702. **Knicker Biker** does much of the same. ~ 1123 Central Avenue, Great Falls; 406-454-2912.

HIKING

All distances listed for hiking trails are one way unless otherwise noted.

GREAT FALLS   **River's Edge Trail** (5 miles) follows an abandoned railway bed through Great Falls, along the east and south shores of the Missouri River. The trail begins at Oddfellows Park, just under the Warden Street Bridge, and continues to Giant Springs/Heritage State Park. It connects with several other parks along the way, and draws bicyclists, in-line skaters and runners as well as day hikers.

ROCKY MOUNTAIN FRONT   **Mill Falls Trail** (.1 mile) is a short stroll from the Mill Falls Campground to a cascade surrounded by fir and spruce trees. It begins about 30 miles west of Choteau off Forest Road 109.

Clary Coulee Trail (6 miles), which begins 26 miles west of Choteau off Canyon Road, climbs more than 1200 feet above the North Fork of the Teton River and along the eastern ridge of Choteau Mountain, yielding far-reaching, panoramic views of the Great Plains.

Mortimer Gulch National Recreation Trail (5 miles) zigzags up a 550-foot ridge above Gibson Reservoir; deer, elk and bighorn sheep are often seen in spring, and the views are wonderful year-round. It begins 35 miles west of Augusta via Sun River Road.

WESTERN HI-LINE   The **Sweet Grass Hills**, about 15 miles east of Sunburst just south of the Canadian border, offer numerous hiking opportunities. The BLM administers them as a special recreation management area; there's a steep 2-mile climb to the summit of 6983-foot West Butte and a slightly easier 3-mile ascent past the Devils Chimney Cave on 6958-foot East Butte.

FORT BENTON AREA Windy Mountain/Briggs Creek Trail (7 miles) is a loop trek through the Highwood Mountains, 42 miles east of Great Falls in Lewis and Clark National Forest. The trail climbs gradually up a creek bed and descends a mountain slope.

KINGS HILL The **Porphyry Peak-Ranch Creek Trail** (10 miles) climbs 1.2 miles from Kings Hill Pass to the fire lookout (manned in summer) above the Showdown Ski Area, then descends Mizpah Ridge, circumventing a steep cirque to Ranch Creek.

Equipment **Big Horn Wilderness Equipment** is the best place to fill your hiking needs before hitting the trail. ~ 600 Central Avenue, Great Falls; 406-453-2841.

▼▼▼▼▼▼▼▼▼▼▼
Transportation

Four principal highways provide the thread that binds north central Montana. Great Falls is at the easternmost point of **Route 15**, which extends north from Helena to the Canadian border. **Route 87**, though not a freeway, directly connects Great Falls with Billings, 230 miles southeast, and with Havre, 112 miles northeast. **Route 89** runs north from Yellowstone National Park through White Sulphur Springs and Great Falls en route to Glacier National Park. Finally, **Route 2**, the Hi-Line, extends east from Glacier National Park through Havre and on to North Dakota.

CAR

Great Falls International Airport, the region's principal terminal, is served by Delta, Northwest and Horizon Airlines. ~ 406-727-3404. **Havre City County Airport** is a regional airport served by Big Sky Airlines from Great Falls—as are Miles City, Glendive, Lewistown, Glasgow, Wolf Point and Sidney. ~ 406-265-4671.

AIR

Rimrock Trailways serves all of Montana's major cities and many of its smaller ones. ~ 800-255-7655. In Great Falls, it arrives and departs from the Union Bus Depot. ~ 326 1st Avenue South; 406-453-1541.

BUS

Amtrak's (800-872-7245) Seattle–Chicago "Empire Builder" makes several stops on the Hi-Line east of Glacier National Park. They are in Cut Bank at 1029 East Railroad Street, 406-873-2171; in Shelby at 198½ Burlington Street, 406-434-5031; in Havre at 235 Main Street, 406-265-5381; and in Malta at 51 South 1st Street; 406-654-1622.

TRAIN

Great Falls International Airport has the following rental agencies: **Avis Rent A Car** (800-331-1212), **Budget Rent A Car** (800-527-0700), **Hertz Rent A Car** (800-654-3131) and **National Interrent** (800-328-4567). At the Havre Airport you'll also find **Budget Rent A Car** (800-527-0700).

CAR RENTALS

PUBLIC TRANSIT

Great Falls Transit, known by the acronym GFT, has extensive bus networks throughout the city and its suburbs. Adult fares are less than $1. Buses run from 6 a.m. to 7 p.m. Monday through Friday and from 9:30 a.m. to 5:30 p.m. on Saturday. ~ 406-727-0382.

TAXIS

In Great Falls, dial **Diamond Cab,** which also operates wheelchair-accessible vans. ~ 1005 11th Street North; 406-453-3241. In other area towns, call **Shelby Taxi.** ~ 1000 Ash Avenue, Shelby; 406-434-5790. Or try **Havre Taxi.** ~ 335 1st Street, Havre; 406-265-1287.

FIVE

Southwest Montana

Mining discoveries near the crest of the Continental Divide provided the initial impetus for Montana's growth. More than a century and a quarter later, that mining heritage remains the unifying theme throughout southwest Montana.

The Montana Territory was established in 1862 after major gold discoveries at Bannack and Virginia City—the former now a ghost town, the latter saved from that fate by tourism. Statehood was granted in 1889; the capitol has remained for more than 100 years in another gold-boom town, Helena. Its main street is still called Last Chance Gulch, and nearby Victorian mansions attest to its former affluence.

Soon after Montana became a state, world demand for copper turned Butte into "the richest hill on earth." At the turn of the century, more than 100,000 people lived in the city. Today, its population is barely a third that large. But Butte's stately and historic downtown (more properly referred to as "Uptown" for its hillside location) is more reminiscent of 19th-century San Francisco than of any other town in the Rockies. Butte's copper mines continue to be America's most productive.

If you want to see what *might* have happened to Butte, pay a visit to one or more of the myriad ghost towns on either side of the Continental Divide. Some, like the former territorial capitals of Bannack (now a state park) and Virginia City (a bustling tourist mecca), are well preserved. Many others are no more than names on maps and perhaps a foundation or two.

In addition to the historical value of the region's cities, ghost towns and battlefields, southwest Montana offers sterling natural features (such as the Gates of the Mountains on the Missouri River near Helena), manmade attractions (including Butte's World Museum of Mining), wildlife viewing and outdoor-sports opportunities throughout its national forests and wilderness areas.

Helena Area

▼▼▼▼▼▼▼▼▼▼ An 1864 gold strike in Last Chance Gulch led to the founding of Helena, nestled between the Continental Divide and the Missouri River. Dubbed the "Queen City of the Rockies" because of its grand architecture and cultural sophistication, Helena became the capital of the Montana Territory within a year of its founding and ultimately was chosen as the state capital.

Aside from its urban enticements, the city is an access point to numerous ghost towns and scenic attractions, including Helena National Forest and the Gates of the Mountains Wilderness, where the Missouri River leaves the mountains and heads into the northeastern plains.

Helena's gold rush lasted for about two decades, a period during which, in today's dollars, an estimated $3.6 billion worth of the mineral was taken from Last Chance Gulch. Today, Last Chance Gulch is the historic main street of this colorful town of 25,000, and the three-block stretch from 6th Avenue to Wong Street is a pedestrian mall. Markers describe buildings of historical and architectural significance, including an old bordello, and statues.

SIGHTS

Self-guided walks of **Last Chance Gulch** and the surrounding **Capital City Historic District** are described in brochures available from the Helena Chamber of Commerce. ~ 201 East Lyndale Street, Helena; 406-442-4120. Or take the **Last Chance Tour Train,** a four-car trolley that offers one-hour city tours from mid-May through September. Trips begin more or less hourly from outside the Montana Historical Society, opposite the State Capitol. Fare. ~ 6th Avenue and Roberts Street, Helena; 406-442-4120.

Within the historic district, more distinctive even than the capitol, is the **St. Helena Cathedral,** its two gothic spires towering high above Last Chance Gulch. Modeled after the famous cathedral of Cologne, Germany, and the Votive Church of Vienna, Austria, the cathedral was completed in 1913. Its $66-million stained-glass windows (by F. X. Zettler of Munich) represent the second most expensive art collection in Montana. Interior furnishings, including pews, are of hand-carved oak; the lighting fixtures are bronze; and marble statues stand throughout the cathedral. ~ 530 North Ewing Street, Helena; 406-442-5825.

The **Montana State Capitol** and the surrounding capital district lie about a mile east of Last Chance Gulch. Completed in 1902 and expanded ten years later, the imposing neoclassical capitol building features a copper-faced dome that rises 165 feet above its 14-acre grounds. Its exterior is of Montana sandstone and granite; the interior is decorated in French Renaissance style. Of particular note are panels by noted painters depicting themes from the state's past. A mural by Charles M. Russell is among the artist's masterpieces: *Lewis and Clark Meeting the Flathead Indians at Ross'*

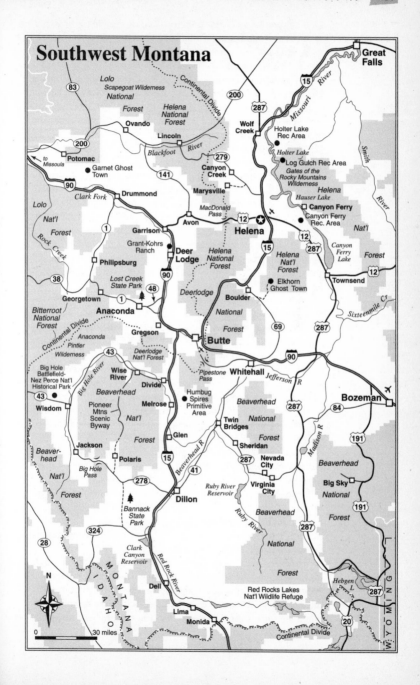

Southwest Montana

83 Lolo
Scapegoat Wilderness
National
Forest
Helena
National
Forest
Ovando
Lincoln
200
287
Wolf
Creek
200
15 River
Great
Falls
Holter Lake
Rec Area
to
Missoula
Potomac
Garnet Ghost
Town
141
90
Clark Fork
Drummond
Blackfoot River
279
Canyon
Creek
Marysville
Holter Lake
Log Gulch Rec Area
Gates of the
Rocky Mountains
Wilderness
Helena
Hauser Lake
Canyon Ferry
Smith
River
Lolo
Nat'l
Forest
1
Garrison
Grant-Kohrs
Ranch
Rock Creek
Philipsburg
38
1
Georgetown
Lost Creek
State Park
48
Anaconda
Deer
Lodge
90
MacDonald
Pass
Avon
12
Helena
15
Helena
National
Forest
Helena
Nat'l
Forest
12
287
Canyon Ferry
Rec. Area
Nat'l
Forest
Canyon
Ferry
Lake
Townsend
12
Elkhorn
Ghost Town
Boulder
National
Forest
69
287
Sixteenmile Cr.
Bitterroot
National
Forest
Continental Divide
Anaconda
Pintler
Wilderness
Gregson
Deerlodge
Nat'l Forest
Butte
90
43
Big Hole
Battlefield-
Nez Perce Nat'l
Historical Park
43
Wisdom
Big Hole River
Wise
River
Beaverhead
Divide
Pioneer
Mtns
Scenic
Byway
Nat'l
Melrose
Humbug
Spires
Primitive
Area
Pipestone
Pass
Whitehall
Jefferson R.
Beaverhead
287
National
84
Bozeman
191
Beaver-
head
Nat'l
Forest
Jackson
Big Hole
Pass
Polaris
278
Beaverhead R.
Glen
Twin
Bridges
Sheridan
287
Nevada
City
Forest
Madison R.
Beaverhead
Big Sky
National
191
28
324
Bannack
State
Park
41
Dillon
Ruby River
Reservoir
Virginia
City
Beaverhead
287
Forest
Hebgen
L.
287
Clark
Canyon
Reservoir
Red Rock River
Dell
Lima
Monida
Red Rocks Lakes
Nat'l Wildlife Refuge
Ruby River
National
Forest
Continental Divide
20

MONTANA
IDAHO
WYOMING

N

0   30 miles

Hole covers the wall above the rostrum of the House of Representatives. Hourly tours are offered every day in summer; self-guided tours are encouraged at other times. ~ 6th Avenue at Washington Drive, Helena; 406-444-2511.

Opposite the capitol is the excellent museum of the **Montana Historical Society**. Its largest permanent gallery traces the history of the state, from prehistory through World War II; there are also galleries of Russell's art and F. Jay Haynes' photography. The state archives are also housed here, and there's a museum store. ~ 225 North Roberts Street, Helena; 406-444-2694.

The official residence of Montana's governor has moved, but the **Original Governor's Mansion** is open April through December afternoons for guided hourly tours. Built in 1888, the Victorian mansion three blocks above Last Chance Gulch was the home of nine governors between 1913 and 1959. Other impressive late-19th-century mansions can be glimpsed on a driving or walking tour of the **mansion district**, located northwest of Last Chance Gulch, mainly west of Benton Avenue and south of Hauser Boulevard. Tours run from April through December. ~ 304 North Ewing Street, Helena; 406-442-3115.

Other historic attractions in downtown Helena include the **Helena Civic Center**, a former Shrine temple built in exotic Moorish style with a needle-slim minaret, now the home of a large auditorium and municipal offices. ~ Benton and Neill avenues; 406-447-8481. The **Old Fire Tower**, erected in 1876, is one of five of its type still standing in the United States. ~ Congress and Pine streets. The **Pioneer Cabin**, Helena's oldest structure, was built in 1864 and still houses many original furnishings. ~ 200 South Park Street; 406-443-7641. Just off Last Chance Gulch, the **Holter Museum of Art** features changing exhibits of contemporary and historical art. ~ 12 East Lawrence Street; 406-442-6400.

Looming 1300 feet above Last Chance Gulch is **Mount Helena**, which offers seven separate hiking trails to its peak. For more information see the "Hiking" section in this chapter.

A series of Missouri River reservoirs, created by early-20th-century dams, provide wide recreational opportunities east of Helena. **Holter Lake**, **Hauser Lake** and **Canyon Ferry Lake** attract walleye, trout, kokanee salmon and perch fishermen, as well as boaters, waterskiers and board sailors.

Holter Lake offers access to one of the Helena area's preeminent attractions: the **Gates of the Mountains**. Narrated commercial **tour boats** that depart from the Upper Holter Lake marina, 20 miles north of Helena, ply a steep canyon whose quarter-mile-high limestone walls seemed to open and close before the eyes of the advancing Lewis and Clark expedition in 1805. Beyond these "gates," as the explorers dubbed them, were the Missouri River

HIDDEN ►

headwaters and the crest of the Rockies. Tours operate from Memorial Day through September. Fare. ~ Route 15 Exit 109; 406-458-5241.

The canyon's western slopes make up the **Gates of the Mountains Game Preserve**; to the east lies the **Gates of the Mountains Wilderness**. Both are vehicle-free parcels of **Helena National Forest**. ~ 2800 Skyway Drive, Helena; 406-449-5201. Rocky Mountain goats, deer, bighorn sheep, osprey, eagles and occasional bear—as well as ancient American Indian petroglyphs—can be seen from the tour boat.

Further upstream on the Missouri River, northeast of Helena, visitors can try mining for sapphires. Among the gem sites are two beside Hauser Lake. Check out **Spokane Bar Mine**. ~ 5360 Castles Drive; 406-227-8989. Or try your luck at **Love Stone Mine**. ~ Hart Drive; 406-227-6076. Rockhounds pour buckets of concentrates from gravel bars onto riffle jig machines, which separate the gravel and sort out any precious stones.

Due east of Helena is 25-mile-long, four-mile-wide Canyon Ferry Lake, whose **Canyon Ferry Recreation Area** is the state's most popular for water-sports enthusiasts. Admission. ~ Canyon Ferry Road; 406-444-4475. Located at the lake's southern head is **Townsend**, 32 miles from Helena via Route 12. The highway turns east here across the Big Belt Mountains to the town of White Sulphur Springs.

South of Helena, a half-hour's drive in the direction of Butte on Route 15, is the town of **Boulder**. Worth a look is the **Jefferson County Courthouse**, built in 1889 and on the National Register of Historic Places: It features gargoyles perched on 24-inch-thick stone walls above its three-story entrance.

Just east are the **Boulder Hot Springs**, noted for their high content of radon, a mining byproduct considered helpful by sufferers of arthritis, emphysema and other ailments. Hot (104°F) and cold

◆◆◆

✔ CHECK THESE OUT—UNIQUE SIGHTS

- Board a boat to retrace Lewis and Clark's voyage through the **Gates of the Mountains**, a Missouri River gorge north of Helena. *page 132*
- Tour the working acreage of **Grant-Kohrs Ranch National Historic Site**, once the headquarters of a million-acre cattle ranch. *page 142*
- Ride an old mine train or watch an old stamp mill in action at Butte's **World Museum of Mining**. *page 146*
- Wander the streets of **Bannack State Park** and explore five dozen preserved 1860s buildings, dating to the town's heyday as a lawless territorial capital. *page 156*

soaking pools, salt scrubs and therapeutic massages are offered at the health resort here, built in 1888 and currently undergoing restoration. ~ Route 69; 406-225-4339.

HIDDEN ▶   One of Montana's finest ghost towns is **Elkhorn**, reached by traveling seven miles southeast of Boulder on Route 69, then following signs north another 11 miles. ~ Forest Road 258; 406-444-4720.

Sixteen miles west of Helena, atop the Continental Divide at 6320-foot MacDonald Pass, is an authentic replica of a pioneer village. **Frontier Town** was built of hand-hewn logs beginning in the late 1940s by John Quigley, a direct descendant of early Montana settlers. Unfortunately, new owners have put more energy into a gift shop, restaurant and unique Western bar than into the neglected town itself, which seems full of possibilities. Closed November to March. ~ Route 12; 406-442-4560.

A real-life frontier town is **Marysville**, about 22 miles northwest of Helena off Route 279. At its zenith, this boom town near the Drumlummon Mine (said to have produced as much as $50 million in gold) supported a population of 2000 with six hotels, four general stores, two churches and a school. Today, only the presence of the nearby Great Divide ski area and other sports options in the surrounding Helena National Forest preserve it as a "living" ghost town. ~ Marysville Road.

Route 279 crosses the Continental Divide at Flesher Pass, then follows the upper reaches of the Blackfoot River into **Lincoln**. The ranching community is the gateway to National Forest recreation at several small lakes as well as the **Scapegoat Wilderness**, which borders the south end of the famed Bob Marshall Wilderness. No road, in fact, crosses the Divide between Lincoln and Route 2, which traces the southern boundary of Glacier National Park 100 miles to the north.

LODGING   The **Sanders—Helena's Bed & Breakfast** occupies a three-story 1875 mansion overlooking Last Chance Gulch and the cathedral, just a block from the Original Governor's Mansion. The home has seven restored bedrooms, all with period antiques, private baths and air-conditioning. Gourmet breakfasts are served in a lovely dining room. ~ 328 North Ewing Street, Helena; 406-442-3309. MODERATE TO DELUXE.

A block away, and with very similar flavor, is the **Barrister Bed & Breakfast**, with five rooms in a three-story 1874 Victorian estate. All rooms have private baths and televisions, with phones available on request. Full breakfasts are served each morning, and in the evening, guests gather to talk around an elaborate fireplace. ~ 416 North Ewing Street, Helena; 406-443-7330. MODERATE TO DELUXE.

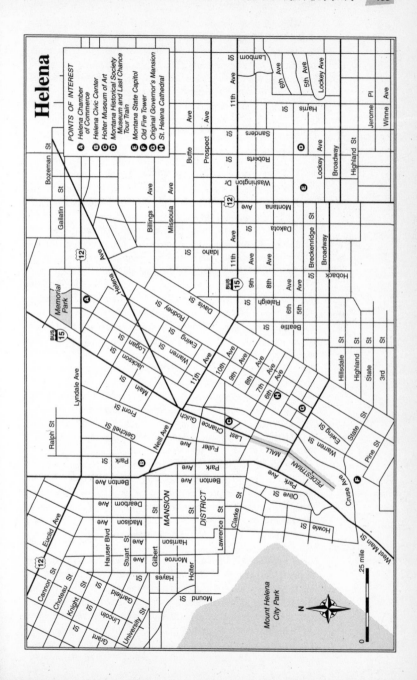

Helena

POINTS OF INTEREST

- Ⓐ Helena Chamber of Commerce
- Ⓑ Helena Civic Center
- Ⓒ Holter Museum of Art
- Ⓓ Montana Historical Society Museum and Last Chance Tour Train
- Ⓔ Montana State Capitol
- Ⓕ Old Fire Tower
- Ⓖ Original Governor's Mansion
- Ⓗ St. Helena Cathedral

Within hailing distance of the Last Chance Gulch pedestrian mall is the **King's Carriage Inn**. Its 125 comfortable rooms all have standard amenities. There's a 24-hour restaurant here, a casino-lounge, an outdoor swimming pool, steambaths and saunas. A good value. ~ 910 North Last Chance Gulch, Helena; 406-442-6080, fax 406-449-4131. BUDGET TO MODERATE.

The **Park Plaza Hotel** is in the heart of historic downtown. It doesn't have a pool, but it *does* have a restaurant, nightclub and lounge. Its 71 guest rooms are standard issue with queen-size beds and air-conditioning. ~ 22 North Last Chance Gulch, Helena; 406-443-2200, 800-332-2290, fax 406-442-4030. MODERATE.

The Windbag Saloon was "one of the cleanest, most respected bordellos in all of Montana" until "Big Dorothy" was closed down in 1973.

Helena's largest and most luxurious lodging is the **Best Western Colonial Inn**, just off Route 15. This two-story motel's 149 spacious rooms have just what you'd expect from an upscale property, including king- or queen-size beds and air-conditioning: some have microwaves and refrigerators. A restaurant and lounge are located off the elegant atrium lobby, and the motel contains two swimming pools, a hot tub, a sauna and a coin laundry. ~ 2301 Colonial Drive, Helena; 406-443-2100, 800-442-1002, fax 406-442-0301. MODERATE.

Spread across 6000 acres of forest and rangeland, the **Grassy Mountain Ranch** is a low-key retreat on the eastern slope of the Big Belt Mountains, 50 miles from Helena. A working cattle ranch that welcomes families, it is especially popular among horse lovers, who may ride daily. Guests may work with the ranch's wranglers, swim, fish and hike. For kids, there's an overnight camping trip and campfire sing-alongs. Twelve lodging units are housed in four log cabins, all with rock fireplaces and private baths. Hearty meals are served buffet-style in the main lodge. ~ P.O. Box C, Townsend, MT 59644; 406-547-3402. MODERATE.

An hour's drive west of Helena, surrounded by ponderosa pines and within view of the Scapegoat Wilderness is **Leeper's Motel**. This clean little bargain has private baths, cable TV and coffeemakers in all 15 rooms, kitchenettes in four. A spa and sauna are available for guest use. ~ Route 200 West, Lincoln; 406-362-4333. BUDGET.

DINING

For atmosphere, it's hard to outdo the **Stonehouse Restaurant** in a restored 19th-century brick building at the entrance to a historic shopping and artisans' mall. The staff even dresses as they might have 100 years ago. The menu focuses on steak and seafood dinners. ~ 120 Reeder's Alley at South Park Avenue, Helena; 406-449-2552. MODERATE TO DELUXE.

The **Queen City Cafe** has a relaxing garden atmosphere and an interesting daily menu of Continental and international cuisine, from chicken Parisienne and fresh grilled seafood to jambalaya and lasagna. ~ 42 South Park Avenue, Helena; 406-442-3354. MODERATE.

Northern Italian cuisine is the menu mainstay at **On Broadway**, lodged in an 1889 grocery store refurbished in art deco style. A wide choice of chicken, seafood and vegetarian dishes—as well as a handful of meat dishes—share the spotlight with one of the city's best wine lists. ~ 106 Broadway, Helena; 406-4431929. MODERATE.

You can get two pounds of beef ribs for $12.95 at **The Windbag Saloon**. This is steak lover's paradise, and there are lots of chicken and fish dishes as well. The desserts are local legend. ~ 19 South Last Chance Gulch, Helena; 406-443-9669. BUDGET TO MODERATE.

Bert & Ernie's Saloon and Eatery offers a wide variety of sandwiches and salads, and a handful of nightly dinners. The best things here are the eclectic antique decor and the extensive list of microbrews and wines by the glass. ~ 361 North Last Chance Gulch, Helena; 406-443-5680. BUDGET.

Overland Express, off the freeway between the Colonial Inn and the Super 8 Motel, offers generous steaks, chicken and seafood in a modern rustic atmosphere that families enjoy. ~ 2250 11th Avenue, Helena; 406-449-2635. BUDGET TO MODERATE.

West of Helena near the banks of the Blackfoot River, the atmosphere is even more rustic, the food even more meat-and-potatoes. Behind log-cabin walls, the **Seven-Up Ranch Supper Club** prepares what some swear is the best prime rib between Great Falls and Missoula. ~ Route 200, Lincoln; 406-362-4255. MODERATE.

Perhaps the most interesting shopping, from a visitor's standpoint, is at **Reeder's Alley**, a short block west of Last Chance Gulch at Wong Street. Built as an inn for miners and laborers during the early gold-rush era, it was largely constructed of brick freighted up the Missouri River from St. Louis. Until recently an arts center, it has undergone extensive and authentic restoration and has re-opened as a block of arts and crafts galleries and retail specialty shops. ~ 100 South Park Avenue, Helena.

SHOPPING

Potters from all over the world come to work and study at the **Archie Bray Foundation**. The public gallery offers outstanding traditional and contemporary pottery, sculpture and ceramics, at premium prices. Studio tours are by appointment. ~ 2915 Country Club Avenue, Helena; 406-443-3502.

◄ HIDDEN

Two Bears Gifts, in Capital Plaza, though a good mile removed from the Last Chance Gulch pedestrian mall, may be the best option for made-in-Montana souvenirs. Look for jewelry and other artwork, glassware, shirts and hats, books and huckleberry products. ~ 511 North Sanders Street, Helena; 406-442-8241.

State legislators peruse the racks at the **Main News Smoke Shop**. Local and national newspapers and more than 800 magazine titles are sold here. ~ 9 North Last Chance Gulch, Helena; 406-442-6424.

HIDDEN ►

Certainly one of the Helena area's most intriguing stores is **The Prospector's Shop**, five miles west on the MacDonald Pass highway. On display are all manner of mining equipment and supplies, from metal detectors to sluice boxes and gold dredges. It's fascinating just to stop and browse a while. ~ 6312 Route 12 West, Helena; 406-442-1872.

The **Capital Hill Mall** is Helena's largest shopping mall. It is anchored by the **JC Penney** and **Hennessy's** department stores; shops include **Waldenbooks**. ~ 11th Avenue between Roberts and Lamborn streets, Helena; 406-442-0183.

NIGHTLIFE

Since its earliest days of gold-rush affluence, Helena has been a magnet for performing artists of national renown. Today the **Myrna Loy Center for the Performing Arts**, occupying the renovated Lewis and Clark County Jail, showcases music, theater and dance, as well as films, conferences and festivals. ~ 15 North Ewing Street, Helena; 406-443-0287.

Local thespians perform Thursday through Saturday nights in the historic brownstone **Grandstreet Theater**, close by Last Chance Gulch. ~ 325 North Park Street, Helena; 406-443-3311. And the **Helena Orchestra and Symphony Chorale** makes its home beneath the exotic minaret of the Moorish-style Helena Civic Center. ~ Benton and Neill avenues, Helena; 406-442-1860.

For late-night revelers in Helena, **JD's** is a disco-nightclub in the Park Plaza Hotel that attracts a mostly mid-to-late-20s crowd. ~ 22 North Last Chance Gulch, Helena; 406-443-2200. **Jeff's Joint**, though cozy, features live rock bands. ~ 101 North Last Chance Gulch, Helena; 406-443-2200. **The Windbag Saloon**, lodged in a former brothel, offers a rustic atmosphere for conversation and acoustic music. ~ 19 South Last Chance Gulch, Helena; 406-443-9669.

Like other Montana cities, Helena has numerous casinos with low-stakes poker and keno machines. Among the more popular is the **Last Chance Casino**, which also features live keno and serves three square meals a day. ~ 1001 North Last Chance Gulch, Helena; 406-442-4474.

PARKS

MOUNT HELENA CITY PARK 🧍🚲 This small mountain is noteworthy not for its elevation (only 5468 feet), but for its proximity to the State Capitol. Seven trails rise to the summit, a quarter-mile above Last Chance Gulch. Easiest is the gradually ascending 1906 Trail. The Prairie Trail is especially attractive during spring and early summer wildflower season; the winding Prospect Shafts Trail passes old mining sites. Many visitors climb one path and descend on another. Restaurants and groceries are in downtown Helena. ~ Nearest access is west six blocks on Lawrence Street, south three blocks on Harrison Avenue, then west on Adams Street to its end; 406-442-4120.

HOLTER LAKE RECREATION AREA

Located at the lower (north) end of the Missouri River reservoir that flows between the lofty limestone cliffs of the Gates of the Mountains, this area is especially popular with boating and fishing enthusiasts. Facilities include picnic areas and restrooms. Day-use fee $2. Groceries are in Wolf Creek, and there are restaurants in Helena. ~ Take Route 15 north from Helena for 33 miles to Wolf Creek exit 226; go east three miles on Recreation Road to the Wolf Creek Bridge; then drive south three miles on Beartooth Road; 406-494-5059.

▲ There are 50 RV/tent sites (no hookups), $6 per night; 14-day maximum stay. Nearby Log Gulch, administered by the Bureau of Land Management, has 100 RV/tent sites available on the same basis.

GATES OF THE MOUNTAINS WILDERNESS AREA

A handful of trails traverse the rugged backcountry east of the Missouri River between Elkhorn and Beaver creeks, providing spectacular views of the Gates of the Mountains canyon, especially from the sheer slopes of 7190-foot Willow Mountain. This 28,500-acre preserve is rich in wildlife, including bighorn sheep and mountain goats. Groceries and restaurants are in Helena. ~ There are several trailheads on Beaver Creek Road, 20 miles northeast of Helena via York Road and York-Nelson Road. The Meriwether picnic area on the Missouri River also offers trail access; the Gates of the Mountains tour boat will drop hikers at that spot; 406-449-5201.

▲ Primitive only.

CANYON FERRY RECREATION AREA

The most popular and largest of Montana's 46 state recreation areas consists of 24 units around the 76-mile shoreline of Canyon Ferry Lake. All but six of the sites are within a few miles of the Canyon Ferry Dam (tours available) at the reservoir's north end; the park visitors center is located in adjacent Canyon Ferry Village, along with lodging and RV resorts, restaurants, a grocery store and other facilities. Wildlife viewing around the lakeshore is excellent, especially from November to January, when several hundred bald eagles make their winter homes here. Facilities include picnic areas, restrooms, showers, three marinas with boat rentals and concessions. Restaurants and groceries are located in Helena and Townsend. ~ For park headquarters, take Route 12/287 ten miles east from Helena; then turn north on Route 284 (Canyon Ferry Road) and continue eight miles to Canyon Ferry Village; 406-475-3310.

▲ There are 383 RV/tent sites (no hookups) in eight developed and three undeveloped campgrounds; the largest is Hellgate (130 RV/tent sites), nine miles southeast of Canyon Ferry Village on Hellgate Gulch Road. No charge to $6 per night.

HELENA NATIONAL FOREST 🎿 🚴 🐎 🎣 🏕 ⛷ 🎿 Three principal units make up this 975,000-acre national forest, one of ten in the state. The largest segment takes in both sides of the Continental Divide west of Helena, from the Scapegoat Wilderness nearly to Boulder. Smaller parcels include the Big Belt Mountains, east of Canyon Ferry Lake, and the Elkhorn Mountains, south of the capital. The forest includes 730 miles of trails and 1600 miles of backroads. Facilities include picnic areas and restrooms. Restaurants and groceries are in Helena, Townsend, Boulder, Lincoln and other towns. ~ Principal highways are Route 200, through Lincoln; Route 12, west of Helena and east of Townsend; York Road and several connecting roads, east of Hauser and Canyon Ferry lakes; 406-449-5201.

▲ There are 135 RV/tent sites plus seven tents-only sites, none with hookups, in nine campgrounds; no charge to $6 per night. Four recreational cabins within the forest are available by reservation for $20 per night.

SCAPEGOAT WILDERNESS AREA 🎿 🐎 🎣 The southernmost of three contiguous wilderness areas that extend south 100 miles along the crest of the Rockies from Glacier National Park, the 240,000-acre Scapegoat features striking alpine scenery, massive limestone cliffs along its eastern front and numerous small lakes and trout-rich streams. Restaurants and groceries are in Lincoln. ~ Lincoln, on Route 200, is the gateway community. Nearest trail access is from the Snowbank Creek campground in Helena National Forest, on Cooper Creek Road 15 miles northeast of Lincoln; 406-362-4265.

▲ Primitive only.

▼▼▼▼▼▼▼▼▼▼▼▼▼▼▼
Pintler Scenic Route

The Pintler Scenic Route, which follows Route 1 through historic mining towns and the Deerlodge National Forest, combines with Route 90 through Deer Lodge to make a 150-mile driving loop that can easily take up a full day. Butte is 41 miles southeast via Route 90 from Deerlodge. From Helena, the most direct access is via Route 12 west across MacDonald Pass to Garrison, a 46-mile drive; from Butte, the loop is accessed 18 miles northwest at the Anaconda exit from Route 90.

It's nine miles from the interstate into **Anaconda**, a city of 10,000 founded by Marcus Daly when he erected a copper smelter and reduction works in 1883. Though it ceased operating in 1980, the 585-foot **Anaconda Smelter Stack**, on a hill south of town, remains the city's landmark and a state historic park. Once known as the Washoe Stack, it is one of the world's tallest freestanding brick structures. A Jack Nicklaus–designed golf course is scheduled to open around the old smelter works in spring 1997.

The downtown **Anaconda Historic District** is worthy of exploration. Vintage tour buses depart twice daily from the **Anaconda Visitors Center,** housed in a replica of an old train depot that once served the Anaconda Copper Mining Company. Brochures describing a self-guided walking tour are available here. Admission. ~ 306 East Park Street, Anaconda; 406-563-2400.

The Anaconda Smelter Stack is one of the world's tallest free-standing brick structures—taller even than the Washington Monument.

Among the district's significant buildings is the **Hearst Free Library,** built in 1898 and donated to the city by Phoebe Hearst, wife of Anaconda investor George Hearst and mother of San Francisco publisher William Randolph Hearst. ~ Main and 4th streets; 406-563-6932. The **Copper Village Museum and Arts Center** housed the Anaconda City Hall from 1895 to 1982. ~ 401 East Commercial Street; 406-563-2422. The copper dome of the **Deer Lodge County Courthouse** towers above Anaconda. ~ 800 South Main Street; 406-563-8421. The **Washoe Theater** is a 1000-seat art deco theater built in 1937. The Smithsonian Institution rates the theater's elaborate interior as one of the most beautiful in the nation. ~ 305 Main Street; 406-563-6161.

◄ *HIDDEN*

The 10,000-foot-high peaks of the Anaconda-Pintler Wilderness rise to the south as Route 1 follows Warm Springs Creek west from Anaconda to **Georgetown Lake,** a year-round recreation area in Deerlodge National Forest. Kokanee salmon and rainbow trout draw anglers in summer; the Discovery Basin ski area, only five miles north of the lake, caters to winter enthusiasts. The lake freezes over in winter to the delight of snowmobilers and ice fishermen.

At Georgetown Lake, the Pintler Scenic Route turns north and follows Flint Creek to the Clark Fork River. About ten miles north of the lake, it's a short detour into **Philipsburg,** an 1860s silver-mining town and now (in its entirety) a national historic district. The many circa-1890s brick businesses along Broadway, the town's colorful main street, have been restored and now house a variety of shops and restaurants.

Twenty-one ghost towns lie within 40 miles of Philipsburg, so it's appropriate that the town's **Granite County Museum and Cultural Center** is the home of the Ghost Town Hall of Fame. Here you can find photographs of, and information on, such lost communities as Granite, Southern Cross, Princeton and Red Lion. Closed January through April. Admission. ~ 135 South Sansome Street, Philipsburg; 406-859-3388.

Philipsburg is still a sapphire-mining center. Learn about the precious gems at the **Sapphire Gallery**. ~ 119 East Broadway, Philipsburg; 406-859-3236. Dig through buckets of gravel concentrate to find a few; then get directions to the **Gem Mountain Sapphire Mine**. Closed from mid-September to mid-May. ~ 24 miles southwest on Route 38 at Rock Creek; 406-859-3530.

Route 1 rejoins the interstate at Drummond, 26 scenic miles north of Philipsburg. Missoula is 48 miles northwest. Turn left here on Route 90 to Bearmouth, the next exit, 15 miles west, and detour to **Garnet**, one of the best-preserved of Montana's myriad ghost towns. You must travel six miles east on a frontage road and ten miles north on a narrow, steep, decidedly backcountry byway to reach the ruins of this community.

HIDDEN ▶

After an 1897 gold strike, Garnet was home to about 1000 men, women and children. Four hotels, 13 saloons and a school were among its buildings. But after the claims were mined out, the population dwindled and disappeared. Today the Bureau of Land Management and the nonprofit Garnet Preservation Association operate a small visitors center and maintain a couple of dozen log structures. Two of these cabins can be rented in winter by snowmobilers or cross-country skiers, and some mining still continues in the area. A trail leads about 300 yards to the townsite from the picnic ground near the parking area. ~ Bear Creek Road; 406-329-3914.

If you choose to bypass Garnet and turn southeast (right) at Drummond instead, you'll follow Route 90 about 31 miles past Goldcreek and Garrison to **Deer Lodge**, home of several important tourist attractions.

Chief among them is the **Grant-Kohrs Ranch National Historic Site**. For more than a century the headquarters of a cattle empire that once controlled one million acres of the northern Rockies, the ranch was set aside by the federal government in 1972 to illustrate the history of the ranching industry. Half-hour guided tours of the elegant 23-room Kohrs home, built in 1862 and expanded in 1890, begin at the visitors center. Guests may take themselves through interpretive displays in a bunkhouse row and buggy shed, tack room, blacksmith shop and more. Cattle graze and draft horses still work the remaining 1500 acres of the ranch. Admission. ~ Route 10 North, Deer Lodge; 406-846-2070.

Within the walls of the **Montana Territorial Prison** are three separate museums. The foreboding **Old Montana Prison**, with its massive gray stone walls and crenelated guard towers, was in active use for 108 years until 1979. Guided and self-guided tours give glimpses of the cellblocks and maximum-security corridors. The **Towe Ford Museum** features more than 100 perfectly restored Ford automobiles from 1903 to the 1960s; the **Law Enforcement Museum** is a memorial to Montana officers who have died in the line of duty. The prison and Ford museum are closed December and January; the law-enforcement museum is closed November to mid-May. Admission. ~ 1106 Main Street, Deer Lodge; 406-846-3111.

Also in Deer Lodge, the **Powell County Museum,** which displays artifacts and photographs from local history, is open from Memorial Day to Labor Day. ~ 1193 Main Street, Deer Lodge; 406-846-3294. **Yesterday's Playthings** exhibits more than a thousand dolls and a century's worth of toys. Admission. ~ 1017 Main Street, Deer Lodge; 406-846-1480.

LODGING

Three miles off Route 90 near Anaconda is the **Fairmont Hot Springs Resort.** Set in picturesque surroundings at the foot of 10,600-foot Mount Haggin, the resort attracts hot-spring soakers and swimmers with four indoor and outdoor pools, one with a twisting, 350-foot water slide. Golfers are drawn to its 18-hole golf course, one of Montana's best. There's even a petting zoo for the kids. There are 158 spacious rooms and suites with standard furnishings and amenities, two restaurants and a lounge/casino. ~ 1500 Fairmont Road, Gregson; 406-797-3241, 800-443-2381, fax 406-797-3337. MODERATE TO DELUXE.

On a ridgetop overlooking Georgetown Lake, 25 miles west of Anaconda and just off the Pintler Scenic Route, is **The Summit Bed & Breakfast Inn,** which surely has one of Montana's finest views. Newly constructed but furnished with Victorian antiques, the inn has four guest rooms, all with queen-size beds and private bathrooms (with clawfoot tubs). Full breakfasts are served each morn-

✔ **CHECK THESE OUT—UNIQUE LODGING**

- *Budget:* Stay in spartan accommodations at the **Metlen Hotel,** a Dillon residential hotel that has survived since 1897. *page 157*
- *Moderate:* Admire hand-painted fresco ceilings and dine on fine crystal and silver when you stay at the **Copper King Mansion.** *page 148*
- *Moderate:* Don't forget your camera when you visit the **Lakeview Guest Ranch;** you're practically guaranteed to see whooping cranes. *page 158*
- *Moderate to deluxe:* Go water-sliding, golfing or horseback riding when you stay at the **Fairmont Hot Springs Resort.** *page 143*

Budget: under $50 Moderate: $50–$90 Deluxe: $90–$130 Ultra-deluxe: over $130

ing. No smoking is permitted inside the inn. ~ P.O. Box 217, Anaconda, MT 59711; 406-563-6578. MODERATE.

Scharf's Motor Inn meets basic requirements for travelers who want to spend a night near the Grant-Kohrs Ranch and Montana Territorial Prison. Rooms are clean and comfortable if nothing fancy, and the motel has its own family restaurant and lounge. A couple of kitchens are available for families. ~ 819 Main Street, Deer Lodge; 406-846-2810, 800-341-8000. BUDGET.

DINING

If you're in Anaconda anytime before mid-afternoon, drop by **Rose's Tea Room** for Scottish scones and traditional black or herbal teas. Calico curtains and white-tablecloth service add class to this café, which also serves breakfasts, light lunches and dessert specials. ~ 117 East Park Street, Anaconda; 406-563-5060. BUDGET.

For steak and seafood, Anaconda locals head to the **Barclay II Supper Club & Lounge**. This low-lit, informal restaurant has full bar service but a firm no-smoking policy. Dinner only. ~ 1300 East Commercial Street, Anaconda; 406-563-5541. MODERATE.

The place to go in Deer Lodge is the **Broken Arrow Casino & Steakhouse**. This candlelit steakhouse in the heart of downtown, between the Territorial Prison and the Grant-Kohrs Ranch, serves up dinners in a rustic ambience. There's an adjoining casino-lounge. ~ 317 Main Street, Deer Lodge; 406-846-3400. MODERATE.

SHOPPING

Anaconda is a good place to look for hard-to-find antiques. Two of Montana's largest antique shops are located here. **Brewery Antiques** is a great spot to find Western paraphernalia. ~ 125 West Commercial Street, Anaconda; 406-563-7926. **Park Street Antique Mall** has a fine selection of art pottery. ~ 113 East Park Street, Anaconda; 406-563-3150.

The Old Book Shoppe is an excellent antiquarian shop. ~ 101 Main Street, Anaconda; 406-563-7962.

HIDDEN ► Further up the Pintler Scenic Route, the **Sapphire Gallery** is a natural stop for gems. But the shop also displays and sells an intriguing variety of international artworks, as well as framed fossils-as-art. ~ 119 East Broadway, Philipsburg; 406-859-3236.

NIGHTLIFE

In Deer Lodge, the **Old Prison Players** perform musical comedies and melodramas Wednesday through Sunday evenings, late June through late August, behind the walls of Montana Territorial Prison. Admission. ~ 1106 Main Street, Deer Lodge; 406-846-3111.

PARKS

LOST CREEK STATE PARK 🏃‍♂️ 🚣 A short nature trail leads to the base of Lost Creek Falls, which makes a spectacular drop from the HIDDEN ► 1200-foot-high limestone cliffs of the Flint Creek Range north of Anaconda. Rocky Mountain goats and bighorn sheep are frequently seen here; bring binoculars. Facilities include picnic areas and restrooms; restaurants and groceries are in Anaconda. ~ From Anaconda, take Route 1 east for one and a half miles, Route 273 north for two miles, then Forest Road 635 west for six miles; 406-542-5500.

▲ Twenty-five primitive sites; no charge; 14-day maximum stay.

ANACONDA-PINTLER WILDERNESS AREA 🚶 🐎 ⛵ High rocky peaks, several of them over 10,000 feet, speckled with alpine lakes, meadows and forests, are the feature of this 159,000-acre wilderness. It extends for some 40 miles on both sides of the Continental Divide southwest of Anaconda and encompasses parts of three national forests: the Deer Lodge, Beaverhead and Bitterroot. As in all wilderness areas, no vehicular travel is permitted. Restaurants and groceries are in Anaconda, Philipsburg and other towns. ~ Popular access points are East Fork Reservoir and Moose Lake, south of Georgetown Lake; Pintler and Lower Seymour lakes, in the Big Hole Valley on the east slope of the wilderness; and the East Fork of the Bitterroot River near Sula, off Route 93 on the west; 406-832-3178.

▲ Primitive only.

Butte

At the turn of the 20th century, few cities in western North America were larger than Butte, which stretches down a long slope on the west side of the Continental Divide. Urbane and cosmopolitan, "the richest hill on earth" had a population of more than 100,000, a powerful position in the national labor movement and a cast of millionaires.

Though the city was founded on gold in the 1860s and thrived on silver in the 1870s, copper was king. During the 1880s, Butte became the world's greatest copper producer. In succeeding decades, some 19 *billion* pounds of the ore were taken from underground by hard-rock miners, and state-of-the-art smelters extracted the metal for shipment around the nation and overseas.

"Copper kings" like Marcus Daly and William Andrews Clark fought for control of the city's wealth. (Daly's Anaconda Copper Mining Company amalgamated with John Rockefeller's Standard Oil and dominated Butte into the 1970s.) Irish and Cornish miners, followed by dozens of other nationalities—among them Italians, Finns, Serbians, Croatians, Germans, Chinese and Mexicans—came to Butte and created their own distinctive ethnic communities.

After the First World War, demand for copper decreased and an exodus from Butte began. The population declined further after 1955, when labor-intensive hard-rock mining was abandoned in favor of more cost-efficient open-pit mining, changing the face of

Butte forever. Whole neighborhoods on the city's east side were evacuated and razed to allow the hillside to be excavated. The first hole, the Berkeley Pit, was exhausted and closed in 1982; other adjacent mines are currently being worked.

Today, Butte is a city in transition. Though only about 33,000 people now make their homes here, its history is evident everywhere.

Uptown Butte is the city's downtown. It is reminiscent of parts of San Francisco without its cable cars; built on a hillside at about 5700 feet, it has preserved an eclectic turn-of-the-century architecture and clings to a big-city ambience in a small-town environment. Black headframes that once towered over the entrances to hardrock mines are a unique accent on the city skyline. About six square miles, encompassing 4500 buildings, have been designated a national historic landmark district—one of the largest such districts in the United States.

The hillsides that surround Butte, wasted of vegetation in an era when copper smelters spewed toxic sulfurous fumes into the atmosphere, are finally recovering. The city, meanwhile, is diversifying its economy to include medical and energy research, education and tourism.

SIGHTS A 90-minute introductory tour of the city on **Old No. 1,** a motorized replica of an open electric trolley, is offered several times daily throughout the summer from the **Butte-Silver Bow Chamber of Commerce**. Admission. The chamber also provides free brochures for a walking tour of the mansions, churches and other buildings of historic Uptown. ~ 2950 Harrison Avenue, Butte; 406-494-5595.

Start a self-guided tour of Butte at the **Berkeley Pit,** 7000 feet wide, more than a mile long and 1800 feet deep. The pit has been filling with ground water since its pumping system was shut down with the mining operation; the chemical content of the resulting body of water is an ecological hell for the Environmental Protection Agency and the mine's owner, the Atlantic Richfield Company (ARCO). A public tunnel leads to a viewing stand with taped narrations, open March through November; a visitors center/gift shop outside the tunnel is open daily in summer. ~ 200 Shields Street; 406-782-8117.

For a more thorough look at Butte's mining history, head west two miles on Park Street to the **World Museum of Mining**. The free 12-acre museum, re-creates a circa-1899 mining camp complete with mine entrances, machinery and a fully furnished, three-square-block village (known as "Hell Roarin' Gulch") where miners and their families lived, shopped and enjoyed various services and entertainments. The museum headquarters building has two floors of exhibits and a gift shop. Closed December to March. ~ At the junction of West Park and Granite streets; 406-723-7211.

From a platform behind the Hell Roarin' Gulch schoolhouse, the **Neversweat and Washoe Railroad** takes passengers on a one-hour guided tour to the defunct Anselmo Mine Yard, Wednesdays through Sundays in summer. Admission. ~ 406-723-8343.

On the nearby campus of the Montana College of Mineral Science & Technology (Montana Tech), the **Mineral Museum** displays more than 1500 mineral specimens, including a 27.5-ounce gold nugget found in the surrounding mountains. A statue of Marcus Daly stands in the middle of Park Street at the entrance to the campus. ~ Next to Main Hall, off West Park Street; 406-496-4414.

Daly's archrival, William A. Clark, is likewise commemorated by the **Copper King Mansion**. His elegant former home—a three-story, 32-room manor in the heart of Uptown Butte—has been preserved, inside and out, as it was in the 1880s. Though in use year-

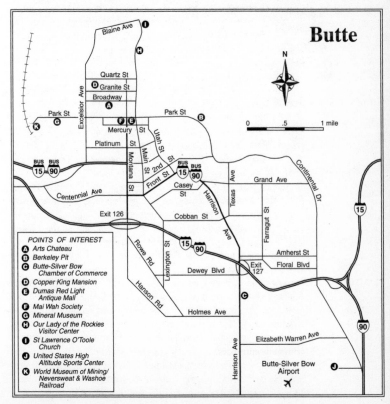

Butte

POINTS OF INTEREST
- **A** Arts Chateau
- **B** Berkeley Pit
- **C** Butte-Silver Bow Chamber of Commerce
- **D** Copper King Mansion
- **E** Dumas Red Light Antique Mall
- **F** Mai Wah Society
- **G** Mineral Museum
- **H** Our Lady of the Rockies Visitor Center
- **I** St Lawrence O'Toole Church
- **J** United States High Altitude Sports Center
- **K** World Museum of Mining/ Neversweat & Washoe Railroad

round as a bed and breakfast, the mansion is open daily for tours from May through September and other times by appointment. Admission. ~ 219 West Granite Street; 406-782-7580.

Two blocks away, another mansion, this one built in 1898 for William Clark's son Charles, has been converted to a heritage museum. The four-story **Arts Chateau**, designed in the style of France's Loire River castles, houses permanent and changing exhibits of regional art and the George Grant collection of 700 handwoven fishing flies. Admission. ~ 321 West Broadway; 406-723-7600.

HIDDEN ▶

High above Butte, overlooking the city from an elevation of 8510 feet on the crest of the Continental Divide, a 90-foot statue of **Our Lady of the Rockies** is said to represent all women "regardless of religion." It was built by volunteers in 1985 and is maintained by a nonprofit organization. Daily summer bus tours begin from an information center and gift shop in the former St. Mary's Church. Admission. ~ 434 North Main Street; 406-782-1221.

The Berkeley Pit, 1800 feet deep, has been filling with ground water since its pumping system was shut down, creating Montana's deepest body of water.

Farther up Main toward the Butte hilltop is the **St. Lawrence O'Toole Church**. The miners' church, built in 1897, features hand-carved altars, some of marble and brass, and 40 frescoes. Open Friday and Sunday. ~ 1308 North Main Street, Walkerville; 406-782-9220.

HIDDEN ▶

Two small museums sit in the heart of the historic district. The **Mai Wah Society** displays artifacts and photographs from Butte's once-bustling community of Chinese miners. Closed October to April. Admission. ~ 17 West Mercury Street; 406-494-5595. The **Dumas Red Light Antique Mall** preserves the last of the city's "Venus Alley" brothels that operated from the late 19th century until 1982. ~ 45 East Mercury Street; 406-782-3808.

On the plains at the southeast edge of Butte is the **United States High Altitude Sports Center**, an Olympic training facility and the site of world-class speed-skating competitions. In the audience you might even run into Butte's best-known native son of the 1960s and 1970s: motorcycle daredevil Evel Knievel. ~ 1 Olympic Way, off Continental Drive; 406-723-7060.

LODGING

HIDDEN ▶

For a taste of Victorian luxury without modern amenities, William A. Clark's **Copper King Mansion** is a real find. Five exquisite bedrooms (two with private baths, the others with shared baths) display the likes of hand-painted fresco ceilings, sycamore and walnut woodwork and other turn-of-the-century touches. A gourmet breakfast is served in a dining room whose cupboards brim with the finest crystal and silver. The mansion is entirely deserving of its listing as a national historic site. ~ 219 West Granite Street; 406-782-7580. MODERATE.

Ghost

Towns

The thing about mining boom towns is, as soon as the ore is worked out of the hills or streams, there's nothing left to hold a town there. Thus it has been throughout the Rocky Mountain foothills of southern Montana, where settlements that thrived with thousands of people in the latter half of the 19th century dwindled to nearly nothing by the early 20th.

A visit to one of these abandoned communities can be a poignant experience. You can almost see the miners carrying their gold dust to the assay office, almost hear the rowdy shouts and raucous music as you stroll by the old saloon.

The two most accessible ghost towns are Bannack and Nevada City, both gold-mining communities dating from the 1860s. They are very different. **Bannack**, a Montana state park, has been left mostly unrestored, except to prevent the ravages of time and nature from taking their course too quickly. **Nevada City**, a privately owned museum, has been fully and carefully restored as it probably appeared in its heyday, right down to the interior furnishings of its 100-or-so buildings.

Hidden treasures await backroad explorers with time and perhaps a four-wheel-drive vehicle.

Elkhorn was an 1880s silver-mining town whose smelter produced as much as $30,000 worth of ore in a single month. Its ruins, some still scarred with bullet holes, contain fine examples of frontier architecture. To get there, take Route 69 seven miles southeast from Boulder; then follow signs east and north another 11 miles. ~ Forest Road 258, south of Helena.

Situated east of Missoula, **Garnet** was home to about 1000 men, women and children after an 1897 gold strike. Four hotels, 13 saloons and a school were among its buildings. A couple of dozen of the town's vacated log structures are preserved today. ~ Exit Route 90 at Bearmouth; follow the frontage road about six miles east; then turn north on steep and narrow Bear Creek Road.

Castle, southeast of White Sulphur Springs, was a silver boom town of the 1880s. Today all that remain are weathered homes and various outbuildings. ~ Take Route 89 south from White Sulphur Springs for 17 miles; follow Route 294 east for 15 miles; turn north and continue eight miles on Forest Road 581.

For an overview of Montana's ghost towns, stop to see the **Ghost Town Hall of Fame** at the Granite County Museum and Cultural Center on the Pintler Scenic Route west of Butte. ~ 135 South Sansome Street, Philipsburg; 406-859-3388. In the Sapphire, Flint Creek and other ranges surrounding Philipsburg are no fewer than 21 ghost towns with names like Granite, Princeton, Red Lion and Southern Cross.

The ten-story **Finlen Hotel and Motor Inn,** with its mansard roof, is a massive presence in the Uptown skyline. Modeled after New York's Astor, it opened in 1924 and was long the favored hotel in this mining city. The Finlen fell on hard times and was turned into senior residential housing but has since undergone renovation: 16 cozy rooms on the tower's second and third floors have been reopened to travelers. Another 34 are in an adjoining two-story motor inn. ~ 100 East Broadway; 406-723-5461, 800-729-5461. BUDGET.

The **Capri Motel,** like the Copper King and Finlen, is in Uptown Butte, within walking distance of many of the city's attractions and better restaurants. This well-kept, two-story lodge has 68 rooms with TVs; a continental breakfast is included. Within the motel are a guest laundry and hot tub. ~ 220 North Wyoming Street; phone/fax 406-723-4391, 800-342-2774. BUDGET.

The **War Bonnet Inn** may be more distant, but it's also more upscale. Kids stay free at this 134-unit motor inn, whose facilities include a full-service restaurant and lounge, a heated indoor pool, a hot tub, sauna and workout room. A park across the street has tennis courts and a running track, and a van provides airport transportation. ~ 2100 Cornell Avenue; 406-494-7800, 800-443-1806, fax 406-494-2875. MODERATE.

Butte's finest is the **Best Western Copper King Park Hotel.** Though its 150 rooms are four miles south of the Uptown historic district, opposite the airport on Route 2, they are spacious and tastefully furnished. There are separate restaurants for fine dining and casual meals. Beneath a two-story atrium roof are a swimming pool, a hot tub, a sauna and an exercise room. Adjoining is the CopperDome, a 24,000-square-foot facility beneath an inflated roof used for indoor tennis, major concerts, trade shows and conferences. ~ 4655 Harrison Avenue; 406-494-6666, 800-332-8600, fax 406-494-3274. MODERATE TO DELUXE.

✔ CHECK THESE OUT—UNIQUE DINING

- *Budget:* Feast on superb biscuits and gravy at the 1863 **Star Bakery,** Montana's oldest restaurant extant. *page 162*
- *Budget to moderate:* Enjoy dessert at Helena's **Windbag Saloon.** (As recently as the 1970s, this building was a bordello.) *page 137*
- *Moderate to deluxe:* Return to gold-rush days at Helena's **Stonehouse Restaurant,** where servers dress in 19th-century outfits. *page 136*
- *Deluxe:* Dine on elegant Continental-style dishes at the **Uptown Café** in Butte. *page 151*

Budget: under $8   Moderate: $8–$16   Deluxe: $16–$24   Ultra-deluxe: over $24

DINING

Creative Continental dining in an old mining town? That's what you get at the **Uptown Café**. There's a heavy emphasis on seafood (from *cioppino* to coquilles Saint-Jacques) at this elegant gallery-style eatery, but look for chicken, beef, veal and pasta dishes as well. The wine list is small but enlightened. Closed Sunday; no lunch Saturday, and no dinner Monday. ~ 47 East Broadway; 406-723-4735. DELUXE.

At the **Metals Banque Restaurant**, you can actually eat in the vault of a restored bank tower. In an atmosphere of Italian marble, African mahogany and solid copper window frames, choose from steak, seafood or Mexican specialties. Full bar and microbrews. ~ 8 West Park Street; 406-723-6160. BUDGET TO MODERATE.

◄ *HIDDEN*

If the **Pekin Noodle Parlor** isn't Butte's oldest restaurant, it's close. Established a century ago in what was then a bustling China-town, it remains a "hole in the wall." Guests are served heaping helpings of chow mein, chop suey and egg foo yung. ~ 117 South Main Street; 406-782-2217. BUDGET.

◄ *HIDDEN*

Just around the corner is a veritable Butte institution, **Pork Chop John's**. Though John's has since extended its little empire to Billings and Bozeman, this tiny chop shop—a streetside takeout window and a half-dozen counter stools inside—is the original. (There's another outlet at 2400 Harrison Avenue.) ~ 18 West Mercury Street; 406-782-0812. BUDGET.

On the south side of town is the **Red Rooster Supper Club**, which serves elegant five-course dinners of steak, chicken or seafood. In business since 1930—people who ate here as children now bring their grandchildren—it has an adjoining casino with keno and poker. ~ 3636 Harrison Avenue; 406-494-4974. MODERATE.

Four miles further south—indeed, at the edge of town—is **Lydia's Supper Club**, which has a distinctly Italian flavor. Antipasto appetizers precede, and pasta accompanies, each entrée; cappuccinos follow. Lydia's is fully licensed, but a smoke-free policy helps preserve the restaurant's beautiful collection of antique stained-glass windows, illumined by candlelight. ~ 4915 Harrison Avenue; 406-494-2000. MODERATE.

SHOPPING

Right in the Copper City itself, the **Butte Copper Co.** boasts that it has "anything and everything in copper." Its stock includes copper jewelry, other semiprecious metals and gems, and various less pricey souvenirs. ~ 3015 Harrison Avenue; 406-494-2070.

Art lovers are well served at the gift shop and sales gallery at the **Arts Chateau**. Paintings, prints, pottery, jewelry, crafts and books are among the items available for purchase. ~ 321 West Broadway; 406-723-7600.

Butte's premier bookstore is **Books and Books**, which offers an extensive selection of current and classic literature and occasional appearances by authors. ~ 205 West Park Street; 406-782-9520.

Whitehead's Cutlery Store is worth a visit if only to view its vast collection of weaponry. This is the place to buy home and commercial cutlery, pocket and hunting knives. ~ 73 East Park Street; 406-723-9188.

Butte Plaza is the region's only full-size shopping mall, with some 30 stores and a six-plex cinema. ~ 3100 Harrison Avenue; 406-494-3362.

NIGHTLIFE   The focus of the arts in Butte, and the home of the Butte-Silver Bow Arts Foundation, is the striking **Arts Chateau**. In addition to its permanent art collection, the Chateau sponsors year-round performances by visiting chamber orchestras and ballet troupes; on summer Wednesdays, from mid-June to mid-August, it stages its own marionette theater for children and adults alike in the Arts Chateau ballroom. Admission. ~ 321 West Broadway; 406-723-7600.

Community theater and music have rallied around **Broadway 215**, which organizes a year-round schedule of events. ~ 215 West Broadway; 406-782-3207. The **Troupe du Jour** stage company has a strong local following. ~ 406-723-8232.

At this writing, visiting classical artists typically perform at the **Butte Civic Center**. ~ 1340 Harrison Avenue; 406-723-8262. Restoration of the old Fox Theater is nearing completion, at which point the **Butte Center for the Performing Arts** will take over the magnificent art deco theater in the heart of Uptown Butte. ~ 315 West Park Street.

Popular concert entertainers on tour often appear at south Butte's **CopperDome**. ~ 4655 Harrison Avenue; 406-494-6666.

In the adjoining Best Western Copper King Inn, **Jox** has established itself as the city's most upscale nightclub with live rock bands on weekends, and comedy nights midweek. Occasional cover. ~ 4655 Harrison Avenue; 406-494-1616.

EVEL KNIEVEL

Perhaps Butte's most famous celebrated native son of the 1960s and 1970s was Evel Knievel, a motorcycle daredevil who leaped to international fame and faded from view nearly as quickly. One of his most famous stunts was an attempted jump of the Snake River Canyon at Twin Falls, Idaho, on a rocket-powered cycle in 1974. Knievel was traveling up a launch ramp at 350 miles per hour when his safety parachute flew open, propelling him upward 1000 feet before he drifted downward almost 1500 feet to the canyon floor. He suffered only facial cuts and bruises.

Bands also perform at the **Cavalier Lounge**. ~ Finlen Hotel, 100 East Broadway; 406-723-5171. Check out the live performances at the **Silver Dollar Saloon**, which is discreetly frequented by gays and lesbians. ~ 133 South Main Street; 406-782-7367. For atmosphere and colorful drinking companionship, visit **Charlie's New Deal Bar**. ~ 333 South Arizona Street; 406-723-9968. There's also the **M & M Bar**. ~ 9 North Main Street; 406-723-7612. Or try the **Helsinki Bar & Steam Bath**, one of two surviving businesses left over from Butte's once-thriving Finntown. ~ 402 East Broadway; 406-723-9004.

Butte's largest casino, open 24 hours daily, is the **Gold Rush Casino**. It boasts casino machines, live poker and keno games. ~ 22 West Galena Street; 406-723-3211.

DEERLODGE NATIONAL FOREST Straddling the Continental Divide and eight separate mountain ranges, this 1.2-million-acre national forest surrounds Butte on all sides. Ranging over 10,000-foot peaks and rolling grasslands, the forest includes 140 lakes, 630 miles of trails and the Discovery Basin ski area. The Sheepshead Mountain Recreation Area, on Maney Lake 19 miles north of Butte via Route 15 and Forest Road 442, has a campground, picnic area, fishing pier and sports fields designed specifically for the disabled. Facilities include picnic areas and restrooms; restaurants and groceries are in Butte and many other towns. ~ Forest areas can be reached from interstate freeway exits in all directions from Butte, as well as Route 2 (Harrison Avenue South) through Pipestone Pass and Route 1 (the Pintler Scenic Route) to Georgetown Lake; 406-496-3400.

▲ There are 266 RV/tent sites plus 80 for tents only, none with hookups, at 22 campgrounds; no charge to $6 per night; 14-day maximum stay. The national forest also has four recreational cabins that can be reserved at $15 to $20 a night.

PARKS

Southwest of Butte, Route 43 is the principal thoroughfare to the remote, often-snowbound Big Hole Valley. Best known for its hay-fattened cattle, the Big Hole is rarely visited except by trout fishermen, big-game hunters and travelers following the most direct route between Boise and Butte.

▼▼▼▼▼▼▼▼▼▼▼▼
Big Hole Valley

The valley is reached by traveling on Route 15 west and south from Butte some 25 miles to the town of Divide. A series of country roads follow the lower Big Horn some 50 miles around McCartney Mountain to its confluence with the Jefferson River near Twin Bridges; for tourists, the main point of interest on this route is the **Humbug Spires Primitive Area**, reached from a freeway interchange about three miles south of Divide. The Humbug Spires—

SIGHTS

ancient, 600-foot granite towers—are much loved by rock climbers. ~ Moose Creek Road, Divide; 406-494-5059.

Route 43 begins at Divide and proceeds westerly 77 miles to its junction with Route 93 at Lost Trail Pass on the Idaho border. En route, the highway transits but two villages: **Wise River** (12 miles from Divide), junction point of the Pioneer Mountains Scenic Byway through Beaverhead National Forest, and **Wisdom** (51 miles from Divide), the Big Hole Valley's largest community with a whopping 180 citizens.

The **Pioneer Mountains Scenic Byway** (Forest Road 484) runs 40 miles south from Wise River to Route 278 west of Dillon. Most of the road (gravel for all but its last 12 miles) is open for car travel only from June or July to October, as snow comes early and stays late. (In winter, the route is open to snowmobiles.) But during the peak summer season, it provides access to outstanding landscapes and outdoor recreational activities.

There are several attractions along the Pioneer Mountains Scenic Byway. Visitors may dig for quartz, garnets and amethysts at **Crystal Park**. ~ Route 484, Polaris; 406-683-3900. An abandoned narrow-gauge railroad can still be seen in the ghost town of **Coolidge**, a 1920s silver-mining community. ~ Forest Road 2465. Also in the area are the **Canyon Creek Charcoal Kilns**, which demonstrate how dependent miners were upon wood to fuel their smelters and steam engines, and prehistoric Indian sites and Depression-era campgrounds built by the Civilian Conservation Corps. ~ Forest Road 7401. On the paved route, open year-round, are two resorts. **Elk Horn Hot Springs** offers a mineral pool, restaurant and rustic lodge. ~ Route 484, Polaris; 406-834-3434. **Maverick Mountain** is a popular local ski resort. ~ Route 484, Polaris; 406-834-3454.

At **Wisdom**, Route 43 meets Route 278, which leaves you two options. Turn west toward Idaho (it's just 26 miles to Lost Trail Pass, at the head of the Bitterroot Valley south of Missoula), or continue south and east across Big Hole Pass to Dillon, 65 miles east.

If you choose the westbound route, you're 11 miles from **Big Hole National Battlefield**, just beneath 7264-foot Chief Joseph Pass. The pass was named for the Nez Perce Indian leader who in 1877 led his people on an ill-fated exodus from their tribal lands in northeastern Oregon and central Idaho. The party of about 800 was camped at what is now the national battlefield site when U.S. cavalrymen attacked before dawn on August 9. The tribe fought back for the next 24 hours before withdrawing and continuing their long march. But Nez Perce casualties were high and their spirit was broken. Less than two months later—at Bear's Paw, Montana, near Chinook—they surrendered and were either forced onto a reservation or exiled, as in the case of Chief Joseph.

The tragedy of the Nez Perce is related in displays and a video program at the national battlefield's visitors center and museum. Several trails begin at a picnic area and wind through the battle-ground, which is one of Montana's three units of the Nez Perce National Historical Park. Admission in summer. ~ Route 43, Wisdom; 406-689-3155.

Proceed south on Route 278 toward the headwaters of the Big Hole River and you'll pass through **Jackson**, another tiny village, and cross 7360-foot Big Hole Pass. A junction on your left turns north toward Polaris and Wise River (the Pioneer Mountains Scenic Byway); it's 30 miles more from here to Dillon.

LODGING

The 70-year-old **Elk Horn Hot Springs Lodge** offers eight lodge rooms and nine log cabins in very rustic environs. The Elk Horn has two outdoor hot-spring pools, a pair of saunas heated by the springs, and a restaurant; there are no individual phones here, but the lodge has a pay phone! ~ P.O. Box 514, Polaris, MT 59746; 406-834-3434. BUDGET.

The **Sundance Lodge** comprises a handful of modern riverside cabins, some of them with fireplaces, one with cooking facilities. There's also a home-cooking restaurant, and despite temperatures that are sometimes the coldest in the United States, it's open year-round. ~ Route 43, Wise River; 406-689-3611. BUDGET.

DINING

There are plenty of small cafés in the Big Hole Valley. The **Wise River Club** serves three meals a day every day, with locally grown steaks its specialty. ~ Route 43, Wise River; 406-832-3258. BUD-GET. **Fetty's Bar & Cafe** offers breakfast all day long for late risers. ~ Route 43, Wisdom; 406-689-3260. BUDGET. **Rose's Cantina** serves hearty enchiladas in a most unlikely location. ~ Route 278, Jackson; 406-834-3100. BUDGET.

PARKS

HUMBUG SPIRES PRIMITIVE AREA White granite outcrop-pings, 70 million years old, rise like steeples 600 feet into the sky at this 8000-acre Bureau of Land Management preserve. Backpackers and rock climbers are drawn to the scenic location. Groceries are in Divide, six miles northwest, and restaurants are in Butte and Dillon. ~ Take Route 15 south from Butte 28 miles or north from Dillon 37 miles to Exit 99 at Moose Creek; then drive three miles northeast on Moose Creek Road to the Humbug Spires trailhead; 406-494-5059.

▲ Primitive only at Humbug Spires. There are 20 RV/tent sites, none with hookups, at the BLM's Divide Bridge campground, six miles west off Route 15 Exit 99; $4 per night; 14-day maximum stay.

BIG HOLE NATIONAL BATTLEFIELD One of three Montana parcels of the widespread Nez Perce National Historical

Park, the Big Hole battlefield was the site of an August 1877 fray between Chief Joseph's Nez Perce and the U.S. cavalry. Facilities include picnic areas, restrooms and a visitors center, all wheelchair accessible. Restaurants and groceries are in Wisdom. ~ On Route 43, 11 miles west of Wisdom; 406-689-3155.

▼▼▼▼▼▼▼▼▼▼▼▼▼
Dillon & the Red Rock River Valley

The southernmost reach of Montana is focused around Dillon, an old Union Pacific railroad town of 4000 people that has become a center for ranching and summer recreation. An hour's drive south of Butte and a similar distance north of the Idaho border on Route 15, Dillon is located on the Beaverhead River, a short drive from Montana's most authentic ghost town, Bannack, and not far from the laid-back scenery of the Red Rock River Valley.

SIGHTS

The **Dillon Visitors Information Center**, housed in an old train depot, offers a brochure for a walking tour of the Dillon's historic late-19th-century downtown. ~ 125 South Montana Street, Dillon; 406-683-5511. The most intriguing building is the **Beaverhead County Courthouse**, whose four-faced Seth Thomas clock looks in all directions from a 60-foot tower. ~ Pacific and Bannock streets, Dillon; 406-683-2383.

Next door to the visitors center is the **Beaverhead County Museum**, a log building that boasts an impressive and well-organized collection of artifacts and memorabilia from American Indian (mainly Shoshone) and pioneer history. A quarter-mile-long boardwalk leads past a homesteader's cabin and Dillon's first flush toilet (in an outhouse, of course). ~ 15 South Montana Street, Dillon; 406-683-5027.

Western Montana College has a Victorian main hall built in 1896. ~ 710 South Atlantic Street; 406-683-7011. Don't miss the campus art gallery/museum, featuring the Seidensticker Wildlife Collection of trophy game from Africa, Asia and North America. Closed Saturday and Sunday. ~ 406-683-7126.

No visit to Dillon would be complete without a side trip to **Bannack State Park**, 25 miles west via Route 278. This is an 1860s ghost town at its authentic best: preserved but mostly unrestored, except to ward off Mother Nature and Father Time. Its 60-odd hand-fashioned buildings of rough-hewn logs and brick masonry contain little more than the memories and shattered dreams of their former owners.

The town was founded in 1862 on Grasshopper Creek, site of the first major gold strike in the future Montana. Bannack was briefly the territory's first capital (before Virginia City) and claimed its first school, first hotel and first jail.

As Bannack grew to 3000, so did its reputation for lawlessness. But one of the West's most remarkable chapters was written here and in Virginia City by a league of law-abiding vigilantes in 1864. When the vigilantes realized that their sheriff, Henry Plummer, was secretly the leader of a gang of murderous "road agents" known as The Innocents, they hunted the gang down, administered hasty trials and hung them on gallows built by Plummer himself.

> The Red Rock Lakes National Wildlife Refuge winter populations of trumpeter swans may reach as high as 1500.

The gallows can still be seen on a walking tour of Bannack, as well as the imposing Meade Hotel and courthouse, Skinner's Saloon, the Methodist church, the Masonic temple, Bachelor's Row and other sites. Rings for leg irons remain in the floor of the Bannack jail. Guided tours are offered three times daily, on weekends and holidays. Closed September through May. Admission. ~ 4200 Bannack Road, Bannack; 406-834-3413.

From Bannack, you can return directly to Dillon or loop back via the **Clark Canyon Recreation Area.** Clark Canyon Reservoir, which attracts anglers from miles around for its excellent trout fishing, was formed by the damming of the Red Rock River and Horse Prairie Creek. Traces of Lewis and Clark's Camp Fortunate can be found on its northwest shore. Dillon is 20 miles north of the dam. ~ Route 15 and 324; 406-684-6573.

South of Clark Canyon, Route 15 follows the gently rising Red Rock River Valley through the communities of **Dell** and **Lima.** Both are old railroad towns with a number of historic buildings.

At Monida, on the Idaho border, turn east onto Centennial Valley Road for 28 miles to reach the remote **Red Rock Lakes National Wildlife Refuge.** Established in 1935 to protect nesting grounds of the rare trumpeter swan, it is also home to sandhill cranes, great blue herons and other striking waterfowl, as well as raptors, moose, elk and antelope. Today it is estimated that between 400 and 500 swans make this Montana-Idaho-Wyoming border area their home. ~ Centennial Valley Road, Lakeview; 406-276-3536.

◄ HIDDEN

The **Metlen Hotel** may be on "the other side of the tracks," and it has definitely seen better days, but it's a magnet for the true low-fare traveler. Built in 1897, this three-story white elephant has survived nearly a century as a residential hotel. Most of the 20-some rooms share down-the-hall bathrooms; a handful of rooms have private baths but minimal furnishings. ~ 5 South Railroad Avenue, Dillon; 406-683-2335. BUDGET.

LODGING

The **Sundowner Motel** is a friendly property at the edge of downtown Dillon with 32 spacious rooms, queen-size beds, a swimming pool and a playground. Refrigerators are available by request. ~ 500 North Montana Street, Dillon; 406-683-2375, 800-524-9746. BUDGET.

The most upscale property in Beaverhead County is the **Best Western Paradise Inn,** located at Dillon's north end at Route 15 Exit 63. The two-story motor inn has 65 rooms with queen-size beds and air-conditioning. A restaurant serves three meals daily, and there's a lounge and casino, an indoor swimming pool, a whirlpool and an exercise room. ~ 650 North Montana Street, Dillon; 406-683-4214, 800-528-1234, fax 406-683-4216. MODERATE.

Whooping crane sightings are practically guaranteed at the **Lakeview Guest Ranch,** adjacent to the Red Rock Lakes. You'll get everything here from horsemanship and professional outfitters schools to photography workshops and cross-country skiing. Facilities are rustic but the setting makes up for any shortcoming. (In winter, contact the ranch owners at 2905 Harrison Avenue, Butte; 406-494-2585.) ~ Monida Star Route, Lima; 406-276-3300 (summer), and 406-494-2585 (winter). MODERATE.

DINING

Dillon was never a mining town per se, but **The Mine Shaft** has captured a smidgen of that atmosphere, with antique mining equipment displayed on rough-hewn walls in the basement of a historic building opposite the Beaverhead County Museum. Steaks and chicken are popular at lunch and dinner. ~ 26 South Montana Street, Dillon; 406-683-6611. MODERATE.

Located opposite Western Montana College is the **Crosswinds Restaurant.** A family-style eatery open from early till late, it serves breakfast anytime, offers an expansive salad bar and has special menus for the kids. ~ 1008 South Atlantic Street, Dillon; 406-683-6370. BUDGET TO MODERATE.

For breakfast and lunch, a popular choice is **Anna's Oven.** Open only until 4 p.m., this café across the street from the Dillon Visitors Center specializes in gourmet openers as well as baked goods and deli-style sandwiches. ~ 120 Montana Street, Dillon; 406-683-5766. BUDGET.

Twenty miles south of Dillon near Clark Canyon Reservoir is the **Buffalo Lodge.** The rural getaway, popular among hunters and fishermen, is known locally for its steaks and burgers. ~ 19975 Route 15 South, Dillon; 406-683-5535. BUDGET TO MODERATE.

SHOPPING

The **Southwest Montana Artists Gallery** is a cooperative run by regional artisans. Located on the second floor of the city hall building, it presents paintings, sculptures and crafts in a range of artistic media. ~ 125 North Idaho Street, Dillon; 406-683-4245.

NIGHTLIFE

The **Short Line Players/Wapiti Theatre** offers dinner-theater performances ranging from comedy to drama on select weekend nights between Memorial Day and mid-September at the Dillon Elks Lodge. ~ 27 East Center Street, Dillon; 406-683-6402. The

Old Depot Theatre presents vaudeville nightly except Mondays at the old Union Pacific Depot. ~ 125 South Montana Street, Dillon; 406-683-5511.

BEAVERHEAD NATIONAL FOREST

Cloaking 2.1 million acres of southwestern Montana from the Bitterroots to the Madison Range, the Beaverhead forest has more than 1500 miles of hiking trails and well over 100 lakes. It is readily explored on the Pioneer Mountains National Scenic Byway and on the Gravelly Range Road, which climbs to elevations of nearly 10,000 feet south of Virginia City. There are picnic areas and restrooms; restaurants and groceries are in Dillon and many smaller towns. ~ Routes 43 (through the Big Hole Valley), 278 (Dillon to Wisdom) and 287 (through Virginia City), as well as the Pioneer Mountains and Gravelly Range roads, provide the most direct access; 406-683-3900.

▲ There are 197 RV/tent sites plus 94 for tents only, none with hookups, at 33 campgrounds; no charge to $6 per night; 14-day maximum stay. Within the forest are 12 recreational cabins, which can be reserved for $15 to $20 per night.

BANNACK STATE PARK

This true ghost town preserves the main street and more than 60 buildings of Montana's first territorial capital. Picnic areas, restrooms and a visitors center round out the amenities. Restaurants and groceries are in Dillon. Day-use fee, $3. ~ Take Route 278 west from Dillon 21 miles; then turn south on Route 5 and continue for four miles to Bannack Road; 406-834-3413.

▲ There are 30 RV/tent sites, none with hookups; $7 to $8 per night May to September, $7 per night October to April; 14-day maximum stay.

CLARK CANYON RECREATION AREA

Waterskiing and fishing (in winter, ice fishing) are the most popular pursuits on 6600-acre Clark Canyon Reservoir. A full marina, with an RV park and numerous campgrounds, makes this area readily accessible. Facilities include picnic areas, restrooms and a marina. Groceries are available at the marina shop, and there are restaurants in Dillon. ~ Located 20 miles south of Dillon on Routes 15 and 324; 406-683-6472.

▲ Nine campgrounds, most without designated sites, none with hookups, no charge; 38 sites with hookups at Beaverhead Marina and RV Park (406-683-5556) with fees ranging $8 to $15 per night.

RED ROCK LAKES NATIONAL WILDLIFE REFUGE

◄ HIDDEN

Framed on two sides by the Continental Divide, this remote refuge is a crucial nesting area for the rare trumpeter swan. Located more than 15 miles in any direction from paved roads, it is also ideal haven for waterfowl, songbirds, raptors, moose, elk and antelope. About three-quarters of the preserve's 43,500 acres is designated wilderness. You'll find restrooms here; restaurants and groceries are in Lima and West Yellowstone. ~ From Dillon, take Route 15 south 63 miles to Monida on the Idaho state border; then turn east for 20 miles on gravel Centennial Valley Road (formerly Red Rock Pass Road); 406-276-3536.

▲ Primitive only.

▼▼▼▼▼▼▼▼▼▼▼
Alder Gulch

The discovery of the richest deposit of placer gold on earth took place in the valley of a tiny creek 70 road miles southeast of Butte. The Alder Gulch mining district yielded some $130 million in gold nuggets, gold flakes and gold dust in the decades that followed the original strike in 1863. After the gold ran out, Virginia City persisted, first as Montana's territorial capital, today as the tourism-oriented seat of Madison County. Nearly 100 buildings in nearby Nevada City have been completely restored, while the roads surrounding Alder Gulch offer myriad reminders of the boom era.

The area is an almost essential detour on the road from Butte to Bozeman. Follow Butte's Harrison Avenue south past the airport, where it becomes Route 2 and climbs across the Continental Divide at 6453-foot Pipestone Pass. Turn south again on Route 41 and continue to Twin Bridges, a small town on the Jefferson River 42 miles from Butte; then bear left (southeast) on Route 287.

SIGHTS

On the banks of the Ruby River halfway between Twin Bridges and Nevada City, look for a large brown building with a historical marker sign nearby. **Robber's Roost** was a roadhouse (read *saloon-bordello*) where villains and ne'er-do-wells gathered in the 1860s and 1870s when stagecoaches that ran between Virginia City and Bannack were subject to regular holdups. ~ 2841 Route 287, Sheridan; 406-842-5936.

Nevada City, 29 miles from Twin Bridges, and Virginia City, little more than another mile up Alder Gulch, grew up around the 1863 gold strike in the Tobacco Root Mountains. When President Abraham Lincoln created the Montana Territory the following year, Virginia City was chosen as its capital and remained so until Helena wrested that status away in 1875. But long after other mining towns were abandoned, Alder Gulch continued to produce gold.

By World War II, though, Nevada City was a ghost town and Virginia City was getting decidedly long in the tooth. A team of historic preservationists headed by Charles and Sue Bovey restored and furnished original buildings wherever possible; in the case of

Nevada City, they moved several complete structures in from other areas.

Today, **Nevada City** has the authentic flavor of an early-day mining camp. Officially known as the **Nevada City Museum**, it consists of five streets with nearly 100 buildings, including homes, shops and schoolhouses. There's also a cozy hotel, cabins and a restaurant. Mock gunfights occur on the streets of the town, hearkening back to an era when desperadoes used real bullets. Not surprisingly, the town is also a favorite of movie companies; such films as *Little Big Man* and *Return to Lonesome Dove* were shot here. Closed from October to April. Admission. ~ Route 287; 406-843-5377.

The Nevada City music hall contains a remarkable collection of machines that produce music ranging from the harmonic to the cacophonic.

Across the highway from the open-air museum, the **Alder Gulch River of Gold** allows visitors to try their hands at gold panning, rocking and sluicing. The business also has a gift shop and mining museum, including a historic dredge. Admission. ~ Route 287, Nevada City; 406-843-5526.

While Nevada City is a re-creation, **Virginia City**, a national historic landmark district, remains very much alive. Every building along the three-block stretch of Wallace Street west of Broadway is of original construction. No other main street in the American West can make that claim.

Walking-tour brochures are available from numerous merchants as well as the **Virginia City Area Chamber of Commerce**. ~ 302 West Wallace Street, Virginia City; 406-843-5377. Wallace Street is the main drag; in addition to several restaurants and numerous fine shops worth a browse, its buildings of special note include the 1863 **Montana Post** print shop, whose old typesetting equipment is a reminder that the territory's first newspaper was printed here; **Ranks Drug** (1865), Montana's oldest continuously operating business; **Stonewall Hall** and **Content Corner** (both 1864), once original territorial government buildings; the **E. L. Smith General Store** (1863); and the **Sauebier Blacksmith Shop** (1863).

Pioneer artifacts and historical photographs and documents are displayed at the **Thompson-Hickman Memorial Museum**. ~ 218 East Wallace Street, Virginia City; 406-843-5346. Other events of historical significance are recorded at the **Madison County Museum**. ~ 219 West Wallace Street, Virginia City; 406-843-5321. Atmospheric **Boot Hill Cemetery** is just two blocks north of Wallace Street. ~ Jackson and Jefferson streets, Virginia City.

The **Alder Gulch Shortline** narrow-gauge railroad, located at West Wallace and Main streets in Virginia City, runs all summer long between the 1901 Northern Pacific Depot at Virginia City's west end and the **Steam Railroad Museum** (Route 287), lodged in restored railcars in Nevada City and displaying outstanding steam cars of the time. Admission. ~ 406-843-5377.

To proceed to Bozeman after leaving Virginia City, continue 13 miles east to Ennis, on the Madison River. Take Route 287 north 16 miles to Norris; then turn east on Route 84 for the final 38 miles into Bozeman.

LODGING

A variety of lodgings, all with the rustic flavor of a 19th-century mining camp, are available in the Alder Gulch area. When you book with the **Fairweather Inn,** you can opt for Victorian hotel rooms with private or shared baths, upscale suites with period antiques or 125-year-old cabins (Virginia City's Daylight Village, Nevada City's Miners' Cabins) whose interiors have been restored but whose exteriors have hardly been touched. ~ 305 West Wallace Street, Virginia City; 406-843-5377, 800-648-7588, fax 406-843-5377. BUDGET.

An alternative is the **Virginia City Country Inn,** a pleasant bed-and-breakfast establishment just a block south and uphill from the highway through town. A quaint wood-frame Victorian house built in 1879, it has five spacious bedrooms with antique furnishings and a separate efficiency cabin. A full breakfast is served in the dining room, and guests can relax on three porches, in the TV room or beside a fireplace. Bathrooms are shared. ~ 115 Idaho Street, Virginia City; 406-843-5515. MODERATE.

DINING

En route to Alder Gulch, the family-oriented **Blue Anchor Restaurant** offers three meals a day, seven days a week. Lunch and dinner specials frequently include Cajun-style barbecues. ~ 102 North Main Street, Twin Bridges; 406-684-5655. BUDGET TO MODERATE.

The **Star Bakery** boasts "the best biscuits and gravy in town." Built in 1863 and considered to be the oldest surviving eating establishment in Montana, it's open for breakfast and lunch. ~ Route 287, Nevada City; 406-843-5377. BUDGET.

Virginia City's **Bale of Hay Saloon** was a grocery during the town's boom years, but it was restored as this saloon in 1945. Always rustic and often lively, with live music and antique music machines, it has summer patio dining and a mesquite grill to which area fishermen often bring their fresh catches. ~ 330 West Wallace Street, Virginia City; 406-843-5510. BUDGET TO MODERATE.

SHOPPING

There are plenty of souvenir shops in the restored mining towns of Alder Gulch, but the **Vigilante Gift Shop** may be the biggest and friendliest of the bunch. ~ 115 West Wallace Street, Virginia City; 406-843-5345.

NIGHTLIFE

From June to mid-September, the **Virginia City Players**—Montana's oldest summer-stock troupe—act out 19th-century melodramas nightly except Mondays at the Virginia City Opera House. ~ 350 West Wallace Street, Virginia City; 406-843-5377. The **Brewery Players** offer cabaret-style follies every night but Tuesday at the Gilbert Brewery. ~ Hamilton and Jefferson streets, Virginia City; 406-843-5377.

Fishing is not just a sport in Montana. To many, it's a religion.

Outdoor Adventures

Cold-water species such as trout, whitefish and arctic grayling thrive in the high-elevation streams and lakes on either side of the Continental Divide in southern Montana. In nationally famous streams like the Big Hole and Beaverhead, anglers cast for three species of trout—brook, brown and rainbow— as well as mountain whitefish. Many rivers also have the rarer cutthroat trout; a few may have bull trout. Georgetown Lake, west of Anaconda, offers kokanee salmon. A few high-elevation lakes, such as Holter, have walleye and yellow perch, but these are mainly low-elevation species.

FISHING

For fishing tackle or information on guided expeditions, try **Fran Johnson's Sport Shop**. ~ 1957 Harrison Avenue, Butte; 406-782-3322. In Dillon, contact **Fishing Headquarters**. ~ 610 North Montana Street, Dillon; 406-683-6660. Or try **Montana Troutfitters Orvis Shop**. ~ 1716 West Main Street, Bozeman; 406-587-4707. One regional flyfishing specialist is **Fish-On Fly & Tackle**. ~ 3346 Harrison Avenue, Butte; 406-494-4218. For more information, contact the **Montana Department of Fish, Wildlife & Parks**. ~ 1420 East 6th Avenue, Helena; 406-444-2535.

Because southwest Montana is mainly a high plateau on the eastern flank of the Bitterroot Range, its rivers don't offer the same level of whitewater rapids as some in other parts of the state. But flatwater paddlers, especially canoeists, appreciate the tranquility and wildlife-watching opportunities of the region. The Big Hole River (from Wisdom to Wise River) and Jefferson River (from Twin Bridges to Three Forks), as well as the remote Red Rock Lakes, are among the most appealing stretches.

RIVER RUNNING

For guided river trips, contact **Pioneer Outfitters**. ~ Alder Creek Ranch, Wise River; 406-832-3128. You may also contact **Alder Gulch Outfitters**. ~ 215 West Wallace Street, Virginia City; 406-843-5442. Rafts and other river equipment are available for renting from **Montana Outdoor Sports**. ~ 708 North Main Street, Helena; 406-443-4119.

HELENA AREA   **Great Divide**, 22 miles northwest of Helena off Route 279, is a midsize day area with 50 runs and a 1520-foot vertical drop from the rim of the Continental Divide. Facilities include three chairlifts and a surface tow. Cross-country and snowmobile

DOWNHILL SKIING

trails also extend from the base area into Helena National Forest. ~ Marysville Road, Marysville; 406-449-3746.

BUTTE AREA For sheer scenic beauty, it's hard to top **Discovery Basin**. Looking across Georgetown Lake toward the Anaconda Range, 20 miles west of Anaconda and 45 miles from Butte, it has three chairlifts and two surface tows running from just below the summit of 8187-foot Rumsey Mountain. There are 30 runs with a 1300-foot vertical. ~ Forest Road 65, Georgetown; 406-563-2184.

DILLON AREA **Maverick Mountain** is among the most isolated of Montana's ski areas. Located in Beaverhead National Forest near Elk Horn Hot Springs on the Pioneer Mountains National Scenic Byway, 35 miles west of Dillon and about 100 miles southwest of Butte, it appeals to committed skiers with 15 trails, averaging more than a mile in length, and a 2120-foot vertical drop. There's one chairlift; a surface tow serves a beginner's bowl. ~ Route 484, Polaris; 406-834-3454.

Ski Rentals Many stores throughout the region offer equipment rentals and information. **The Outdoorsman** offers both downhill and cross-country rentals. ~ 2700 Harrison Avenue, Butte; 406-494-7700. A shop specializing in cross-country equipment is **Montana Outdoor Sports**. ~ 708 North Main Street, Helena; 406-443-4119. In Butte, contact **Pipestone Mountaineering**. ~ 829 South Montana Street, Butte; 406-782-4994.

CROSS-COUNTRY SKIING West of Butte, the **Mt. Haggin Nordic Ski Area**, created by the Mile High Nordic Ski Club, offers groomed trails at the foot of the Anaconda Range; it operates by donation and volunteer energy. ~ Route 274, Anaconda; 406-782-0316.

For information on renting equipment, see the ski-rental section in "Downhill Skiing" above.

✦✦✦

✔ CHECK THESE OUT—UNIQUE OUTDOOR ADVENTURES

- Cast a fishing line for landlocked kokanee salmon at Georgetown Lake, west of Anaconda. *page 163*
- Challenge wild elk on the 649-yard fifth hole, perhaps the toughest golf in Montana, at the Fairmont Hot Springs Resort. *page 165*
- Play tennis within Butte's CopperDome Racquet Club and keep warm even if outside temperatures are subzero. *page 165*
- Get a bird's-eye perspective on the Montana State Capitol when you hike one of seven trails to the top of Mount Helena. *page 166*

Public courses in southwest Montana include **Bill Roberts Munici-pal Golf Course.** ~ Benton and Cole avenues, Helena; 406-442-2191. Practice your golf swing at **Deer Lodge Golf Club.** ~ Deer Lodge; 406-846-1625. In Dillon, play at **Beaverhead Golf Club.** ~ 1200 Route 41, Dillon; 406-683-9933. In addition, Anaconda's new Jack Nicklaus-signature course is scheduled to open by June 1997.

Wild elk can be a hazard when they graze on the greens at **Fairmont Hot Springs Resort,** an 18-hole, par-72 public course. The 649-yard fifth hole of this course is regarded as one of the most challenging in the state. ~ 1500 Fairmont Road, Gregson; 406-797-3241.

Perhaps the most intriguing place to charge a Montana net is within **The CopperDome Racquet Club.** The inflated Copper-Dome is attached to the Best Western Copper King Inn opposite the Butte airport, but guest fees are waived for first visits by guests of *any* Butte hotel, not just the Copper King. Reservations are accepted daily; rentals are also available. ~ 4655 Harrison Avenue, Butte; 406-494-6666.

Elsewhere, city parks and recreation offices have exhaustive listings of municipal courts. In Helena, call 406-447-8463.

Horses go with Montana like salsa with nachos, like Bogie with Bacall, like dogma with religion. It's hard to imagine having one without the other.

Riding options are as diverse as the stables, ranches and out-fitters that offer them. Rides may be available by the hour or the day, as breakfast trips at sunrise or dinner steak grills around a campfire.

For daytrippers, **Peterson's Fairmont Corral,** located a mile south of the Fairmont Hot Springs resort outside of Butte, empha-sizes guided breakfast and dinner trail trips; riders can also rent horses for backcountry expeditions. ~ Star Route East, Anaconda; 406-797-3377. **Rush's Lakeview Guest Ranch** has a summer horse-manship school, photography workshops and other year-round programs on the edge of the remote Red Rock Lakes National Wildlife Refuge. ~ Red Rock Lakes, Lima; 406-276-3300.

There are dozens of outfitters in the region. **Red Mountain Out-fitters** specializes in the Scapegoat and Bob Marshall wildernesses. ~ P.O. Box 24, Lincoln, MT 59639; 406-362-4360. **Pintler Wilder-ness Outfitting** covers the rugged reaches of the Anaconda-Pintler Wilderness. ~ 9010-3 Route 1, Anaconda; 406-563-7567. **Coyote Outfitters** focuses on the Tobacco Root and Ruby ranges. ~ 318 South Madison Street, Twin Bridges; 406-684-5769.

BIKING

Mountain bikers enjoy roads and trails in national forests throughout southwest Montana. Guided mountain-bike tours are offered by **Dave Willborn Outfitter.** ~ 775 Medicine Lodge Road, Dillon; 406-681-3117. Vehicles are not permitted in wilderness areas, but some highway loops—including the Pintler Scenic Route and the Big Hole Valley road—make excellent road trips.

Bike Rentals   One of the region's best bike shops is **Great Divide Cyclery**, which offers rentals and repair service as well as retail sales. ~ 827 South Montana Street, Butte; 406-782-4726.

HIKING

The national forests, wilderness areas and other public lands of southwest Montana contain literally thousands of miles of trails that offer an astounding range of choices for hikers of all experience and ability levels.

Following are a few of the region's more popular trails. All distances listed are one way unless otherwise noted.

HELENA AREA   Mount Helena is a 900-acre city park that has seven separate trails to its 5468-foot peak. The reward for climbers is a bird's-eye view of the capital's Last Chance Gulch, a quarter-mile below the summit. Many hikers take the easy **1906 Trail** (2 miles) to the summit and descend on a steeper path, like the **Prospect Shafts Trail** (1.5 miles) past old mining sites or the **Prairie Trail** (2.5 miles), which is especially colorful during the spring and early-summer wildflower seasons. Nearest trailhead to downtown Helena is at the west end of Adams Street.

Refrigerator Canyon Trail (2 miles) offers access into the eastern part of the Gates of the Mountains Wilderness. After climbing dramatically through a narrow limestone canyon, the trail levels out to several excellent viewing points. The trailhead is on Beaver Creek Road north of Hauser Lake.

Hanging Valley National Recreation Trail (6 miles) in Helena National Forest northeast of Hauser Lake, climbs rapidly through limestone cliffs on the west side of the Big Belt Mountains before dropping into a valley of giant Douglas fir. The trail, which involves a 2260-foot elevation gain, begins at the Vigilante campground near York.

PINTLER SCENIC ROUTE   The **Continental Divide National Scenic Trail** (45 miles) is actually part of a 3100-mile Canada-to-Mexico trek; the segment through the Anaconda-Pintler Wilderness from Storm Lake, south of Georgetown Lake, to East Fork Road, east of Sula, offers a challenging backpack and spectacular views along the boundaries of Beaverhead, Deerlodge and Bitterroot national forests.

BUTTE   The **Sheepshead Trail System** (5 miles) is a system of paved paths that provide handicapped access to the outdoors. These Deerlodge National Forest trails traverse meadows and wooded hills, and loop around a small lake. Trails begin at the Sheepshead Mountain Recreation Area, 19 miles north of Butte via Route 15 to Elk Park.

The **Bear Gulch Trail** (4 miles), which begins about 22 miles north of Butte off Route 15 exit 151, is an easy hike through an alpine meadow at about 6500 feet elevation. Beginning at the end of Forest Road 8481, it follows a small creek to the wildflower-rich grassland between Sullivan and Bear mountains in Deerlodge National Forest.

BIG HOLE VALLEY **Humbug Spires Trail** (2 miles) enters a fascinating geological preserve of 600-foot Mesozoic granite columns. Rock climbers often gather at this Bureau of Land Management sanctuary, 40 miles north of Dillon.

Big Hole Battlefield National Recreation Trail (3.8 miles) traces the route along the Continental Divide by which Chief Joseph is thought to have led his Nez Perce warriors after they fled this 1877 battleground.

The **Pioneer Loop National Recreation Trail** (35 miles) follows the spine of the West Pioneer Mountains, with spectacular views across the upper Big Hole Valley. There are many alpine tarns and small creeks en route. You can walk the entire trail between Forest Roads 1213 (west of Wise River) and 75 (east of Jackson), or join it midway from the Pioneer Mountains Scenic Byway via the Lacy Creek Road (Forest Road 90). This is a moderately strenuous hike.

DILLON AND THE RED ROCK RIVER VALLEY **Lion Creek Trail** (9 miles) is one of the most attractive routes into the Pioneer Mountains. The path winds through meadows and forests to alpine lakes surrounded by 9800-foot peaks. The trailhead is in the Beaverhead National Forest west of Melrose, 30 miles north of Dillon.

The **Upper Rattlesnake Trail** (5.5 miles) is a relatively short but rugged track through a district of at least a dozen small lakes in the East Pioneer Mountains. Reach it via the Birch Creek Road (Forest Road 192 off Route 801) at Route 15 exit 74, about 12 miles north of Dillon.

ALDER GULCH **Louise Lake National Recreation Trail** (1.7 miles) switchbacks 3000 feet up two steep ridges to a shimmering lake cradled between the sheer cliffs of the Tobacco Root Mountains. Wildlife viewers often spot mountain goats. The trailhead is in Deerlodge National Forest at the end of South Boulder Road, south of Whitehall; it can also be reached from Twin Bridges via Wisconsin Creek Road.

Equipment For backpacking gear, visit **The Base Camp**. ~ 333 North Last Chance Gulch, Helena; 406-443-5360. In Butte, try **Pipestone Mountaineering**. ~ 829 South Montana Street, Butte; 406-782-4994.

▼▼▼▼▼▼▼▼▼▼▼▼

Transportation

Montana's two principal interstate highways, **Route 15** and **Route 90**, cross and briefly converge at Butte, making this area, in a sense, Montana's transportation hub.

CAR

Route 90 runs 548 miles east and west across Montana, connecting many of its largest cities (Missoula, Butte, Bozeman and Billings) with points west (Seattle) and east (Chicago and Boston). Route 15 runs 385 miles north and south, from the Canadian border through Great Falls, Helena and Butte to Pocatello, Idaho, and points south (Salt Lake City and San Diego).

For road reports, call 800-332-6171 statewide, or call for local information in Helena (406-444-6354) or Butte (406-494-3666).

AIR

Butte's **Bert Mooney Airport** is served by Horizon and SkyWest. Delta, Horizon and SkyWest fly to the **Helena Municipal Airport**.

BUS

Greyhound Bus Lines offers service to the larger towns along the Route 90/94 corridor, including Butte and Deer Lodge. ~ 800-231-2222. **Intermountain Transportation Co.** connects Helena, Butte, Dillon and other towns of southwestern Montana. ~ 406-563-3841.

The central bus terminal in Helena is at 5 West 15th Street. ~ 406-442-5860. In Butte, it is at 105 West Broadway. ~ 406-723-3287.

CAR RENTALS

Helena has nine agencies and Butte has eight. At Helena Regional Airport there are **Avis Rent A Car** (800-331-1212), **Hertz Rent A Car** (800-654-3131) and **National Interrent** (800-328-4567). At Butte's Bert Mooney Airport, you will find **Avis Rent A Car** (800-331-1212), **Hertz Rent A Car** (800-654-3131) and **Budget Rent A Car** (800-527-0700).

PUBLIC TRANSIT

The **Butte-Silver Bow Transit System** runs an extensive route system through Butte and surrounding areas, with nominal fares. No other southern Montana town has a public transportation system. ~ 406-723-8262.

TAXIS

All cities and larger towns in southern Montana have taxi services. In Butte, call **City Taxi**. ~ 406-723-6511.

SIX

South Central Montana

Southwest Montana grew around mining, southeast Montana around ranching. South central Montana evolved from both economies, but from early in its development, it had something even more important: Tourism.

Credit the Northern Pacific Railroad with opening this section of the state to settlement in 1882. Its major towns, Bozeman and Livingston, were established by rail construction crews, as were other communities like Three Forks, Big Timber and Columbus. More importantly, credit the U.S. Congress with establishing Yellowstone as the nation's first national park a full decade earlier. As soon as the railroad was completed, a spur line from Livingston to Gardiner began carrying tourists to the new park, and the future of south central Montana as a center for outdoor recreationists was assured.

All four of Montana's access routes to Yellowstone originate in this part of the state. Three of them extend up river valleys: the Madison from Three Forks, the Gallatin from Bozeman and the Yellowstone from Livingston. A fourth, from Red Lodge, circles the spectacular Absaroka-Beartooth Wilderness Area on the Wyoming border. Many tourists combine a visit to Yellowstone with a loop trip on any two of these highway routes, which they can extend from 200 to 450 miles or even more.

Apart from the river canyons and wilderness mountains that abut Yellowstone, south central Montana has other attractions worthy of note. Bozeman, home of Montana State University (MSU) and its impressive Museum of the Rockies is only a 45-minute drive from the spectacular Lewis and Clark Caverns and from Three Forks, where the Jefferson, Madison and Gallatin rivers join to form the Missouri River headwaters. Livingston, once the home of "Calamity Jane" Canary, has preserved the historical integrity of its late-19th-century downtown. Red Lodge retains the feel of a cosmopolitan coal-mining town of 100 years ago, while Big Timber is best known for the Greycliff Prairie Dog Town to its east. Many of the region's streams draw anglers and rafters from far reaches of the country. Skiers, meanwhile, delight in the Big Sky, Bridger Bowl and Red Lodge Mountain resorts.

▼▼▼▼▼▼▼▼▼▼▼
Bozeman Area

Bozeman is an oasis of sophistication in the center of a thriving agricultural area. Located at the foot of the Bridger Range in the Gallatin River Valley, this city of 25,000 has become a darling of affluent young (or young-at-heart) visitors.

Named for John Bozeman, a 19th-century wagon master, this is Montana's "yuppie" city. A hangout for such Hollywood luminaries as actress Meryl Streep and actor Steven Seagal, its prices are higher than those in other Montana cities.

SIGHTS

The one attraction in Bozeman that no visitor should miss is the **Museum of the Rockies** at the edge of the MSU campus. The museum's dinosaur exhibit is world-class; paleontologists offer summer field courses at Egg Mountain (northwest of Great Falls), where the first known dinosaur eggs were discovered in North America. Programs at the Taylor Planetarium are comparable to those in much larger cities. Exhibits focus on American Indian culture, contemporary western art, American history with a Rockies perspective and scientific discoveries. The museum operates a pioneer homestead and a nature center, and has an excellent gift shop. Admission. ~ 600 West Kagy Boulevard, Bozeman; 406-994-2251.

Montana State University, with an enrollment of about 10,800, is a national leader in agricultural research and education, physical science and technology. Visitors can attend any of the university's cultural and sporting events, including the annual College National Finals Rodeo in June. ~ South of College Street and west of South 7th Avenue, Bozeman; 406-994-0211.

East of the campus is the **South Willson Historic District**. Four dozen houses, from small cottages to large mansions, may be viewed in this residential area. Some of the large homes, which date back to the 1880s, are now fraternity and sorority houses. ~ South Willson Avenue, Bozeman.

A walking-tour guide to the South Willson Historic District is available from the Museum of the Rockies or the **Bozeman Area Chamber of Commerce**. ~ 1205 East Main Street, Bozeman; 406-586-5421.

There's more early Bozeman history at the **Gallatin County Pioneer Museum**. A county jail from 1911 to 1982, the building now holds audiences captive with displays of agricultural implements, American Indian artifacts and the jail's original gallows room (complete with noose and drop floor). ~ 317 West Main Street, Bozeman; 406-585-1311.

The **American Computer Museum**, on the ground floor of a downtown office building, claims to be the "world's second museum of its type." Visitors can trace the computer's history from the abacus and early mechanical calculators through the develop-

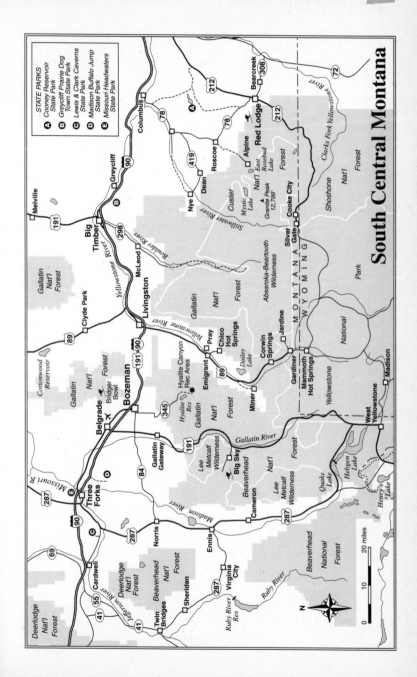

South Central Montana

STATE PARKS
A Cooney Reservoir State Park
B Greycliff Prairie Dog Town State Park
C Lewis & Clark Caverns State Park
D Madison Buffalo Jump State Park
E Missouri Headwaters State Park

ment of the microchip. Guided tours and videos are geared for all ages and levels of computer knowledge. (That Bozeman should have a museum devoted to the evolution of the computer may be more an ode to the reach of the modem than to any particular role the city has played in the history of technology.) Admission. ~ 234 East Babcock Street, Bozeman; 406-587-7545.

At the **Fish Technology Center**, visitors can observe U.S. Fish and Wildlife Service research into the health, nutrition, reproduction and management of fish in hatcheries and in the wild. The center, established in 1965, also works with threatened species such as the Colorado greenback cutthroat trout and the Big Hole arctic grayling. Other species can also be seen. ~ 4050 Bridger Canyon Road, Bozeman; 406-587-9265.

Beyond the Fish Center northeast of Bozeman, Bridger Canyon Road (Route 86) climbs gradually through a short, rocky canyon to a mountain valley surrounded by the peaks of the Bridger Range. A smattering of ranches and new homes have been built in this valley, reminiscent of some in Switzerland. En route, look for directional signs to **Coffrin's Old West Gallery**, which displays a remarkable set of photographs of Sioux and early settler life taken by pioneer cameraman L. A. Huffman between 1878 and 1920. ~ 8118 Rolling Hills Drive, Bozeman; 406-586-0170.

Sixteen miles from Bozeman at the head of the valley is **Bridger Bowl**, a popular local ski resort within Gallatin National Forest. ~ 15795 Bridger Canyon Road; 406-587-2111.

GALLATIN VALLEY HIGHWAY   Gallatin National Forest dominates Gallatin County south of Bozeman. Route 191 follows the Gallatin River, one of the three headwater streams of the Missouri, upstream nearly to its source in Yellowstone National Park. Through much of its course, the Gallatin, a favorite of whitewater rafters and kayakers, follows a narrow gorge between the Spanish Peaks on its west and the Gallatin Range on its east. The magnifi-

✔ CHECK THESE OUT—UNIQUE SIGHTS

- Inspect the findings of Montana State University paleontologists, including dinosaur eggs, at the **Museum of the Rockies**. *page 170*
- Scramble three-quarters of a mile (some of it on hands and knees) through the **Lewis and Clark Caverns** to see a fantastic set of limestone caves inhabited by bats. *page 180*
- Safely observe the natural behavior of fearsome grizzly bears at West Yellowstone's **Grizzly Discovery Center**. *page 183*
- Stroll among the burrows of hundreds of curious rodents at **Greycliff Prairie Dog Town State Park**. *page 193*

cent 82-mile drive to West Yellowstone passes two parcels of the **Lee Metcalf Wilderness Area** and a turnoff to the Big Sky resort before entering the northwest corner of Yellowstone Park. See Chapter Seven for more information. ~ Federal Building, 601 Nickles Drive, Bozeman; 406-587-6920.

Below the head of the canyon, 14 miles southwest of Bozeman, is the old railroad town of Gallatin Gateway and its famous **Gallatin Gateway Inn**. The imposing, mission-style hotel, which is listed on the National Register of Historic Places, was built in 1927 by the Chicago, Milwaukee & St. Paul Railroad. ~ Route 191, Gallatin Gateway; 406-763-4672.

On the south side of the 10,000-foot Spanish Peaks, 48 miles from Bozeman, is the **Big Sky Ski & Summer Resort**. Established in the 1970s by a group of investors (including Montana native Chet Huntley, the late network newscaster), Big Sky has grown into two separate year-round villages. Both Meadow Village and Mountain Village, six miles apart, have lodging and dining facilities as well as shopping. Recreational activities range from skiing and snowmobiling in winter to golf, tennis, horseback riding, mountain biking, hiking, rafting and fishing in summer. ~ Big Sky Road, Big Sky; 406-995-4211.

In 1955, before Big Sky was even so much as a brainstorm, a **Soldier's Chapel** was built as a Second World War memorial just south of today's road junction. The nondenominational chapel offers a striking view of 11,188-foot Lone Mountain. ~ Route 191, Big Sky; 406-995-4292.

If you want to get a closer look, you can take a **gondola** from Mountain Village to the 9500-foot level of the mountain. Operating summers as well as winters, the gondola affords memorable panoramas of the surrounding terrain. Admission.

From Big Sky, you can continue up the Gallatin River on Route 191, skirting the corner of Yellowstone National Park. The park's west entrance is at West Yellowstone, 39 miles south of Big Sky.

LODGING

In the heart of the South Willson Historic District, three blocks from downtown Bozeman, is the **Voss Inn**, a restored 1883 Victorian with elegant hardwood floors. Its six rooms all have private baths and contain such period antiques as clawfoot tubs, carved armoires, and brass or iron beds. Rooms are air-conditioned or have fans. Gourmet breakfasts are delivered to the rooms each morning; afternoon tea and evening sherry are served in the parlor, which has a piano and small library. ~ 319 South Willson Avenue, Bozeman; 406-587-0982. MODERATE.

Several economy motels are located along Main Street in Bozeman. I like the **Alpine Lodge**, which has 14 units in the Tyrolean-style, yellow-and-brown main building and adjacent cabins. All have full kitchens, private baths and standard motel amenities. ~ 1017 East Main Street, Bozeman; 406-586-0356. BUDGET.

The **Sacajawea Hostel** is a find for backpackers. It has a dozen bunk beds in three dorm rooms; hostellers share toilets, showers and kitchen facilities. Unlike many hostels, this one is open year-round and doesn't have a curfew. ~ 105 West Olive Street, Bozeman; 406-586-4659. BUDGET.

The chateau-like tower of the **Best Western GranTree Inn** is a landmark for visitors arriving off Route 90. This pleasant two-story property has a restaurant and coffee shop, a lounge and casino, an indoor pool, a jacuzzi and a coin laundry. Its 103 rooms, all reached from inside corridors, are spacious and well lit, with wood furniture. ~ 1325 North 7th Avenue, Bozeman; 406-587-5261, 800-624-5865, fax 406-587-9437. MODERATE TO DELUXE.

Bozeman's largest motel, and one of its best bargains, is the **Holiday Inn**. Located north of the interstate off of 7th Avenue, this two-story lodging has an art deco appeal that extends from its restaurant and lounge to its 178 rooms, all with standard furnishings. The motel has an indoor pool, a jacuzzi, a Nautilus exercise area, a coin laundry and a game room. Many motels offer free lodging to children under 12 accompanied by a parent; here, the age limit is 18. ~ 5 Baxter Lane, Bozeman; 406-587-4561, 800-366-5101, fax 406-587-4413. MODERATE.

A three-story granite fireplace greets guests in the lobby of the seven-story slope-side Huntley Lodge at Big Sky.

For a taste of old-time luxury, visit the **Gallatin Gateway Inn**, a restored railroad hotel listed on the National Register of Historic Places. Built in Spanish Colonial style in 1927, the inn has a cavernous lobby with a huge fireplace and a grand piano beneath mahogany ceiling beams. Its 35 rooms are cozy but comfortable; most have full private baths. The 15-acre grounds include a year-round swimming pool, a hot tub, a tennis court, a fly-casting pond and mountain-bike rentals and trails. The inn's gourmet restaurant draws dinner guests from Bozeman, 14 miles north. ~ 76405 Route 191 South, Gallatin Gateway; 406-763-4672, fax 406-763-4672 ext. 313. MODERATE TO DELUXE.

The most prestigious place to stay at the Big Sky resort complex is **The Huntley Lodge at Big Sky**, which also has a fine restaurant and a lounge with live entertainment. The 300 rooms are modern and spacious. On-site recreation includes golf, tennis, horseback riding, mountain biking and fishing; the lodge has two swimming pools, saunas, whirlpools, a steam room and an exercise room. There are children's programs and a playground, a coin laundry and ski and sports shops. ~ 1 Lone Mountain Trail, Big Sky; 406-995-4211, 800-548-4486, fax 406-995-4860. DELUXE.

Montana's Yellowstone country has many friendly guest ranches. One of the longest established is the **Lone Mountain**

Ranch, homesteaded as a cattle ranch in 1915 and attracting paying guests since the 1940s. Guests stay in 23 log cabins with full baths and fireplaces; gourmet meals are served family-style in an elaborate log-and-stone dining hall. Activities on the 4000-acre ranch include horseback riding, trout fishing and hiking in summer, cross-country skiing in winter. Closed in spring and fall. ~ P.O. Box 69, Big Sky, MT 59716; 406-995-4644, fax 406-995-4670. DELUXE.

DINING

The Rocky Mountain Pasta Company is much more a classic northern Italian restaurant than a noodle dispensary. Located on the ground floor of the 1929 Baxter Hotel in the heart of downtown, it serves fine food and wines in a warm, elegant atmosphere. ~ 105 West Main Street, Bozeman; 406-586-1314. MODERATE.

The adjoining **Bacchus Pub** offers salads, sandwiches and other light fare. BUDGET.

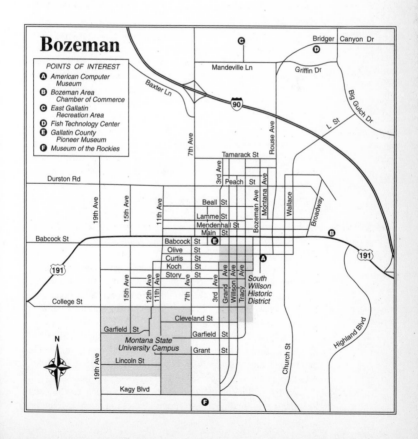

John Bozeman's Bistro boasts "world cuisine with Montana style," and it delivers on that promise. Housed in a historic downtown brewery building, it offers up innovative preparations of steaks, seafoods and other popular dishes, often with Asian culinary twists. Lunch and dinner are offered Tuesday through Sunday, breakfasts on weekends only. ~ 242 East Main Street, Bozeman; 406-587-4100. MODERATE TO DELUXE.

Fred's Mesquite Diner is just what its name implies: a small downtown diner with a mesquite charcoal grill. The result: steaks, chicken, ribs and other foods with gourmet taste and low price tags. The patio is a great place for people watching. ~ 451 East Main Street, Bozeman; 406-585-8558. BUDGET.

The menu at the **Hearthstone Whole Grain Bakery & Café** may be *too* healthy for some. Located next door to the Chamber of Commerce, this spacious café features a three-meals-a-day menu of tofu burgers on homemade whole-wheat buns and other vegetarian specialties. ~ 1211 East Main Street, Bozeman; 406-586-4031. BUDGET TO MODERATE.

HIDDEN ▶   Order hearty soups and healthy salads at **Community Food Co-op**. This small, casual deli also features a menu board of sandwiches and entrées, as well as daily ethnic specials such as sweet potato *quesadillas*, Anasazi eggplant stew and tempeh stir-fry. A great deal at a low price. ~ 908 West Main Street, Bozeman; 406-587-4039. BUDGET.

South of Bozeman, a mile south of the Big Sky junction in a Best Western motel, **Buck's T-4** offers two attractive alternatives to resort restaurants. Buck's dining room specializes in wild game, from pheasant to wild boar, moose and antelope, at exotic prices. Steaks and seafood are also available. In the same location, the **Gameroom Grill** serves pizzas and other lighter, low-priced fare. ~ Route 191, Big Sky; 406-995-4111. BUDGET TO DELUXE.

SHOPPING   It's fun to browse downtown Bozeman's 100-or-so retail stores, including eight galleries and five antique shops. Among the newest shopping meccas is the **Emerson Cultural Center**, a nonprofit arts center whose tenants include craftspeople (jewelers, ceramicists, woodworkers and clothiers) and cultural organizations. Some three dozen artisans have their studios in this former school, built in 1919; many of them welcome visitors. ~ 111 South Grand Avenue, Bozeman; 406-587-9797.

To see the work of noted regional artists like Gary Carter and Russell Chatham, check out the **Beall Park Art Center**, four blocks north of Main Street. ~ 409 North Bozeman Street, Bozeman; 406-586-3970.

For true 19th- and 20th-century Western classics, you can't beat the top-of-the-line selection (with prices to match) at **Thomas**

Nygard Inc. If you've ever had a hankering for a Charles Russell or an Albert Bierstadt, Nygard can help you out. ~ 127 East Main Street, Bozeman; 406-586-3636.

The Antique Mall claims to be Montana's largest antique mall, with 14,000 square feet of furniture, glassware, art and memorabilia. ~ 612 East Main Street, Bozeman; 406-587-5281.

Readings by celebrated authors are regular features of **The Country Bookshelf**, an excellent, comprehensive bookstore in Bozeman. ~ 28 West Main Street, Bozeman; 406-587-0166.

Bozeman's largest enclosed shopping center is **Main Mall**, about a mile west of downtown. Among its five dozen retailers are **Bon Marché**, **JC Penney** and **B. Dalton Bookseller**. ~ 2825 West Main Street, Bozeman; 406-586-4565.

The city also has a **Farmers Market** on summer Saturdays from about 9:30 a.m. to noon. ~ Bogart Park, 325 South Church Street, Bozeman; 406-587-4724.

In large part because of Montana State University, Bozeman is a very culturally active city.

NIGHTLIFE

The **Bozeman Symphony Orchestra and Symphonic Choir** has a fall-through-spring season. ~ 104 East Main Street, Bozeman; 406-585-9774. The **Intermountain Opera Association** mounts two productions each year. ~ 104 East Main Street, Bozeman; 406-587-2889. Every Christmas season the **Montana Ballet Company** performs Tchaikovsky's *Nutcracker*. ~ 221 East Main Street, Bozeman; 406-587-7192. All three organizations perform at the Willson School auditorium. ~ 404 West Main Street, Bozeman.

Summer also brings **Shakespeare in the Parks** to Bozeman. The company presents two plays—typically a tragedy and a comedy—almost nightly in a 12-week tour, mid-June to Labor Day, of 48 Montana communities. The tour begins and ends in Bozeman and returns to its home stage (the MSU Campus Grove) three other times. ~ 406-994-5885.

The summer **Bozeman Stage Company** and spring-to-fall **Vigilante Theatre Company**, offer several shows throughout the year, including dramas, comedies and musicals. Both companies are based in the Emerson Cultural Center. ~ 111 South Grand Avenue, Bozeman; 406-586-3897.

There's a variety of popular nightlife hot spots in Bozeman. **Rock's Bar** features rock, reggae or rhythm-and-blues bands most nights. ~ 321 East Main Street, Bozeman; 406-585-8851.

At **Little John's Bar** free dance lessons precede appearances by country bands. ~ 515 West Aspen Street, Bozeman; 406-587-1652.

The **Cat's Paw** hosts comedians on Thursday nights and live bands on Friday and Saturday. ~ 721 North 7th Avenue, Bozeman; 406-586-3542.

For a quiet drink, there's the **Spanish Peaks Brewery**, a restaurant and microbrewery that has developed a solid regional reputation with its Black Dog Ale. ~ 120 North 19th Avenue, Bozeman; 406-585-2296. Coffeehouses have gotten big among nondrinkers here; **The Leaf and Bean** often hosts acoustic musicians, poets and other throwbacks to the Beat days of Greenwich Village. ~ 35 West Main Street, Bozeman; 406-587-1580.

PARKS

EAST GALLATIN STATE RECREATION AREA

A local park that surrounds little Glen Lake near the confluence of Bridger and Bozeman creeks, East Gallatin owes its existence to community volunteers. Watersports lovers of all kinds appreciate their efforts. Fishing is good for trout, perch and sunfish. Facilities include picnic areas and restrooms; restaurants and groceries are in Bozeman. Day-use fee, $2. ~ Located on Manley Road, off Griffin Drive (between 7th and Rouse avenues) north of the Bozeman city limits; 406-994-4042.

HYALITE CANYON RECREATION AREA

Covering 34,000 acres of Gallatin National Forest southeast of Bozeman, this wheelchair-accessible park area is popular among anglers, hikers, and mountain bikers and anglers seeking cutthroat trout and arctic grayling. The reservoir, created in the 1940s, has a "no-wake" rule that restricts motorboaters to low speeds. Trails include a half-mile hard-surfaced track to Palisade Falls, a one-and-a-quarter-mile gravel track to Grotto Falls, and a strenuous five-and-a-half-mile ascent of 10,299-foot Hyalite Peak. There are picnic areas and restrooms; restaurants and groceries are in Bozeman. ~ From downtown Bozeman, take South 19th Avenue seven miles south to Hyalite Canyon Road (Route 62), an extension of Fowler Lane. It's ten miles from here to Hyalite Reservoir, twelve to the Palisade Falls trailhead; 406-587-6920.

▲ There are 39 RV/tent sites at three campgrounds, none with hookups; $8 per night; 14-day maximum stay. A rental cabin is also available.

GALLATIN NATIONAL FOREST

Stretching east and west across the Absaroka, Gallatin and Madison ranges, this 1.7-million-acre forest includes large parts of two wilderness areas (the Absaroka-Beartooth and the Lee Metcalf), the upper reaches of four important trout rivers (the Yellowstone, Gallatin, Madison and Boulder), and the Big Sky and Bridger Bowl ski resorts. Picnic areas and restrooms round out the amenities. Restaurants and groceries are in Bozeman, Livingston, West Yellowstone and other towns. ~ Route 191, south of Bozeman, and Route 89, south of Livingston, traverse the forest, and numerous other spur roads provide access; 406-587-6791.

▲ There are 558 RV/tent sites plus 89 for tents only at 30 campgrounds, none with hookups; no charge to $8 per night; 14-day maximum stay. Reservations (800-283-2267) are accepted at four summer-only campgrounds near West Yellowstone. Also, 23 recreational cabins can be reserved for use by hikers or skiers at $20 per night.

LEE METCALF WILDERNESS AREA 🏃 🐎 🛶 ⚲ Four parcels, totaling nearly a quarter million acres, include the spectacular Spanish Peaks area rising to more than 11,000 feet north of Big Sky; the crest of the Madison Range southwest of Big Sky as far as Quake Lake; the Monument Mountain region adjoining the northwest corner of Yellowstone National Park; and steep Beartrap Canyon on the Madison River downstream from Ennis Lake. There's fine hiking and horseback riding, as well as rafting on the Madison. ~ Access from Big Sky, off Route 191 south of Bozeman; from Routes 191 and 297, north of West Yellowstone; and from Beartrap Canyon on the Madison River, off Route 84 west of Bozeman; 406-587-6701.

▲ Primitive only.

Traveling west from Bozeman, Route 90 bypasses a series of small Gallatin Valley towns whose names speak of founders from a variety of backgrounds:

▼▼▼▼▼▼▼▼▼▼▼▼
Three Forks Area

Belgrade (Serbian), Churchill (British), Amsterdam (Dutch), Manhattan (New Yorker!).

At Route 90 Exit 283, 25 miles west of Bozeman, a secondary road leads seven miles south to **Madison Buffalo Jump State Park**. This site preserves a cliff over which American Indians stampeded bison as long as 2000 years ago. Interpretive displays describe how buffalo meat and hides were thus obtained on a mass scale before the mid-16th century, when horses altered the Plains Indians' hunting practices. Admission. ~ Buffalo Jump Road, Logan; 406-994-4042.

SIGHTS

At the valley's west end, located near the point where three rivers come together to form the Missouri River about 30 miles from Bozeman, is the intriguing town of **Three Forks**. Three Forks' colorful history as a tribal crossroads, trading post and rail center is related in exhibits at its **Headwaters Heritage Museum**, which dates from 1910: You'll find, faithfully re-created, a settler's home, a railroad office, a schoolroom and a blacksmith's shop. ~ Main Street; 406-285-3495.

Just across the street, the **Sacajawea Inn** was constructed the same year. Recently restored, the handsome rail-junction hotel is on the National Register of Historic Places. ~ 5 North Main Street; 406-285-6515.

Five miles from town, **Missouri Headwaters State Park** is located at the convergence of the Gallatin, Madison and Jefferson rivers. "All of them run with great velocity and throw out large bodies of water," wrote Captain Meriwether Lewis in 1805. Admission. ~ Trident Road, Three Forks; 406-994-4042.

Lewis and Clark Caverns State Park, 18 miles west of Three Forks, may be the most impressive limestone caves in the northwestern United States. A fairyland of ancient stalactites, stalagmites and other wonders of the underground, created over millions of years, highlights the 90-minute guided tour (offered May to September). Visitors should be modestly fit: They climb a gradually sloping three-quarter-mile paved trail to the cavern entrance; descend another three-quarters of a mile through the fascinating subterranean chamber; then return one-half mile to the visitors center. The route includes more than 600 steps leading through hands-and-knees crawl space, narrow rock slides and cathedral-size chambers inhabited by bats. The cave's interior is a constant 50°F. Admission. ~ Route 2, Cardwell; 406-287-3541 or 406-287-5424 in summer.

MADISON VALLEY HIGHWAY   From Route 2 between Three Forks and Cardwell, Route 287 cuts south through Norris and Ennis to West Yellowstone and Yellowstone National Park. It's 107 miles from the Route 2 junction to the park entrance, most of it up the scenic valley of the Madison River. Flanked on the east by the 11,000-foot peaks of the Madison Range and on the west by the 10,000-foot Tobacco Root and Gravelly ranges, the route offers ready access to the Beaverhead National Forest and several parcels of the Metcalf Wilderness.

At Norris, 19 miles from the route's start, Route 84 from Bozeman (38 miles east) joins the Madison Valley highway. Six miles east from here is the **Trail Creek Access Recreational Area**, which provides access for the handicapped to the Metcalf Wilderness where the Madison River emerges from Beartrap Canyon. There's fishing, picnicking, whitewater rafting and hiking. ~ Route 84, Norris; 406-683-2337.

Ennis is in the heart of the Madison Valley, on the east side of the Tobacco Root Mountains, just 13 miles from the historic mining town of Virginia City (see "Alder Gulch," above). Ennis (pop. 800) is a hunting and fishing center whose three blocks of downtown businesses boast Old West–style facades. When visiting, keep your eyes open for media mogul Ted Turner and his actress wife Jane Fonda, who own a massive private ranch in the vicinity.

Twelve miles south, visitors are welcome at the **Ennis National Fish Hatchery**, at the foot of the Gravelly Range. The hatchery breeds 23 million rainbow trout hatchlings each year to stock streams throughout the U.S. ~ Varney Road; 406-682-7635.

Thirty miles before West Yellowstone, a visitors center commemorates the devastating earthquake of August 1959, which took 28 lives and created Quake Lake. See the "West Yellowstone Area" section in this chapter for details.

A historic railroad hotel built in 1910, the three-story **Sacajawea Inn** is a pleasant place to lay one's head on the road west from Bozeman. Its 33 restored guest rooms are small but clean, each with a private bath. The hotel has a romantic restaurant and small espresso bar; smoking is not permitted. Rates include a Continental breakfast. ~ 5 North Main Street, Three Forks; 406-285-6515, 800-821-7326, fax 406-285-6515. MODERATE.

LODGING

A simple lodging is the **Broken Spur Motel**. The two-story motel has 21 neat, clean rooms with TVs and phones, but no frills. ~ 124 West Elm Street, Three Forks; 406-285-3237, fax 406-285-6514. BUDGET.

In the heart of the Madison River Valley is the riverside **Rainbow Valley Motel**. Its 24 rooms have log-cabin decor; several are two-bedroom units with efficiency kitchens. Facilities include a swimming pool, a barbecue area and a coin laundry; there are even horse corrals for those intending backcountry excursions. ~ Route 287 South, Ennis; 406-682-4264, 800-341-8000, fax 406-682-5012. MODERATE.

The **Lost Fork Ranch**, located about 40 miles south of Ennis and two miles west of Route 287's junction with Route 87 from Henry's Lake, Idaho, was built in 1989 for two types of outdoors lovers: riders and anglers. Four duplex cabins and a log-and-stone lodge with a couple of more rooms sit beside Pine Butte Creek. Daily horsemanship and fly-fishing programs are offered, while family-style or buffet meals are served nightly. Kids enjoy the weekly rodeos. ~ Route 287, Drawer K, Cameron, MT 59720; 406-682-7690, fax 406-682-7515. MODERATE.

◆◆

✔ **CHECK THESE OUT—UNIQUE LODGING**

- *Budget:* Rest your backpack at Bozeman's **Sacajawea Hostel**, which offers shared kitchens and no curfew. *page 174*
- *Moderate to deluxe:* Join the likes of Buffalo Bill Cody and William Jennings Bryan on the guest list at Red Lodge's **Pollard Hotel**. *page 197*
- *Moderate to deluxe:* Stay in Spanish Colonial–style luxury at the **Gallatin Gateway Inn**, a restored railway hotel. *page 174*
- *Deluxe:* Indulge in a total-fitness vacation at the **Rock Creek Resort**, at the foot of the Beartooth Highway. *page 197*

Budget: under $50   Moderate: $50–$90   Deluxe: $90–$130   Ultra-deluxe: over $130

DINING

Who could resist a stop at a Montana fast-food establishment called **Custer's Last Root Beer Stand**? Located at a fork in westbound Route 2 as it heads out of Three Forks toward Lewis and Clark Caverns, this small but jumpin' joint has good burgers and *great* root beer. ~ 23 West Date Street, Three Forks; 406-285-6713. BUDGET.

The **Schoolhouse Restaurant** near the Route 84 junction is housed in, you guessed it, an old schoolhouse. The fare here is Mexican, prepared in delectable homemade fashion. ~ Route 287, Norris; 406-685-3200. BUDGET.

HIDDEN ▶

Perhaps the fine French, Cajun and Creole cuisine dished up at the **Continental Divide Restaurant** is a legacy of the Louisiana Purchase. Otherwise, it's hard to explain how a place this good could have found itself behind an Old West facade in an area that caters mainly to outdoor sportsmen and tourists. If you're staying in Virginia City, it's worth driving the 13 miles to dine here. ~ Yellowstone Highway, Ennis; 406-682-7600. DELUXE.

PARKS

MADISON BUFFALO JUMP STATE PARK 🚶🚲 Using a primitive but highly efficient hunting method, American Indians stampeded herds of bison over this cliff for some 1500 years—until they obtained horses and guns in the mid-16th century. Interpretive displays describe the buffalo's importance to the Plains Indians' way of life. Picnic areas, restrooms; restaurants and groceries in Three Forks. ~ From Logan Exit 283 off Route 90, five miles east of Three Forks, take Buffalo Jump Road south for seven miles; 406-994-4042.

MISSOURI HEADWATERS STATE PARK 🚶🛶🚤⛵ Located where the Gallatin, Madison and Jefferson rivers flow together to create the Missouri River, this park offers fishing and hiking, wildlife viewing, camping and picnicking. Exhibits discuss the site's importance as a gathering place for American Indians long before the Lewis and Clark expedition stumbled upon it in 1805. Facilities include picnic areas and restrooms. Restaurants and groceries are in Three Forks. Day-use fee, $3. ~ Take Exit 278 from Route 90 at Three Forks; follow Route 205 east for two miles and then Route 286 (Trident Road) north for three miles; 406-994-4042.

▲ There are 21 primitive sites, none with hookups; $4 to $5 per night for Montana residents, $7 to $8 for nonresidents; 14-day maximum stay.

LEWIS AND CLARK CAVERNS STATE PARK 🚶🛶⛵ Deep limestone caves, some of the most impressive in North America, are the highlight of Montana's first state park. The park is open year-round, but cavern tours operate from May through September only. Bats inhabit the caves, while deer and other animals live on the nearby slopes. Picnic areas, restrooms, showers, visitors center, and an amphitheater round out the amenities. There's a restaurant at the park, and groceries are in Cardwell or Three Forks. Day-use fee, $3. ~ Take Route 2 (off Route 90) from Three Forks (18 miles east of the park) or from Cardwell (ten miles west); 406-287-5424 in summer, 406-287-3541 the rest of the year.

▲ There are 50 RV/tent sites, none with hookups; $7 to $9 per night; 14-day maximum stay. Three primitive cabins are available for $25 to $39 per night depending upon season.

West Yellowstone Area

With about 900 full-time residents, West Yellowstone, is the primary "suburb" of Yellowstone National Park. Founded in 1907 as a Union Pacific railroad terminus where Yellowstone visitors could transfer to stagecoaches for their tour of the national park, it gradually grew into the tourism- and outdoor recreation–focused community it is today.

SIGHTS

The train stopped running to West Yellowstone as private automobiles came into common use after World War II. The imposing stone Union Pacific Depot, damaged by the massive 7.1-magnitude 1959 earthquake but restored in 1972, is now the **Museum of the Yellowstone**. Permanent displays on regional history and wildlife are complemented by annually changing exhibits; there's also a bookstore and a theater showing documentary videos. Closed from November to April. Admission. ~ Yellowstone and Canyon avenues, West Yellowstone; 406-646-7814.

Located almost across the street, the **Yellowstone IMAX Theatre** presents *Grizzlies, Geysers, Grandeur* on its six-story screen with Dolby sound. The 35-minute film is shown hourly between 9 a.m. and 9 p.m. from May to September; times vary the rest of the year. Admission. ~ Canyon Avenue, West Yellowstone; 406-646-4100.

> The great earthquake of August 1959 dropped the north shore of Hebgen Lake 18 feet.

Next door to the theater, on the south side, is the **Grizzly Discovery Center** where visitors can observe the natural behavior of grizzly bears in an outdoor viewing area constructed with minimal barriers. Several bears reside here; they have been orphaned, born in captivity or taken in as habitual "problem bears." The center also has museum displays and a gift shop. Admission. ~ Canyon Avenue, West Yellowstone; 406-646-7001.

North of West Yellowstone, two miles up Route 287, is the **Interagency Aerial Fire Control Center**, where summer visitors can make reservations for a facility tour, including a closer look at smokejumping techniques. ~ Route 287; 406-646-7691.

The **West Yellowstone Visitors Information Center,** open year-round, is one of the most comprehensive you'll find. Besides providing basic information on the town and the national park, chamber of commerce representatives locate lodging for tourists who arrive without reservations, and forest rangers advise on nearby camping when "Full" signs cover the campground board at Yellowstone's west entrance. ~ 100 Yellowstone Avenue, West Yellowstone; 406-646-7701.

One of the most popular places to send campers is **Hebgen Lake,** less than five miles northwest of the town. Numerous recreation areas and campgrounds speckle the south and west shores of the 15-mile-long lake, created by the damming of the Madison River. Hebgen is especially popular among boaters, fishermen and wildlife watchers, who keep their eyes peeled for moose and trumpeter swans.

The great earthquake of August 17, 1959, had its epicenter just west of Hebgen Lake. The tremor caused a landslide that blocked the Madison River canyon, creating adjacent Quake Lake. Twenty-eight campers died. The **Madison Canyon Earthquake Area and Visitor Center,** at the west end of Quake Lake, marks the quake's epicenter. ~ Route 287; 406-646-7369.

LODGING   Doing Yellowstone on the cheap? The **Madison Hotel Youth Hostel** is a good place to start. The hotel can accommodate as many as two dozen backpackers in dormitories (smoking and non-smoking) and a few private rooms. Shared facilities include toilets and showers, a TV lounge and a coffee bar. There's no kitchen, unfortunately. Closed from mid-October to the end of May. ~ 139 Yellowstone Avenue, West Yellowstone; 406-646-7745, 800-521-5241. BUDGET.

◆◆

✔ CHECK THESE OUT—UNIQUE DINING

- *Budget:* Consider that **The Round Barn,** a smorgasbord-style eatery near Red Lodge, was once a dairy farm's milking parlor. *page 198*
- *Moderate:* Don your lederhosen for Bavarian-style schnitzels and trout at **Alice's Restaurant,** on the Montana–Idaho border. *page 185*
- *Moderate:* Feel free to get rough and rowdy at **Calamity Jane's Steakhouse** in Livingston, a Wild West town that the noted frontierswoman found a bit too tame. *page 191*
- *Deluxe:* Treat your gourmet taste buds to New Orleans–style cuisine at the exquisite **Continental Divide Restaurant** in Ennis. *page 182*

Budget: under $8 Moderate: $8–$16 Deluxe: $16–$24 Ultra-deluxe: over $24

If you can live with the fact that rooms at **Al's Westward Ho Motel** don't have phones or air-conditioning, you'll find this off-the-main-drag lodging to be a real bargain. Thirty-three rooms, including several with kitchens, are located just north of the park entrance. There's cable TV and full bath facilities. ~ 16 Boundary Street, West Yellowstone; 406-646-7331. BUDGET.

West Yellowstone's best bet is the **Travelers Lodge**. This two-story motor hotel has 46 rooms of varying sizes: from small units by the park entrance to suites with king-size beds. All have televisions and room safes; some have refrigerators. Facilities include a sauna, a whirlpool, a heated pool, and a coin laundry. In winter, the lodge offers snowmobile rentals. ~ 225 Yellowstone Avenue, West Yellowstone; 406-646-9561, 800-831-5741, fax 406-646-7965. MODERATE.

The **Stage Coach Inn** is one of the nicest motels around. A shingle-roofed lodging with a rock facade and a balcony that surrounds its large, knotty pine-paneled lobby and stone fireplace, it looks as if it came straight out of a storybook. The 86 guest rooms are cozy but nicely decorated. The inn has an upscale dining room, coffee shop, casino-lounge, spa and sauna, game room for the kids and guest laundry. ~ 209 Madison Avenue, West Yellowstone; 406-646-7381, 800-842-2882, fax 406-646-9575. MODERATE TO DELUXE.

DINING

Regional game dishes—including elk and buffalo—are available outside the park's west entrance at the **Rustler's Roost** in the Best Western Pine Motel. Rainbow trout, chicken and prime rib are also on the menu at this family establishment, which offers a soup-and-salad bar and a children's menu as well. ~ 234 Firehole Avenue, West Yellowstone; 406-646-7622. MODERATE.

The **Three Bear Restaurant**, located in a motor lodge of the same name, serves breakfast and dinner daily from mid-May to mid-October and mid-December through February. The nonsmoking, family-style restaurant touts its salad bar, prime rib and home-made pastries. The Grizzly Lounge is attached. ~ 205 Yellowstone Avenue, West Yellowstone; 406-646-7811. MODERATE.

◄ HIDDEN

Alice's Restaurant is eight miles west of the park entrance on Route 20, but many folks find it worth the drive for its Bavarian atmosphere and excellent German-style cuisine. Schnitzels and grilled rainbow trout highlight the menu. The restaurant is located at the foot of the Continental Divide just east of the Idaho border. ~ 1545 Targhee Pass Highway, seven and a half miles west of West Yellowstone; 406-646-7296. MODERATE.

SHOPPING

Outside the park's west entrance in West Yellowstone, check out **Eagle's Store** for Western wear, outdoor equipment and American

Indian crafts. ~ 3 Canyon Avenue; 406-646-9300. **Madison Gift Shop** carries a large selection of souvenirs. ~ 139 Yellowstone Avenue; 406-646-7745. **Oak N Pine** features custom lodge-style furniture and handmade quilts. ~ 124 Canyon Avenue; 406-646-9657. Visit the **Book Peddler** for volumes about the West as well as espressos and baked goods. ~ 106 Canyon Avenue; 406-646-9358.

NIGHTLIFE   The **Musical Moose Playhouse** focuses on vaudeville revues presented "nearly year-round." ~ 124 Madison Avenue; 406-646-9710. The **Playmill Theatre** has presented a summer season of melodrama and musical comedy since 1964. ~ 29 Madison Avenue; 406-646-7757.

Nine miles north on Route 191 (just past the Route 287 junction) is **Eino's Tavern,** which has a grill alongside Hebgen Lake, big-screen TV and even fuel for snowmobilers. ~ 8955 Gallatin Road; 406-646-9344.

PARKS   **HENRY'S LAKE STATE PARK** 🚶🚲🛶🎣🚤🛥️⛵ Henry's Lake is a quiet mountain oasis just 15 miles west of West Yellowstone, on the Idaho side of Targhee Pass. Sheltered on three sides by the Continental Divide, the lake fills an alpine valley of about 12 square miles. The 585-acre park, on the southeast shore near its outlet to Henry's Fork of the Snake River, is ideal for trout-fishing enthusiasts. Facilities include picnic areas and restrooms. Restaurants and groceries are in West Yellowstone and Island Park. Day-use fee, $2. ~ From West Yellowstone, take Route 20 west 13 miles to Goose Bay Road; turn northwest two miles to the park entrance; 208-558-7532.

▲ All 50 RV/tent sites have hookups; $12 per night for RVs, $6 for tents; 14-day maximum stay. Open Memorial Day weekend to September.

▼▼▼▼▼▼▼▼▼▼▼
Livingston Area

East of Bozeman, interstate Route 90 crosses a low pass in the Bridger Range and descends to the Yellowstone River Valley, where it enters the historic rail town of Livingston. The hub of the upper Yellowstone Valley, Livingston is a place where wilderness meets the Wild West. Founded in 1882 by the Northern Pacific Railroad and named for a director of that line, the town was the original gateway to Yellowstone National Park. Tourists changed trains here from the main east–west line to a spur line that followed the Yellowstone River upstream to Gardiner at the park's north entrance.

The community quickly became a trading center for farmers, ranchers and miners of the Yellowstone Valley, and by 1905 a thriving city of about 5000 people had emerged. Since then, growth has been modest: Modern Livingston's population hovers around 6700. But 436 buildings from that turn-of-the-century boom era are preserved; its downtown historic district and three residential districts are on the National Register of Historic Places. Among them is a log cabin that once was the home of notorious frontiers-woman Martha "Calamity Jane" Canary. (When a public disturbance led to her being jailed, she became disenchanted with Livingston and left town.)

The place to begin a walking tour, or to gather information on area attractions, is the **Livingston Chamber of Commerce**. ~ 212 West Park Street, Livingston; 406-222-0850. The Chamber and adjoining **Livingston Depot Center** are located in the 1902 Northern Pacific station, designed in Italian villa–style by the same architectural firm that created New York's Grand Central Station. The Depot Center is a satellite museum for the Buffalo Bill Historical Center in Cody, Wyoming; exhibits include rail history, Yellowstone exploration, Western art and more. It's open daily from mid-May to mid-October and doubles as a performing arts center. Admission. ~ 200 West Park Street, Livingston; 406-222-2300.

SIGHTS

In winter, Absaroka Dog-sled Treks takes couples or small groups on canine-powered trips into the Emigrant Peak area. ~ Chico Hot Springs; 406-333-4933.

There are more history exhibits across the tracks and two blocks north at the **Park County Museum**. Located in an early-20th-century schoolhouse, it's open daily in summer and by appointment. Admission. ~ 118 West Chinook Street, Livingston; 406-222-3506. Taxidermy enthusiasts will appreciate the **Lone Wolf Wildlife Museum**, a mile south of the city center. Admission. ~ Sleeping Giant Trade Center, Route 89, Livingston; 406-222-6140.

PARADISE VALLEY The Route 89 corridor upriver to Yellowstone Park, 53 driving miles south of Livingston, follows the scenic **Paradise Valley** beneath the constant gaze of the Absaroka Range. The Yellowstone River—the longest free-flowing (undammed) river in the United States—is considered a blue-ribbon trout stream through this portion, which is also popular among whitewater rafters.

Twenty miles south, near the small towns of Emigrant and Pray, are the **Chico Hot Springs**. A resort here provides access to natural mineral hot springs and other health therapies. ~ Chico Road, Pray; 406-333-4933.

Farther south, via Sixmile Creek Road, **Dailey Lake** is as popular among board-sailing enthusiasts as with trout and walleye fishermen. Trailheads above the lake lead into the Absaroka-Beartooth Wilderness Area.

Climbing the Yellowstone valley from Emigrant, Route 89 circles 8600-foot Dome Mountain, home of a historic winter elk range. West of the hamlet of Miner (38 miles from Livingston),

Text continued on page 190.

Choosing a Guest Ranch

Only two states, Colorado and Wyoming, have more guest ranches than does Montana, and perhaps no one region in either of those states boasts more of these rural resorts than south central Montana.

The bible of the guest-ranch genre, *Gene Kilgore's Ranch Vacations*, lists 15 of them in this part of Montana, and official state tourism rolls triple the figure.

The earliest guest ranches (then better known as "dude ranches") were established around the turn of the century in Montana, Wyoming and Colorado for easterners enthralled by the idea of Buffalo Bill–style adventure and romance.

With railroads traversing the continent and the hostile Indian tribes subjugated, working cattle ranchers often found themselves besieged by requests from friends and relatives who wanted to come and visit for weeks at a time. Some of these ranchers saw an opportunity to increase their revenues, and so began advertising accommodations and charging guests.

By the 1920s, 35 of them in the greater Yellowstone National Park area banded together to form **The Dude Ranchers' Association**, which today remains the most respected of all guest-ranch coalitions.

In recent years, membership in the association has more than tripled to 109 ranches in 13 western states and two Canadian provinces. That figure represents only a fraction of the total number of guest ranches. ~ Box 471, La Porte, CO 80535; 970-223-8440.

In 1994, according to the Tourism Works for America Council in Washington, D.C., visitors spent $31 million for U.S. guest-ranch vacations, paying anywhere from $550 to $1895 per week for the privilege. A 1994 survey by the council indicated that five percent of the adult U.S. population had at some time visited a dude or cattle ranch.

In the text of this chapter, you may already have read about the Boulder River, Lone Mountain, Lost Fork and Mountain Sky ranches. But there are many others.

For instance, there's the historic **Beartooth Ranch**, at the edge of the Absaroka-Beartooth Wilderness in the canyon of the Stillwater River, which has been hosting guests since 1904. The ranch is a charter member of The Dude Ranchers' Association. ~ HC 54, Box 350, Nye, MT 59061; 406-328-6194.

The **C-B Cattle and Guest Ranch**, 20 miles southeast of Ennis, has no planned activities but attracts scores of anglers each summer to fly-fish the renowned waters of the Madison River. ~ Box 604, Cameron, MT 59720; 406-682-4954.

There's the **Diamond J Ranch**, surrounded by the Lee Metcalf Wilderness, whose family orientation is clear in the number and variety of children's programs it offers: from horseback riding and wrangling to fishing, swimming and mountain biking.

In the foothills northeast of Bozeman is the **G Bar M Ranch**, a working cattle ranch that has welcomed guests since the 1930s. Guests spend most of their week herding cattle, repairing fences, milking cows and basically paying for the chance to be ranch hands. ~ Box AE, Clyde Park, MT 59018; 406-686-4423.

That's just a sampling of the options available. But how do you, as a first-time potential guest, determine which ranch experience is best for you and your family?

Not the least factor is price range. You can expect to pay anywhere from $75 to $275 per person per night. At the low end, your accommodation will be quite rustic and you may be cooking your own meals. At the top end, you will live in luxury and dine on gourmet cuisine. Many ranches require a one-week minimum stay for their guests, especially during summer; others may allow guests to stay on a nightly basis.

Also consider the range and choice of activities, the existence of children's programs, the level of staff involvement, the number of other guests with whom you'll be sharing your visit, and the accessibility of the ranch.

Rock Creek Road extends nine miles to a trailhead for the **Gallatin Petrified Forest**, whose fossilized specimens include still-upright tree trunks estimated to be between 35 and 55 million years old. Another nine miles past Miner, near the small tourist center of **Corwin Springs**, bright-red **Devils Slide** is an unmistakable geological feature: The exposed sedimentary rocks at the base of Cinnabar Mountain are about 200 million years old.

Gardiner, astride the Yellowstone River just five miles north of Mammoth Hot Springs in Yellowstone National Park, began life as an entertainment boomtown for soldiers stationed at Mammoth in the late 19th century. By the time the army turned over its responsibilities to the National Park Service during World War I, the saloons, gambling halls and cigar factory were less important to Gardiner than its position as a terminus for the Yellowstone rail spur from Livingston. As at West Yellowstone, tourists changed from train coaches to stagecoaches at Gardiner to explore the park.

Today, more than one million visitors a year stream through the Roosevelt Arch to the North Entrance, the only park entrance open year-round. The town, while retaining some of its Wild West flavor, has a tidy tourist infrastructure of motels, restaurants, bars, a cinema and plenty of outfitters. For more information contact the **Chamber of Commerce**. ~ P.O. Box 81, Gardiner, MT 59030; 406-848-7971.

HIDDEN ►

Six miles northeast of Gardiner on a rutted dirt road is **Jardine**, where miners struck gold in 1866. Various century-old mining structures can be seen by ambitious visitors to this not-quite-a-ghost-town: Since 1989, the Mineral Hill Mine has pulled about 42,000 ounces of gold a year from the side of Palmer Mountain. ~ Forest Road 493; 406-848-7971.

LODGING

It seems only natural to stay in historic hotels throughout historic communities. The **Murray Hotel**, in the heart of town, has 43 recently renovated rooms with simple decor, private baths and standard amenities. There's also a restaurant and bar. ~ 201 West Park Street, Livingston; 406-222-1350, fax 406-222-6547. BUDGET TO MODERATE.

The **Mountain Sky Guest Ranch** is one of the grand old dude ranches of Montana. Located 32 miles southwest of Livingston, five miles west of Route 89 in the Paradise Valley, it has 28 cabins—some rustic, some modern—and a rebuilt lodge with three stone fireplaces and a grand piano. Guests must book a full week's stay, during which they get three gourmet meals daily, evening entertainment, top-class horseback riding and fly-fishing. ~ Big Creek Road, Emigrant; 406-333-4911, 800-548-3392, fax 406-587-3977. ULTRA-DELUXE.

Six miles north of Mammoth Hot Springs, the two-story **Yellowstone Village Motel** is all rustic wood on the outside but virtually brand-new inside (it opened in 1992). The rooms include 40 standard-size units and two family condominium suites with full kitchens. The motel also has an indoor pool and sauna, a game arcade and a guest laundry. ~ Route 89 North, Gardiner; 406-848-7417, 800-228-8158. BUDGET TO MODERATE.

The **Winchester Cafe**, in the 19th-century Murray Hotel, is the region's best fine-dining experience. Though the Victorian atmosphere is casual, you'll be treated to dinners of steaks and seafood, chicken and prime rib at reasonable prices. Breakfast and lunch are also served. ~ 201 West Park Street, Livingston; 406-222-2708. MODERATE.

DINING

Calamity Jane's Steakhouse, in the heart of Livingston's historic district, pays tribute to the rowdy late-19th-century frontierswoman who moved into a log cabin in this old rail town but found the sedentary lifestyle too tame. Buffalo steaks, chicken and seafood are hits at dinner here; soups and sandwiches are served at lunch, both inside and on the patio. ~ 106 East Park Street, Livingston; 406-222-2255. MODERATE.

At the north entrance of the park, the **Yellowstone Mine Restaurant**, in the Best Western by Mammoth Hot Springs, offers a fine steak-and-seafood menu amid the recreated ambience of a 19th-century mine. There's a children's menu, and breakfast is served as well. ~ Route 89 at Hellroaring Street, Gardiner; 406-848-7336. MODERATE.

Among Livingston's art galleries is the **Paradise Gallery**, where the art of Carol Newbury Howe and other wildlife artists is presented. ~ East River Road, Livingston; 406-222-6297. **Books Etc.** is the leading book dealer. ~ 106 South Main Street, Livingston; 406-222-7766.

SHOPPING

In Gardiner, **Kellem's Montana Saddlery** may be the most intriguing store outside the north entrance to Yellowstone Park; its inventory runs from handmade saddles and other cowboy gear to clothing, silver jewelry and Montana-made gifts. ~ 222 Main Street, Gardiner; 406-848-7776. The **Yellowstone Outpost Mall** puts ten shops, restaurants and the Chamber of Commerce under one roof at the north end of town. ~ Route 89 at Hellroaring Street, Gardiner; 406-848-7220. For literature and espresso, try **High Country Books**. ~ Park Street, Gardiner; 406-848-7707.

Livingston has a pair of noteworthy stage groups. The **Firehouse 5 Playhouse** presents melodrama and vaudeville Tuesday through Saturday nights and Sunday afternoons through the summer, and

NIGHTLIFE

a variety of community musicals and holiday specials during the winter. ~ Sleeping Giant Trade Center, Route 89, Livingston; 406-222-1420. The **Blue Slipper Theatre**, now in its fourth decade as a community theater, serves up comedies, mysteries, dramas and other more serious productions in a season lasting from fall through spring. ~ 113 East Callender Street, Livingston; 406-222-7720.

Imbibers will enjoy the **Livingston Bar & Grille**'s extensive beer menu. ~ 130 North Main Street, Livingston; 406-222-7909.

Seven miles north of Gardiner, the professional **Paradise Players** present family-oriented dinner theater from June to September. ~ Route 89, Corwin Springs; 406-848-7891.

The most historic bar in the greater Yellowstone area is Gardiner's **Two-Bit Saloon**, a mining-era relic that remains open 18 hours a day, year-round. ~ 2nd Street between Main and Park streets, Gardiner; 406-848-7743.

PARKS   **SACAJAWEA PARK** ⌐ Located beside the Yellowstone River, this Livingston municipal park is one of the nicest in Montana. At its broad riverine lagoon, children can fish or feed ducks and geese. Within the park is Livingston Civic Center, where indoor scenes from Robert Redford's 1992 *A River Runs Through It* were filmed. Picnic areas, restrooms, band shell, tennis courts, a playground and wading pool round out the amenities. ~ From downtown Livingston, follow South Yellowstone Street to its south end; 406-222-8155.

▼▼▼▼▼▼▼▼▼▼▼▼▼
Big Timber Area   Big Timber—33 miles east of Livingston and an hour's drive from Bozeman at the foot of the Crazy Mountains—is at a geographical transition point. West of the town, the Absaroka Range rises to lofty heights, while east stretch the vast Great Plains. A livestock-producing and recreational center surrounded by Gallatin National Forest, Big Timber has several sites of interest.

SIGHTS   A historical museum—the **Crazy Mountain Museum**—features a miniature reproduction of Big Timber as it appeared in 1907, when it was known as Cobblestone City. Exact down to the finest architectural details, it covers more than 12 blocks of the old town at a scale of $\frac{1}{16}$ inch to one foot. Fewer than 20 percent of the 184 buildings represented in the model still stand in downtown Big Timber. Open summers only. ~ Frontage Road, Route 90 Exit 367, Big Timber; 406-932-5126.

Nearby is the **Victorian Village**, a museum and antique store. Exhibits include a complete hot-metal print shop, millinery and dry-goods shops, a harness barn, a carpenter's shop and a chapel.

Open summers only. Admission. ~ Frontage Road, Route 90 Exit 367, Big Timber; 406-932-4378.

Also in Big Timber, firearms aficionados enjoy weekday tours of the **Shiloh Rifle Manufacturing Co.** ~ 201 Centennial Drive, Big Timber; 406-932-4454. Sharps and Winchester rifles and accessories circa 1870 are on display at the **C. Sharps Arms** showroom. ~ 100 Centennial Drive, Big Timber; 406-932-4353. The **Yellowstone River Trout Hatchery** is open year-round for visits. ~ Fairgrounds Road, Big Timber; 406-932-4434.

The **Crazy Mountains**, a small but rugged Rockies subrange whose jagged summits rise to more than 11,000 feet, is located to the north of Big Timber. The range is mostly contained within Gallatin National Forest. The most direct access is via Big Timber Canyon Road, which begins 11 miles north of Big Timber off Route 191.

Columbus is the home of Montana Silversmiths, the world's largest manufacturer of silver jewelry, belt buckles and other cowboy-style trappings. ~ Route 78 South; 406-322-4555.

South of Big Timber, Route 298 (Boulder Road) follows the **Boulder River** more than 40 miles upstream from its confluence with the Yellowstone River to near its source in the Absaroka-Beartooth Wilderness. A good number of national-forest campgrounds are located along this corridor; more than a dozen trails extend into the wilderness, where vehicular travel is forbidden. A highlight along this route is the **Boulder River Falls**, 27 miles south of Big Timber. The impressive 90-foot falls once cascaded through a natural stone bridge at low water, but the arch collapsed in 1988 after centuries of erosion.

Sheep and cattle ranchers have waged a successful war against prairie dogs, which compete with stock for grasses and forage, and whose burrowing creates holes that often cause leg injuries to livestock. The prairie dog's range is now less than 20 percent its original size. The **Greycliff Prairie Dog Town State Park**, nine miles east of Big Timber, is a 98-acre park that preserves a traditional prairie-dog colony, albeit tiny compared to the huge cities of these ground squirrels that once spread across the plains. Admission. ~ Route 90 Exit 377, Greycliff; 406-252-4654.

The town of **Columbus**, an old stage and rail station on Route 90 where the Stillwater River joins the Yellowstone, lies about halfway between Big Timber and Billings. Aside from being the junction of Route 78, which threads its way 48 miles through the foothills of the Beartooth Range to Red Lodge, Columbus is the gateway to the Stillwater Mining Company, largest platinum mine in the United States, 35 miles west near Nye. The **Museum of the Beartooths** here has one of the finest collections of homestead-era farm and household machinery you'll ever find. ~ 440 East 5th Avenue North, Columbus; 406-322-4588.

LODGING Big Timber's best lodging is the **C. M. Russell Lodge** at the west end of town. The two-story motor hotel has 42 rooms with interior corridors, cable TV, a guest laundry and a gift shop. There's also a restaurant and lounge. Smoking is not permitted. ~ Route 90 Exit 367, Big Timber; 406-932-5244. BUDGET.

One of Montana's longest established guest ranches is the **Boulder River Ranch**. Situated at 5000 feet in an Absaroka Mountain canyon, the ranch—which is open only from June to mid-September, and accepts payment by cash or check only—first opened to guests in 1918. Today it's run by the third- and fourth-generation Aller family, and boasts 15 rustic cabins, family-style meals and a wide range of riding and fishing activities. ~ Route 298, McLeod; 406-932-6406. BUDGET TO MODERATE.

DINING The best place to dine in Big Timber is the two-story, red-brick **Grand Hotel**. Built in 1890, the historic hotel's Victorian restaurant serves outstanding steaks, lamb and pan-roasted salmon. Perhaps because of the fire danger, smoking is not permitted in the restaurant or in the adjacent bar. ~ 139 McLeod Street, Big Timber; 406-932-4459. MODERATE.

HIDDEN ▶ If you're traveling from Columbus up the Stillwater River road to Nye, you can plan on a meal at **Montana Hanna's Trout Hole Restaurant**. Open daily for lunch and dinner, this casual eatery offers great trout, as well as ribs and chicken, in a rustic setting with a view upon the Beartooth Range. No smoking. ~ Route 419, Dean; 406-328-6780. MODERATE.

SHOPPING The **Zemsky-Hines Gallery** features the works of resident Western artists Jessica Zemsky and Jack Hines along with other regional artists. ~ 108 East 3rd Street, Big Timber; 406-932-5307.

PARKS **GREYCLIFF PRAIRIE DOG TOWN STATE PARK** 🏃 Located just off the freeway, this park preserves a traditional colony of common black-tailed prairie dogs. Visitors can stroll among the burrows and observe the animals' behavior, especially their community warning system, but they are actively discouraged from feeding the squirrel-like rodents, who remain wary of intrusions. Picnic areas, restrooms and interpretive displays are among the facilities. Restaurants and groceries are in Big Timber. ~ From Big Timber, take Route 90 east nine miles to Exit 377; 406-252-4654.

▼▼▼▼▼▼▼▼▼▼▼
Red Lodge Area An hour's drive southwest from Billings on Route 212, or two hours southeast from Livingston via Routes 90 and 78, brings travelers to the foot of Montana's loftiest mountains. Granite Peak, at 12,799 feet the highest of the high, crowns the plateau that towers above the historic mining town of

Red Lodge. It and numerous smaller communities provide access to the lakes and streams of Custer National Forest and the Absaroka-Beartooth Wilderness.

Red Lodge, which lists its elevation as 5555 feet, is the logical portal to the region. Its 2000 residents live in a lovely town whose appearance may not be a lot different from what it was during its coal-mining boom of 1890–1910.

Six blocks of Broadway (the main street) from 8th to 14th streets and numerous side streets make up the **Red Lodge Historic District**. ~ 406-446-1718. Nearly all the buildings date from the boom period. Among them are the Theatorium, decorated with imported Italian marble statues; the 1889 railroad station; the 1893 Spofford (now Pollard) Hotel, which hosted such historical figures as "Buffalo Bill" Cody, "Calamity Jane" Canary and John "Liver Eatin'" Johnston; the 1899 Carbon County Courthouse; and the 1897 Finnish Opera House.

The Finns were one of many European groups who settled in their own small enclaves near the banks of Rock Creek. Others included Irish, Scots, Italians, Germans and Slavs. Today, those roots are celebrated each August during the nine-day Festival of Nations.

Much of the region's history is retold through artifacts and memorabilia south of town at the **Carbon County Museum**. ~ Route 212, Red Lodge; 406-446-3914. The old homestead cabin of "Liver Eatin'" Johnston, upon whose life the Robert Redford movie *Jeremiah Johnson* was based, stands intact on the grounds.

Five miles north of Red Lodge, the **Beartooth Nature Center & Children's Petting Zoo** exhibits native Montana animals in their natural habitats. The park also has a playground, picnic area and

SIGHTS

SAVING THE BEARTOOTH PLATEAU

In 1996, President Clinton negotiated a solution to a potential environmental crisis that had made Cooke City a hot topic in the region for years. A Canadian mining conglomerate obtained rights to Custer National Forest land outside the Absaroka-Beartooth Wilderness Area, two and a half miles from Yellowstone Park, and planned to begin extracting precious metals from 10,000-foot Crown Butte. Led by the Greater Yellowstone Coalition, conservationists maintained that mining in so fragile an ecosystem would severely pollute three major tributaries of the Yellowstone River, all of which have their sources on or near Crown Butte. Clinton, a regular visitor to nearby Jackson Hole, Wyoming, succeeded in trading land in less sensitive precincts for the Beartooth Plateau property.

concessions. Open daily in summer. Admission. ~ Coal Miners' Memorial Park, Route 212, Red Lodge; 406-446-1133.

The hills around Red Lodge were always rich in coal, but perhaps none more so than those flanking **Bearcreek**, over the hill to the east. In 1943, though, the mining industry—already on the wane—heard its death knell. An underground explosion in the Smith Mine killed 74 men near Washoe, four miles from Red Lodge. A tipple and several outbuildings still stand as sober reminders of Montana's worst coal-mining disaster.

Red Lodge's coal industry never recovered from the Smith Mine tragedy. Since World War II, tourism has been the economic mainstay of the area. In summer, Red Lodge is a northeastern gateway to Yellowstone National Park; in winter, the **Red Lodge Mountain Ski Area**, with 2000 feet of vertical terrain just six miles west of town, is a popular destination. ~ 101 Ski Run Road; 406-446-2610.

Spectacular mountain scenery lies west of Red Lodge off Route 78 via Roscoe. Particularly sterling is **East Rosebud Lake**, about 32 miles from Red Lodge. Above this small alpine lake, accessible by foot or horseback, East Rosebud Creek has carved a canyon reminiscent of Yosemite's glacial grandeur.

From mid-October to May, when the Beartooth Highway is closed, the area's towns are virtually isolated, reachable by only a 113-mile one-way road from Livingston, via Mammoth Hot Springs and Tower Junction.

The Yellowstone gateway route is the **Beartooth Highway** (Route 212 West). Officially opened in 1936, this 70-mile designated scenic byway through Custer and Shoshone national forests has been called "the most beautiful drive in America" by CBS television correspondent Charles Kuralt. The trip through isolated Cooke City to the park entrance may take up to three hours because of the highway's elevation (nearly 11,000 feet at its high point) and its prodigious number of switchbacks. For more information, contact the U.S. Forest Service (406-446-2103).

But *breathtaking* is not the only descriptive word that applies here. Numerous trails leave the highway to enter the Beartooth Plateau portion of the **Absaroka-Beartooth Wilderness**. Nearly a million acres in size, this wilderness area includes some two dozen mountains over 12,000 feet in elevation. Traveling around the rim and over the top of the Beartooth Plateau, visitors get spectacular vistas across magnificent glaciated peaks and pristine alpine lakes. (Note: Because snow stays late and returns early, the Beartooth Highway normally is open only from June to the middle of October.)

Sixty-six miles across the Beartooth Plateau from Red Lodge, and accessible only after a 35-mile passage through a corner of Wyoming, is the Montana town of **Cooke City**. Located just four miles from Yellowstone's northeast entrance, the village goes about life in peaceful seclusion. Only a few hundred people live here and in the hamlet of **Silver Gate**, three miles west.

Cooke City is perhaps best regarded as a stepping-off point for wilderness excursions. There's fishing, hunting and mountain climbing in the adjacent mountains, as well as horseback and back-packing trips. The town also has a **Yellowstone Wildlife Museum** that displays more than 100 animals and birds in lifelike dioramas. Admission. ~ Route 212; 406-838-2265. For more information, contact the **Cooke City Chamber of Commerce.** ~ P.O. Box 1146, Cooke City, MT 59020; 406-838-2272, 406-838-2244.

Of particular note is the 14-mile trail to **Grasshopper Glacier**   ◄ *HIDDEN* in the Absaroka-Beartooth Wilderness Area. The glacier, one of the largest ice fields in the continental United States, takes its name from the millions of grasshoppers (of a now-extinct species) frozen in a sheer 80-foot cliff of glacial ice. Nearby is **Granite Peak**, at 12,799 feet Montana's tallest.

One of the region's classiest resorts is undoubtedly the **Rock Creek**   **LODGING** **Resort**, five miles south of Red Lodge at the foot of the Beartooth Highway. The handsome Beartooth Lodge and adjacent Grizzly Condos have 75 rooms (32 with kitchens) designed in contempo-rary rustic style with balconies. The Old Piney Dell restaurant serves exquisite American and Continental cuisine. The resort of-fers tennis and mountain biking as well as an indoor swimming pool, a sauna, a jacuzzi and a fitness club; golf, horseback riding, snowmobiling and skiing are available nearby. Kids have a play-ground and game room. ~ Route 212 South, Red Lodge; 406-446-1111, fax 406-446-3688. DELUXE.

Red Lodge's **Pollard Hotel**, built in 1893, once hosted the likes   ◄ *HIDDEN* of "Buffalo Bill" Cody and William Jennings Bryan. Now a cen-tury old, it's undergone a total facelift and is the only hotel in the northern Rockies to be accepted as a member of the select Historic Hotels of America. Entirely nonsmoking, the Pollard has 36 rooms and suites, some with indoor balconies, others with parlors and hot tubs, all with private bathrooms. Fare in the upscale restaurant is creative Continental; a full fitness club has saunas and a racquet-ball court. ~ 2 North Broadway, Red Lodge; 406-446-0001, 800-765-5273, fax 406-446-3733. MODERATE TO DELUXE.

For economical lodging in Red Lodge, check out the **Yodeler Motel**. The Yodeler's Scandinavian-style decor, and its willingness to take in dogs as well as people, make it a travelers' favorite. There are 22 rooms with coffeemakers and cable TV; rooms with steam baths, jacuzzis (and one kitchen) are available on request. ~ 601 South Broadway, Red Lodge; 406-446-1435, fax 406-446-1020. MODERATE.

In Cooke City, the **All Seasons Mine Co. Hotel & Casino** has a little of everything. Most of the 32 guest rooms have queen-size or double beds; all have full baths and Western-style decor. The hotel's restaurant is open for three meals daily, and there's a casino, hot tub and heated indoor pool; a snowmobile dealer (with rentals, of course) adjoins the hotel. ~ Route 212, Cooke City; 406-838-2251, 800-527-6462. MODERATE.

DINING

Pius' International Room is an elegant Continental restaurant that serves gourmet food and sophisticated wine in rustic surroundings. This is fine dining, priced to match. There's a pleasant bar as well. ~ 115 South Broadway, Red Lodge; 406-446-3333. DELUXE.

Just a block away, **17 Broadway: The Restaurant** has a lunch and dinner menu of new American cuisine in the casual setting of a late-19th-century Victorian library. Sunday brunch is popular here. No smoking. ~ 17 South Broadway, Red Lodge; 406-446-1717. MODERATE.

Two miles north, **The Round Barn** is a bargain for big eaters. Nightly except Tuesday it offers a smorgasbord of salads, main courses and desserts to hungry families. The 64-foot-diameter brick barn was once a milking parlor for a dairy farm; today, the upper story is a dinner theater where vaudeville, family musicals and visiting instrumentalists appear throughout the summer. ~ Route 212, Red Lodge; 406-446-1197. BUDGET.

Near Yellowstone Park's remote northeast corner is **Joan & Bill's Restaurant**, certainly a throwback to another era. Three meals are served daily in a relaxed and rustic family-style atmosphere in the heart of the old mining town of Cooke City. ~ Route 212, Cooke City; 406-838-2280. BUDGET.

NIGHTLIFE

Red Lodge locals spend a lot of time at the **Snow Creek Saloon**. ~ 124 South Broadway, Red Lodge; 406-446-2542. On weekends, they often travel eight miles east to the **Bear Creek Saloon**, where pig races and enchiladas are the big events on hot summer nights. ~ Route 308, Bearcreek; 406-446-3481.

PARKS

ABSAROKA-BEARTOOTH WILDERNESS AREA 🏃 🏇 🛶 Abutting Yellowstone National Park's northern edge, and nearly half as large as the park itself, this 944,000-acre wilderness comprises two distinctly different mountain ranges: in its western half, the rugged, forested Absarokas; in the east, near Red Lodge, the alpine meadows and plateaus of the Beartooths. Several Absaroka peaks top 11,000 feet, but more than two dozen Beartooth summits exceed 12,000, including Granite Peak, Montana's highest mountain at 12,799 feet. A unique feature is the Grasshopper Glacier, a remote ice field named for the millions of ancient grasshoppers frozen into the face of a sheer 80-foot ice cliff. Seven species of trout inhabit the small lakes of the Beartooth Plateau. The wilderness features nearly 1000 alpine lakes and more than 700 miles of hiking trails. Horseback riders are welcome; vehicles are not. Restaurants and groceries are in Red Lodge, Livingston and other towns. ~ The Absaroka-Beartooth has many gateways, including Mill Creek Road, off Route 89 south of Livingston; the Boulder River road from McLeod, south of Big Timber; East and West Rosebud roads, off Route 78 south of Absarokee; and Route 212 (the Beartooth Highway) southwest of Red Lodge; 406-587-6747.

▲ Primitive only.

COONEY RESERVOIR STATE PARK Fishing, boating, swimming and wildlife watching are the hobbies of choice at this irrigation reservoir, south of the Yellowstone River in the shadow of the Beartooth Range. Facilities include picnic areas and restrooms. Groceries are located at the park; restaurants are in Red Lodge and Columbus. Day-use fee, $3. ~ From Red Lodge, head north 21 miles on Route 212 to Boyd, then go west eight miles on Cooney Dam Road; 406-445-2326.

▲ There are 75 RV/tent sites, none with hookups; $7 per night; 14-day maximum stay.

Outdoor Adventures

The whitewater streams that flow northward from the Yellowstone caldera—the Madison, Gallatin, Yellowstone, Boulder and Stillwater rivers, as well as Rosebud and Rock creeks and other rivulets—are all internationally renowned, blue-ribbon trout streams. No fewer than seven species of trout, including rainbow, brook, brown, cutthroat, bull, lake and golden, are taken from their waters, as well as arctic grayling and mountain whitefish. At lower elevations, Dailey and some other lakes offer walleye pike, yellow perch and other species.

FISHING

There are two good places to purchase tackle and inquire about guided expeditions. **Montana Troutfitters Orvis Shop** is one. ~ 1716 West Main Street, Bozeman; 406-587-4707. **Bud Lilly's Trout Shop** is the other. ~ 39 Madison Avenue, West Yellowstone; 406-646-7801. Fly-fishing specialists include **The Rivers Edge**. ~ 2012 North 7th Avenue, Bozeman; 406-586-5373. Also try **Jacklin's Outfitters for the World of Fly-Fishing**. ~ 105 Yellowstone Avenue, West Yellowstone; 406-646-7336. In Emigrant, contact **Big Sky Flies & Guides** for fly-fishing information. ~ Route 89, Emigrant; 406-333-4401.

RIVER RUNNING

There's outstanding whitewater rafting and kayaking in the upper reaches of the Madison, Gallatin, Yellowstone, Boulder and Stillwater rivers, south of Bozeman. The Madison boasts Beartrap

Canyon, with alternating calm water and rapids through the Lee Metcalf Wilderness below Ennis Lake. The Gallatin, squeezed into a narrow canyon above Big Sky, has the region's most challenging whitewater. The Yellowstone, above Emigrant, appeals to families with wildlife viewing, hot springs and a handful of exciting-but-not-too-exciting rapids.

Flatwater paddlers enjoy the gentler stretches of the Jefferson River (Twin Bridges to Three Forks) and Yellowstone River (Pray to Livingston).

Keep in mind that rivers are higher in June, when snow is still melting in the summits, than in August. That means the water is usually colder and more wild in spring, but rocks pose more of a hazard in late summer.

Leading outfitters in the region include **Montana Whitewater**. ~ P.O. Box 1552, Bozeman, MT 59715; 406-763-4465. Also try **Yellowstone Raft Company**. ~ P.O. Box 160262, Big Sky, MT 59716; 406-995-4613. In Red Lodge, contact **Beartooth Whitewater**, which runs the Stillwater. ~ 601 North Broadway, Red Lodge; 406-446-3142. Many outfitters also offer guided kayaking expeditions.

DOWNHILL SKIING

BOZEMAN AREA   Just 16 miles from Bozeman, an easy distance for a day destination, is **Bridger Bowl**. The resort's "mogul-cutter" grooming equipment and its steep Bridger Ridge—looming 500 feet above the upper lifts, for those willing to hike a bit—make it a favorite mountain for expert skiers and snowboarders. But there are plenty of groomed bowls and powder glades for novice and intermediate skiers. The Gallatin National Forest resort has 2000 acres of terrain and a 2000-foot vertical drop from its 8100-foot summit. Fifty runs are served by five chairlifts and one surface tow. ~ 15795 Bridger Canyon Road, Bozeman; 406-586-2389, 800-223-9609.

The **Big Sky Ski & Summer Resort**, in the Madison Range less than an hour's drive south of Bozeman, is beginning to get its due as a major national destination for winter-sports lovers. Established in the 1970s, the ski resort boasts a vertical drop of more than 3000 feet (the state's longest) from the 10,000-foot level of Lone Mountain to the Mountain Village complex at its base. Two gondolas, five chairlifts and three surface tows serve 55 runs that weave across 2100 acres of skiable terrain. All levels of skiing ability are well served. ~ Big Sky Road, Big Sky; 406-995-4211, 800-548-4486.

RED LODGE AREA   **Red Lodge Mountain**, at the edge of the Beartooth Plateau just outside the old coal-mining town of Red Lodge, is little more than an hour's drive from Billings. Five chairlifts ascend to the summit of 9416-foot Grizzly Peak, from which

35 runs drop 2016 feet to the base lodge. The ski resort is in Custer National Forest. Lodging is in Red Lodge. ~ Red Lodge Mountain Road; 406-446-2610, 800-444-8977.

Ski Rentals For downhill and cross-country equipment rentals or purchases and information, visit **Chalet Sports**. ~ 108 West Main Street, Bozeman; 406-587-4595. Or try **Sir Michael's Sport Shoppe**. ~ 21 North Broadway, Red Lodge; 406-446-1613. **World Boards Inc.** is the place for snowboarders. ~ 601 West Main Street, Bozeman; 406-587-1707. A cross-country specialist is the **Cache Creek Outdoor Shoppe**. ~ 131 West Main Street, Bozeman; 406-587-0975.

CROSS-COUNTRY SKIING

The region's leading nordic center is the **Bohart Ranch Cross-Country Ski Center**, just up the road from the Bridger Bowl downhill area. Bohart Ranch has 30 kilometers of groomed and tracked trails, as well as a year-round biathlon training range and a warming cabin. ~ 16621 Bridger Canyon Road, Bozeman; 406-586-9070. At Big Sky, the **Lone Mountain Ranch** caters to cross-country skiers with 75 kilometers of groomed and tracked trails for all ability levels. ~ Big Sky; 406-995-4644. Just outside the boundary of Yellowstone National Park, **The Rendezvous Ski Trails** offer 26 kilometers of groomed trails, and another eight kilometers ungroomed, from November through April. The U.S. national cross-country and biathlon (skiing and shooting) teams train here each year. ~ West Yellowstone; 406-646-7701.

For information on renting equipment, see the ski-rental section in "Downhill Skiing" above.

GOLF

Eighteen-hole public golf courses include **Bridger Creek Golf Club**. ~ 2710 McIlhattan Road, Bozeman, 406-586-2333. In Big Sky there's the Arnold Palmer–designed **Big Sky Golf Course**. ~ Meadow Village, Big Sky; 406-995-4706. Also try the **Red Lodge Mountain**

✔ **CHECK THESE OUT—UNIQUE OUTDOOR ADVENTURES**

- Play catch-and-release with seven species of trout that inhabit the blue-ribbon streams flowing north from Yellowstone Park. *page 199*
- Challenge the Gallatin River's rugged whitewater as it rushes through a narrow gorge at the foot of the Spanish Peaks. *page 200*
- Indulge your passion for winter sports at the Big Sky Resort, where downhill and Nordic skiers are equally delighted. *pages 200, 201*
- Hike the Granite Peak Trail around Montana's highest mountain to the Grasshopper Glacier, where millions of prehistoric grasshoppers are frozen into the face of an ice cliff. *pages 205*

Golf Course. ~ 828 Upper Continental Drive, Red Lodge; 406-446-3344.

TENNIS

City parks and recreation offices have exhaustive listings of municipal courts. In Bozeman, try **Bogart Park**. ~ 325 South Church Avenue. Or for more information, call 406-587-4724.

RIDING STABLES

The **Grace Meadows Equestrian Center** has horses available for country canters. ~ 1021 Cobb Hill Road, Bozeman; 406-585-9345. **Beartooth Mountain Wagon Trains & Cattle Drives** climb into high country along the Meeteetse Trail in the foothills of the Beartooth Range. ~ P.O. Box 63, Red Lodge, MT 59068; 406-446-2179. Proficient riders can rent steeds for unguided trips from **Lone Rider Stables**. ~ 1111 Targhee Pass Highway, West Yellowstone; 406-646-7900.

PACK TRIPS & LLAMA TREKS

Overnight pack trips from a night to a week or longer can be set up for fishermen, hunters, photographers or nature lovers. Most trips are guided, but some outfitters can arrange "wilderness drop trips": They'll pack you in and out, but you're on your own during the interim.

There are dozens of outfitters in the region. **Cayuse Outfitters** offers Absaroka tours that focus on archaeology. ~ P.O. Box 1218, Livingston, MT 59047; 406-222-2100. **Jake's Horses** climbs into the Madison Range near the Big Sky resort complex, off Route 191. ~ Doe Creek Road, Big Sky; 406-995-4630. **Diamond P Ranch** offers pack trips into Yellowstone National Park. ~ 4865 Targhee Pass Highway, West Yellowstone; 406-646-7246. **Medicine Lake Outfitters** offers much of the same. ~ 3246 Linney Road, Belgrade; 406-388-4938.

The Absaroka-Beartooth and Lee Metcalf wildernesses—between Bozeman/Livingston and Yellowstone National Park—are extremely popular for pack trips. Visitors centers can offer extensive lists of outfitters.

Wilderness llama-trekking expeditions are offered by **Yellowstone Llamas**. ~ P.O. Box 5042, Bozeman, MT 59717; 406-586-6872.

BIKING

Bozeman is the biking center of the southern Montana region. Bicyclists and runners share numerous urban trails, chief among them the one-and-a-half-mile **Gallagator Linear**, which connects the Museum of the Rockies, on Kagy Boulevard near South 3rd Avenue, with Bogart Park, at South Church Avenue and Story Street. An extension of the Gallagator is under construction at this writing. Also popular is the **Painted Hills Trail**, off Kagy Boulevard in the southeast corner of Bozeman. (In winter, cross-country

skiers enjoy the same trails that bikers do when there's no snow.)
Inquire locally for the "Bozeman Area Bike Trail Map."

Mountain bikers enjoy roads and trails in national forests
throughout southern Montana. Among the most popular areas are
the seasonal alpine and Nordic ski trails at the **Big Sky Ski & Summer Resort**, south of Bozeman. ~ Big Sky Road, Big Sky; 406-995-4211. Bicycle tours through Yellowstone National Park are offered
by **Yellowstone Eco Tours**. ~ 555 Yellowstone Avenue, West Yellowstone; 406-646-9009.

Bike Rentals   The region has several leading bike shops. Check
out **Bangtail Bikes**. ~ 508 West Main Street, Bozeman; 406-587-4905. Also try **Yellowstone Bicycles**. ~ 132 Madison Avenue, West
Yellowstone; 406-646-7815. In Livingston, contact **Livingston
Cycle**. ~ 117 West Callender Street, Livingston; 406-222-2628. If
you're in the Red Lodge area, try **Wacky Spoke & Hackle**. ~ 1500
South Broadway, Red Lodge; 406-556-2138.

HIKING

The greater Yellowstone ecosystem is one of the most environmentally remarkable in North America, with its mountains and
river canyons, hot springs and alpine meadows, and its vast array
of wildlife. Hikers can explore the backcountry in a way that drivers never will. And they have the opportunity to take advantage of
several dozen recreational cabins available (by reservation) from
the U.S. Forest Service at a cost of $15 to $30 per night. Contact
specific National Forest offices.

Following are a few of the region's more popular trails. All distances listed are one way unless otherwise noted.

BOZEMAN AREA   Bridger Foothills National Recreation Trail
(20.8 miles) begins at the foot of Montana State University's hillside "M" at Bozeman's northern city limits, and follows the rim of
the Bridger Range through Gallatin National Forest. It ends after
a 2640-foot elevation gain at Fairy Lake campground, at the foot
of 9665-foot Sacajawea Peak, highest summit in the Bridgers.

Palisades Falls National Recreation Trail (.6 mile) is designed
for visually impaired hikers. Beginning about 20 miles south of
Bozeman off East Fork Road, above Hyalite Canyon, the hard-surfaced Gallatin National Forest trail climbs just over 500 feet to
the 900-foot waterfall. There are descriptive signs in both English
and Braille.

Hyalite Peak Trail (7.2 miles) ascends to the peak of 10,299-foot
Hyalite Peak, high point of the Gallatin Range south of Bozeman.
The trailhead for this strenuous climb is at 7000 feet, three miles
south of Hyalite Reservoir at the end of Hyalite Canyon Road.

THREE FORKS AREA   Potosi Trail (3 miles) begins at the Beaverhead National Forest's Potosi Campground, on South Willow Creek

Road 13 miles southwest of Harrison off Route 287. Moderately difficult, it climbs a couple of steep ridges to an alpine plateau with wonderful views over a series of small lakes and streams.

Indian Creek Trail (17 miles) links the Madison and Gallatin river valleys with a route across the Madison Range through the Lee Metcalf Wilderness Area. The best entrance is from Taylor Fork Road (at 7000 feet) off Route 191 between Big Sky and West Yellowstone; the path ascends Taylor Creek, transits an 8500-foot saddle just past the Cache Creek Ranger Station, then descends Indian Creek to Bear Creek Road (at 6000 feet) southeast of Cameron off Route 287.

WEST YELLOWSTONE AREA The best trails in this vicinity are in Yellowstone National Park itself. **Yellowstone Eco Tours** offers guided walks on many of them. ~ 555 Yellowstone Avenue, West Yellowstone; 406-646-9009. If you're on your own, check out **Skyline Ridge Trail** (21 miles) through the Cabin Creek Recreation and Wildlife Management Area north of Hebgen Lake. This track, which follows the base of a 10,000-foot ridge across an alpine meadow, is reached via Forest Road 986 (off Route 191) or Forest Road 985 (off Route 287).

LIVINGSTON AREA **Pine Creek Trail** (5 miles) follows steep, rocky Pine Creek from the Pine Creek campground, 14 miles south of Livingston, past Pine Creek Falls to glacial Jewell Lake. The alpine gem lies at 9032 feet in the Absaroka-Beartooth Wilderness. There's a 3400-foot elevation gain on this trail.

Rock Creek North Trail (4 miles) climbs 2000 feet into the Crazy Mountains from a Gallatin National Forest trailhead off Rock Creek Road North, northeast of Livingston. It ends at Rock Lake, resting in a saddle between 11,214-foot Crazy Mountain and 10,737-foot Conical Peak, the highest points in the stark, craggy range.

BIG TIMBER AREA **Elk Mountain Trail** (14 miles) begins in the Boulder River watershed off Forest Road 31A, nine miles south of McLeod; follows Elk Creek to the ruins of an abandoned mining community on the flank of Elk Mountain; then crosses more Gallatin National Forest highlands before descending Lodgepole Creek to Limestone Road, near the huge platinum mine eight miles west of Nye.

RED LODGE AREA **Lake Fork Trail** (18 miles) offers a good glimpse of the Absaroka-Beartooth Wilderness. The trail begins at about 8000-foot elevation, one and a half miles west of Route 212, 14 miles south of Red Lodge; proceeds upstream past alpine lakes to Sundance Pass, at about 10,500 feet; then drops rapidly to the West Fork of Rock Creek, ending at about 7600 feet at the end of Route 71.

Granite Peak Trail (12 miles) is one of the three most often used routes to the summit of Montana's highest mountain, 12,799-foot Granite Peak in the Absaroka-Beartooth Wilderness. The trail begins at East Rosebud Lake and circles Froze to Death Mountain; from there, narrow rock ledges, glacial snow bridges and vertical climbs make this one for experienced mountaineers.

▼▼▼▼▼▼▼▼▼▼

Transportation

CAR

Route 90 is the east–west interstate artery through south-central Montana. Three Forks, Bozeman, Livingston, Big Timber and Columbus are all about a half-hour's drive, each from the last, along this route, which continues west to Butte and beyond, and east to Billings (and, ultimately Chicago and Boston). North–south **Route 287** (through Three Forks), **Route 191** (Bozeman), **Route 89** (Livingston) and **Route 212** (Red Lodge) tie the region's main towns to Yellowstone National Park.

AIR

Bozeman's **Gallatin Field Airport** is served year-round by Continental, Delta, Horizon, Northwest and SkyWest. From May to September, the **Yellowstone Airport** in West Yellowstone is served by SkyWest commuter flights and by charters.

BUS

Greyhound Bus Lines offers service to the all of the larger towns along the Route 90/94 corridor. In summer, it also stops at West Yellowstone, on a spur route south from Bozeman to Idaho Falls. ~ 800-231-2222.

Karst Stage (406-586-8567) and the **Montana Motor Coach Ltd.** (406-586-6121) offer seasonal service between Bozeman and West Yellowstone, Livingston and Gardiner, and Yellowstone National Park.

Gray Line offers seasonal charter service and guided tours through Yellowstone Park from West Yellowstone. ~ 633 Madison Avenue; 406-646-9374, 800-733-2304.

The central bus terminal in Bozeman is located at 625 North 7th Avenue. ~ 406-587-3110. In Livingston, it's at 332 South Main Street. ~ 406-222-2231. In West Yellowstone the terminal is at 127 Yellowstone Avenue. ~ 406-646-7666.

CAR RENTALS

Bozeman has 12 car-rental agencies. At Gallatin Field Airport, you'll find **Avis Rent A Car** (800-331-1212), **Budget Rent A Car** (800-527-0700), **Dollar-Rent-A-Car** (800-800-4000), **Hertz Rent A Car** (800-654-3131), **National Interrent** (800-227-7368) and **Thrifty Car Rental** (800-367-2277).

Outside the airport, rentals can also be found in Big Sky at **Gallatin Car Rental** (Big Sky Road; 406-995-4577), in Livingston at **Cranky Ranky's Livingston Auto Rentals** (207 South Second

Street; 406-222-8600) and in West Yellowstone at **Yellowstone Car Rentals** (Madison Street and Electric Avenue; 406-646-9332).

TAXIS   For cab service, consult Bozeman's **City Taxi** (406-586-2341), Big Sky's **Mountain Taxi** (406-995-4895) or Livingston's VIP **Taxi** (406-222-0200).

SEVEN

Yellowstone National Park

Yellowstone, the world's first national park, which overlaps Montana's southern border, remains first on nearly every visitor's list of Most Remarkable Places.

Nowhere else on earth is there as large and varied a collection of hydrothermal features—erupting geysers, bubbling mud caldrons, hissing fumaroles, gurgling mineral springs. The park is estimated to contain 10,000 thermal features, including more than 200 active geysers. Sites like Old Faithful Geyser and Mammoth Hot Springs have become part of the American lexicon, if not the American identity.

No other place in the contiguous 48 states has as great a concentration of mammals as does Yellowstone, or as extensive an interactive ecosystem. The park is home to an amazing five dozen species of mammals, including eight hoofed animals (bighorn sheep, pronghorn antelope, mountain goat, bison, elk, moose, mule deer and white-tailed deer) and two bear (black and grizzly).

Then there's the magnificent Grand Canyon of the Yellowstone, with its spectacular waterfalls: 136-square-mile Yellowstone Lake, the largest lake in North America at so high an elevation; rugged mountains reaching above 10,000 feet in all directions. It's no wonder folks didn't believe the first stories they heard coming out of the West.

The park's 2.2 million acres were set aside by Congress as a national park on March 1, 1872. But convincing Washington had not been easy.

The heart of Yellowstone was once a giant volcanic caldera, 28 miles wide, 47 miles long and thousands of feet deep. Some geologists think the explosion that created this crater 600,000 years ago may have been 2000 times greater than that of Mount St. Helens in 1980. Three ice ages sculpted the modern landscape, but they couldn't quiet the earth beneath. Nomadic tribes, who lived and hunted in the area for thousands of years thereafter, apparently avoided the most active geothermal areas, as did the Lewis and Clark expedition of 1804. Ever respectful of native superstition, William Clark noted that Indians who visited the region had "frequently heard a loud noise like thunder, which makes the earth tremble. . . . They conceive it possessed of spirits, who were adverse that men should be near them."

John Colter, a wayward member of the Lewis and Clark party, spent the winter of 1807 trapping and wandering throughout the area; he apparently was the first white man to observe the natural wonders of Yellowstone. But no one back East believed him. It didn't help when Jim Bridger, a mountain man as famous for his tall tales as for his knowledge of wilderness survival, claimed that "a fellow can catch a fish in an icy river, pull it into a boiling pool, and cook his fish without ever taking it off the hook."

Finally, in 1870, a group of respected Montana citizens set out to explore the area and put an end to rumor. Astonished by their discoveries (including Old Faithful), the Washburn-Langford-Doane party convinced Dr. Ferdinand Hayden, U.S. Geological Survey director, to investigate. In June 1871, Hayden took a survey party of 34 men, including painter Thomas Moran and photographer William Henry Jackson, to northwestern Wyoming. Their visuals and Hayden's 500-page report helped convince Congress to set aside this remarkable wilderness the following year. By the early 20th century, when rail access to the north entrance became possible, tourists were flooding in.

With 3472 square miles of terrain, Yellowstone—its name derives from the yellow rock cliffs of the Yellowstone River, which originates in the park—measures 54 miles east to west and 63 miles north to south, making it bigger than the state of Delaware. Its elevation ranges from 11,358 feet, atop Eagle Peak in the Absarokas, to 5314 feet, at the north entrance. The park has 370 miles of paved roads and more than 1200 miles of marked backcountry trails. In summer, when three million tourists visit, its population is greater than that of St. Louis or Cleveland. Its rainfall varies from 80 inches a year, in the southwestern Falls River Basin, to ten inches at Mammoth Hot Springs. Snow can fall in any month of the year.

Generally speaking, the park is open only from May through October, and many of its lodges and campgrounds have shorter seasons than that. But a second, the winter season—running from mid-December to mid-March—attracts snowmobilers and cross-country skiers to the Old Faithful and Mammoth Hot Springs areas. Ironically, although 96 percent of the park is in Wyoming, only two of its five entrances—from Jackson (south) and Cody (east)—are in this state. Three entrances—West Yellowstone (west), Gardiner (north) and Cooke City (northeast)—are in Montana, which contains only 3 percent of the park. Idaho has the other 1 percent.

The following touring itinerary assumes that you're entering Yellowstone from Mammoth Hot Springs, at its northern boundary. It proceeds clockwise around the park circuit for 141 miles and returns to Mammoth, but it can be easily picked up from any other gateway.

SIGHTS   **MAMMOTH HOT SPRINGS AREA** Where the North Entrance Road enters the park, it passes beneath the 30-foot stone **Roosevelt Arch**, dedicated in 1903 by President Theodore Roosevelt and inscribed "For the Benefit and Enjoyment of the People." It then swings by the steaming, subterranean outlet where the **Boiling River** flows into the Gardiner River and transits 600-foot-deep **Gardiner Canyon**.

The **Mammoth Hot Springs**, truly one of Yellowstone's high-lights, are a spectacular series of steaming travertine terraces in a steady state of metamorphosis. Super-heated ground water rises to the surface as carbonic acid, dissolving great quantities of natural limestone. As it seeps through cracks in the earth, it deposits the limestone, which solidifies again as travertine (calcium carbonate). This white mineral provides a habitat for colorful bacterial algae (cyanobacteria), whose varying pastel hues reflect the temperature of the water they inhabit: White bacteria live in the hottest water,

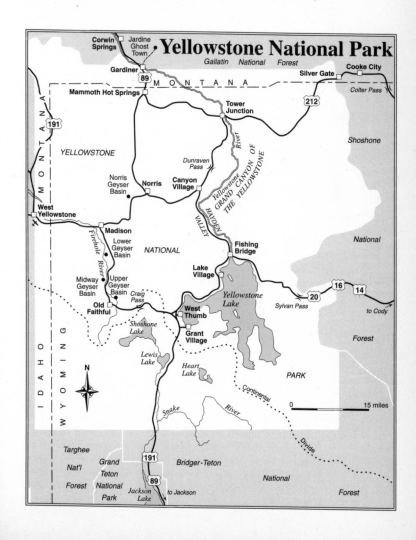

Yellowstone National Park

followed, in descending order, by yellow, orange, brown and, in the coolest, green.

The result of this thermal dynamism on the lower slopes of Terrace Mountain is a lopsided wedding cake of a hillside. About 500 gallons of water flow from the springs per minute; by some estimates, two tons of dissolved limestone are deposited each day. But the springs and terraces are constantly changing, new ones emerging while others become dormant.

Probably the best place to view the entire Mammoth area is from the **Lower Terrace Overlook** off the Upper Terrace Loop Drive. Boardwalk trails lead a half mile downhill through the main terrace region to the village beyond. Features like **Minerva Spring** and **Jupiter Spring** go through cycles of activity and dormancy lasting years at a time. **Opal Terrace**, at the foot of the hill, deposits as much as a foot of travertine per year in its most active periods. **Liberty Cap**, a cone formed by a long-extinct hot spring, marks the north end of the Mammoth Hot Springs; it is 37 feet high and 20 feet in diameter at its base.

At the south end of the Mammoth Hot Springs area is the one-and-a-half-mile **Upper Terrace Loop Drive**, a narrow, one-way route that turns right off the Grand Loop Road about a mile and a half south of Mammoth village. The thermal landscape here is highly varied: Some terraces have been inactive for five centuries, others have come back to life after decades of dormancy, and still others have erupted from verdant forest in relatively recent times—even as park rangers and frequent visitors watched.

One of the most surprising aspects of these hot springs is their apparent allure to elk. Dozens of the magnificent antlered creatures bed down in the terraces, seemingly oblivious to tourists who pass within a few feet. They can be seen wandering throughout the village as well, more tame than wild.

Mammoth was the first settlement in Yellowstone National Park. Park headquarters are lodged in the gray stone buildings of the former **Fort Yellowstone**, a cavalry post during the three decades the park was administered by the U.S. Army, from 1886 to 1916. ~ 307-344-7381. Also in the historic fort is the **Horace M. Albright Visitors Center**, whose exhibits explain the army's role during those early years. There are also excellent wildlife displays and a slide program on park ecology, philosophy and history. ~ 307-344-2263.

Other village facilities, open year-round, include a hotel, restaurants, a general store and other shops, a gas station with towing and repair services, a medical clinic, a post office, a campground and an amphitheater for evening programs. There's even a corral for trail riders.

East of Mammoth Hot Springs, the Grand Loop Road continues 18 miles to Tower Junction. En route, about four miles from

Mammoth, it passes **Undine Falls**, which drop 60 feet between perpendicular cliff walls on Lava Creek.

TOWER-ROOSEVELT AREA   About three and a half miles before Tower Junction you'll pass **Garnet Hill**. The rocks here are Precambrian granite gneiss estimated to be roughly 2.7 billion years old, formed before the first primitive lifeforms even began to appear on the planet. Imperfect garnets can be found in this ancient formation.

A short side road a little over a mile west of Tower Junction leads to a **petrified tree**, enclosed by a tall iron fence to prevent the vandalism that consumed its former neighbors. Petrified trees—like this upright 20-foot redwood stump—were fossilized 50 million years ago after falling volcanic ash covered them. They can be found in isolated locations throughout northern Yellowstone, especially nearby **Specimen Ridge**, where between nine and twelve separate petrified forests—one on top of another—have been identified. Rangers lead all-day hikes along the ridge trail southeast of Tower Junction.

◄ *HIDDEN*

Tower Junction takes its name from the unusual basalt pinnacles that rise above the Yellowstone River canyon just south of here. **Tower Fall** is about two miles south of the junction off the Grand Loop Road; it plummets 132 feet from the palisades into **The Narrows**, at 500 feet the deepest part of this section of the canyon, and its most confined. A trail that leads to the foot of the waterfall reveals more steam vents and hot springs, including **Calcite Springs**, where the geothermal waters deposit calcite, gypsum and sulfur.

At Tower Junction itself are a ranger station, a service station, horse corrals and the **Roosevelt Lodge**, a rustic 1920s log building (with cabins and a restaurant) named for Teddy Roosevelt. The environmentalist president favored this area's rolling hills for camping around the turn of the 20th century.

◆◆◆

YELLOWSTONE NATIONAL PARK EXPERIENCES

- Wander paths among geysers, hot springs, mud pools and silica terraces at the **Norris Geyser Basin**, considered "one of the most extreme environments on earth." *page 218*
- Watch the world's most famous geyser erupt from the deck of the **Old Faithful Inn**, a massive and historic lodge. *page 221*
- Sit back in 1920s wicker furniture in the **Lake Yellowstone Hotel Dining Room** and view the sun's reflection on the lake. *page 222*
- Assault the craggy 13,000-foot walls of the **Teton Range** with instruction from renowned mountaineers. *page 230*

There are really two junctions at Tower Junction: that of the Grand Loop Road with the **Northeast Entrance Road**, and that of the **Lamar River** with the Yellowstone River. The Northeast Entrance Road follows the Lamar Valley upstream for the first half of its 29-mile run to the park's Northeast Entrance, closely paralleling an old American Indian route, the Bannock Trail. Bison and elk winter in the broad, open meadows of this glacial valley. **Buffalo Ranch**, ten miles east of Tower Junction, was used as a breeding preserve for bison for a half century after its establishment in 1907, during which time it helped Yellowstone's once-rare bison population increase from 25 to a modern estimate of 2500. It's now home to the **Yellowstone Institute**, a nonprofit academy specializing in wildlife and natural-history education for day or resident students. Some courses earn university credit. ~ 307-344-2294. There are two park campgrounds along this route: **Slough Creek campground** and **Pebble Creek campground**. Beyond are the isolated communities of Silver Gate and Cooke City and the rugged Beartooth Plateau.

South of Tower Junction, the Grand Loop Road passes Tower Fall, then begins a 12-mile ascent into the Washburn Range, a stretch that is Yellowstone's highest road. The area southeast of the highway, between Antelope Creek and the rim of the Yellowstone canyon, is a refuge for grizzly bears. Any human travel (even by foot) is prohibited in the area.

Trails from 8859-foot **Dunraven Pass** lead through groves of gnarled whitebark pine and subalpine fir to the fire lookout atop 10,243-foot **Mount Washburn**, a summer range for bighorn sheep. There are magnificent views from here across the Yellowstone caldera to the Red Mountains, 35 miles away, and on clear days to the Teton Range, 100 miles to the southwest.

CANYON AREA From Dunraven Pass the Grand Loop Road makes a five-mile descent through dense stands of lodgepole pine to **Canyon Village**.

The lodge here is among the park's newest; visitors also find dining facilities and a lounge, a campground and an amphitheater, riding stables and a general store, service station, post office and ranger station. Exhibits at the **Canyon Visitors Center** describe the creation of the Yellowstone River canyon by lava, glaciers and floods as well as other aspects of park geology. ~ 307-242-2550.

While the **Grand Canyon of the Yellowstone** extends 24 miles to The Narrows, just past Tower Fall at its northern end, the truly "grand" part is its first couple of miles, which include the Upper and Lower Yellowstone Falls. For your first view of the falls (you'll want more than one), take the two-and-a-half-mile, one-way North Rim Drive east and south from Canyon Village.

Your first stop is **Inspiration Point,** where you can park and descend several dozen steps to a lookout. To the southwest (about 1.4 miles) is the **Lower Falls,** at 308 feet Yellowstone's highest waterfall. (Around the corner to the south, out of view from this point, are the 109-foot **Upper Falls.**) The canyon is about 1000 feet deep at this point (it ranges from 800 to 1200), while the distance from here to the South Rim is about 1500 feet. Farther downriver are places where it widens out to about 4000 feet.

Yellowstone's population of flying insects is kept in check by the violet-green swallows who make their home in the canyon's cliffs.

The vivid hues of the canyon walls—yellow, red, orange, brown and even blue—are proof of ancient hydrothermal action on rhyolite, a fine-grained volcanic rock heavy in silica, and its mineral oxides. Though the cliffs still exude steam and seem forbidding, they make a fine home for ospreys, which scan for fish from their huge summer nests built on rock porches high above the Yellowstone River.

Less than a half mile south, after Grand Loop Road crosses Cascade Creek (whose own **Crystal Falls** empty into the Yellowstone just below this point), look for a turnout to the Upper Falls. The trail to the brink of these falls is almost a stairway, and it's only a couple of hundred yards in either direction.

Just over a half mile from the Upper Falls turnout, and about 2.3 miles south of Canyon Village, cross the Chittenden Bridge to Artist Point Road, which branches northeast along the canyon's South Rim. It ends 1.6 miles beyond at **Artist Point,** directly opposite Grandview Point but with a strikingly different perspective on the canyon.

The contrast between the reckless river that rushes through the Yellowstone canyon and the quiet, tranquil stream that meanders through the **Hayden Valley** is quite striking. Yet only about three miles separate these two opposite faces of the Yellowstone River. Whereas the canyon is hostile to most wildlife, the lush, six-mile valley between Alum and Trout creeks is a natural sanctuary.

Bison, moose, elk, bear and other large animals wander the former lakebed while trumpeter swans, sandhill cranes, great blue herons, white pelicans and other stately waterfowl abound in the marshes. Fishing is prohibited in the valley.

Numerous roadside parking areas have been created to accommodate wildlife viewing. Nevertheless, traffic jams are common. Park officials continually warn visitors to view large animals only from a distance, even if they're in their cars. The ferocity of grizzly bears is well documented, but bison, though they may seem docile, can be unpredictable and temperamental as well.

An intense thermal area beyond Elk Antler Creek marks the south end of the Hayden Valley, about 11 miles from Canyon Village. The varied features here are arguably the park's most foul smelling. The stench of hydrogen sulfide gas emanates from the constantly churning caldron of murky **Mud Volcano**. Rising volcanic gases continually bubble to the surface of **Black Dragon's Caldron**, which erupted in 1948 with such frenzy that it flung pitch-black mud dozens of feet around; Sour Lake, whose acid water has killed nearby trees; Dragon's Mouth, whose bursts of steam roar and echo within its cavern; and Sulphur Caldron, its water yellow with sulfur.

YELLOWSTONE LAKE AREA   Spawning cutthroat trout leap up the cascades at **Le Hardy Rapids** on the Yellowstone River in June and July, making their final approach to nearby Yellowstone Lake. **Lake Junction** is just three miles south from this point.

The first of three communities situated along the lake's northwest shore is **Fishing Bridge**, whose facilities (just east of Lake Junction) include a full-service garage, a general store, a ranger station and a park for hard-sided recreational vehicles. A camping restriction was imposed because of the area's popularity among park bears.

Despite its name, the bridge—which spans the Yellowstone River at its outlet from Yellowstone Lake—was closed to fishing in 1973. Visitors now use it primarily for watching the summer spawning spectacular of native cutthroat trout returning to the lake to lay their eggs. Pelicans, gulls and even bears are a part of the show. Exhibits at the **Fishing Bridge Visitors Center** focus on the geology and bird and fish life of the Yellowstone Lake area. ~ 307-242-2450.

Here also, you'll get your first panoramic view of Yellowstone Lake. Measuring 20 miles from north to south, 14 miles from east to west, and with 110 miles of shoreline, this is the highest (7733 feet) large lake in the Western Hemisphere outside of South America's High Andes.

If you want, you can turn off the Grand Loop Road at Lake Junction and take the park's **East Entrance Road** toward Cody, Wyoming, 77 miles distant. It's 26 miles from Fishing Bridge, through the dense evergreen forests surrounding 8530-foot Sylvan Pass in the Absaroka Range, to the East Entrance station.

EVERYTHING YOU EVER WANTED TO KNOW ABOUT RANGERS

Less than a mile north of the Norris Junction, at the entrance to the Norris campground, is the **Museum of the National Park Ranger**. Housed in a restored log cabin built in 1897 as a U.S. Army outpost, the museum contains exhibits explaining how park protection began as a domestic military function and evolved into the highly specialized occupation it is today. ~ 307-344-7353.

For its first nine miles, the East Entrance Road traces the north shore of Yellowstone Lake. Moose often browse in the fens and sedge meadows of the **Pelican Creek Flats,** one to three miles east of Fishing Bridge. Although there's no immediate cause for alarm, the earth in this area is rising by as much as an inch per year. This is a warning of future volcanic activity, perhaps along the line of what exists in the Norris Geyser Basin today.

A short spur road climbs 600 feet to the **Lake Butte Overlook** for one last panoramic glimpse of Yellowstone Lake. Then it's back to the East Entrance Road and up the west side of the Absaroka Range. Look for marmots and pikas on the rocky slopes at higher elevations. Beyond **Sylvan Pass,** 20 miles from Fishing Bridge, the highway descends nearly 1600 feet in seven miles to **East Entrance.**

The turnoff from the Grand Loop Road to **Lake Village** is less than two miles south of Lake Junction. Lake Village is the home of the park's oldest lodging, the **Lake Yellowstone Hotel,** which opened to visitors in 1891. Though renovated, it has kept its historic flavor and is still going strong. Lake Village also has cabins, restaurants, stores, a ranger station and a hospital. Another two miles south is **Bridge Bay,** the lake's primary abode for tent campers and, with 420 sites, the park's largest campground.

GRANT VILLAGE–WEST THUMB AREA   Much of southern Yellowstone bears the scars of the terrible 1988 forest fires that ravaged about 36 percent (793,000 acres) of the park's vegetation and that took 25,000 firefighters about three months and $120 million to quell. But exhibits at the **Grant Village Visitors Center,** beside the lakeshore amphitheater, explain fire's role not only as a destructive force but also as a creative one. It clears areas for the growth of new vegetation, which in turn serves to nurture a greater diversity of wildlife. Naturalists say major fires such as these occur once or twice a century when nature is allowed to take its course. ~ 307-242-2650.

Grant Village, located a mile east of the highway and a couple of miles south of West Thumb junction, lies on Yellowstone Lake's **West Thumb,** a bay so named because early surveyors thought the lake was shaped like a hand. (In our my opinion, it's shaped more like a tired backpacker, and this bay is his or her drooping head.) The southernmost park community was named for Ulysses S. Grant, who as president signed the bill that created Yellowstone National Park in 1872. It has a 299-room hotel, restaurants, campgrounds, boat ramps, several shops, service station, post office and other facilities.

The **West Thumb Geyser Basin,** noted for the vivid colors of its springs, is less than two miles north of Grand Village on the lakeshore. A walkway winds past features like the **Thumb Paint Pots,** the intensity and hue of whose colors seem to change seasonally

with the light; **Abyss Pool**, with a deep, cobalt blue crater of remarkably clear water; **Fishing Cone**, a spring whose volcanolike
mound is surrounded by lake water; and **Lake-
shore Geyser**, which spouts up to 60 feet high when
it's not submerged by Yellowstone Lake.

The namesake of Lewis
Lake is explorer
Meriwether Lewis
although he never
set foot within 100
miles of it.

If you're heading south toward Grand Teton National
Park and Jackson, Wyoming, you'll turn south at West
Thumb, past Grant Village, on Route 89/191. Six miles
south of Grant you'll find yourself on the east shore of
Lewis Lake, a pretty three-mile-long, two-mile-wide fa-
vorite of fishermen. The lake lies just within the ancient
Yellowstone caldera.

The outflow from Lewis Lake is the **Lewis River**, which flows
through a steep-sided canyon with its black lava walls 600 feet
high. Look for turnouts for **Lewis Falls,** a 37-foot drop, and **Moose
Falls,** a split waterfall that enters the Lewis from Crawfish Creek.
The Lewis River joins the Snake River just before the South
Entrance ranger station. From here, you can cover the 64 miles to
Jackson in about 90 minutes on the **John D. Rockefeller, Jr.,
Memorial Parkway**, a busy highway with lots of junctions and
turnouts.

If you're continuing on the Grand Loop Road, you'll want to
take the westbound fork from West Thumb junction. It crosses the
Continental Divide twice—the first time at 8391 feet elevation—
en route to Old Faithful.

OLD FAITHFUL AREA In a saddle between the crossings of the
Divide, you can turn off at Shoshone Point for a view down Delacy
Creek to Shoshone Lake, the park's second-largest body of water,
three miles south. This is moose country. In the far distance, on
clear days, you can see the towering spires of the Grand Tetons.

It's about 17 miles from West Thumb to the cloverleaf junction
for **Old Faithful Geyser**, Yellowstone's best-known sight and the
world's most famous geyser. While not the largest, the highest or
the most regular geyser in the park, Old Faithful has demonstrated
remarkably consistent behavior since its 1870 discovery. It erupts
19 to 21 times per day at intervals averaging about 75 minutes,
varying by 30 minutes on either side. Eruptions, lasting from 90
seconds to five minutes, eject between 4000 and 8000 gallons of
boiling water to heights of up to 180 feet. The **Old Faithful Visitors
Center**, next to the Old Faithful Inn by the west parking area, can
tell you when to expect the next discharge. Normally, the shorter
and smaller the last eruption, the less time you'll have to wait before for next one. ~ 307-545-2750.

The park community of Old Faithful is one of Yellowstone's
largest villages, with three overnight lodges; several restaurants,
cafeterias and snack bars; numerous stores and shops; a full-service

garage; a 24-hour medical clinic; a post office and other community facilities.

It's also the focal point of Yellowstone's spectacular **Upper Geyser Basin**, the world's single largest concentration of geysers. Weaving from the visitors center through the basin, on either side of the aptly named **Firehole River**, are about four miles of boardwalks and paved, wheelchair-accessible trails as well as many more miles of dirt paths. The geysers of Upper Geyser Basin are a motley group whose very *un*predictability makes Old Faithful's consistency seem all the more remarkable.

◄ *HIDDEN*

Directly opposite Old Faithful, overlooking the northeast bank of the river, is the Geyser Hill Group. It includes the **Anemone Geyser**, which bubbles explosively every seven to ten minutes; the **Plume Geyser**, which has erupted to 25 feet high every 30 to 50 minutes since 1942, when it first became active; the **Beehive Geyser**, which shoots water 180 feet or higher at irregular intervals of one to ten days; the four **Lion Geysers**, connected underground, which gush two or three times a day; and the **Giantess Geyser**, which erupts violently once or twice an hour, for 12 to 42 hours, two to six times a year, and then returns to dormancy.

Downstream is the **Castle Geyser**, probably the oldest in the park. Its ancient cone is 120 feet around. Castle's twice-daily explosions rise to 90 feet, last about 20 minutes and are followed by another 30 to 40 minutes of furious steaming. Nearby **Grand Geyser**, the world's tallest predictable geyser, erupts like a fountain up to 200 feet high every 7 to 15 hours.

Upper Geyser Basin also includes several attractive springs and pools, the best known of which is **Morning Glory Pool**, reached by a one-and-a-half-mile stroll from the visitors center. Labeled in 1880 for its likeness to its namesake flower, the hot spring began to cloud because of vandalism (mainly trash thrown in the pool) and geological changes created by a 1959 earthquake, its epicenter just west of the park, that measured 7.1 on the Richter scale. Thanks to a harder line on park vandalism, the pool has begun to recover its original deep blue color. The vivid colors of these pools—yellow, orange, brown and green—are due to the presence of photosynthetic algae on the submerged earth. There are several more geyser basins along the Grand Loop Road as it proceeds north from Old Faithful toward the Madison junction.

The principal features of **Midway Geyser Basin** are **Excelsior Geyser** and **Grand Prismatic Spring**. Excelsior Geyser erupted in 1888 (to a height of 300 feet) and again in 1985 (nonstop for two days, to a height of 55 feet. If you missed it then, don't hold your breath). At all other times, it's like a pot of scalding water that continually boils over—at a rate of five million gallons *per day*. When the air cools at sunset, the geyser's steam fills the entire basin.

Grand Prismatic Spring is Yellowstone's largest hot spring at 370 feet in diameter; it has azure blue water at its center, colorful algae around its edges.

Two miles past Midway, a turnoff down the three-mile, one-way **Firehole Lake Drive** marks the beginning of **Lower Geyser Basin**. This basin covers more ground than some of the others but its geysers are not as striking, with the exception of the **Great Fountain Geyser**, whose hour-long eruptions reach heights of 100 to 230 feet; intervals between eruptions vary from 7 to 15 hours. Where the drive rejoins the Grand Loop Road you'll see the **Fountain Paint Pots**, a multicolored collection of gurgling mud pools that vary in size, color and intensity.

MADISON AREA–WEST ENTRANCE   Grand Loop Road follows the Firehole River downstream another six and a half miles to Madison. Two miles before Madison, the river drops into a deep, dark canyon. Coming from the south, you must proceed to a turnoff for one-way **Firehole Canyon Drive**, about a half mile from Madison, and then backtrack. The two-mile route penetrates the 800-foot, black lava walls of the canyon, reaching its climax where the 40-foot **Firehole Falls** tumble and churn into the **Firehole Cascades**. Above the falls is a big swimming hole; the miles of geothermal activity upstream raise the river's temperature about 30 degrees higher than normally would be expected at this elevation and latitude.

Madison is one of the park's smaller communities. It doesn't offer overnight lodging, stores or service stations, but it does have a campground, a ranger station, an amphitheater and the **Explorer's Museum**, with exhibits that tell the saga of the park's creation. ~ 307-344-7381.

If you're ready for a sidetrip, a left turn at the junction will take you down the **West Entrance Road** 14 miles to the bustling town of West Yellowstone, Montana. The route closely parallels the Madison River and is excellent for wildlife viewing.

To continue your tour, turn right at Madison and remain on the park's Grand Loop Road. About four and a half miles ahead, and right beside the highway, is **Gibbon Falls**, a veil-like 84-foot drop over a rock face. The route continues to ascend through the minor Monument and Gibbon geyser basins to Norris, 14 miles northeast of Madison.

NORRIS AREA   For many visitors, Yellowstone's most intriguing thermal area is not the Upper Geyser Basin around Old Faithful but the **Norris Geyser Basin**. In a walk of less than two miles beginning just a few hundred yards west of the road junction, you can take in dozens of geysers, hot springs, mud pools and silica terraces in "one of the most extreme environments on earth," as it's called by some park publications.

HIDDEN ▶

Thermal activity seems to be on the increase here. After a moderate earthquake struck the area in March 1994, long-dormant geysers surged back to life, and geologists monitored dramatic increases in ground temperature in certain parts of the basin.

Start your visit at the rustic **Norris Geyser Basin Museum**, where displays interpret hydrothermal geology. Then set out on the one-and-a-half-mile loop trail through patchily forested Back Basin (to the south) or the three-quarter-mile loop around the more open Porcelain Basin (to the north). ~ 307-344-2812.

The Norris Geyser Basin is pervaded by the perpetual, pungent smell of hydrogen sulfide.

Back Basin has two highlights. **Steamboat Geyser** is the world's tallest active geyser—when it is, indeed, active. Its eruptions, though spectacular, are *highly* unpredictable. After its 1969 eruption, Steamboat lay dormant for nine years, until 1978; it spewed several times between then and 1991 but has again been dormant up to the time of this writing. When the geyser does blast, it sends a shower of water 300 feet into the air for as long as 40 minutes.

Echinus Geyser is far more dependable. Its explosions come every 35 to 75 minutes, and they last anywhere from six minutes to an hour, with water rising skyward 40 to 60 feet. Small crowds gather on benches around its cone much as they do (on a larger scale!) around Old Faithful. Echinus is also the largest acid-water geyser known, with a pH level between 3.3 and 3.6—almost as high as vinegar. Acid-water geysers are extremely rare; most of those known to exist on earth are in the Norris Geyser Basin.

From an overlook northeast of the Norris museum you can get a good panorama of **Porcelain Basin**, which appears as a steaming sheet of whitish rock. Silica and clay are responsible for the milky color characteristic of this area's various springs and geysers; some are rimmed with orange, indicating the presence of iron compounds.

From Norris junction, the **Norris Canyon Road** proceeds 12 miles east to Canyon Village, effectively dividing the Grand Loop Road into two smaller loops. En route, about three miles east of Norris, it passes the pretty **Virginia Cascades**, where the Gibbon River slides through a narrow canyon and drops 60 feet. Most of the route is densely forested.

The **Museum of the National Park Ranger** is housed in a restored log cabin—a former U.S. Army outpost built at the turn of the century. Exhibits detailing the genesis of park protection (which began as a domestic military function) and its development into a highly specialized field are featured. ~ Located less than a mile north of the junction, at the entrance to the Norris campground; 307-344-7353.

The Grand Loop Road north from Norris to Mammoth Hot Springs, a distance of about 21 miles, passes several interesting geothermal features. Vents in the slopes of **Roaring Mountain**, five miles from Norris, hiss and steam at the side of the road. A glossy black volcanic glass from which ancient Native Americans made utensils and tools forms 200-foot-high **Obsidian Cliff**, nine miles from Norris. **Sheepeater Cliff**, 14 miles from Norris, is composed of pentagonal and heptagonal columns of basalt, another volcanic byproduct.

This region of low-lying streams and small lakes is a favorite of moose, who feed on willow shrubs and underwater plants, and who often wander through the **Indian Creek campground**, located just to the southwest of Sheepeater Cliff.

The Grand Loop Road begins its descent to Mammoth Hot Springs and the park's north entrance at **Golden Gate Canyon**, so named for the yellow lichen that paints its otherwise-barren rock walls.

LODGING

Yellowstone National Park probably offers more accommodations and more hotels of historic value than any other park. In all, Yellowstone boasts nine properties with 1043 hotel rooms and 1159 cabin units. *Note:* All accommodations must be booked through **TW Recreational Services**. ~ Yellowstone National Park; 307-344-7311, fax 307-344-7456.

Only two park accommodations are open in both winter and summer. One is at Old Faithful; the other is the **Mammoth Hot Springs Hotel,** built in 1937, which incorporates a wing of an earlier inn from 1911 (during the heyday of Fort Yellowstone). Its 223 rooms and cabin units come either with (moderate) or without (budget) private baths; four deluxe suite-style cabins have private hot tubs. Facilities include a dining room, fast-food outlet, lounge, gift shop and guest laundry. A decorative highlight is a huge United States map made of 15 woods from nine different countries. Open mid-May to late September and mid-December to early March. ~ Mammoth Hot Springs; 307-344-5400. BUDGET TO MODERATE.

The rustic **Roosevelt Lodge and Cabins**, so named because of its proximity to President Teddy Roosevelt's favorite camping areas, has the feel of an earlier era. Its 69 cabins are of simple frame construction; some have electric heat and private baths, but most have wood-burning stoves and share a bathhouse. In the main lodge are two stone fireplaces, a family-style restaurant, a lounge and a gift shop. Open mid-June to late August. ~ Tower Junction; 307-344-5273. BUDGET TO MODERATE.

Not far from the Grand Canyon of the Yellowstone is the 609-room **Canyon Lodge & Cabins**. The new three-story lodge has hotel-style rooms with private baths; cabins are single-story four-plex units, all with private toilets and showers. In the main lodge are a dining room, cafeteria, snack shop, lounge and gift shop. Open early June to late August. ~ Canyon Village; 307-242-3900. MODERATE.

The grande dame of Yellowstone hostelries is the **Lake Yellowstone Hotel & Cabins**. First opened in 1891 and listed on the National Register of Historic Places, the 296-room hotel has been fully renovated and again boasts its long-sequestered 1920s wicker furniture. The Sun Room, which has great lake views (especially at sunrise!), offers evening cocktail service and frequent piano or chamber-music performances. Other facilities include a lakeside dining room, deli and gift shop. Guests choose between deluxe hotel rooms, less expensive annex rooms or cabins with private baths. Open mid-May to early October. ~ Lake Village; 307-242-3700. MODERATE TO DELUXE.

Relax in rocking chairs on the lodge porch of the **Lake Lodge and Cabins** to take in a sweeping view of Yellowstone Lake to the east. The Lake Lodge has 186 cabins, some cozy, some spacious, all with private baths. In the classic log lodge are a big fireplace, a cafeteria, a lobby bar and a gift shop. There's also a guest laundry. Open mid-June to mid-September. ~ Lake Village; 307-242-3800. BUDGET TO MODERATE.

Old Faithful Inn was built of pine logs from the surrounding forests and volcanic rock from a nearby quarry.

Grant Village, built in 1984, is the newest of the park hotels. Open from late May to late September, it has 299 standard rooms, all with private bathrooms and showers. Facilities include a dining room and separate steakhouse, a lounge, a gift shop and a guest laundry. ~ West Thumb; 307-242-3400. MODERATE.

The massive yet rustic **Old Faithful Inn** was acclaimed a National Historic Landmark in 1987. This 325-room hotel is said to be the largest log structure in the world. The gables on its steeply pitched roof were a trademark of architect Robert Reamer. In the enormous lobby are a stone fireplace and a clock handcrafted from copper, wood and wrought iron. The inn has deluxe suites, moderately priced rooms with private baths and budget-priced rooms with shared toilets and showers down the hall. Open early May to mid-October. ~ Old Faithful; 307-545-4600. BUDGET TO DELUXE.

From the **Old Faithful Lodge and Cabins**, just a couple of hundred yards south of the famous geyser, it seems as if you can reach out and touch the park landmark. The 130 rustic cabins include "frontier" units, with private toilets and showers, and "rough rider" units that share a common bathhouse. Open mid-May to mid-September. ~ Old Faithful; 307-545-4900. BUDGET.

Winter activities in this thermal basin center around the **Old Faithful Snow Lodge & Cabins**, with 65 rooms. Most cabins have private baths; the lodge has shared toilets and showers. Open mid-December to mid-March and mid-May to early October. ~ Old Faithful; 307-545-4800. BUDGET TO MODERATE.

DINING

Most restaurants within Yellowstone National Park are in the hotels and lodges themselves. Reservations are highly recommended at hotel dining rooms and the Old West Dinner Cookout.

Patrons of the **Mammoth Hotel Dining Room** can enjoy three American-style meals a day amid the steaming travertine terraces for which the area is named. ~ Mammoth Hot Springs; 307-344-5400. MODERATE. In the same lodge, **The Terrace Grill** dishes up cafeteria-style fast food and snacks. BUDGET.

For a taste of how things used to be, look no further than the **Old West Dinner Cookout**. Adventurous diners mount horses or clamber aboard a wagon and ride a short distance to Yancey's Hole, where they are served a hearty chuck-wagon dinner of steak, corn-on-the-cob, baked beans, corn muffins, cole slaw and more. ~ Roosevelt Lodge, Tower Junction; 307-344-7311. MODERATE.

The **Canyon Lodge Dining Room** offers American-style breakfasts and steak-and-seafood dinners daily in a forested setting just a half mile from the north rim of the Grand Canyon of the Yellowstone. ~ Canyon Village; 307-242-3900. MODERATE.

Yellowstone's top-end culinary experience is at the **Lake Yellowstone Hotel Dining Room**. Prime rib, steak, seafood, chicken and vegetarian meals, as well as daily specials, are served in a classic lakeside setting of etched glass and wicker furniture. Breakfast and lunch are also available. ~ Lake Yellowstone Hotel, Lake Village; 307-242-7647. DELUXE.

The **Steakhouse** serves up choice sirloins and filets mignon along with a sterling view across Yellowstone Lake. Seafood and chicken entrées are also on the dinner menu, and full breakfasts are served as well. ~ Grant Village, West Thumb; 307-242-3400. MODERATE.

The **Bear Pit Dining Room** offers a gourmet menu of prime rib, steak, seafood and poultry beneath the log beams and braces of this immense lodge. Etched glass panels are replicas of carved-wood murals. Three meals a day are served. MODERATE. The hotel's **Pony Express** serves a take-out lunch and dinner menu. ~ Old Faithful Inn, Old Faithful; 307-545-4600. BUDGET.

Made-to-order deli sandwiches, homemade soup and other light fare are the specialties of the **Four Seasons Deli**. ~ Near Old Faithful Snow Lodge, Old Faithful. BUDGET.

PARKS

YELLOWSTONE NATIONAL PARK 🚶 🚴 🐎 🎣 ⛵ 🚤 🛶 Superlatives rule in Yellowstone's 2.2 million acres: the largest and most varied hydrothermal region on earth, the largest lake in North America at so high an elevation (7700 feet), the greatest diversity of wildlife in the Lower 48—the list goes on. Set within the park are nine overnight lodges, 17 restaurants and snack shops, nine general stores and numerous other shops, 48 picnic areas, restrooms, five visitors centers, three museums, 11 amphitheaters, two marinas, 1200 miles of hiking and horse trails with 85 trailheads (permits required on some trails); $20 weekly vehicle pass (includes Grand Teton National Park). Swimming is prohibited in thermal features and discouraged in Yellowstone and other lakes because of the high risk of hypothermia from the freezing waters. Park fishing permits ($10 for ten days) can be obtained at ranger stations, visitors centers and general stores. Regulations vary in park waters; for example, no fishing is allowed in a six-mile stretch of the Hayden Valley. Boating permits can be obtained at Grant or Lake villages. Cutthroat trout and mountain whitefish are native to Yellowstone waters, and rainbow trout have been introduced to all. ~ There are five different park entrances: South Entrance (via Route 89/191 from Jackson and Route 287 from Dubois); West Entrance (via West Yellowstone, Route 20 from Idaho Falls, Route 191 from Bozeman and Route 287 from Ennis); North Entrance (via Gardiner, Route 89 from Livingston); Northeast Entrance (via Cooke City, Route 212 from Red Lodge and Billings); and the East Entrance (Route 14/16/20 from Cody); 307-344-7381.

▲ There are 2198 units (1853 for tents or RVs, 345 for RVs only) at 12 campgrounds (hookups at Fishing Bridge only), plus 330 backcountry campsites (tents only). Numbers of sites, open dates and fees are listed below. National Park Service campgrounds: *Lewis Lake* (85, early June to October 31, $10); *Norris* (116, mid-May to late September, $12); *Indian Creek* (75, early June to mid-September, $10); *Mammoth* (85, year-round, $12); *Tower Fall* (32, late May to mid-September, $10); *Slough Creek* (29, mid-May to October 31, $10); *Pebble Creek* (36, early June to early September, $10). TW Recreational Services campgrounds: *Grant Village* (414, late June to mid-October, $12); *Madison* (292, May 1 to October 31, $12); *Canyon* (280, early June to early September, $12); *Bridge Bay* (420, late May to late September, $14.50; reservations for stays from early June to Labor Day through DESTINET, 800-365-2267); *Fishing Bridge* (345, RVs only, full hookups, mid-May to mid-September, $25). Funding restrictions may force the National Park Service to close down some of these campgrounds or raise their fees significantly.

GRAND TETON NATIONAL PARK

Anyone who has ever laid eyes upon the stunning heights of the Teton Range has come away awestruck. Even people whose only glimpse of these dramatic mountains has been in photographs or paintings find themselves haunted by their beauty.

Climaxed by the 13,770-foot **Grand Teton**, this commanding range boasts 16 peaks of 11,000 feet or higher in a north–south stretch of less than 20 miles, towering over a string of conifer-shrouded lakes. Despite its close proximity to Yellowstone, the 485-square-mile Teton Park is very different from its famous sister. Teton doesn't have premier attractions like Yellowstone; its allure is scenery that seems so close you can reach out and touch it. But the park demands active effort to fully appreciate it. Mountaineers are challenged by the Grand Teton and other peaks, while water-sports enthusiasts enjoy floating the upper Snake River and scanning its shores for wildlife. Within the park are lodges, restaurants, stores, picnic tables, restrooms, amphitheaters, visitors centers and marinas. A $20 weekly vehicle pass includes Yellowstone National Park. Swimming is permitted everywhere; there are designated beaches at Colter Bay and Signal Mountain Lodge. If your aim is to do some fishing, the park's lakes and rivers yield mountain whitefish and brown, cutthroat and lake trout. Flyfishing for trout in the upper Snake River is an angler's dream. ~ Take Route 26 north from Jackson or west from Dubois, or Route 89/191 north from Jackson or south from Yellowstone National Park; 307-739-3399.

▲ There are 850 RV/tent sites at five park campgrounds (trailers allowed; no hookups); $14.50 per night; Jenny Lake has 49 tent sites; open from May to October. There are 334 units at three privately owned campgrounds; $17 to $25 per night: Colter Bay RV & Trailer Park (112 trailer sites with hookups; 307-543-2811); Colter Bay Tent Village (72 sites for tents only; 307-543-2811); Grand Teton Park KOA (36 tent sites, 114 RV sites with hookups; 307-733-1980). Reservations accepted; open from May to September.

▼▼▼▼▼▼▼▼▼▼▼▼▼
Outdoor Adventures

FISHING

Within the boundaries of Yellowstone National Park, all anglers regardless of residency must buy a ten-day park license, which costs $10; a season permit is $20. Anyone fishing elsewhere in Wyoming, including Grand Teton National Park, must obtain a state license. For more information, call the Jackson regional office of the **Wyoming Game and Fish Division**. ~ 307-733-2321.

Yellowstone Lake is renowned for its cutthroat trout, as is the upper portion of the Yellowstone River between Fishing Bridge and the Hayden Valley. Rainbow and brook trout and grayling are native to waters on the west side of the Continental Divide, including Shoshone and Lewis lakes, the Gallatin and Madison rivers and their tributaries, and Hebgen Lake, outside the park near West Yellowstone, Montana.

Jackson Lake and other Grand Teton National Park lakes have excellent cutthroat and mackinaw (lake trout) fisheries. The Snake River is considered superb for cutthroat and brook trout.

Within Yellowstone National Park, you can buy or rent complete fishing gear at marinas on Yellowstone Lake; guides are generally available at the marinas as well. Contact the **Lake Yellowstone Hotel** for fishing equipment. ~ Lake Village; 307-242-3700. Or try **Grant Village** for your supplies. ~ West Thumb; 307-242-3400. Tackle is also available at **Hamilton Stores** located throughout the park. ~ Mammoth Hot Springs; 307-344-7702.

BOATING

Marinas on Yellowstone and Jackson lakes offer full boat-rental services and guided lake trips. In Yellowstone, 40-passenger excursion boats leave the **Bridge Bay Marina** several times daily on lake cruises; there are also twilight trips and individual motorboat rentals. ~ Bridge Bay; 307-344-7381. The marina at **Grant Village** also has rentals. ~ West Thumb; 307-242-3400. Ranger stations provide boat-operating permits on request. In Grand Teton, visit the **Colter Bay Marina**, which is administered by the park and features twice-a-week dinner cruises. ~ Rockefeller Parkway, Moran; 307-543-3594. Or try the privately owned **Signal Mountain Lodge**. ~ Teton Park Road, Moran; 307-733-5470. Shuttles across little Jenny Lake are operated by the **Teton Boating Company**. ~ South Jenny Lake, Moose; 307-733-2703.

RIVER RUNNING

The best rivers in the greater Yellowstone area for whitewater rafting and kayaking are the Snake, south of Jackson, and the Gallatin, north of Yellowstone in Montana. For tranquil float trips or easy canoeing with spectacular scenery and abundant wildlife, it is hard to top the upper Snake River through Grand Teton National Park.

Most of the rafting outfitters that operate in the rivers north of Yellowstone National Park are based in Bozeman, Livingston or Big Sky. An exception is the **Yellowstone Raft Company**, which runs the Yellowstone, Gallatin and other rivers on the north side of the park. ~ P.O. Box 46, Gardiner, MT 59030; 406-848-7777.

Also, the **Grand Teton Lodge Company** offers scenic float trips, including lunch and dinner voyages, along a ten-and-a-half-mile stretch of the upper Snake from mid-May through September. ~ Jackson Lake Lodge, Moran; 307-543-2811. Numerous other outfitters, including **National Park Float Trips**, put in at Deadman's Bar, south of Moran, and take out at Moose Visitors Center. ~ Moose; 307-733-6445.

CROSS-COUNTRY SKIING

Yellowstone National Park has hundreds of miles of marked cross-country ski trails, including groomed tracks near Old Faithful and the Grand Canyon of the Yellowstone (see "Winter Wonderland" in this chapter.)

Just outside the park boundaries, **The Rendezvous Ski Trails** offer 26 kilometers of groomed trails, and another eight kilometers ungroomed, from November through April. The U.S. national cross-country and biathlon (skiing and shooting) teams train here each year. ~ West Yellowstone; 406-646-7701. Some 65 kilometers of marked but ungroomed trails are open to cross-country skiers in **Grand Teton National Park**; maps are available at the Moose Visitors Center, open daily in winter. ~ Moose; 307-733-2880.

Ski Rentals   Nordic specialists with rentals available include **Skinny Skis**. ~ 65 West Deloney Street, Jackson; 307-733-6094. Also contact **Wilson Backcountry Sports** for equipment rentals. ~ 1230 Ida Drive, Wilson; 307-733-5228.

ICE SKATING

The **Mammoth Hot Springs Hotel** has an outdoor rink with skate rentals open throughout the winter. ~ Mammoth Hot Springs; 307-344-5400.

RIDING STABLES

Three stables in Yellowstone National Park and two in Grand Teton offer park visitors ample opportunities for one- and two-hour guided rides in off-the-road wilderness. Private outfitters throughout the region provide many more options. Half-day, full-day and extended overnight trips are available. Some outfitters offer riding lessons; more commonly, novice riders will be matched with gentler horses.

One- and two-hour guided trail rides depart from corrals at **Mammoth Hot Springs** (307-344-5400), **Roosevelt Lodge** (307-344-5273) and **Canyon Village** (307-242-3900) throughout the day. Roosevelt visitors can also ride to Yancey's Hole for an Old West dinner cookout or hop aboard a horse-drawn stagecoach for half-hour rambles around the Tower Junction area. Schedules vary; the summer riding season is longest at lower-lying Mammoth than at the other two sites.

Proficient riders can rent steeds for unguided trips from **Lone Rider Stables**. ~ 1111 Targhee Pass Highway, West Yellowstone; 406-646-7900. In Grand Teton National Park, the Grand Teton Lodging Company offers all manner of trail rides from both the **Colter Bay Village Corral**. ~ Rockefeller Parkway, Moran; 307-543-3594. There is also the **Jackson Bay Lodge Corral**. ~ Rockefeller Parkway, Moran; 307-543-2811.

PACK TRIPS & LLAMA TREKS

Guided pack trips through Yellowstone's backcountry and the nearby wilderness area are offered by **Hell's a Roarin' Outfitters**, who have more than 300 horses in their stables. ~ Route 89 North, Gardiner; 406-848-7578. **Wilderness Connection** is another option. ~ Cinnabar Basin Road, Gardiner; 406-848-7287. **Beartooth Plateau Outfitters** specializes in five-day-long fishing trips; all sup-

Winter
Wonderland

If anything, the natural wonders of Yellowstone National Park are more spectacular in winter than in summer. Imagine, for instance, the steam from hot springs and geysers filling the frigid Rocky Mountain air as snow falls all around.

From mid-December to mid-March, Yellowstone is a paradise for cross-country skiers, snowmobilers and snowshoers. Although the park is accessible by car only at its north entrance, via Gardiner, Montana—this route, through Mammoth Hot Springs to Tower Junction and Cooke City, Montana, on the Beartooth Plateau, is kept open year-round—there are other ways to get there.

Heated, ten-passenger snowcoaches (track vans) run from the south and west entrances as well as from Mammoth Hot Springs. Coaches operated by **TW Recreational Services** depart from the south entrance for Old Faithful every afternoon, returning every morning. The journey takes three and a half hours. ~ Mammoth Hot Springs; 307-344-7311. Similar trips connect Old Faithful and Canyon Village with West Yellowstone and Mammoth Hot Springs. Other snowcoaches are run by **Sno-Vans of Yellowstone**. ~ 530 Madison Avenue, West Yellowstone; 406-646-7276. Also try **Yellowstone Alpen Guides**. ~ 555 Yellowstone Avenue, West Yellowstone; 406-646-9591.

Mammoth Hot Springs Hotel and Old Faithful Snow Lodge are the only park accommodations open during winter, although warming huts throughout the park provide shelter. Old Faithful, like the rest of the park, can be reached only across snow. But like the Mammoth hotel, the Snow Lodge serves three good meals daily and offers both Nordic skiing and snowshoeing equipment rentals and lessons. It's a good base for winter exploration of the park.

Hundreds of miles of cross-country ski trails are marked in Yellowstone, and the most popular are groomed. Those include the geyser basin trails at Old Faithful and the canyon rim trail at the Grand Canyon of the Yellowstone. Trail maps are available at visitors centers.

For guided cross-country skiing expeditions, talk to TW Recreational Services or **Yellowstone Nordic Guides**. ~ 511 Gibbon Avenue, West Yellowstone, Montana; 406-646-9333.

Snowmobiles are restricted to 300 miles of park roads, groomed daily. Expect a four-foot snowpack beside highways. TW Recreational Services rents snowmobiles with helmets and all appropriate clothing.

plies and gear are included. ~ Main Street, Cooke City; 406838-2328.

The llama is more a hiking companion than a mode of transportation; it carries all the gear while you proceed on foot. Guided four- and five-day llama treks through Yellowstone Park or the nearby Jedediah Smith Wilderness are the specialty of **Jackson Hole Llamas**. Routes range from moderate to strenuous. ~ P.O. Box 7375, Jackson, WY 83001; 307-733-1617.

BIKING Mountain bikes have become a common sight in recent years, joining touring bikes on and off the roads of northwestern Wyoming. Many of the routes here are narrow and dangerous, so helmets and rear-view mirrors, small tool kits, first-aid kits and (if you're venturing into the backcountry) emergency survival kits are essential accessories.

YELLOWSTONE NATIONAL PARK Bicycling through Yellowstone can be an exhilarating experience but it is not without peril. There are no bicycle lanes along park roads, and because roads are narrow and winding, high-visibility clothing and helmets are recommended. Keep an eye out for campers and RVs passing you from behind; their projecting mirrors pose a particular safety threat. Though a few bike paths do exist around park communities, bicycles are not permitted on boardwalks or backcountry trails.

Bicycle tours through Yellowstone are offered by **Yellowstone Eco Tours**. ~ 555 Yellowstone Avenue, West Yellowstone; 406-646-9009. You can also try **Yellowstone Mountain Bike Tours and Rentals**. ~ P.O. Box 840, Gardiner, MT 59030; 406-848-7600.

Grand Teton National Park roads and other valley highways are great for touring; hundreds of miles of trails and dirt roads head into adjacent national forests. Wilderness areas are off-limits. The 15-mile **RKO Road** in Grand Teton National Park, a dirt road along a bluff on the west side of the Snake River from Signal Mountain to Cottonwood Creek, is a good bet for a moderate day ride.

Bike Rentals In the Yellowstone area, a good full-service bicycle shop is **Yellowstone Bicycles**. ~ 132 Madison Avenue, West Yellowstone; 406-646-7815.

HIKING All distances listed for hiking trails are one way unless otherwise noted.

YELLOWSTONE NATIONAL PARK Yellowstone contains more than 1200 miles of marked hiking trails and 85 trailheads. Trails include the boardwalks and handicapped-accessible trails at **Upper Geyser Basin** (Old Faithful), **Norris Geyser Basin** and **Mammoth Hot Springs**, among others.

For youngsters, the **Fountain Paint Pot Nature Trail** (.5 mile) in the Lower Geyser Basin and the **Children's Fire Trail** (.5 mile) east of Mammoth Hot Springs have several interpretive stations to help teach about thermal activity and forest fires, respectively.

Backcountry permits are required for all overnight hikes and some day hikes in Yellowstone Park. They can be obtained at no charge from ranger stations within 48 hours before you start your hike. Topographic maps are sold at Hamilton Stores.

Avalanche Peak Trail (2.5 miles) is a strenuous ascent to a 10,566-foot summit, a mile west of Sylvan Pass on the East Entrance Road. Look for the unsigned trailhead opposite the Eleanor Lake picnic area. The trail transits several eco-zones before achieving the peak, which provides spectacular views across Yellowstone Lake to the Tetons and beyond.

Mount Washburn Trail (3 miles) leads to another panoramic point, but the climb isn't as steep as Avalanche Peak. Bighorn sheep are often seen on top. There are trailheads on the Grand Loop Road (north of Canyon Village) at the Dunraven Pass picnic area and the Chittenden Road parking area.

> Backcountry permits are required for all overnight hikes and some day hikes in Yellowstone National Park.

Seven Mile Hole Trail (5.5 miles) offers an impressive way to see the Grand Canyon of the Yellowstone . . . close up. Beginning on the Inspiration Point spur road a mile east of Canyon Village, it clings to the rim of the gorge for the first mile and a half, then swings into the pine forest and drops rapidly for three miles to the canyon floor near Sulphur Creek. Perhaps needless to say, the return climb is harder than the descent.

Bechler River Trail (32 miles) traverses the park's rarely visited southwest corner. It begins at Old Faithful, crosses the Continental Divide three times and then descends steep-sided Bechler Canyon, passing dazzling waterfalls and hot springs. The trail crosses Bechler Meadows, a low-lying haven for moose, black bear and trumpeter swans, and ends at Bechler River Ranger Station, off Cave Falls Road 25 miles east of Ashton, Idaho.

For guided hikes through the park, contact **Yellowstone Eco Tours**. ~ 555 Yellowstone Avenue, West Yellowstone; 406-646-9009.

GRAND TETON NATIONAL PARK **Hidden Falls Trail** (2.5 miles) is an easy two-mile walk around the southwest shore of Jenny Lake from the South Jenny ranger station and a strenuous half-mile uphill scramble to the secluded cascade. If you want to continue, there's another half-mile climb to Inspiration Point and then six and a half more through Cascade Canyon to lovely Lake Solitude. Boat shuttles across Jenny Lake are available to return tired hikers from near Hidden Falls to the South Jenny ranger station.

Two Ocean Lake Trail (12.2 miles) circles the three-mile-long lake in the park's northeastern corner, skirts adjacent Emma

Matilda Lake and climbs to a panoramic outlook toward Jackson Lake at Grand View Point. It's of moderate difficulty.

Teton Crest Trail (27 miles) has many feeder trails and many spurs. One popular if strenuous circuit of the Grand Teton begins at Jenny Lake Lodge (6900 feet), climbs west on the Paintbrush Canyon Trail to Lake Solitude, then turns south along the upper slopes of Mount Owen and the high Tetons. The trail crests at about 11,000 feet before descending again on switchbacks through Death Canyon to Phelps Lake and Teton Village (6300 feet).

All overnight backcountry camping requires a permit, which can be obtained free at ranger stations.

MOUNTAIN CLIMBING

The Teton Range is considered one of the world's finest tests for experienced climbers. Yet even first-timers can master the apparently insurmountable 13,770-foot Grand Teton itself, given that they have good physical strength, determination and expert instruction.

The latter element can be provided by Jackson Hole's two internationally renowned climbing schools. One is **Exum Mountain Guides.** ~ South Jenny Lake, Moose; 307-733-2297. Another highly respected school is **Jackson Hole Mountain Guides.** ~ 165 North Glenwood Street, Jackson; 307-733-4979.

Teton Mountaineering has the largest inventory of equipment and clothing in the area. ~ 170 North Cache Street, Jackson; 307-733-3595.

▼▼▼▼▼▼▼▼▼▼▼
Transportation

CAR

To reach Yellowstone, take **Route 89/191** north from Jackson; **Route 14/16/20** west from Cody; **Route 212** southwest off Route 90 near Billings, Montana; **Route 89** south at Livingston, Montana, or **Route 191** south at Bozeman, Montana, off 90; **Route 287** southeast off 90 near Butte, Montana; or **Route 20** northeast off **Route 15** at Idaho Falls.

AIR

From May to September, the **West Yellowstone Airport** in West Yellowstone, at the west entrance to Yellowstone National Park, is served by regular SkyWest commuter flights and by charters. The airport closes during the winter.

Jackson Hole Airport has regular daily nonstop arrivals from and departures to Chicago, Denver and Salt Lake City, with connecting flights from many other cities. It is served by American Airlines, Continental Express, Delta Air Lines, SkyWest Airlines and United Express. Regional charters and scenic flights are available at the airport.

Limousines and taxis take visitors to and from the airport. Try calling **Jackson Hole Transportation** (307-733-3135) or **All Star Transportation** (307-733-2888).

Greyhound Bus Lines serves West Yellowstone, Montana (between Idaho Falls, Idaho, and Bozeman, Montana), in summer. ~ 800-231-2222.

BUS

Gray Line (800-733-2304) offers seasonal charter service and guided tours through Yellowstone Park from Jackson Hole (330 North Glenwood Street, Jackson; 307-733-4324) and West Yellowstone (633 Madison Avenue, West Yellowstone; 406-646-9374).

In addition, **Karst Stage** offers seasonal bus service into the park at its west (West Yellowstone) and north (Gardiner) entrances from Bozeman. ~ 406-586-8567.

Backroads Tours and **Access Tours** offer multiday van tours of the northwestern Wyoming region and elsewhere in the Rockies for travelers with disabilities. ~ Both are at P.O. Box 2985, Jackson, WY 83001; 307-733-6664.

In West Yellowstone, you'll find **Avis Rent A Car** at the Yellowstone Airport. ~ 800-331-1212. **Big Sky** rents cars in town. ~ 415 Yellowstone Avenue; 406-646-9564. **Budget Rent A Car** also has rentals available in town. ~ 131 Dunraven Street; 800-527-0700 are in town.

CAR RENTALS

Rental agencies at the Jackson Hole Airport are **Alamo Rent A Car** (800-327-9633), **Avis Rent A Car** (800-331-1212), **Budget Rent A Car** (800-527-0700) and **Hertz Rent A Car** (800-654-3131). A locally owned agency, worth checking out is **Jackson Hole Car Rental**. ~ 75 South Glenwood Street, Jackson; 307-733-6868, 800-722-2002.

Guided all-day motorcoach tours of Yellowstone National Park are offered from various park lodgings by BTW **Recreational Services**. ~ 307-344-7311.

PUBLIC TRANSIT

EIGHT

Southeast Montana

Southeast Montanans truly have a home "where the buffalo roam, where the deer and the antelope play."

It was once that way, at least. Two centuries ago, tens of millions of American bison, in herds of thousands, cavorted through these mountains and prairies and down the Yellowstone River valley. Deer and pronghorn antelope remain in large numbers, but the bison were hunted to near-extinction in the 19th century and have made only a modest comeback in the 20th.

The bison nearly met the same fate as their Jurassic predecessors, whose bones and other fossil remains have been found en masse from the Rockies' eastern slope to the Makoshika Badlands near Montana's boundary with North Dakota. In fact, more skeletons of *Tyrannosaurus rex*, believed to have been the largest dinosaur ever to walk the earth, have been found in Montana than in all other discovery areas put together.

As far as human habitation goes, this has always been a land more suited to outdoors lovers and implacable individualists than to genteel urbanites. The American Indians—primarily Crow (Sioux) and Cheyenne—who lived in this region before the arrival of whites were horsemen and hunters who relied heavily on bison to provide food and hides for clothing and shelter.

When the white man arrived in the 19th century, relations with the American Indians were at first mutually tolerant, if not cordial. But as settlers' demands for land increased—for railroads, for ranches, for riches promised by gold, silver and copper strikes in the nearby mountains—hostilities flared. Tribes stepped up a campaign of raids against white settlements to protect their traditional hunting grounds.

The U.S. cavalry tried to suppress the uprisings and restrict the native people to reservations. At first, they were unsuccessful. In 1876, American Indians scored their greatest triumph at the Battle of the Little Bighorn (southeast of modern Billings), where a combined force of Sioux and Cheyenne annihilated more than 200 soldiers under the command of Lieutenant Colonel George Custer.

It was to be their last hurrah, as they were soon overwhelmed and subjugated. Today the Crow and Northern Cheyenne indian reservations stretch side by side from the Pryor Mountains to the Tongue River.

Modern Billings is a thriving community of 90,000 that dominates the region; it owes its existence to railroads and ranching. Through Billings flows the Yellowstone River, the longest undammed river in the contiguous 48 states. Only one other community in the region—Miles City, with a population of 8500—has more than 6000 people.

Billings Area

Montana's largest city nestles between sandstone cliffs in the valley of the Yellowstone River, within the shadow of the Rockies but with an outlook toward the Great Plains. Billings is the urban hub for a vast and sparsely populated region that includes eastern Montana, northern Wyoming and the western Dakotas.

Called "The Magic City" because it sprang up almost overnight after its founding as a railroad town in 1882, Billings grew as an agricultural, trade and transportation center. Now oil and medicine are major industries as well, and two colleges (Montana State University-Billings and Rocky Mountain College) attract a young population and enliven the city's cultural life.

For Rocky Mountain travelers, Billings is a gateway to such attractions as Little Bighorn Battlefield National Monument, the Bighorn Canyon National Recreation Area, the mountain town of Red Lodge and its spectacular Beartooth Highway, which travels past Montana's highest peaks to Yellowstone National Park. The Yellowstone, Musselshell and Bighorn rivers are acclaimed fishing streams, and there are unique geological and cultural features throughout southeastern Montana's "Custer Country."

SIGHTS

Many visitors get their first impression of Billings at the **Visitors Center and Cattle Drive Monument**, a few blocks off Route 90 Exit 450. The bronze sculpture in front of the modern building was commissioned to commemorate Montana's centennial cattle drive of 1989 to Billings from Roundup, 50 miles north. ~ 815 South 27th Street, Billings; 406-252-4016.

If that sculpture isn't enough to convince you of Billings' importance as a cow town, swing by the **Branding Wall**. Ranchers and celebrities burned their brands into this wooden wall, on the west side of Bert & Ernie's Saloon & Eatery, to record their participation in that "Drive of '89." They were supplemented by other brands important in Montana's pioneer history. ~ 2824 2nd Avenue North, Billings; 406-248-4313.

Perhaps the most notable of Billings' downtown attractions is the **Moss Mansion**. Built in 1902 by famed architect Henry Janeway Hardenbergh for bank president Preston B. Moss, this elegant three-story mansion features a Moorish entryway (inspired by Spain's Alhambra), a formal French parlor and an English Tudor dining room. Elaborate original furnishings provide a glimpse of the Mosses' Victorian lifestyle. Guided tours are offered from March through October and during the Christmas season. Admission. ~ 914 Division Street, Billings; 406-256-5100.

Two museums are worth a visit. The **Western Heritage Center**, in an imposing Romanesque sandstone structure at the corner of 29th Street, focuses on American Indian and pioneer history throughout the Yellowstone valley region. The center also has a gift shop and theater, and it offers a continuing calendar of educational programs. ~ 2822 Montana Avenue, Billings; 406-256-6809. The **Yellowstone Art Center** has a permanent collection of work by regional artists, from the days of exploration to modern times. Changing exhibits (about 15 a year) showcase leading contemporary artists. There's a gift shop here as well. Admission. ~ 401 North 27th Street, Billings; 406-256-6804.

You can get a good feel for Billings' layout by driving the **Black Otter Trail** along the rim of its overlooking sandstone cliffs—"The Rimrocks"—north of downtown, carefully avoiding the potholes as you do so. The route begins just west of Main Street (Route 87) in the Billings Heights area, above the grounds of the MetraPark exhibition center.

Boothill Cemetery is all that remains of the short-lived town of Coulson (1877–85). Among the graves is that of H. M. "Muggins" Taylor, who as an army scout first carried the news of Custer's defeat at Little Bighorn to the outside world. He was later gunned down while serving as Coulson's sheriff.

A short distance farther west along the Black Otter Trail is the **grave of Yellowstone Kelly**, a famed frontier scout whose lifespan (1849–1928) paralleled the pioneering and development of the American West. On a clear day, five Rocky Mountain spur ranges (the Big Horn, Pryor, Beartooth, Crazy and Snowy) can be seen from the gravesite.

The Black Otter Trail rejoins Airport Road just before busy Billings-Logan International Airport. Facing the terminal from the city side of the parking area is the **Peter Yegen, Jr., Yellowstone County Museum**. Its displays include a diorama of pioneer life, an authentic roundup wagon and, outside, a life-size statue, *The Range Rider of the Yellowstone*, facing the metropolis at the foot of the Rimrocks. ~ Airport Road at North 27th Street, Billings; 406-256-6811.

If the *Range Rider* could see far enough into the bluffs on the far side of the valley, he might spot **Pictograph Cave State Park** just southeast of Billings. An estimated 4500 years ago, prehistoric hunters lived in three different caves at this site; some 30,000 arti-

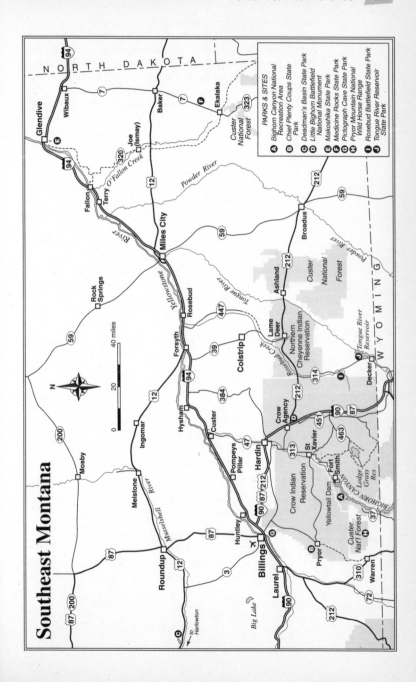

Southeast Montana

PARKS & SITES

- **A** Bighorn Canyon National Recreation Area
- **B** Chief Plenty Coups State Park
- **C** Deadman's Basin State Park
- **D** Little Bighorn Battlefield National Monument
- **E** Makoshika State Park
- **F** Medicine Rocks State Park
- **G** Pictograph Cave State Park
- **H** Pryor Mountain National Wild Horse Range
- **I** Rosebud Battlefield State Park
- **J** Tongue River Reservoir State Park

NORTH DAKOTA

Glendive
Wibaux
Baker
Ekalaka
Custer National Forest

Terry
Fallon
Joe (Ismay)
O'Fallon Creek
Powder River

Miles City
Rock Springs
Rosebud
Forsyth
Ashland
Broadus
Custer National Forest

Colstrip
Lame Deer
Northern Cheyenne Indian Reservation
Decker
Tongue River Reservoir
WYOMING

Hysham
Custer
Crow Agency
St Xavier
Fort Smith
Lodge Grass Res

Ingomar
Pompeys Pillar
Hardin
Crow Indian Reservation
Yellowtail Dam
Bighorn Canyon

Mosby
Melstone
Musselshell River
Huntley
Pryor
Warren

Roundup
Billings
Laurel
Big Lake
to Harlowton

Yellowstone River
Tongue River
Rosebud Creek
Powder River

40 miles
20
0
N

facts, including distinctive rock paintings (pictographs), have told archaeologists a great deal about the hunters' way of life. Short trails lead to the caves; there are also interpretive signs and a picnic area. Take Exit 452 (Lockwood) from Route 90 and follow Coburn Road seven miles south. Closed from mid-October to mid-April. Admission. ~ Coburn Road, Billings; 406-252-4654.

HIDDEN ►

There's more history in southwest Billings at **Oscar's Dreamland**. This pioneer town and agricultural museum is a tribute to the efforts of one man, Oscar Cooke, to preserve Montana's early-1900s homesteading era. An old train circles the 19-acre grounds that also include an early carousel and Ferris wheel, a garage full of Model-T Fords and hundreds more rare and antique vehicles and farm machines. Take the South Frontage Road three miles along Route 90 from Exit 446; then turn south one mile on Wise Lane. Closed October to May. Admission. ~ Wise Lane and Storey Road, Billings; 406-656-0966.

Still in the development process in west Billings is **ZooMontana**. Canyon Creek runs through the 70-acre park, which opened in 1993 as Montana's first big zoo but which is still under construction at this writing. Waterfowl, river otters and other native North American animals were to be joined on display by Siberian tigers and more exotic creatures. A botanical garden for the visually impaired and a children's zoo are also in the works. Admission. ~ 2100 South Shiloh Road, Billings; 406-652-8100.

Animals are also the reason to visit **New Horizon Horse World**, 16 miles west of Billings. Fifteen breeds of horses, from appaloosas and Arabians to quarterhorses and thoroughbreds, are on display; visitors can view demonstrations of the horses' different abilities, go on hayrides and just hang out in the stables. Closed in winter; otherwise open daily except Monday in summer. ~ Route 212 near Thiel Road, Laurel; 406-628-4436.

Also in Laurel is the **Chief Joseph Statue and Canyon Creek Battlefield Marker**. Chief Joseph and his fugitive band of Nez Perce

SOUTHEAST MONTANA EXPERIENCES

- Quaff a custom-brewed beer with a sandwich at the **Montana Brewing Company**, housed in a 19th-century power-company building. *page 242*
- Spend a week in a teepee at **Sacred Ground** and learn tribal crafts and wisdom from Crow tribal elders. *page 248*
- Explore the juniper-studded badlands of **Makoshika State Park**, where paleontologists have uncovered many complete dinosaur skeletons. *page 254*
- Shed your "city slicker" mentality by going on a week-long **cattle drive** with any of several outfitters. *page 258*

fled before the U.S. Cavalry near here in 1877, in the penultimate skirmish before their subsequent surrender at Bear's Paw, near Havre. (The actual Canyon Creek battleground is seven and a half miles north on Route 532.) ~ Firemen's Park; 406-628-8105.

THE MUSSELSHELL VALLEY North of Billings, the **Musselshell River** parallels the Yellowstone for about 150 miles, at a distance of about 35 to 40 miles, from its sources in the Crazy and Little Belt mountains until it turns abruptly north to flow into the Missouri. Route 12 follows the famed trout and catfish stream east from White Sulphur Springs downstream to Melstone, where it makes its northerly bend; then Route 12 crosses the prairies to join Route 94 at Forsyth.

Harlowton, 92 miles northwest of Billings, was once the terminus of the world's longest electrified rail line, connecting it with the silver-mining town of Castle (now a ghost town) in the Castle Mountains to the west. The last E-57B engine to run on that line is now the centerpiece of **Electric Engine Park** in the heart of this small town. ~ Route 12 and Central Avenue, Harlowton.

The **Upper Musselshell Museum** recalls some of the boom times in its early-1900s re-creations of a general store, schoolroom and homestead. Other displays include dinosaur bones, American Indian artifacts, farm tools and vintage clothing. Closed Monday during summer; closed the rest of the year except by appointment. ~ 11 South Central Avenue, Harlowton; 406-632-5519.

From Harlowton, the Musselshell River flows past **Deadman's Basin State Park** and through the Golden Valley, so named for the autumn colors that line the river. ~ Deadman's Basin Road, Shawmut; 406-252-4654.

Pause in **Roundup**, another small town 66 miles east of Harlowton and 50 miles north of Billings, at the crossroads of Routes 12 and 87, to see the **Musselshell Valley Historical Museum**. Open summers, it has 7000 square feet of exhibits including a five-room pioneer home and a simulated coal-mine shaft. ~ 524 1st Street West, Roundup; 406-323-1403.

Every year since Montana's 1989 statehood centennial, when 3500 riders and 250 wagons herded 3000 head of cattle to Billings, the **Roundup Cattle Drive** has attracted would-be cowpokes on a six-day, five-night mid-August adventure with hands-on experience assured. It's *City Slickers* without the pathos or drama. ~ Roundup; 406-323-3434.

Route 12 pursues the course of the Musselshell as far as tiny Melstone, then cuts southeasterly across the plains to Forsyth, 100 miles from Roundup on the Yellowstone River. The Musselshell turns due north at Melstone; Route 500, a backcountry road, follows the river in the direction of Fort Peck Lake.

LODGING   The **Josephine Bed & Breakfast** is one of only two B & Bs in greater Billings, and the other is in a country cornfield. The Josephine offers three bright, antique-filled bedrooms in a 1915 home a short walk from the downtown hub. It *is* old-fashioned, however: None of the rooms has air-conditioning and all share bathrooms. Smoking is not permitted inside the house. ~ 514 North 29th Street, Billings; 406-248-5898. MODERATE.

North of downtown en route to the airport and MSU-Billings, the **Rimrock Inn** has all the basics and more, such as a free continental breakfast, a fitness area with a hot tub and a restaurant and lounge. The guest rooms are no-frills. ~ 1203 North 27th Street, Billings; 406-252-7107, 800-624-9770, fax 406-252-7107 ext. 305. BUDGET.

Downtown Billings' finest accommodations are at the **Radisson Northern Hotel**. More than five decades old, the ten-story, 160-room hotel has been fully remodeled with a contemporary Western flair. Some rooms have refrigerators. There's a restaurant, a lounge and an exercise room; guests get golf privileges at a nearby course. ~ 19 North Broadway, Billings; 406-245-5121, 800-822-3384, fax 406-259-9862. DELUXE.

Also downtown, a step down in price, is the **Best Western Ponderosa Inn**. This motel has 130 guest rooms in a pair of two-story buildings. One building faces an outdoor courtyard with a swimming pool; the other looks toward a 24-hour restaurant and cellar lounge. Each standard room has a double bed and hideaway sofa, a full bathroom, a desk, air-conditioning and complimentary coffee. In addition to the pool, the Ponderosa has a sauna, fitness room and coin laundry. ~ 2511 1st Avenue North, Billings; 406-259-5511, 800-628-9081, fax 406-245-8004. MODERATE.

Conveniently located off Route 90 for travelers arriving from the west, the **Holiday Inn Billings Plaza** is the region's largest. With 316 guest rooms in seven stories adjoining the biggest exposition hall in the northern Great Plains, it has everything you'd expect a convention hotel to have, such as a full-service restaurant, room service and a lounge-casino featuring live entertainment and dancing. A waterfall tumbles past twin glass elevators in the atrium; there's an indoor pool, a spa, a sauna, an exercise room and a video-game parlor for the children. Softly lit, tastefully decorated rooms come with all the amenities. ~ 5500 Midland Road, Billings; 406-248-7701, 800-637-3670, fax 406-248-8954. MODERATE TO DELUXE.

There's adequate lodging in the Musselshell Valley at the **Corral Motel**. This is an older ma-and-pa establishment with 18 small rooms; six of them are two-bedroom units, three have kitchens, and the entire place is kept neat and clean. ~ Routes 12 and 191, Harlowton; 406-632-4331. BUDGET.

DINING

Top of the line in southeastern Montana is **Juliano's**, which serves up generous portions of fresh game and Continental cuisine in a converted turn-of-the-century livery stable behind The Castle, a medieval-looking sandstone manor, and on an outdoor patio. The restaurant does its own baking and has an extensive wine list. ~ 2912 7th Avenue North, Billings; 406-248-6400. DELUXE.

Also atmospheric, but in a more magisterial sort of way, is **Walkers Grill**, which occupies the ground floor of Billings' renovated Old Chamber Building opposite the Yellowstone County Court House. Dinner is a creative affair, with Italian, Mexican, Cajun and Asian influences in various seafood and meat dishes; lunch is simpler, with a focus on soups, salads and pastas. ~ 301 North 27th Street, Billings; 406-245-9291. MODERATE.

For straight beef and seafood, it's hard to top **Jaker's Steak & Fish House** in the heart of downtown Billings. A large salad bar complements meals amid the garden decor of the main restaurant, and a lighter menu is served in the wood-and-brass Good

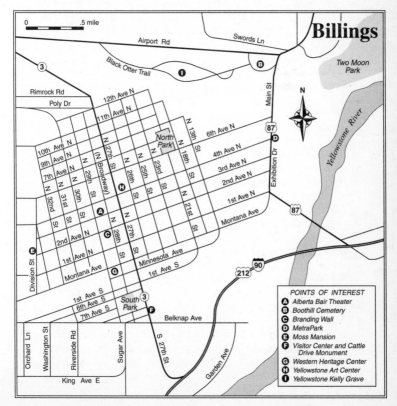

Billings

POINTS OF INTEREST

- **Ⓐ** Alberta Bair Theater
- **Ⓑ** Boothill Cemetery
- **Ⓒ** Branding Wall
- **Ⓓ** MetraPark
- **Ⓔ** Moss Mansion
- **Ⓕ** Visitor Center and Cattle Drive Monument
- **Ⓖ** Western Heritage Center
- **Ⓗ** Yellowstone Art Center
- **Ⓘ** Yellowstone Kelly Grave

Text continued on page 242.

Custer's
Last Stand

By the 1870s, U.S. government policy toward the proud native peoples of the Great Plains had changed from aggressive domination to pseudo-accommodation. Deciding it "cheaper to feed than to fight the Indians," Congress had pledged in 1868 to defend them from further hostility, designating a large part of the Wyoming territory, including the Black Hills, as a permanent reservation for Sioux (Crow), Cheyenne and other tribes.

It seemed that treaties were made to be broken. Following an 1874 gold strike in the Black Hills, thousands of anxious argonauts poured onto reservation lands despite the cavalry's feeble efforts to keep them out. The Indians, who still wished to honor the treaty, refused to cede this portion of their sacred hunting grounds, and the Sioux and Cheyenne stepped up a campaign of hostile raids against mining settlements, pioneer homesteads and ill-fated travelers.

When the renegade clans, led by chiefs Sitting Bull and Crazy Horse, defied a direct order from the Commissioner of Indian Affairs to restrict themselves to reservation lands, the U.S. Army launched a three-pronged campaign against them in the spring of 1876. Since the order was issued in the dead of winter, it is unlikely that many families could have made it back to the reservation by the end of January, as specified, under any circumstances.)

The first of the three expeditions, from Fort Fetterman, Wyoming Territory, was turned back June 17 on Rosebud Creek, about 40 miles southeast of Sitting Bull's encampment on the Little Bighorn River. A joint Sioux-Cheyenne force sent General George Crook into retreating after substantial losses; this Rosebud Battlefield site is now a Montana state park.

The other two prongs of the attack—Colonel John Gibbon's troops from Fort Ellis, Montana Territory, and General Alfred Terry's column from Fort Abraham Lincoln, Dakota Territory—met on the banks of the Yellowstone River. Unaware of Crook's failure, Terry designated Lieutenant Colonel George Armstrong Custer, a Civil War hero, to lead the 600 men of the 7th Cavalry up Rosebud Creek, then cross a saddle of land and slip into the Little Bighorn from the southeast. Terry and Gibbon, meanwhile, would circle in from the Bighorn River to the northwest.

Custer arrived at least 36 hours earlier than Terry and Gibbon, and located Sitting Bull's camp at about dawn June 25. Probably underestimating the tribes' strength, Custer put five 45-man battalions under his direct command and assigned three each to Major Marcus Reno and Captain Frederick Benteen. (A twelfth was assigned to guard the pack train.)

Benteen was charged with scouting the bluffs south of the Indian camp as Custer and Reno headed toward the village. Custer intended to invade the camp from its lower, northern end, while Reno was to strike at the high end of the camp. But the Sioux detected Reno's approach and sent a large force to stop his advance. Outflanked and overwhelmed, Reno's men retreated in disorder and took up defensive positions in the bluffs with Benteen.

Where had the impetuous Custer gone? When heavy gunfire began sounding from the north, Reno and Benteen concluded that the colonel, too, had come under attack. By the time they had distributed ammunition to their troops and moved them northward, however, all activity had ceased. Further Indian attacks caused them to withdraw once again to the bluffs, where they held their defenses until the columns under Terry and Gibson arrived on the afternoon of the following day, June 26.

Custer's precise movements, after he separated from Benteen and Reno, will forever be conjecture. But not a man among the 225 who followed Custer into battle survived the skirmish with the Cheyenne and Sioux. (A single horse, Comanche, was left standing; for years thereafter, he was saddled but left riderless as he marched in military parades to commemorate the massacre.) Battle accounts rendered by Indians who participated told how Custer's battalions were surrounded and exterminated.

Said Chief Two Moon of the Northern Cheyenne: "The shooting was quick, quick. Pop-pop-pop very fast. Some of the soldiers were down on their knees, some standing. . . . The smoke was like a great cloud, and everywhere the Sioux went the dust rose like smoke. We circled all around him—swirling like water around a stone. We shoot, we ride fast, we shoot again. Soldiers drop, and horses fall on them."

Of the men under the command of Reno and Benteen, 47 were killed and 52 wounded, bringing total fatalities probably to 272. No more than one hundred Sioux and Cheyenne were killed. After the Indians removed their dead from the battlefield, the village broke up, with tribes scattering in different directions.

Little Bighorn Battlefield National Monument and Custer National Cemetery are today surrounded by the expansive Crow Indian Reservation. On its eastern border is the Northern Cheyenne reservation. Together, the reservations stretch well over 100 miles from the Pryor Mountains to the Tongue River.

Time Bar. ~ 2701 1st Avenue North, Billings; 406-259-9375. MODERATE.

The Granary serves prime rib, Alaskan king crab and Cajun cuisine in a building constructed as a mill by the former Billings Polytechnic Institute in 1935. The original machinery is still on display. Students enjoy the outdoor patio lounge. ~ 1500 Poly Drive, Billings; 406-259-3488. MODERATE.

Billings' first brewpub is the **Montana Brewing Company**. This downtown establishment has taken over the first floor of an old power company building, retaining and restoring the original century-old architecture. Besides designer beers, the pub offers salads, sandwiches and pizzas in a friendly, casual atmosphere. ~ 113 North Broadway, Billings; 406-252-9200. MODERATE.

The **Great Wall Restaurant** boasts the best Chinese food in Montana, and few are they who argue. A wide variety of pork, beef, chicken and shrimp dishes, in varied Cantonese, Mandarin and Szechuan styles, are prepared at this west Billings restaurant. ~ 1309 Grand Avenue, Billings; 406-245-8601. BUDGET TO MODERATE.

HIDDEN ► Next door to the Great Wall is a surprise: **Khanthaly's Eggrolls**, a Laotian fast-food restaurant in the middle of the prairie. Because Laos is wedged between Thailand, Vietnam and China, its food bears influences from all three traditions. ~ 1301 Grand Avenue, Billings; 406-259-7252. BUDGET.

Bruno's Italian Specialties is a longtime Billings favorite for its pizza and homemade Italian sausage. The spacious restaurant on the north side of downtown has a full bar and casino machines. A second shop is at 1523 Broadwater (406-252-1616). ~ 1002 1st Avenue North, Billings; 406-248-4146. BUDGET.

As anyone who travels the highways of Montana will tell you, Roundup's **Busy Bee** has something for everyone. Located on the west side of town on routes 12 and 87, and open 24 hours a day, the Bee serves a wide-ranging country-style menu in a pair of homey dining rooms. There's a big salad bar; beer and wine are served, but no spirits. ~ 317 1st Avenue West, Roundup; 406-323-2204. BUDGET.

HIDDEN ► If you're traveling east on Route 12 from Roundup to Miles City, don't fail to stop at the **Jersey Lilly Bar & Cafe**. You can't miss it: It's the only business in town. People drive many miles to eat its famous pinto-bean chili and to meet the old bar's legendary owner. ~ Route 12, Ingomar; 406-358-2278. BUDGET.

SHOPPING   As the commercial center of a four-state region, Billings is a magnet for shoppers. **Rimrock Mall** has more than 100 shops, anchored by two major department stores. ~ 300 South 24th Street West, Billings; 406-656-3205. Somewhat nearer to downtown is

West Park Plaza; Montana's first mall when it opened in the early 1960s, West Park has 45 stores. ~ 1603 Grand Avenue, Billings; 406-252-8684. Downtown Billings has many blocks of specialty stores and an indoor mall at **Market Square**. ~ 207 North Broadway, Billings; 406-259-6435.

An excellent place to find regional arts and crafts is at the **Yellowstone Art Center**. ~ 401 North 27th Street, Billings; 406-256-6804. Also check out the **Western Heritage Center**. ~ 2822 Montana Avenue, Billings; 406-256-6809.

> The mainstay of community theater is the Billings Studio Theatre, which performs five plays during a September-to-May season.

Other spots of special interest downtown include **Collector's Emporium**, an antique mall of 14,000 square feet. ~ 114 North 29th Street; 406-259-2338. **Billings Army/Navy Surplus** is the largest of its kind in the northwestern United States. ~ 15 North 29th Street; 406-259-8528. **Stillwater Traders** features all manner of cowboy kitsch. ~ 2nd Avenue North and North 29th Street; 406-252-6211. **Center Lodge Native Arts** offers modern and traditional American Indian arts and crafts. ~ 121 North 29th Street; 406-252-9994.

The **Alberta Bair Theater for the Performing Arts** is Montana's largest concert hall. A renovated former Fox theater on the corner of Broadway downtown, it has been acoustically redesigned and is now in use more than 110 nights a year. Touring professional ballet, opera, theater and symphony companies appear here. ~ 2801 3rd Avenue North at Broadway, Billings; 406-256-6052. The Bair Theater is the venue for performances presented by the **Billings Community Concert Association**. ~ 1603 Grand Avenue, Billings; 406-245-0460. The **Billings Symphony Orchestra and Chorale** presents concerts at the Bair monthly in a September-to-April season. ~ 401 North 31st Avenue, Billings; 406-252-3610.

NIGHTLIFE

Big-name concerts of country and popular musical artists usually are held at **MetraPark Arena**. The greatest concentrations take place in mid-August during the Montana Fair. ~ 308 6th Avenue North, Billings, Billings; 406-256-2422.

The **Billings Studio Theatre** performs at Rocky Mountain College. The troupe stages five plays of different genres (often including a musical, a comedy, a drama and a Shakespearean classic). ~ 1500 Rimrock Road, Billings; 406-248-1141.

Billings' rock-and-rollers appreciate **The Bungalow**, which boasts live music nightly except Monday, a huge dance floor, an outdoor patio and casino gaming. ~ 925 South 27th Street; 406-254-2800. **Casey's Golden Pheasant** brings blues, bluegrass and zydeco to downtown Billings. ~ 109 North Broadway; 406-256-5200. Country-and-western dancers head out to **Drifters Tavern**. ~ 3953 Montana Avenue; 406-259-8619. Or they head to the **Corral Bar** to do their two-stepping. ~ 5005 Route 312 East; 406-373-5345.

A popular downtown gathering place is **The Billings Club**, with microbrews on tap in an outdoor beer garden and satellite TV in every corner of the indoor sports bar. ~ 2702 1st Avenue North, Billings; 406-245-2262.

Casino lovers can check out **Doc & Eddy's** at two locations: west of downtown at 711 15th Avenue West, 406-259-0881; and in Billings Heights located at 1403 Main Street, 406-248-4336.

PARKS

LAKE ELMO STATE PARK A 64-acre irrigation reservoir on Billings' northern city limits, Lake Elmo attracts city residents for swimming, fishing (for panfish) and nonmotorized boating. Boat rentals and boardsailing lessons are available from June through August. There are restrooms and concessions; restaurants and groceries are in Billings. Day-use fee, $1 from May through September. ~ Head north on Main Street (Route 87) through Billings Heights; turn left on Pemberton Lane, then right for one-half mile on Lake Elmo Drive; 406-256-6205 (summer) or 406-252-4654.

CUSTER NATIONAL FOREST Montana's most diverse national forest extends across nearly 2.5 million acres of the southern part of the state, in seven different parcels reaching from the Stillwater River, west of Red Lodge, to Capitol Rock, southeast of Ekalaka on the border of South Dakota. In between, it includes a large chunk of the Absaroka-Beartooth Wilderness as well as the Pryor Mountains, west of Bighorn Canyon, and the Ashland District lands, east of the Tongue River. Picnic tables and restrooms are among the facilities. Groceries and restaurants are in Billings, Red Lodge, Ashland, Ekalaka and many other towns. ~ Main approach roads for the Beartooth region are Routes 212 and 78 from Red Lodge, or Route 419 from Absarokee. Enter the Pryor Mountains via Crow Reservation Road 11, off Route 5 between Pryor and Warren; the Ashland District from Route 212 or Otter Creek Road; and the Ekalaka District from county roads south and east of Ekalaka, at the end of Route 7; 406-657-6361.

▲ There are 277 RV/tent sites, none with hookups, plus 91 for tents only at 20 campgrounds; no charge to $7 per night; 14-day maximum stay. A recreational cabin, available at $15 per night, is located at Beaver Creek in the Ashland District.

DEADMAN'S BASIN STATE PARK Trout fishing and other water sports are widely pursued at this prairie irrigation reservoir, located just north of the Musselshell River. There are picnic tables and restrooms; groceries and restaurants are in Harlowton and Ryegate. Day-use fee $3. ~ Twenty miles east from Harlowton on Route 12, then one mile north on Deadman's Basin Road; 406-252-4654.

▲ Primitive only.

▼▼▼▼▼▼▼▼▼▼▼

The Big Horns and Beyond

Route 90 connecting Billings with Sheridan, Wyoming, 130 miles southeast, is an avenue to many of the leading attractions of southeastern Montana. Traversing the Crow Indian Reservation, it passes directly by the Little Bighorn Battlefield of "Custer's Last Stand" fame and comes within a short drive of Bighorn Canyon National Recreation Area.

SIGHTS

◄ HIDDEN

At the northwest corner of the Crow Indian Reservation is **Hardin**, a farming and ranching center of 3000 people. Twelve months a year, the best reason to visit Hardin is to see its **Big Horn County Historical Museum** at the **State Visitors Center**. Located at the east end of town, the free museum carefully preserves more than a dozen homestead-era buildings from all over Big Horn County. Picnic grounds surround the 24-acre "village," which includes a farm home and outbuildings, railroad depot, service station, mercantile shop, school and church (still used for services on summer Sundays). Antique farm implements and machinery are on display. ~ Route 90 Exit 497; 406-665-1671.

Hardin lives hard by its memories of Little Bighorn. While the battlefield is 18 miles southeast of here, the Custer's Last Stand Reenactment takes place five times each year, in a field six miles west of Hardin, during Little Big Horn Days, the weekend nearest June 25. Thousands attend the hour-long spectacle; advance tickets can be purchased from the **Hardin Area Chamber of Commerce**. ~ 21 East 4th Street; 406-665-1672.

Little Bighorn Battlefield National Monument is where the *real* action took place, however, and there's no better way to understand the maneuvers and tactics of the best known of all American Indian battles than to spend some time here. The clash, which took place on June 25 and 26, 1876, memorializes one of the Plains Indians' last armed attempts to defend their life against the intrusion of white settlement. Admission. ~ Battlefield Road, Crow Agency; 406-638-2621.

Museum displays and dioramas in the visitors center and ranger-led talks and tours describe the chain of events that led Sioux and Cheyenne warriors to vanquish a corps of 260 U.S. Army cavalrymen. Not a soldier survived the massacre; among the dead was their leader, Lieutenant Colonel George Armstrong Custer.

The national monument, reached off Route 212 at Exit 510 from Route 90, includes the **Custer National Cemetery** (for veterans of the armed services) and a four-and-a-half-mile tour road that winds through the sage-covered hills overlooking the Little Bighorn River.

Given that the Indians were fighting for their ultimate freedom, it's ironic that the national monument is now within the **Crow Indian Reservation**. The vast (2.3-million-acre) reservation is home to about 5200 Apsalooké ("Children of the Large-Beaked Bird"), or Crow, a Sioux tribe. Stretching 55 miles north and south, from Billings to the Wyoming border, and 83 miles east and west, from West Pryor Mountain to Rosebud Creek, the tribe leans upon tourism for its economic wherewithal. ~ Crow Agency; 406-638-2601.

The mustangs roaming the Pryor Mountains National Wild Horse Range are believed to be descendants of a herd that has lived in this area for more than two hundred years.

After Little Bighorn Battlefield, the Crow Indian Reservation's second ace-in-the-tourism-hole is the **Bighorn Canyon National Recreation Area**. The park spans two states, stretching south well into Wyoming, but it is from Hardin that most Montana visitors reach it. Its central feature is 71-mile-long Bighorn Lake, which fills a dramatic desert canyon whose limestone walls rise a half mile high on either side, revealing millions of years of geologic history. The numerous outdoor stores in tiny **Fort Smith**, at the north entrance to the park 43 miles south of Hardin, make the area's recreational focus abundantly clear. See "Parks" section below, for more information. ~ Fort Smith; 406-666-2412.

Bighorn Lake was created in 1965 by 525-foot-high Yellowtail Dam. Today, the **Yellowtail Dam Visitors Center**, open summers only, describes the construction and operation of the dam. ~ Route 313, Fort Smith; 406-666-3234. The **Fort Smith Visitors Center** has displays that focus on wildlife and geography and sponsors evening programs at a nearby campground. ~ Afterbay Road, Fort Smith; 406-666-2339.

The best vista of the meandering reservoir and gorge is from the **Devil Canyon Overlook**, a course that requires drivers to backtrack more than 100 miles through Lovell, Wyoming. Those who do are rewarded with a magnificent view where Bighorn Canyon cuts through the Pryor Mountains. ~ Route 37; 406-548-2251.

Those same Pryor Mountains, on the west side of Bighorn Canyon, are the site of the 44,000-acre **Pryor Mountain National Wild Horse Range**. About 130 mustangs freely roam this rugged desert land administered by the Bureau of Land Management. Backcountry roads penetrate the range from Route 310 east of Warren. ~ Route 37 via Lovell, Wyoming; 406-657-6262.

Just inside the Crow Indian Reservation's western boundary is **Chief Plenty Coups State Park**, which preserves the log home, medicinal spring and grave of the last Crow chief. Plenty Coups deeded the land, 35 miles south of Billings, to the Crow nation in 1928. It is now an interpretive center for Crow tribal history as well as a memorial to the chief himself. Admission. ~ Route 416, Pryor; 406-252-1289.

The Crow Indian Reservation is bordered on the east by the wooded mesas and creek beds of the **Northern Cheyenne Indian Reservation**. Covering 445,000 acres west of the Tongue River, the reservation is home to 5600 Northern Cheyenne, who call themselves the "People of the Morning Star." ~ Reservation headquarters, Lame Deer; 406-477-6253. Also located in Lame Deer is the **Northern Cheyenne Arts and Crafts Center**, which displays beadwork and other handicrafts. ~ Route 212; 406-477-6284.

More impressive is the **Plains Indian Museum at St. Labre Indian School**, on the reservation's eastern frontier 21 miles from Lame Deer. The modern museum has a colorful and varied collection of clothing and artifacts from Cheyenne, Sioux and other plains tribes. The school, founded as a mission in 1884, is notable for its stylized stone church, built in the shape of a teepee but with a metal cross protruding in place of the center supporting pole. ~ Tongue River Road, Ashland; 406-784-2741 2200.

◄ HIDDEN

Rosebud Battlefield State Park, 44 miles southwest of Lame Deer, marks the spot where Sioux warriors took on a cavalry division in June 1876, setting the stage for the Battle of the Little Bighorn eight days later. ~ Route 314, Decker; 406-232-4365.

It's an hour's drive north from Lame Deer to Route 94 west of Forsyth. Not quite halfway, Route 39 passes through the town of **Colstrip**, a modern coal-mining boom town that bills itself as the "Energy Center of Montana." The **Colstrip Visitors Center** will show you videos about the town's history, the operation of a coal-fired power plant, and the workings of an open-pit mine; then a guide will take you on a free tour of the Rosebud mine (by reservation). ~ Route 39, Colstrip; 406-748-3746. The **Big Sky Mine** also offers tours by appointment. ~ Colstrip; 406-748-2321.

The little town of **Broadus**, a 44-mile drive east from Ashland on Route 212, has one of the most memorable local museums to be found in the northern Rockies. The **Powder River Historical Museum** is actually two museums in one. The main building, located two blocks off the highway, displays a well-organized homestead-era collection including a complete general store, a ranch's chuck wagon, the original Powder River jail and many antique vehicles.

If those don't grab you, ask to see **Mac's Museum** in a rear building. Until his death in 1986, pioneer resident R. D. "Mac" McCurdy devoted most of his waking hours to his personal collection of arrowheads, fossils, rocks, insects, birds' eggs and more. But those pale in comparison to his 200,000 seashells from throughout the world. Many of them are no larger than pinheads,

◄ HIDDEN

but McCurdy identified all by their exact genera and species. Scientists visit from all over North America to study McCurdy's collection. Open from Memorial Day to Labor Day or by appointment. ~ 102 West Wilson Street, Broadus; 406-436-2276.

Also in Broadus, the **Powder River Taxidermy Wildlife Museum** has assembled some 150 wildlife trophies—"everything from a mouse to a moose"—along with antique guns and local art. There's not much more to see east of here until Route 212 leaves Montana for Wyoming's Devils Tower and South Dakota's Black Hills. ~ 708 South Park Street, Broadus; 406-436-2538.

LODGING   Near the Little Bighorn Battlefield, in downtown Hardin, an early-20th-century boarding house has been restored as a bed-and-breakfast home. The **Kendrick House Inn** is a handsome Georgian with seven guest rooms decorated in late-Victorian style. Each room has a pedestal sink, but the bathrooms (two of them) must be shared. There are full breakfasts in the dining room and TV in the library. ~ 206 North Custer Avenue, Hardin; 406-665-3035. MODERATE.

The **Western Motel** isn't flashy, but the price tag is right. The two-story property has 28 rooms (four of them two-bedroom family suites) with outdated furnishings but private baths in every unit. ~ 830 West 3rd Street, Hardin; 406-665-2296, fax 406-665-2298. BUDGET.

HIDDEN ▶   A unique experience for cultural adventurers is offered by **Sacred Ground** on the Crow Indian Reservation. Participants spend a full week living Indian-style in teepees in the remote Pryor Mountains, west of Bighorn Canyon. They learn tribal wisdom from Crow elders, study native cooking and crafts, consort with plants and wildlife during hikes and horseback rides through the mountains, and immerse themselves in traditional singing, dancing and (if they wish) sacred ceremonies. Closed October through May. ~ P.O. Box 78, Pryor, MT 59066; phone/fax 406-245-6070. MODERATE.

Ever wanted to be a cowboy? The **Schively Ranch** will give you your chance. There are actually two ranches here, an "upper" and a "lower," located in Montana's Pryor Mountains; the Upper Ranch has small cabins with electric heat and shared shower facilities, while the lower Dry Head Ranch merely has a bunkhouse. This is a real ranching experience, with lots of horseback riding and trailside, chuckwagon meals. Because the ranch's winter feedlot is in Wyoming, early-season (April–May) or late-season (October) guests can join in cattle drives. No credit cards. ~ 106 Road 15, Lovell, WY 82431; 406-259-8866 summer, 307-548-6688 winter. MODERATE.

Lodging options are scarce in the southeasternmost part of the state, but the **C-J Motel** will do in a pinch. Kitchen units are avail-

able in this modest lodging; all rooms have air-conditioning as well
as phones and TV. ~ Route 212 West, Broadus; 406-436-2671.
BUDGET.

Once you get away from Billings, culinary choices are pretty much   **DINING**
limited to steak and potatoes. **The Merry Mixer Restaurant &**
Lounge is a prime example. You can get a good steak or a big slab
of prime rib accompanied by a baked potato, a basic iceberg-
lettuce salad and a hearty cup of coffee. The atmosphere is strictly
red vinyl and low lights, but the service is friendly. ~ 317 North
Center Avenue, Hardin; 208-406-665-3735. MODERATE.

A longtime favorite here is the **Purple Cow**, a family restaurant
open for three meals daily. The Cow offers hearty breakfasts and
generous homemade buffets for lunch and dinner, including a large
salad bar. Soups and pies are also popular. ~ Route 47 North,
Hardin; 406-665-3601. MODERATE.

For American Indian fast food, the **Shake & Burger Hut** is
worth a visit. Ask for a Navajo taco and you'll get ground beef,
cheese and other fixings folded within tasty, pan-fried bread. The
decor of this tiny establishment is strictly Formica-top tables and
video games. ~ Crow Agency; 406-638-2921. BUDGET.

The hangout in the prairies is the **Montana Bar & Cafe**, where
cowhands gather for hot coffee and cinnamon rolls in the morning, and ranch-style lunches and dinners. There's a salad bar here,
too, and a full bar. ~ Broadus; 406-436-2454. BUDGET.

American Indian culture vultures might seek out the **Jailhouse**   **SHOPPING**
Gallery for modern Indian paintings and craftwork. ~ 218 North
Center Street, Hardin; 406-665-3239. The **Little Coyote Gallery**,
on the Crow Indian Reservation, offers more traditional handi-
crafts as well as contemporary works. ~ St. Labre Indian School,
Tongue River Road, Ashland; 406-784-2200.

Montana's largest gambling establishment is the **Little Bighorn**   **NIGHTLIFE**
Casino, a stone's throw from the Little Bighorn Battlefield at the
same exit off Route 90. ~ Route 212, Crow Agency; 406-638-
4444.

Nearly on the Wyoming border is the **Stoneville Saloon**, which
boasts "cheap drinks, lousy food." But the handcarved back bar,
dating from 1865, is worth a look in itself. This is a popular spot
for motorcyclists, as it's a mere hour's drive down the highway
from Sturgis, South Dakota, the late-summer biker capital of
America. ~ Route 212, Alzada; 406-828-9435.

LITTLE BIGHORN BATTLEFIELD NATIONAL MONUMENT 🏃   **PARKS**
🚲 ⚓ Formerly known as Custer Battlefield, this national park-
land commemorates one of the final efforts by American Indians

to defend their homelands. The monument, surrounded by the Crow Indian Reservation, comprises two parcels, three miles apart, that overlook the Little Bighorn River where Sioux, Cheyenne and other warriors camped prior to their June 1876 massacre of Lieutenant Colonel George Custer and his corps of 260 American soldiers. Visitors center displays and films, guided tours and ranger-led programs explain the background, events and aftermath of that battle. Custer National Cemetery is also on the site, and there's fishing in the adjacent Little Bighorn River. (Reservation licenses must be obtained at the office in Crow Agency.) Facilities include picnic areas and restrooms. Day-use fee from April to November is $4 per vehicle, free rest of year. ~ From Route 90, take Exit 510, two miles south of Crow Agency; Battlefield Road enters the national monument about one mile east of the exit off Route 212; 406-638-2621.

BIGHORN CANYON NATIONAL RECREATION AREA 🏃🚴🐎
Prior to 1965 the Bighorn River cut a deep gorge through the Pryor and Big Horn mountain ranges. Since the construction of 525-foot-high Yellowtail Dam, in 1965, Bighorn Lake has stretched 71 miles through the canyon. But the half-mile-high cliffs remain, and boating and fishing enthusiasts have a new playground, and there's a swimming beach at Horseshoe Bend. Fishing is outstanding for trout, walleye, catfish and other species. Visitors centers at Fort Smith, Montana, and Lovell, Wyoming, relate the canyon's geological and natural history. The canyon view is spectacular from Devil Canyon Overlook in the park's southern section, but no direct route connects Fort Smith with Lovell, so a meander of more than 100 miles is required to see both ends of Bighorn Lake. Picnic tables, restrooms, an amphitheater and two marinas round out the amenities. Groceries and restaurants are in Lovell, Hardin and Fort Smith. ~ From Hardin, take Route 313 south 43 miles to the visitors center at Fort Smith. From the visitors center at Lovell, Wyoming, on Route 14A east of Cody, take Route 37 north to Devil Canyon and Barry's Landing; 406-666-2412.

▲ There are 30 RV/tent sites, none with hookups, plus 27 for tents only at four campgrounds; two campgrounds are accessible only by boat; no charge; 14-day maximum stay.

CHIEF PLENTY COUPS STATE PARK 🏃
Plenty Coups, the last Crow chief, understood that he would never defeat the white man, so he led his people to try to adopt the pioneers' lifestyle. This park—an interpretive center for Crow tribal history—includes the chief's log home, his grave, and a spring of medicinal water. Picnic tables, restrooms and a visitors center round out the amenities. Day-use fee, $3. ~ From Pryor, 35 miles south of Billings on the

western edge of the Crow Indian Reservation, take Route 416 west one mile; 406-252-1289.

TONGUE RIVER RESERVOIR STATE PARK
This 12-mile-long lake, set in the prairies amid red shale cliffs and juniper canyons just north of the Wyoming border, is a popular place for camping and water sports. Walleye and northern pike are the most highly sought fish here. There are picnic tables, restrooms, concession stands and groceries. Day-use fee, $3. ~ From Decker, 20 miles north of Sheridan, Wyoming, take Route 314 six miles north, then Route 382 (the Tongue River Dam Road) two miles northeast; 406-232-4365.

▲ There are 20 RV/tent sites, none with hookups; $4 per night; 14-day maximum stay.

▼▼▼▼▼▼▼▼▼▼▼▼▼
Lower Yellowstone Valley

Northeast from Billings, Route 94 follows the Yellowstone River downstream some 223 miles to Glendive, not far from the river's confluence with the Missouri, before turning abruptly east through North Dakota toward Minneapolis and Chicago.

The longest undammed river in the lower 48 states, the Yellowstone—which runs 671 miles from its source in Wyoming's Absaroka Range to the Missouri—in its lower portion is a broad, gently flowing stream. Along with its principal tributaries, the northward flowing Bighorn, Tongue and Powder rivers, it irrigates tens of thousands of square miles of ranchland used in livestock and grain production.

Numerous communities exist along the river's banks, none of them large. This stretch of the Yellowstone may be better known as the home of the paddlefish (see "Outdoor Adventures," at the end of this chapter), a 100-pound-plus living fossil that is basically the same creature it was in the Paleocene era, 70 million years ago.

SIGHTS

Along the south bank of the Yellowstone, stretching 27 miles from Huntley (11 miles east of Billings) to Bull Mountain, the Huntley Irrigation Project embraces 35,000 acres of lush cropland set aside as a federal homesteading project in 1907 and three other small communities. The townsite of Osborn, three miles east of Huntley, is now the location of the **Huntley Project Museum of Irrigated Agriculture**, which preserves 18 buildings and more than 5000 agricultural and household items from the early 20th century. ~ Route 312, Huntley; 406-967-2680.

Near the east end of the Huntley project is **Pompeys Pillar**, a sandstone butte on whose face Captain William Clark carved his name in 1806. That signature is the only direct physical evidence remaining from the Lewis and Clark expedition of 1803–1806, making the 150-foot-high butte a national historic landmark. A boardwalk/stairway leads from a picnic area at the base to Clark's signature and a lookout point atop the butte. A visitors center, operated by the Bureau of Land Management, offers interpretive programs through the summer. Take Exit 23 off Route 94. ~ Route 312, Pompeys Pillar; 406-875-2233.

The village of **Custer**, 52 miles from Billings, is a popular gathering point for fishermen and rockhounds. The anglers come to cast their lines where the Bighorn River meets the Yellowstone, especially during the winter run of eel-like ling. Rockhounds scour the river banks downstream from Custer in search of Montana agates, also called plume or moss agates; geologists remark on the variety of designs sealed inside these stones.

The towns of Hysham and Forsyth are 22 and 45 miles (respectively) northeast of Custer. Each boasts a small pioneer museum; **Hysham** has a wildlife management area in a nearby bend of the Yellowstone River, while **Forsyth** has the neoclassical **Rosebud County Courthouse**. An ornate copper dome caps the two-story building, listed on the National Register of Historic Places; murals and stained glass adorn the top floor and courtroom. ~1200 Main Street, Forsyth; 406-356-7318.

Other than Billings, **Miles City** is the largest community in eastern Montana. Located 145 miles east of the "Magic City," and 94 miles west of the North Dakota border, the town of 8500 people lays claim to the moniker "Montana's Cowboy Capital."

Founded in 1877 near old Fort Keogh at the confluence of the Tongue and Yellowstone rivers, and named (as so many Montana towns were) for an army officer, Miles City became headquarters for the Montana Stockgrowers' Association within three years after the arrival of the Northern Pacific Railroad in 1881. It remains a major ranching and farming center.

Although the open rangeland has long since been fenced, Miles City pays tribute to its cowboy heritage with its annual Breeders Show in February, world-famous Bucking Horse Sale in May and Cattlewomen's Convention in June. The horseracing and rodeo seasons attract tremendous attendance.

TICKET-FREE ZONE

Miles City, by the way, got rid of parking meters years ago. It's a lot more fun to browse the quaint downtown historic district without them. Besides, quarters are essential to poker machines—and like every Montana town, Miles City has its quotient of casinos.

Fort Keogh, once the largest army post in Montana, opened in 1877 following the Little Bighorn uprising and remained of major importance through 1908, when it closed. Several of its original buildings have been incorporated into the Livestock and Range Research Station at Fort Keogh, an applied agricultural science facility two miles from downtown that focuses on genetics, reproduction and nutrition of beef cattle. Tours are offered weekdays by appointment. The old fort's parade grounds are the site of a 19th-century living-history encampment in mid-August each year. ~ Main Street West, Miles City; 406-232-4970.

A miniature replica of old Fort Keogh is displayed at the **Range Riders Museum,** an impressive nine-building complex whose collection also includes a re-creation of the main street of 19th-century Miles City, the Charles M. Russell Art Gallery and a Memorial Hall with hundreds of portraits and plaques remembering pioneer Custer County residents. There's also the Heritage Center, with early photography and American Indian artifacts; a one-room school and log house; and displays of manifold antique vehicles, guns and hats. Open April to October or by appointment, the museum is located just across the Tongue River Bridge from downtown. Admission. ~ Main Street West, Miles City; 406-232-6146.

Custer County Art Center, downriver from the Range Riders Museum where the Tongue enters the Yellowstone, may be the world's only gallery housed in historic water storage tanks. It features a permanent collection of Western art, changing exhibitions of local and regional works, and a gift shop with a wide range of art and books. Open Tuesday to Sunday afternoons year-round. ~ Water Plant Road, Miles City; 406-232-0635.

Terry, equidistant from Miles City and Glendive, boasts the dubious distinction of having "the tallest sign in eastern Montana" at a beside-the-interstate convenience store. Certainly more important, it was the home of British photographer Lady Evelyn Cameron, who moved to Terry in 1894 with her naturalist husband and her 5 x 7 Graflex camera and recorded the lifestyle of eastern Montana homesteaders for the next 34 years. When a Time-Life editor discovered a stash of thousands of Cameron's photos in the basement of a private home, her previously unknown work quickly rocketed to fame. The new Cameron Gallery in the **Prairie County Museum** ◄ *HIDDEN* has an extensive collection of her work. The museum, located in a historic bank building, also displays antique household, farm and business antiques. ~ Terry; 406-637-5782.

A few miles northwest of town via Scenic View Road are the **Terry Badlands,** a 44,000-acre Bureau of Land Management tract containing sandstone spires, buttes, natural bridges and other colorful geological phenomena. There's a scenic overlook, wildlife watching and hiking trails. ~ 406-232-7000.

But badlands lovers will be yet more impressed by the pine-and-juniper-studded terrain at **Makoshika State Park**, located southeast of Glendive, 78 miles northeast of Miles City. In Sioux, *makoshika* means "bad earth"; but to paleontologists, this rippled earth has been very good, yielding the complete fossil remains of such great dinosaurs as triceratops and tyrannosaurus. A new visitors center opened in 1994 at the 8123-acre park. Admission. ~ Makoshika Park Road, Glendive; 406-365-6256.

A mile east of downtown Glendive is the **Frontier Gateway Museum**. Open summers or by appointment, it displays various fossils, Indian and pioneer artifacts, and a replica 19th-century downtown business district. ~ Belle Prairie Frontage Road, Glendive; 406-365-8168.

Anglers call **Glendive** "the paddlefishing capital of the world." Found only in the Yellowstone and Missouri rivers and in China's Yangtze River, paddlefish are prehistoric bottom feeders with two-foot-long, paddle-shaped snouts. See the fishing section in "Outdoor Adventures" at the end of this chapter.

Route 90 turns away from the Yellowstone River at Glendive and makes a beeline for the North Dakota border. Eight miles from the frontier is the small community of **Wibaux**, founded in 1889 by French-born cattle baron Pierre Wibaux. The town office building he constructed in 1892 has been restored and is now the **Pierre Wibaux House Museum**. Besides memorabilia of the cattleman himself, there's a wide variety of turn-of-the-century pioneer items, American Indian artifacts and a classic car display. A state travel information center is across Orgain Street. Closed October through April. ~ Orgain and Wibaux streets, Wibaux; 406-795-2427.

A twice-life-size statue of Pierre Wibaux stands atop a hill at the west end of Orgain Street, overlooking **St. Peter's Catholic**

JOE, MONTANA

Thirty miles west of Baker and five miles north of Route 12 via Ismay Road is a hamlet that wouldn't attract interest had it not changed its name in 1993. **Joe** (formerly Ismay), Montana, now goes by the same name as star professional football quarterback Joe Montana. The community of 22 people said it wanted to raise a couple of thousand dollars to cover the annual operating costs of its volunteer fire department, but within a year the promotion had earned nearly $70,000. So the entire population traveled to Kansas City to watch their namesake play for the Chiefs . . . and to have their photo taken, of course. Montana (the quarterback) retired in 1995, but you can still buy caps, T-shirts and other souvenirs by calling 1-800-HELP-JOE.

Church, which Wibaux built in 1885 with money donated by his father in France. The church has beautiful stained-glass windows and a lava-rock exterior that is covered in summer by climbing vines. ~ West end of Orgain Street, Wibaux.

Baker is 45 miles south of Wibaux via Route 7. This pleasant town of 1800 sits at the crossroads of Route 12, 80 miles east of Miles City. Baker Lake, surrounded by parks and recreational facilities, is right in town. Baker also boasts the **O'Fallon Historical Museum**, which displays the "world's largest steer"—almost six feet high and just under two tons in weight—and a variety of vintage clothing and homestead-era items. ~ 1st Street West and Fallon Avenue, Baker; 406-778-3265.

Medicine Rocks State Park, 25 miles south of Baker, commemorates a place of unusual sandstone rock formations that Sioux hunting parties once visited to conjure sacred spirits and other "big medicine." Wind and water erosion have created a Swiss-cheese landscape where many species of wildlife find a haven. Admission. ~ Route 7, Ekalaka; 406-232-4365.

The town of **Ekalaka**, ten miles south of Medicine Rocks at the end of Route 7, is at the end of the line as far as paved highway is concerned. Livestock production and outdoor sports, mainly deer and bird hunting, provide its economic subsistence. The **Carter County Museum** displays a complete skeleton of an anatosaurus, or duck-billed dinosaur, as well as other prehistoric specimens found in the region. ~ 100 Main Street, Ekalaka; 406-775-6886.

The **Westwood Motor Inn** is a likely stop for travelers headed east from Billings. With 33 rooms, the twin-story hostelry has all essential amenities, including phones and TVs; refrigerators may be available on request. ~ West Main Street at Route 94, Forsyth; 406-356-2038. BUDGET.

LODGING

The **Buckboard Inn** is located in the heart of the Yellowstone valley. The motel's 58 cozy ground-floor guest rooms, spread ranch-style around an outdoor swimming pool, have queen-size beds, and coffee and doughnuts may always be had in the lobby. ~ 1006 South Haynes Avenue, Miles City; 406-232-3550, 800-525-6303. BUDGET.

Miles City's best is the **Best Western War Bonnet Inn**. The 54 rooms are modern and spacious, and facilities at the two-story motel include a sauna, a whirlpool and a small heated pool. Rooms with microwaves and refrigerators may be reserved in advance. A complimentary continental breakfast is included with the room rates. ~ 1015 South Haynes Avenue, Miles City; 406-232-4560, 800-528-1234, fax 406-232-0363. MODERATE.

Approaching the Dakotas, the three-story **Jordan Motor Inn** is an upscale property that offers respite from summer heat in an indoor swimming pool and warm haven from winter's chill in a sauna. All rooms have combination baths; there's also a dining room, separate coffee shop and full lounge. The cafe features an original J. K. Ralston mural and an extensive agate collection. ~ 223 North Merrill Avenue, Glendive; 406-365-5655 3371. MODERATE.

If you find yourself in Baker for the night, you'll find comfortable lodging at the **Sagebrush Inn**. All rooms have queen-size beds, cable TV and direct-dial phones, and the motel has a coin-op laundry. ~ 518 West Montana Avenue, Baker; 406-778-3341, 800-638-3708, fax 406-778-2753. BUDGET.

DINING

A popular local hangout on the eastern plains for more than a century has been Miles City's **Hole in the Wall**. An Old West atmosphere still pervades this steak-and-seafood house; prime rib is a house specialty while a salad bar is a concession to changing tastes. ~ 602 Main Street, Miles City; 406-232-9887. MODERATE.

Another dependable midtown establishment is **Louie's Olive Dining Room**. Located in the old Olive Hotel, Louie's adds a touch of elegance to its steak and seafood dinners. ~ 501 Main Street, Miles City; 406-232-7621. MODERATE.

Twilite Dining & Lounge is not just a twilight restaurant: It serves breakfast and lunch as well as dinner. Montana beef, chicken and deep-fried seafood are the specialties. ~ 209 North Merrill Street, Glendive; 406-365-8705. BUDGET TO MODERATE.

The owners of **Sakelaris' Kitchen** are rightfully proud of the collection of country antiques they've assembled at their restaurant. They're also proud of their home cooking. Open most days at 5:30 a.m., and remaining open for early dinners, this is a great spot for morning cinnamon rolls and midday soups. ~ Montana Avenue, Baker; 406-778-2208. BUDGET.

NIGHTLIFE

If you're traveling east across the prairies, you won't want to miss Miles City's venerable **Montana Bar**. First opened in 1902, it has a classic back bar with beveled leaded glass. Locals will urge you to drink Milestown Draught, brewed just down the street. ~ 612 Main Street, Miles City; 406-232-5809.

PARKS

MAKOSHIKA STATE PARK 🚶 🚲 🏕 Skeletons of the greatest dinosaurs to walk the earth have been discovered amid the deep, barren gullies of these badlands, a few miles southeast of Glendive near the North Dakota border. Grotesquely eroded limestone and sandstone columns are other geological features. Picnic areas, restrooms, visitors center and shooting and archery ranges are among the facilities. Day-use fee, $3. ~ From Glendive, travel southeast on Snyder Avenue to Makoshika Park Road; 406-232-4365.

▲ There are 16 RV/tent sites, none with hookups; $7 to $8 per night; 14-day maximum stay.

MEDICINE ROCKS STATE PARK 🏃🚴🐎🏕 Ancient Sioux believed these pockmarked sandstone rocks to be the home of sacred spirits; they often stopped and prayed for "good medicine." The park is largely undeveloped. Picnic areas and restrooms are available. Day-use fee, $3. ~ Off Route 7, 25 miles south of Baker and ten miles north of Ekalaka; 406-232-4365.

▲ Fifteen nondesignated primitive sites; no charge; 14-day maximum stay.

▼▼▼▼▼▼▼▼▼▼▼▼▼▼

Outdoor Adventures

FISHING

Warmwater fish like bass, walleye, northern pike, catfish and perch do well in the Yellowstone River below Billings; the Musselshell River is famous for both trout and catfish; and Bighorn Lake is home to walleye, catfish and perch as well as brown and rainbow trout and burbot.

The lower Yellowstone River's most unusual species is the paddlefish, an enormous bottom feeder with a two-foot snout that hasn't changed much during 70 million years of evolution. Sought for their delicious meat and caviar-like roe, these fish, which weigh well over 100 pounds at full maturity, must be snagged with huge treble hooks and stout casting gear. The paddlefish season extends from May to July; a popular fishing hole is the Yellowstone Intake Diversion Dam, 17 miles north of Glendive via Route 16.

A good tackle shop in Billings is **The Classic Angler**. ~ 1091 Broadwater Avenue; 406-652-2001. Another is the **Rainbow Run Fly Shop**. ~ 2244 Grand Avenue; 406-656-3455.

BOATING

The most popular place for boating in southeastern Montana is unquestionably Bighorn Lake, in Bighorn Canyon National Recreation Area. There are two marinas on the 71-mile-long reservoir, each offering boat rentals, fuel, and full watersports opportunities. **Ok-A-Beh Marina** is below Yellowtail Dam near Fort Smith. ~ 406-665-2216. **Horseshoe Bend Marina** is north of Lovell, Wyoming. ~ 406-665-2412.

CANOEING

Rentals and guided trips are offered by the **Flowing Rivers Guide Service**. ~ 1809 Darlene Street, Billings; 406-252-5859.

SKIING

East of Red Lodge, you'll find no formal downhill resorts, and cross-country skiing is largely on a choose-your-own-terrain basis. Makoshika and Medicine Rocks state parks are two popular choices with the Nordic types. There are two short, maintained cross-country loops in Custer National Forest, on Route 212 east of Ashland. ~ 406-784-2344. For rentals in Billings and more information, visit **Reiter's Ski Outfit** for downhill skis. ~ 450 Main Street; 406-252-9341. Or try **The Base Camp** for cross-country skis. ~ 1730 Grand Avenue; 406-248-4555.

GOLF

Billings' **Briarwood Country Club** was acclaimed by *USA Today* as one of Montana's best. ~ 3429 Briarwood Boulevard, Billings; 406-245-2966. **Lake Hills Golf Club** also has 18 holes. ~ 1930 Club House Way, Billings Heights; 406-252-9244. **Pryor Creek Golf Club and Estates** has 27 holes, open to the public by invitation only. ~ Route 94, Huntley; 406-256-0626. Roundup, Hardin, Colstrip, Broadus, Forsyth, Miles City, Glendive and Baker have nine-hole courses.

TENNIS

In Billings, look for municipal courts at **North Park**. ~ 6th Avenue North and North 21st Street. The Billings Parks Division has a full listing of city courts. ~ 510 North Broadway; 406-657-8372. In Great Falls, **Montana Park** has a number of courts. ~ 18th Street Southwest and Fox Farm Road. Contact Great Falls Recreation & Park Activities for more information. ~ 2 South Park Drive; 406-771-1265.

RIDING STABLES

The best way for horse lovers to get into the Montana prairies is to join a cattle drive. This normally involves a full week on the trail with real-life cowboys: riding, caring for horses and performing camp chores, as well as sightseeing and enjoying campfire entertainment.

Operators include **Double Rafter Cattle Drives** ~ 419 East Main Street, Laurel, 406-628-2320, 800-704-9268; **Powder River Wagon Train and Cattle Drive** ~ P.O. Box 483, Broadus, MT 59016, 406-427-5317, 800-982-0710; and WSC **Livestock Cattle Drives** ~ 33 Road 253, Glendive, 406-486-5742.

For a complete listing of cattle drive outfitters, contact the **Custer Country Tourism Region**. ~ Route 1, Box 1206, Hardin, MT 59034; 406-665-1671.

BIKING

National Forest roads and trails are generally open to mountain biking, but wheeled vehicles—motorized or not—are not allowed in designated wilderness areas. Local bicycle shops have information on planned activities and mountain-biking routes. A popular trail is the eight-mile route through the badlands of **Makoshika State Park**. ~ Makoshika Park Road, Glendive; 406-365-8596.

You can get bicycle rentals, repairs and information at **Beartooth Bicycle & Sports**. ~ 2160 Central Avenue, Billings; 406-656-2453.

HIKING

While the rolling prairies of Montana's southeast don't excite many hikers, there are interesting trails in mountains, state parks (especially Makoshika and Medicine Rocks) and riverfront areas. Trails at Little Bighorn Battlefield National Monument lead past numerous historical markers, while the three-mile Om-Ne-A Trail descending to Bighorn Lake from the rim of Yellowtail Dam can provide a steep challenge. The Ashland Ranger District of Custer National Forest offers three trails: Cook Mountain, King Mountain and Tongue River Breaks. Call 406-784-2344 for more information. All distances listed for hiking trails are one way unless otherwise noted.

Transportation

CAR

Billings is immediately west of the junction of two interstate highways: **Route 90**, which runs southeast 98 miles to the Wyoming border, continuing east to Chicago and Boston; and **Route 94**, a spur that follows the Yellowstone River northeast (via Miles City) 247 miles to the North Dakota border at Wibaux, and on to Chicago.

Other major east–west routes are **Route 2**, the Hi-Line, from Glacier National Park through Havre and Glasgow to North Dakota, and **Route 212**, which approaches Billings from the west via Yellowstone National Park and Red Lodge, then travels east off Route 94 at Little Bighorn Battlefield, continuing to South Dakota's Black Hills and beyond.

North–south routes include **Route 59**, which extends from Jordan through Miles City and Broadus to northeastern Wyoming; and **Route 87**, which links Billings with Great Falls via Roundup and Lewistown.

AIR

Billings-Logan International Airport is Montana's largest. Four national airlines—Continental, Delta, Northwest and United—and three regional carriers—Big Sky, Horizon and SkyWest—schedule regular arrivals and departures.

Big Sky Airlines provides commuter service between Billings and seven other eastern Montana cities: Miles City, Glendive, Havre, Lewistown, Glasgow, Wolf Point and Sidney.

BUS

Billings-based **Rimrock Trailways** serves all of Montana's major cities and many of its smaller ones. ~ 1206 Cordova Street; 406-245-5392, 800-255-7655.

Larger towns along the Route 90/94 corridor also greet buses of the nationwide **Greyhound Bus Lines**. ~ 2502 1st Avenue North; 406-245-5116, 800-231-2222.

CAR RENTALS

There are 16 car-rental agencies in Billings. Those serving Billings-Logan International Airport are **Avis Rent A Car** (800-331-1212), **Budget Rent A Car** (800-527-0700), **Hertz Rent A Car** (800-654-3131), **National Interrent** (800-328-4567) and **Payless Rent A Car** (406-563-5256).

**PUBLIC
TRANSIT**

Billings Metropolitan Transit, better known as "The MET," has an extensive bus network throughout the metropolitan area. ~ 406-657-8218.

TAXIS

For taxi service and airport shuttle service in Billings, call City Cab. ~ 2713 1st Avenue North; 406-252-8700. Or try Yellow Cab. ~ 3940 1st Avenue South; 406-245-3033.

NINE

Northeast Montana

Montana's vast northeastern quadrant is its most sparsely populated.

Only three states (Alaska, Texas and California) are larger than Montana, yet only two (Alaska and Wyoming) have a lower population density. Statewide, only 800,000 Montanans live on 147,000 square miles of land—about 5.4 people per square mile.

In the northeast, the density is far lower than that.

The eastbound Missouri River is the tie that binds the region together. This broad, slow-flowing stream provides water for the arid farmland, habitat for waterfowl and other wildlife, recreation for the sportsman and sportswoman. Members of the Lewis and Clark expedition were the first white men to travel up-river in the very early 19th century. A generation later, steamboats were plying the Missouri as far as Fort Benton, providing Montana's principal lifeline to the "civilized" East. The Northern Pacific Railroad arrived around 1880, its way cleared by the mass relocation of American Indians to reservations and the mass slaughter of bison by white hunters. Cattle ranching soon became the economic mainstay of the eastern plains; it remains so today. Montana is among the national leaders in cattle and sheep production and is a major grower of barley and wheat.

For someone studying a map of northeastern Montana, the most prominent features are two Indian reservations (Fort Peck and Fort Belknap) and the enormous Charles M. Russell National Wildlife Refuge, encompassing the Missouri's manmade Fort Peck Lake. But for the person passing through—on Route 2, for instance, which follows the Milk River through the grain country of the Hi-Line, or on Route 200, dubbed "the loneliest road in America"—it is the spaces between the small towns, the incredible openness of the prairie skies, that will live longest in memory.

▼▼▼▼▼▼▼▼▼▼
The Hi-Line

From the Rocky Mountain Front to Montana's eastern boundary near the confluence of the Missouri and Yellowstone rivers, Route 2, "the Hi-Line," follows a course between the Missouri Valley and the Canadian border. Paralleled by the Great Northern Railway line, the highway cuts a swath through often-bleak wheat-and-cattle country, first along the Milk River valley (175 miles from Havre to Fort Peck), then following the Missouri (another 125 miles to the Dakotas).

SIGHTS

Leaving Havre, the first community of interest is the small farming town of **Chinook**, 21 miles east. Chinook was named not for salmon but for the warm winter winds that can raise temperatures from 0° to 50°F in a matter of minutes.

Stop at the **Blaine County Museum** to see pioneer re-creations and a multimedia presentation on famous Chief Joseph. ~ 501 Indiana Street, Chinook; 406-357-2590. Then drive 16 miles south to the **Bear's Paw Battleground,** the northeasternmost of 38 Nez Perce National Historical Park sites and one of three units in Montana. This is where Chief Joseph and his band of renegade Nez Perce surrendered to U.S. government forces on October 5, 1877, and where Joseph is said to have uttered his famous words: "From where the sun now stands, I will fight no more, forever." ~ Route 240; 406-357-2590.

Route 2 enters the **Fort Belknap Indian Reservation** at Harlem, about 42 miles from Havre. About 2800 Assiniboine and Gros Ventre tribespeople live on the 700,000-acre reservation. Tours focus on the historic Hays district; arrangements can be made through the **Fort Belknap Tourism Office and Information Center**. ~ Route 2, Harlem; 406-353-2205.

Travelers with time on their hands can visit the southern part of the reservation and take in a couple of old mining communities in the Little Rocky Mountains at the same time. It's about 35 miles from Route 2 at Fort Belknap Agency to Hays. In 1887, the St. Paul's Mission Church was established here; today it serves as a school for kindergarteners through eighth graders. A couple more miles south, scenic Mission Canyon includes a variety of sites of geological intrigue, including Natural Bridge, Needle Eye and Devil's Kitchen.

HIDDEN ►

Outside the reservation boundary, the **Little Rocky Mountains** rise about a half-mile above the surrounding country to the summit of Antoine Butte at 5610 feet. Notorious outlaws Butch Cassidy and Kid Curry are rumored to maintained hideouts in this semiwilderness.

Gold was discovered in the Little Rockies in 1884; about $25 million had been taken from these mountains by the end of World War II. The Pegasus Gold Co. still works a huge open-pit gold mine east of Antoine Butte at **Zortman**. Tours are by reservation on sum-

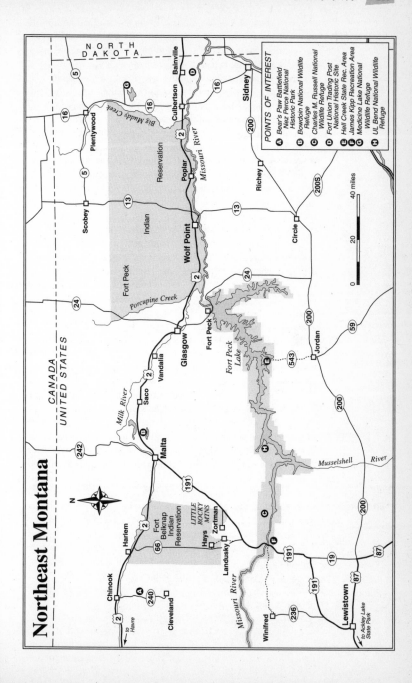

Northeast Montana

NORTH DAKOTA

CANADA
UNITED STATES

POINTS OF INTEREST

- Ⓐ Bear's Paw Battlefield Nez Perce National Historic Park
- Ⓑ Bowdoin National Wildlife Refuge
- Ⓒ Charles M. Russell National Wildlife Refuge
- Ⓓ Fort Union Trading Post National Historic Site
- Ⓔ Hell Creek State Rec. Area
- Ⓕ James Kipp Recreation Area
- Ⓖ Medicine Lake National Wildlife Refuge
- Ⓗ UL Bend National Wildlife Refuge

Bainville

Ⓓ

Culbertson

Sidney

Ⓖ

Plentywood

Big Muddy Creek

Poplar

Missouri River

Scobey

Reservation

Indian

Richey

Wolf Point

Fort Peck

Circle

Porcupine Creek

Fort Peck

Glasgow

Jordan

Vandalia

Fort Peck Lake

Ⓔ

Saco

Milk River

Ⓗ

Ⓑ

Malta

Musselshell River

Ⓒ

Harlem

Fort Belknap Indian Reservation

LITTLE ROCKY MTNS

Zortman

Hays

Ⓕ

Landusky

Chinook

Ⓐ

Cleveland

Missouri River

Lewistown

Winifred

to Ackley Lake State Park

to Havre

N

40 miles

20

0

5

16

16

5

13

2

13

24

200

200S

24

200

59

543

200

242

191

191

66

236

240

2

240

2

19

87

191

87

mer weekdays. ~ 406-673-3252. To the southwest, another old mining town, **Landusky,** is headquarters of the Little Rockies State Recreational Management Area. ~ 406-654-1240. There are undeveloped campgrounds near both communities.

From Zortman, you can return to Route 2 via Route 191, crossing 50 miles of semiarid grassland to **Malta.** A ranching center for a century, Malta (named for the Mediterranean island with which it has virtually nothing in common) has an interesting museum of pioneer history and armaments, the **Phillips County Museum,** housed in a former Carnegie Library building. ~ 133 1st Street West, Malta; 406-654-1037. Eight miles east is the **Bowdoin National Wildlife Refuge,** a nesting place for migratory waterfowl, including the white pelican, and upland game. A brochure on a 15-mile, self-guided auto tour is available from refuge headquarters. ~ Old Route 2; 406-654-2863.

The tiny town of **Saco,** almost midway from Havre to the Dakota border, is an unlikely place for a nationally acclaimed broadcast journalist to have begun his childhood education, but it is indeed where late newsman Chet Huntley learned his ABCs (or was that NBCs?) in the early 20th century. In fact, the one-room **Huntley School** has been restored and is open for visits. Inquire locally.

Glasgow was once best known for its U.S. Air Force base. Today there are only memories. Many of them are displayed in the **Valley County Pioneer Museum,** along with a wildlife collection, fossils, American Indian artifacts and items from railroad and engineering history. ~ Klein Road, Glasgow; 406-228-8692.

Engineering is, indeed, important to the area: **Fort Peck Dam,** on the Missouri River, is just 18 miles south of Glasgow. Built by the U.S. Army Corps of Engineers at the peak of the Great Depression in 1936, it is at 250 feet high and four miles across, one of the largest earth-filled dams on Earth. **Fort Peck Museum** (Powerhouse 1) interprets for visitors the dam's hydroelectric, irrigation and

---

NORTHEAST MONTANA EXPERIENCES

- Walk in the footsteps of mid-19th-century trappers and pioneers at the **Fort Union Trading Post National Historic Site.** *page 266*
- Enjoy a filet of walleye pike pulled fresh from nearby Fort Peck Lake at **Sam's Supper Club** in Glasgow. *page 266*
- Join in tending cattle, sheep and poultry at the **Hell Creek Guest Ranch,** or use it as a base to explore nearby fossil beds. *page 269*
- Take a cruise on **Fort Peck Lake** and drift past the birds and beasts of the Charles W. Russell National Wildlife Refuge. *page 272*

flood-control functions and offers exhibits on geology and paleontology. Free guided tours of the powerhouse are offered from June through September. ~ Route 24; 406-526-3411.

Fort Peck Lake—the reservoir created by the dam—is 134 miles long with 1520 miles of shoreline. Thirteen recreation areas with boat launch sites and campgrounds surround its shores; the vast majority of adjacent land belongs to the **Charles M. Russell National Wildlife Refuge**. Hundreds of species of birds as well as elk, deer, pronghorn antelope and smaller animals make their homes in this million-acre preserve of wetlands, prairies and badlands (see "Parks" in the Heartland section below). ~ Refuge headquarters in Lewistown; 406-538-8706.

Within the Russell refuge is another, more primitive reserve: the **UL Bend National Wildlife Refuge**, located on a prairie peninsula about 75 miles west of the dam. Elk don't need to migrate from this native prairie; it capably supports them year-round. ~ 406-538-8706.

Fort Peck is still a good two-hour drive (in the best of conditions) from North Dakota. This northeasternmost region of Montana is dominated by the two-million-acre (550-square-mile) **Fort Peck Indian Reservation**, home to 10,700 mainly Assiniboine and Sioux tribespeople. Tribal headquarters are in Poplar, 21 miles east of Wolf Point. Its **Fort Peck Assiniboine and Sioux Culture Center and Museum** has permanent exhibits of arts and crafts. ~ Route 2 East; 406-768-5155.

The reservation's largest town is **Wolf Point**, site of two major annual tribal celebrations: the Wild Horse Stampede, which takes place in mid-July, and the Wadopana powwow, held in early August. The **Wolf Point Area Historical Society Museum** focuses on regional farm and ranch history. ~ 220 2nd Avenue South, Wolf Point; 406-653-1912. Farm machinery buffs will definitely want to call ahead to see Louis Toavs' **John Deere Tractor Collection & Museum**, a 15-mile detour north of Wolf Point. ~ Volt Road; 406-392-5224.

Just across Big Muddy Creek at the southeastern corner of the reservation is the agricultural town of **Culbertson**, famous statewide for its late-September threshing bee. About 24 miles north lies the **Medicine Lake National Wildlife Refuge**, home to as many as 230 different species of resident and migratory waterfowl and shorebirds. Motorists can make an 18-mile self-guided drive through the reserve during the warmer months; fishing and picnicking are popular recreational activities here. ~ Route 16; 406-787-5821.

On the north side of the Fort Peck reservation are a series of small towns that seem to have more in common with Saskatchewan province than with the rest of Montana. Worth visiting is the

Daniels County Museum and Pioneer Town, a re-created, 42-building frontier town with stores, homesteads, churches, a library and many antique vehicles. Admission. ~ 7 County Road, Scobey; 406-487-5965. And talk about antiques: The Sheridan County Museum displays 100 old tractors and 34 threshing machines among its collection. ~ Routes 16 and 5, Plentywood; 406-765-2219.

Resting almost exactly on the Montana–North Dakota border, 13 miles southeast of Bainville, is the Fort Union Trading Post National Historic Site. The Missouri River's principal fur-trading post from the 1830s until the Civil War has been restored to depict that era of America's westward expansion. Only the foundations of the original fort remain, but many buildings have been reconstructed and refurbished to their 1850s appearance. A visitors center is open daily, and the site has picnic tables and hiking trails. Admission. ~ Route 327, Bainville-Snowden Road; 701-572-9083.

LODGING

HIDDEN ►

One of the more charming places to stay along the Hi-Line is the Double J Bed & Breakfast, just off Route 2 about 13 miles west of Glasgow. The refurbished ranch, a hit among outdoor recreationists, has a swimming pool, hot tub and satellite TV, and the hosts serve up generous home-cooked meals. ~ P.O. Box 75, Vandalia, MT 59230; 406-367-5353. MODERATE.

On the Fort Peck Indian Reservation, less than an hour's drive east of Fort Peck Dam and Lake, the Sherman Motor Inn is a clean and comfortable three-story property. Its 46 ample rooms have queen-size beds, and desks; there's also a lounge and a restaurant open for three meals daily. ~ 200 East Main Street, Wolf Point; 406-653-1100, 800-962-1100, fax 406-653-3456. BUDGET.

The Cattle King Motor Inn has 31 units just 15 miles south of the Canadian border. All rooms are air-conditioned and have queen-size beds and standard amenities. Two bonuses: The guest laundry facility is free, and the excellent Silver Slipper restaurant is next door. ~ Route 13 South, Scobey; 406-487-5332, 800-562-2775. BUDGET.

DINING

Sam's Supper Club specializes in charbroiled steaks from the surrounding cattle country and filets of walleye pike from nearby Fort Peck Lake. The low-lit restaurant, just off Route 2, also makes its own ice cream and other desserts. Lunch is served Monday to Friday, dinner Tuesday to Saturday. ~ 307 Klein Road, Glasgow; 406-228-4614. MODERATE.

A popular spot in the Fort Peck Indian Reservation is the Stockmen's Bar & Cafe. Great for families, it offers morning pancakes, evening steaks, and other all-American meals three times a day. ~ 220 Main Street, Wolf Point; 406-653-1248. BUDGET.

NIGHTLIFE

The most prominent stage association between the Rocky Mountain Front and the border of the Dakotas is the **Fort Peck Theatre Company**. The summer repertory presents musicals and dramas every weekend of summer at its historic theater near the eastern Montana dam. ~ Missouri Avenue, Fort Peck; 406-228-9219.

▼▼▼▼▼▼▼▼▼▼
The Heartland

Route 200 spans Montana's "Heartland," the state's geographical center, more or less paralleling the Hi-Line. Running east from Great Falls between 50 and 110 miles south of Route 2, it crosses the Judith Basin to Lewistown, the region's largest town; drops to the Musselshell River valley; then races through a couple of hundred miles of "great wide open" before hitting another town with a population of more than a thousand: Sidney, on the Yellowstone River at the North Dakota border.

SIGHTS

The Heartland really begins in the Judith Basin, in the ranching country immortalized by Charlie Russell's art, on the eastern flank of the Little Belt Mountains. A good place to get a feel for regional history is the **Sodbuster Museum**. Open summers, the rural museum displays an eclectic array of American Indian artifacts, old mining tools and pioneer-era tools and furnishings. ~ Route 87/200, 11 miles east of Stanford; 406-423-5358.

Lewistown, whose 6000 people live in the exact center of Montana, 105 miles east of Great Falls, is a ranching and wheat-farming center. The town is rich in late-19th-century pioneer history: Its downtown, Courthouse Square and Silk Stocking District are listed on the National Register of Historic Places. Self-guided tour brochures can be obtained at the **Central Montana Museum**, which chronicles the area. ~ 408 East Main Street, Lewistown; 406-538-5436.

Popular recreational sites in the area include **Ackley Lake State Park**, 30 miles southwest, a favorite of trout anglers. ~ Route 400; 406-454-3441. **Crystal Lake**, 20 miles south in Lewis and Clark National Forest, features hiking to nearby ice caves. ~ Forest Road 275; 406-566-2292. **Judith Peak Recreation Area**, 20 miles northeast, offers 100-mile summit views and access to several ghost towns. ~ Route 81; 406-538-7461. **War Horse National Wildlife Refuge**, which is located about 40 miles east, is noted for its spring waterfowl viewing. ~ Cemetery Road; 406-538-8706.

◆◆◆◆◆◆◆◆◆◆◆◆◆◆◆◆◆◆◆◆◆◆◆◆◆

The James Kipp Recreation Area is the departure point for boat tours and floats of the Upper Missouri National Wild and Scenic River.

Perhaps most interesting to visitors, Lewistown is the headquarters of the **Charles M. Russell National Wildlife Refuge**. The million-acre refuge, which surrounds Fort Peck Lake, supports a rich variety of wildlife and such recreational activities as camping, boating and fishing. ~ Airport Road; 406-538-8706. The primary access point is at the **James Kipp Recreation Area,** 65 miles northeast of Lewistown. ~ Route 191; 406-538-7461.

For a scenic backcountry driving tour of a small portion of the Russell wildlife refuge, depart east from Route 191 on the north side of the river from James Kipp Recreation Area. About ten miles south of the recreation area, Knox Coulee Road leads west to the **Missouri Breaks National Back Country Byway,** a 73-mile loop through badlands along the edge of the refuge to Winifred, a near ghost town on Route 236, 37 miles north of Lewistown. ~ Call the Bureau of Land Management at 406-538-7461 for information.

East from Lewistown on Route 200, it's 130 miles to **Jordan,** once called "the lonesomest town in the world" by a New York radio station. Its **Garfield County Museum** is worth a look for its homesteading-era exhibits and the full-size replica of a triceratops discovered in nearby Hell Creek fossil beds. ~ Route 200, Jordan; 406-557-2517. Another 26 miles north is the lone state park on Fort Peck Lake: **Hell Creek State Recreation Area.** Despite its isolation, this is a popular area, especially for boaters. It has a marina and offers camping and motel lodging. Admission. ~ Hell Creek Road; 406-232-4365.

Jordan gained national notoriety in 1996 as the stronghold of the isolationist Freemen, whose compound—where members engaged in a two-month armed standoff with the federal government—is several miles northwest of the town, near Brusett.

From Jordan, Route 200 continues east through Circle (67 miles) and Richey (96 miles) to Sidney (142 miles), on the Yellowstone River just inside the North Dakota border.

Circle, named for the brand of a long-defunct cattle ranch, is a small ranching center midway between Glendive and Wolf Point. Its **McCone County Museum** is noted for a fine taxidermy collection. ~ 801 Route 200 South, Circle; 406-485-2414. If you drop into the **Richey Museum,** a half hour's drive northeast, you'll want to see its Model A mail car and its unique collection of handmade coats. ~ Route 200, Richey, Circle; 406-773-5656.

The center of a sugar beet–growing area, Sidney is home to the **MonDak Heritage Center,** a re-created pioneer street scene featuring 17 buildings, all displaying historical artifacts. It's a superb exhibit. There are also two art galleries here with changing exhibits. Admission. ~ 120 3rd Avenue Southeast, Sidney; 406-482-3500.

If you have a particular interest in agricultural science, you may want to pay a visit to the **Northern Plains Soil and Water Research Center** in Sidney. Tours can be arranged by the Sidney Chamber of Commerce. ~ 909 South Central Avenue, Sidney; 406-482-1916.

The Heartland's finest lodging is the **Yogo Inn**. Occupying most of a city block in the downtown hub, the two-story inn has 124 guest rooms, their spaciousness accented by high ceilings. Facilities include indoor and outdoor swimming pools, a whirlpool, a dining room, a coffee shop and a lounge. ~ 211 East Main Street, Lewistown; 406-538-8721, 800-437-7275, fax 406538-8969. MODERATE.

LODGING

Twenty-one miles north of isolated Jordan, just outside the Charles M. Russell National Wildlife Refuge, is the **Hell Creek Guest Ranch**. Cattle, sheep and poultry are raised at this working ranch, which offers a central location for exploring the region's wildlife-rich prairies and fossil beds. ~ P.O. Box 325, Jordan, MT 59337; 406-557-2224, fax 406-557-2864. MODERATE.

A stone's throw from North Dakota, the two-story **Richland Motor Inn** has 62 comfortable rooms, all with standard motel furnishings. A few rooms have microwave ovens and refrigerators. There's a game room for the kids, and a continental breakfast is included in the rate. ~ 1200 South Central Street, Sidney; 406-482-6400, fax 406-482-4743. BUDGET.

You can take the whole family to **Whole Famdamily** for healthy home cooking. Soup, giant sandwiches and "international" dinner specials are presented in a home-style atmosphere: The walls are decorated with family portraits. Don't miss the rich desserts. ~ 206½ West Main Street, Lewistown; 406-538-5161. BUDGET.

DINING

Eastern Montana ranchers may not be anxious to ride out to their own south 40 (acres), but they'll make a beeline for Sidney's **South 40**. Huge cuts of prime rib are served in a ranch-style atmosphere, along with hearty homemade soups and a salad bar. ~ 207 2nd Avenue Northwest, Sidney; 406-482-4999. MODERATE.

Take a look at the **Lewistown Art Center** for work by regional artisans. ~ 801 8th Avenue North, Lewistown; 406-538-8278.

SHOPPING

Bar Nineteen combines a steak house with a country-and-western bar—the dancingest for 100 miles in any direction. ~ Fairgrounds Road, Lewistown; 406-538-3250.

NIGHTLIFE

ACKLEY LAKE STATE PARK 🛶 💧 🚤 🐟 Named for an early settler, this lake, at the northern foot of the Little Belt Mountains, is one of the most popular destinations for Heartland watersports lovers. You'll find picnic areas and restrooms; groceries and restaurants are in Lewistown. Day-use fee, $3. ~ From Lewistown, take Route 200 west 22 miles to Hobson; turn south on Route 400 for five miles, then southwest on gravel-surfaced Ackley Lake Road for two miles; 406-454-3441.

PARKS

▲ There are 23 primitive sites; free; 14-day maximum stay.

Text continued on page 272.

The Sport
of Rodeo

The most popular sport in Montana isn't fishing, golfing or skiing. It is rodeo, a cowboy tradition in which few might actually indulge, but all can enjoy watching.

The state's longest-established rodeo is the Wild Horse Stampede, which takes place each July at Wolf Point on the Fort Peck Indian Reservation. But roundups take place throughout northeastern Montana and indeed the entire state, all summer long. Full weekends are devoted to the sport, with parades, barbecues, street dances and country entertainment complementing the main event.

Some of Montana's top annual rodeos include the Professional Rodeo Cowboys Association circuit finals in Great Falls in January; the All Nations Indian Rodeo Championships (Billings, in May); the College National Finals Rodeo (Bozeman, June); the Last Chance Stampede (Helena, July); and the Northern International Livestock Exposition, back in Billings in October.

Rodeo evolved in the late 19th century from cowboys' macho desire to see who was the best calf roper, bronc rider or steer wrestler. Prize money and silver belt buckles were awarded to the winners, who often reinvested their earnings into next year's circuit. Losers usually gained nothing but broken bones.

A rodeo has six principal events: saddle bronc riding, bareback bronc riding, bull riding, steer wrestling, calf roping and women's barrel racing. Scoring is based on difficulty (stronger, more temperamental animals earn the riders higher points) and, in the latter three events, speed. Thus, while skill and courage are essential ingredients, winners also take the luck of the draw in being matched with higher-scoring livestock.

Rides on bucking broncos last but eight seconds: horses are released from chutes (fenced-in enclosures) with riders already aboard. With saddle broncs, cowboys dig in with stirrups and hold onto a thick rope rein; with bareback broncs, there are no stirrups and no reins, only a pair of tightly cinched straps to which the rider clings. The horses buck wildly to throw their passengers off; cowboys who succeed in staying aboard do so with a rhythmic rocking motion. A pickup man rides alongside the bucking horse when the eight-second clock has sounded, and the rider slides off to safety.

Bull riding is considerably more dangerous. Riders must attempt to remain on the back of a 2000-pound bull for eight full seconds while clenching a single thick rope wrapped around its chest. The bull jumps, kicks and rams the wall to throw its rider, then it may turn and attack with its horns or hooves. Some riders have died, and many have been seriously injured. As fallen bull riders attempt to escape their foes, they put their faith in foolish-looking but daring rodeo clowns who put their lives on the line to lure bulls away from the cowboys until they can be recaptured.

In steer wrestling (also known as bulldogging) a cowboy must leap from his horse onto the back of a full-grown steer, grab his horns, and wrestle him to the ground with his feet and head facing the same direction. This involves a two-man team: a mounted "hazer" forces the steer to run straight ahead while the "dogger" gets into position for his leap. A good team can take down a 700-pound steer, running at 25 miles per hour, in less than seven seconds.

Calf roping, perhaps the truest test of a cowboy's skill, is the most highly contested of all events. Riding trained horses, two riders lasso a young heifer (which may weight 250 to 300 pounds)—one by the neck, one by the hind legs. They quickly leap from their horses and tie it (as if for branding); if the calf cannot free itself within six seconds, the time stands and an "untie man" frees the animal.

Barrel racing is a speed and agility event. Competing women ride their horses in a set pattern around a triangular course of three barrels spaced 100 feet apart. Penalty seconds are added to times for any barrels that are knocked over.

CHARLES M. RUSSELL NATIONAL WILDLIFE REFUGE 🏃 🏕

Encompassing one million acres of wetland, prairie and badland surrounding 134-mile-long Fort Peck Lake, this refuge provides a home for hundreds of species of birds and a great many large animals. Thirteen recreation areas along its shores have boat launch sites and campgrounds, including the James Kipp Recreation Area, the main takeout point for floats of the upper Missouri River. The Russell Refuge surrounds the UL Bend National Wildlife Refuge, noted as a wilderness elk sanctuary. Facilities include picnic areas and restrooms; groceries and restaurants in Lewistown, Glasgow and several other communities. ~ Headquarters are in Lewistown; easiest road access, besides Fort Peck Dam, is at the James Kipp Recreation Area on Route 191, 65 miles northeast of Lewistown; 406-538-8706.

▲ There are 72 RV/tent sites, none with hookups, plus 69 sites for tents only at 13 campgrounds; no charge to $8 per night; 14-day maximum stay.

HELL CREEK STATE RECREATION AREA

The only state park on huge Fort Peck Lake, Hell Creek is located about midway down its southern shore. Probably as many visitors arrive by motorboat as by car. Picnic areas, restrooms, a marina, boat rentals, a store and concessions round out the amenities. Restaurants are in Jordan. Day-use fee, $3. ~ Take Hell Creek Road north from Jordan 26 miles to the Hell Creek Arm of Fort Peck Lake; 406-232-4365.

▲ There are 40 RV/tent sites, none with hookups; $7 per night; 14-day maximum stay.

▼▼▼▼▼▼▼▼▼▼▼▼▼▼▼

Outdoor Adventures

Fort Peck Lake is the focal point for anglers in northeast Montana. In this fast body of water can be caught such coldwater species as mountain whitefish and brook and rainbow trout, as well as walleye and northern pike, sauger, burbot, smallmouth bass, channel catfish, and the prehistoric sturgeon and paddlefish.

FISHING

In the far north, the Milk River has an excellent fishery for trout, catfish and perch.

BOATING

The Upper Missouri National Wild and Scenic River is a major draw for river lovers who don't need whitewater to enjoy the scenery. For 149 miles, from Fort Benton to the James Kipp Recreation Area on Fort Peck Lake, this broad, slow-flowing stream meanders past striking geological features and abandoned homesteads, and through the Charles M. Russell National Wildlife Refuge.

Ask about commercial boat tours, or get information about renting a vessel and navigating downstream, at the wild and scenic

river headquarters north of Lewistown. ~ Route 191; 406-538-7461. Or try the **Upper Missouri River Visitors Center.** ~ 1718 Front Street, Fort Benton; 406-622-5185. One of the leading commercial operators is **Missouri River Outfitters.** ~ P.O. Box 762, Fort Benton, MT 59442; 406-622-3295.

The 13 boat launch sites around the 1520-mile shoreline of vast Fort Peck Lake are administered by the Russell Wildlife Refuge. Contact the refuge office for information. ~ Airport Road, Lewistown; 406-538-8706.

Most of the rivers of northeast Montana are too slow for whitewater rafting, and many of them are quite muddy. Independent Missouri River floaters, however, have plenty of river opportunities.

Start your float in the Fort Benton or Virgelle area of the river, northeast of Great Falls, by consulting either **Missouri River Canoe Co.** ~ HC 67 Box 50, Loma, MT 59460; 406-378-3110, 800-426-2926. Or try the **Montana River Outfitters.** ~ 25th Avenue Northeast and Old Havre Highway, Great Falls; 406-761-1677.

RIVER RAFTING & CANOEING

Northeast Montana has eight golf courses, some of them semiprivate but open to nonresident visitors. All are nine-hole courses. Most intriguing, perhaps, is the **Big Muddy Golf Club,** which costs just $2 to play and has sand greens! ~ Outlook Road, Redstone; no phone. Other greens, charging fees of $7 to $12, are the **Marion Hills Golf Club** ~ Route 191, Malta; 406-654-1648; the **Sleeping Buffalo Resort Golf Club** ~ Route 2, Saco; 406-527-3370; the **Sunnyside Golf & Country Club** ~ Cherry Creek Road, Glasgow; 406-228-9519; the **Airport Golf Club** ~ Route 2, Wolf Point; 406-653-2161; the **Scobey Golf Club** ~ Route 13, Scobey; 406-487-5322; the **Plentywood Golf Club** ~ Route 5, Plentywood; 406-765-2532; and the **Sidney Country Club** ~ Route 16, Sidney; 406-482-1894.

GOLF

Summer wagon trains and cattle drives are popular ways for visitors to explore the prairies of northeastern Montana. Package deals are offered by a number of guest ranches. **High Plains Escape** specializes in wildlife trips. ~ P.O. Box 1622, Malta, MT 59538; 406-654-2881. **The Murdock Ranch** is a 20,000-acre red-angus spread. ~ HC 82, Box 9050, Malta, MT 59538; 406-658-2303. Ronnie Korman's **Prairie Schooners** specializes in "learning adventures." ~ 3H Ranch, south of Saco; 406-648-5536. **The Foss Cattle Drive** offers all-inclusive riding vacations near the North Dakota border. ~ HC 69, Box 97, Culbertson, MT 59218; 406-787-5559.

Trail rides are best arranged at the **Sandcliff Ranch,** where daily trips cost just $10 and overnight wagon trains on weekends are the peak of adventure. ~ Sidney; 406-428-2309.

RIDING STABLES

BIKING   The highways and byways of northeastern Montana can be very hot, very cold, and exceedingly windy. They are not regarded as the most favorable geography for bike riding.

HIKING   There's not much in the way of designated hiking trails in northeastern Montana. Backcountry wanderers often make their own paths through the Charles M. Russell National Wildlife Refuge or the Little Rocky Mountains near Zortman. A few suggestions follow. All distances listed for hiking are one way unless otherwise noted.

Mission Canyon Trail (8 miles) takes in a natural rock bridge in the Fort Belknap Indian Reservation, as well as historical and sacred Assiniboine sites around Snake Butte. Arrangements to visit must be made through the reservation office (Harlem; 406-353-2205), and often include an American Indian guide.

Beaver Creek Trail (.5 mile) is a self-guided nature trail off Route 24 near Fort Peck Dam. It offers visitors an opportunity to see wildlife in native habitats, including beavers, muskrats, deer and antelope.

Crystal Lake/Crystal Cascades Trail (6.2 miles) combines an easy 1.7-mile loop around a wooded Lewis and Clark National Forest lakeshore with a moderate climb up a small creek into the Big Snowy Mountains. The cascades flow from a cave and gurgle over a stairstep ledge for nearly 100 feet. The trailhead is 30 miles south of Lewistown on Forest Road 275.

▼▼▼▼▼▼▼▼▼▼▼▼
Transportation

CAR

The two primary routes through northeastern Montana both have east–west orientations. **Route 2** (the Hi-Line) links Williston, North Dakota, with Wolf Point, Glasgow, Malta, Havre and Glacier National Park. **Route 200** runs west from Sidney through the Heartland to Lewistown and Great Falls.

The main north–south roads are **Route 91** (Malta-Lewistown), **Route 87** (Lewistown-Billings), **Route 24** (Glasgow/Fort Peck north to Canada and south to Route 200), **Route 59** (Jordan-Miles City), **Route 13** (Circle-Scobey) and **Route 16** (Sidney-Culbertson-Plentywood).

For road reports—especially important during the unpredictable winter season—call 800-332-6171.

AIR   Most of the region's small airports have direct connections to Billings via the commuter aircraft of **Big Sky Airlines**. Service is available to Havre, Glasgow, Wolf Point, Lewistown and Sidney.

BUS   Billings-based **Rimrock Trailways** serves many of northeastern Montana's small towns. For schedules, fares and information, contact the line's main office. ~ 1206 Cordova Street, Billings; 406-245-5392, 800-255-7655.

Amtrak's (800-872-7245) Seattle–Chicago "Empire Builder" **TRAIN** makes several stops on the Hi-Line east of Glacier National Park. Contact the depot in Malta for more information. ~ 51 South 1st Street; 406-654-1622.

Rentals are available at regional airports in Glasgow, Wolf Point, **CAR** Lewistown and Sidney, as well as nearby Havre and Glendive. **RENTALS**

Index

Absaroka-Beartooth Wilderness Area, 196, 197, 198–99
Ackley Lake State Park, 267, 269
Agnes Vanderburg Cultural Camp, 59
Air travel. See Transportation *in area chapters*
Akamina Parkway, 96
Alder Gulch, 160–63; dining, 162; lodging, 162; nightlife, 162–63; shopping, 162; sights, 160–62
Alder Gulch River of Gold, 161
Alder Gulch Shortline Railroad, 161
Alta Ranger Station, 53
Alzada: nightlife, 249
American Computer Museum, 170
Amtrak. See Transportation *in area chapters*
Anaconda area: dining, 144; lodging, 143–44; shopping, 144; sights, 141; visitor information, 141
Anaconda-Pintler Wilderness Area, 145
Anaconda Smelter Stack, 141
Animals. See Pets; Wildlife
Apgar Village: dining, 92; lodging, 92; shopping, 92; sights, 89
Arts Chateau, 148
Ashland: shopping, 249; sights, 247
Augusta area: lodging, 115; sights, 114

Back Basin, 219
Baker: dining, 256; lodging, 256; sights, 255
Bannack State Park, 149, 156–57, 159
Bearcreek: nightlife, 198; sights, 196
Bears, 15–16, 33, 99
Bear's Paw Battleground, 262
Beartooth Highway, 196
Beartooth Nature Center & Children's Petting Zoo, 195–96
Beaver Creek County Park, 119
Beaverhead County Courthouse, 156
Beaverhead County Museum, 156
Beaverhead National Forest, 159
Bed and breakfasts. See Lodging
Belt: dining, 123; sights, 121
Benton Lake National Wildlife Refuge, 113
Berkeley Pit, 146
Bert Mooney Airport, 168
Big Hole National Battlefield, 154–55, 155–56

Big Hole Valley, 153–56; camping, 155; dining, 155; lodging, 155; parks, 155–56; sights, 153–55
Big Horn area, 245–51; camping, 250, 251; dining, 249; lodging, 248–49; nightlife, 249; parks, 249–51; shopping, 249; sights, 245–48; visitor information, 245
Big Horn County Historical Museum, 245
Big Mountain Ski Area, 66
Big Sky: dining, 176; lodging, 174–75; sights, 173
Big Sky Mine, 247
Big Sky Ski & Summer Resort, 173
Big Sky Waterslide & Miniature Greens, 67
Big Timber area, 192–94; dining, 194; lodging, 194; parks, 194; shopping, 194; sights, 192–93
Bigfork: dining, 63; lodging, 61–62; nightlife, 64; shopping, 63–64; sights, 60
Bigfork Art & Cultural Center, 60
Bigfork Summer Playhouse, 60
Bighorn Canyon National Recreation Area, 246, 250
Biking. See Outdoor adventures *in area chapters*
Billings area, 233–34, 236–39, 242–45; camping, 244, 245; dining, 239, 242; lodging, 238; map, 239; nightlife, 243–44; parks, 244–45; shopping, 242–43; sights, 233–34, 236–37; visitor information, 233
Billings-Logan International Airport, 259
Bison, 14–15
Bitterroot National Forest, 56
Bitterroot Valley, 51–57; camping, 56, 57; dining, 55–56; lodging, 54–55; parks, 56–57; shopping, 56; sights, 51–54
Black Dragon's Caldron, 214
Black Eagle: dining, 110
Black Otter Trail, 234
Blackfeet Indian Reservation, 93
Blaine County Museum, 262
Boat tours, 60
Boating, 38–39. See also Outdoor adventures *in area chapters*
Bob Marshall Wilderness Area, 113, 116
Bob Scriver Museum of Montana Wildlife & Hall of Bronze, 93
Boot Hill Cemetery (Virginia City), 161
Boothill Cemetery (Billings area), 234

Boulder: sights, 133
Boulder Hot Springs, 133–34
Boulder River, 193
Boulder River Falls, 193
Bowdoin National Wildlife Refuge, 264
Box Elder: sights, 118
Bozeman area, 170–79; camping, 178, 179; dining, 175–76; lodging, 173–75; map, 175; nightlife, 177–78; parks, 178–79; shopping, 176–77; sights, 170–73; visitor information, 170
Branding Wall, 233
Bridge Bay, 215
Bridger Bowl, 172
Broadus: dining, 249; lodging, 248–49; sights, 247–48
Broadwater Overlook Park, 106
Browning: dining, 95; lodging, 94; shopping, 95; sights, 93
Buffalo, 14–15
Buffalo Paddocks, 96
Buffalo Ranch, 212
Bus travel. *See* Transportation *in area chapters*
Butte, 145–48, 150–53; camping, 153; dining, 151; lodging, 148, 150; map, 147; nightlife, 152–53; parks, 153; shopping, 151–52; sights, 146–48; visitor information, 146
Bynum: nightlife, 115

C. Sharps Arms showroom, 193
Cabinet Mountains Wilderness Area, 74
Calendar of events, 20–27
Cameron: lodging, 181
Camp Baker, 122
Camping, 36–38. *See also* Camping *in area and town entries*
Canoeing, 78, 124, 257, 273
Canyon area (Yellowstone): dining, 222; lodging, 220–21; sights, 212–14; visitor information, 212
Canyon Creek Charcoal Kilns, 154
Canyon Ferry Lake, 132
Canyon Ferry Recreation Area, 133, 139–40
Canyon Village. *See* Canyon area (Yellowstone)
Car rentals and travel. *See* Transportation *in area chapters*
Carbon County Museum, 195
Cardwell: sights, 180
Carter County Museum, 255
Cascade County Historical Archives, 108
Castle: sights, 149
The Castle, 122
Castle Town, 122
Cattle Drive Monument, 233

Central Montana Museum, 267
Charles M. Russell Museum Complex, 106, 108
Charles M. Russell National Wildlife Refuge, 265, 267–68, 272
Charlo: dining, 62
Charlos Heights: dining, 56
Chester: sights, 117
Chico Hot Springs, 187
Chief Joseph Statue and Canyon Creek Battlefield Marker, 236–37
Chief Plenty Coups State Park, 246–47, 250–51
Children, traveling with, 32–33
Chinook: sights, 262
Choteau: dining, 115; lodging, 114–15; sights, 113–14
Circle: sights, 268
Clark Canyon Recreation Area, 157, 159
Clothes, 28
Coffrin's Old West Gallery, 172
Colstrip: sights, 247; visitor information, 247
Columbia Falls: dining, 69; lodging, 68; nightlife, 70; sights, 67
Columbus: sights, 193
Conrad Mansion, 66
Cooke City: dining, 198; lodging, 198; sights, 196–97; visitor information, 197
Coolidge: sights, 154
Cooney Reservoir State Park, 199
Cooper Village Museum and Arts Center, 141
Copper King Mansion, 147–48
Coram: sights, 85
Corwin Springs: nightlife, 192; sights, 190
Coyotes, 14, 33
Crazy Mountain Museum, 192
Crazy Mountains, 193
Cross country skiing. *See* Outdoor adventures *in area chapters*
Crow Agency: dining, 249; nightlife, 249; sights, 245–46
Crow Indian Reservation, 246–47
Crystal Lake, 267
Crystal Park, 154
Culbertson: sights, 265
Custer: sights, 252
Custer County Art Center, 253
Custer National Cemetery, 241, 245–46
Custer National Forest, 244
Custer's Last Stand, 240–41, 245–46
Cut Bank: lodging, 118; sights, 116

Dailey Lake, 187
Daniels County Museum and Pioneer Town, 265–66

Darby: dining, 56; lodging, 54–55; sights, 53

Darby Historic Ranger Station, 53

Darby Pioneer Memorial Museum, 53

Dayton: sights, 59–60

Deadman's Basin State Park, 237, 244–45

Dean: dining, 194

Decker: sights, 247

Deer Lodge: dining, 144; lodging, 144; nightlife, 144; sights, 142–43

Deer Lodge County Courthouse, 141

Deerlodge National Forest, 153

Dell: sights, 157

Devil Canyon Overlook, 246

Devils Slide, 190

Dillon and the Red Rock River Valley, 156–60; camping, 159, 160; dining, 158; lodging, 157–58; nightlife, 158–59; parks, 159–60; shopping, 158; sights, 156–57; visitor information, 156

Dining, 30–31. See also Dining in area and town entries; see also Dining Index

Disabled travelers, 34

Divide: sights, 154

Downhill skiing. See Outdoor adventures in area chapters

Driving, 31–32. See also Transportation in area chapters

Dude ranches, 188–89. See also Lodging

Dumas Red Light Antique Mall, 148

Dunrave Pass, 212

Earth Science Museum, 120–21

East Gallatin State Recreation Area, 178

East Glacier Park: dining, 94; lodging, 93–94; sights, 93

East Rosebud Lake, 196

Eastern Gateways area (Glacier National Park), 93–95; dining, 94–95; lodging, 93–94; shopping, 95; sights, 93

Eff Mountain fossil field, 114

Ekalaka: sights, 255

Electric Engine Park, 237

Elk Horn Hot Springs, 154

Elkhorn: sights, 134, 149

Emigrant: lodging, 190

Ennis: dining, 182; lodging, 181; sights, 180

Ennis National Fish Hatchery, 180

Essex: lodging, 88; sights, 86

Eureka: lodging, 72; shopping, 73; sights, 72

Explorer's Museum, 218

Fairfield: sights, 114

Fauna, 14–16, 33

Fife: sights, 121

Firehole River, 217

Fish Technology Center, 172

Fishing, 39, 76. See also Outdoor adventures in area chapters

Fishing Bridge, 214

Flathead Indian Reservation, 58

Flathead Indian Reservation and Lake area, 57–66; camping, 64, 65, 66; dining, 62–63; lodging, 61–62; nightlife, 64; parks, 64–66; shopping, 63–64; sights, 57–60

Flathead Lake. See Flathead Indian Reservation and Lake area

Flathead Lake State Park, 59, 64–65

Flathead National Forest, 71

Flathead National Wild and Scenic River system, 86

Flathead Valley, 66–71; camping, 71; dining, 68–69; lodging, 67–68; nightlife, 69–70; parks, 70–71; shopping, 69; sights, 66–67; visitor information, 68

Flora, 13–14

Foreign travelers, 35–36

Forsyth: lodging, 255; sights, 252

Fort Assiniboine, 118

Fort Belknap Indian Reservation, 262

Fort Benton area, 119–21; dining, 121; lodging, 121; sights, 119–21; visitor information, 120

Fort Keogh, 253

Fort Logan, 122

Fort Owens, 52

Fort Peck area: nightlife, 267; sights, 264–66

Fort Peck Assiniboine and Sioux Culture Center and Museum, 265

Fort Peck Dam, 264

Fort Peck Indian Reservation, 265

Fort Peck Lake, 265

Fort Peck Museum, 264–65

Fort Smith: sights, 246

Fort Union Trading Post National Historic Site, 266

Fort Yellowstone, 210

Freemen, 268

Freezout Lake Wildlife Management Area, 114

Frontier Gateway Museum, 254

Frontier Town, 134

Gallatin County Pioneer Museum, 170

Gallatin Field Airport, 205

Gallatin Gateway: lodging, 174; sights, 173

Gallatin Gateway Inn, 173

Gallatin National Forest, 173–74, 178–79

Gallatin Petrified Forest, 190

Garden Wall, 90

Gardiner: dining, 191; lodging, 191; nightlife, 192; shopping, 191; sights, 190; visitor information, 190
Garfield County Museum, 268
Garnet: sights, 142, 149
Garnet Hill, 211
Gates of the Mountains, 132–33
Gates of the Mountains Game Preserve, 133
Gates of the Mountains Wilderness Area, 133, 139
Gay and lesbian travelers, 33–34
Gem Mountain Sapphire Mine, 142
Geology, 4–5
Georgetown Lake, 141
Geraldine: sights, 121
Geysers, 216–20
Ghost Town Hall of Fame, 141–42, 149
Ghost towns, 149. See also specific towns
Giant Springs/Heritage State Park, 106, 112–13
Gibbon Falls, 218
Glacier Maze, 85
Glacier National Park, 89–93; camping, 92–93; dining, 92; lodging, 91–92; map, 87; parks, 92–93; shopping, 92; sights, 89–91; visitor information, 89
Glacier National Park area, 84–104; calendar of events, 20–27; introduction, 84–85; outdoor adventures, 97–103; transportation, 103–104
Glacier Park International Airport, 83, 93
Glacier Park Lodge, 93
Glaciers, 6–7
Glasgow: dining, 266; sights, 264
Glendive: dining, 256; lodging, 255–56; sights, 254
Going-to-the-Sun Road, 89–90
Golden Gate Canyon, 220
Golf. See Outdoor adventures in area chapters
Gondola rides, 173
Grand Canyon of the Yellowstone, 212
Grand Teton, 224
Grand Teton National Park, 223–24
Granite County Museum and Cultural Center, 141–42, 149
Granite Peak, 197
Grant-Kohrs Ranch National Historic Site, 142
Grant Village-West Thumb area (Yellowstone): dining, 222; lodging, 221; sights, 215–16; visitor information, 215
Grasshopper Glacier, 197
Great Bear Adventure, 85
Great Bear Wilderness Area, 88
Great Falls, 106–13; dining, 110; lodging, 109–10; map, 107; nightlife, 112; parks, 112–13; shopping, 110, 112; sights, 106–109
Great Falls International Airport, 127
Greenough Park, 50
Gregson: lodging, 143
Greycliff: sights, 193
Greycliff Prairie Dog Town State Park, 193, 194
Grizzly Discovery Center, 183
Guest ranches, 188–89. See also Lodging
Guides and outfitters, 40

H. Earl Clack Memorial Museum, 118
Hamilton: dining, 55–56; lodging, 54; shopping, 56; sights, 53
Hardin: dining, 249; lodging, 248; shopping, 249; sights, 245
Harlem: sights, 262; visitor information, 262
Harlowton: lodging, 238; sights, 237
Hauser Lake, 132
Havre: dining, 119; lodging, 118–19; nightlife, 119; sights, 117–18
Havre Beneath the Street, 117–18
Havre City County Airport, 127
Hayden Valley, 213–14
Headwaters Heritage Museum, 179
Hearst Free Library, 141
The Heartland (northeast Montana), 267–69, 272; camping, 269, 272; dining, 269; lodging, 269; nightlife, 269; parks, 269, 272; shopping, 269; sights, 267–68
Hebgen Lake, 184
Helena area, 130, 132–30; camping, 139, 140; dining, 136–37; lodging, 134, 136; map, 135; nightlife, 138; parks, 138–40; shopping, 137–38; sights, 130, 132–34
Helena Civic Center, 132
Helena Municipal Airport, 168
Helena National Forest, 133, 140
Hell Creek State Recreation Area, 268, 272
Henry's Lake State Park, 186
Heritage Centre, 95
Heritage Museum, 72
Hi-Line area, 262, 264–67; dining, 266; lodging, 266; nightlife, 267; sights, 262, 264–66. See also Western Hi-Line area
Highwood Mountains, 121
Hiking. See Outdoor adventures in area chapters
Historical Museum at Fort Missoula, 45
History, 5, 8–12
Hockaday Center for the Arts, 66
Holter Lake, 132
Holter Lake Recreation Area, 139
Holter Museum of Art, 132
Hostels, 88, 94, 174, 184

Hotels, 29–30. See also Lodging in area and town entries; see also Lodging Index
House of a Thousand Dolls, 120
House of Mystery, 85
Humbug Spires Primitive Area, 153–54, 155
Hungry Horse: dining, 88; lodging, 86; sights, 85–86
Hungry Horse Dam, 85–86
Huntley: sights, 251–52
Huntley Project Museum of Irrigated Agriculture, 251
Huntley School, 264
Huson: sights, 45–46
Hutterite colonies, 117
Hyalite Canyon Recreation Area, 178
Hysham: sights, 252

I.G. Baker House, 120
Ice skating, 222
Ingomar: dining, 242
Interagency Aerial Fire Control Center, 183
International travelers, 35–36
Izaak Walton Inn, 86

Jackson: dining, 155; sights, 155
Jackson Glacier, 90
Jackson Hole Airport, 230
James Kipp Recreation Area, 268
Jardine: sights, 190
Jefferson County Courthouse, 133
Jewel Basin Hiking Area, 65
Joe (town), 254
John Deere Tractor Collection & Museum, 265
Johnson Bell International Airport, 83
Jordan: lodging, 269; sights, 268
Judith Peak Recreation Area, 267

Kalispell: dining, 68; lodging, 67; nightlife, 70; shopping, 69; sights, 66
Kayaking, 78
Kerr Dam, 59
Kings Hill area, 121–23; camping, 123; dining, 123; lodging, 122–23; parks, 123; sights, 121–22
Kings Hill National Scenic Byway, 121
Kootenai National Forest, 73–74

Lake Como Recreation Area, 57
Lake Elmo State Park, 244
Lake Elwell, 117
Lake Koocanusa, 71–72
Lake Mary Ronan State Park, 65
Lake McDonald, 89
Lake McDonald Lodge, 89

Lake Village. See Yellowstone Lake area
Lake Yellowstone Hotel, 215
Lakeview: sights, 157
Lamar River, 212
Lame Deer: sights, 247
Landusky: sights, 264
Last Chance Gulch, 130
Laurel: sights, 236–37
Law Enforcement Museum, 143
Lee Metcalf National Wildlife Refuge, 52
Lee Metcalf Wilderness Area, 173, 179
Lewis and Clark Caverns State Park, 180, 182–83
Lewis and Clark National Forest, 113, 115
Lewis and Clark State Memorial, 120
Lewis Lake, 216
Lewis River and Falls, 216
Lewistown: dining, 269; lodging, 269; nightlife, 269; shopping, 269; sights, 267
Libby: dining, 73; lodging, 72; nightlife, 73; shopping, 73; sights, 71–72
Libby Dam, 71
Liberty County Museum, 117
Lima: lodging, 158; sights, 157
Lincoln: dining, 137; lodging, 136; sights, 134
Little Bighorn Battlefield National Monument, 241, 245, 249–50
Little Rocky Mountains, 262, 264
Livingston area, 186–87, 190–92; dining, 191; lodging, 190–91; nightlife, 191–92; parks, 192; shopping, 191; sights, 187, 190; visitor information, 187
Livingston Depot Center, 187
Llama treks, 80, 100–101, 165, 202, 228
Lodging, 29–30. See also Lodging in area and town entries; see also Lodging Index
Logan: sights, 179
Logan Pass, 90
Logan State Park, 74
Lolo Hot Springs (town): lodging, 54; sights, 51–52
Lolo Hot Springs, 51–52
Lolo National Forest, 51
Lolo Pass Visitors Information Center, 52
Loma: sights, 120–21
Lone Pine State Park, 70
Lone Wolf Wildlife Museum, 187
Lost Creek State Park, 144–45
Lost Trail Powder Mountain ski area, 53–54
Love Stone Mine, 133
Lovell (Wyoming) area: lodging, 248; sights, 246
Lower Geyser Basin, 218

Lower Yosemite Valley, 251–57; camping, 257; dining, 256; lodging, 255–56; nightlife, 256; parks, 256–57; sights, 251–55

Mac's Museum, 247–48
Madison Area-West Entrance (Yellowstone): sights, 218
Madison Buffalo Jump State Park, 179, 182
Madison Canyon Earthquake Area and Visitor Center, 184
Madison County Museum, 161
Madison Valley Highway, 180–81
Mai Wah Society, 148
Makoshika State Park, 254, 256–57
Malmstrom Air Force Base Museum and Air Park, 108
Malta: sights, 264
Mammoth Hot Springs, 209–10
Mammoth Hot Springs area (Yellowstone): dining, 222; lodging, 220; sights, 208–11
Many Glacier, 90–91
Many Glacier Hotel, 91
Marcus Daly Mansion, 53
Marias Museum of History and Art, 116
Martin City: lodging, 86
Martinsdale: lodging, 123
Marysville: sights, 134
Maverick Mountain, 154
McCone County Museum, 268
McLeod: lodging, 194
Meagher County Museum, 122
Medicine Lake National Wildlife Refuge, 265
Medicine Rocks State Park, 255, 257
Mehmke's Steam Engine Museum, 121
Miles City: dining, 256; lodging, 255; nightlife, 256; sights, 252–53
Mineral Museum, 147
Miracle of America Museum, 59
Mission Mountain Winery, 60
Mission Mountains Wilderness Area, 58, 64
Mission Range (Rockies), 58
Missoula, 42, 44–51; camping, 51; dining, 47–48; lodging, 46–47; nightlife, 49–50; parks, 50–51; shopping, 48–49; sights, 42, 44–46; visitor information, 42
Missoula County Courthouse, 44
Missoula Memorial Rose Garden, 45
Missoula Museum of the Arts, 44
Missouri Breaks National Back Country Byway, 268
Missouri Headwaters State Park, 180, 182
Moiese: sights, 58
Monarch: dining, 123
MonDak Heritage Center, 268

Montana: animals, 14–16; areas, 16–18; calendar of events, 20–27; geology, 4–5; history, 5, 8–12; map, 3; outdoor adventures, 36–40; plants, 13–14; visitor information, 27–28; weather, 18–20. *See also specific areas and towns*
Montana College of Mineral Science & Technology, 147
Montana Cowboys Association Museum, 108
Montana Historical Society Museum, 132
Montana State Capitol, 130, 132
Montana State University, 170
Montana Territorial Prison, 142–43
Moss Mansion, 233–34
Mount Helena, 132
Mount Helena City Park, 138–39
Mount Washburn, 212
Mountain climbing, 230
Museum of the Beartooths, 193
Museum of the National Park Ranger, 214, 219
Museum of the Northern Great Plains, 120
Museum of the Plains Indians, 93
Museum of the Rockies, 170
Museum of the Upper Missouri, 120
Museum of the Yellowstone, 183
Musselshell Valley and River, 237

National Bison Range, 57–58
Neihart: sights, 122
Nevada City: dining, 162; sights, 149, 160–61
Nevada City Museum. *See* Nevada City
Neversweat and Washoe Railroad, 147
New Horizon Horse World, 236
Ninemile Remount Depot, 45–46
Ninepipe National Wildlife Refuge, 59
Norris: dining, 182; sights, 180
Norris Area (Yellowstone): sights, 218–20
Norris Geyser Basin, 218–219
Norris Geyser Basin Museum, 219
North American Wildlife Museum, 85
North central Montana, 105–128; calendar of events, 20–27; introduction, 105; map, 107; outdoor adventures, 123–27; transportation, 127–28
Northeast Montana, 261–75; calendar of events, 20–27; introduction, 261; map, 263; outdoor adventures, 272–74; transportation, 274–75
Northern Cheyenne Arts and Crafts Center, 247
Northern Cheyenne Indian Reservation, 247
Northern Pacific Depot (Missoula), 42

Northern Plains Soil and Water Research Center, 268
Northwest Corner area, 71–74; camping, 74; dining, 73; lodging, 72; nightlife, 73; parks, 73–74; shopping, 73; sights, 71–72
Northwest Montana, 41–83; calendar of events, 20–27; introduction, 41–42; map, 43; outdoor adventures, 75–82; transportation, 82–83
Noxon: lodging, 75
Noxon Rapids Reservoir, 74

O'Fallon Historical Museum, 255
Old Faithful area (Yellowstone): dining, 222; lodging, 221–22; sights, 216–18; visitor information, 216
Old Faithful Geyser, 216
Old Fire Tower, 132
Old Fort Benton, 120
Old Jail Museum, 74
Old Montana Prison, 142–43
Old No. 1 trolley, 146
Old Trail Museum, 113
Older travelers, 34
Original Governor's Mansion, 132
Osborn: sights, 251
Oscar's Dreamland, 236
Our Lady of the Rockies statue, 148

Pablo: sights, 58–59
Pablo National Wildlife Refuge, 59
Pack trips, 80, 100–101, 125, 165, 202, 226
Packing, 28–29
Paddlefish, 254
Painted Rocks State Park, 53, 57
Paradise Valley, 187, 190
Paris Gibson Square, 108
Park County Museum, 187
Pelican Creek Flats, 215
Pendroy: dining, 115
Permits and licenses, 37–38, 39, 40
Peter Yegen, Jr., Yellowstone County Museum, 234
Petrified trees, 211
Pets, traveling with, 33
Philipsburg: shopping, 144; sights, 141–42, 149
Phillips County Museum, 264
Pictograph Cave State Park, 234, 236
Pierre Wibaux House Museum, 254
Pine Butte Swamp Preserve, 114
Pintler scenic route, 140–45; camping, 145; dining, 144; lodging, 143–44; nightlife, 144; parks, 144–45; shopping, 144; sights, 141–43
Pioneer Cabin, 132

Pioneer Mountains Scenic Byway, 154
Placid Lake, 60
Placid Lake State Park, 65–66
Plains Indian Museum, 247
Plants, 13–14
Plentywood: sights, 266
Polaris: lodging, 155; sights, 154
Polebridge: lodging, 88; sights, 86
Polson: dining, 62; lodging, 61; nightlife, 64; shopping, 63; sights, 59
Polson-Flathead Historical Museum, 59
Pompeys Pillar, 251–52
Porcupines, 33
Powder River Historical Museum, 247
Powder River Taxidermy Wildlife Museum, 248
Powell County Museum, 143
Prairie County Museum, 253
Pray: sights, 187
Pryor: lodging, 248; sights, 246–47
Pryor Mountain National Wild Horse Range, 246
Public transit. See Transportation in area chapters

Rafting, 38–39. See also Outdoor adventures in area chapters
Range Riders Museum, 253
Rattlesnake National Recreation and Wilderness, 50–51
Ravalli: sights, 59
Ravalli County Museum, 53
Red Lodge area, 194–99; camping, 199; dining, 198; lodging, 197–98; nightlife, 198; parks, 198–99; sights, 195–97
Red Lodge Mountain Ski Area, 196
Red Rock Lakes National Wildlife Refuge, 157, 159–60
Red Rock Parkway, 96
Red Rock River Valley. See Dillon and the Red Rock River Valley
Restaurants, 30–31. See also Dining in area and town entries; see also Dining Index
Richey Museum, 268
Riding stables. See Outdoor adventures in area chapters
Rising Sun: sights, 90
River running. See Outdoor adventures in area chapters
Riverfront Steamboat Levee, 119–20
Robber's Roost, 160
Rocky Boy's Indian Reservation, 118
Rocky Mountain Elk Foundation, 45
Rocky Mountain Front, 113–16; camping, 115, 116; dining, 115; lodging, 114–15; nightlife, 115; parks, 115–16; sights, 113–14

Rodeos, 270–71
Roe River, 106
Roosevelt Lodge, 211
Rosebud Battlefield State Park, 247
Rosebud County Courthouse, 252
Ross Creek Cedar Grove Scenic Area, 72
Roundup: dining, 242; sights, 237
Roundup Cattle Drive, 237
Russell, Charles M., 106, 108, 111

Sacajawea Inn, 179
Sacajawea Park, 192
Saco: sights, 264
St. Francis Xavier Catholic Church
    (Missoula), 44
St. Helena Cathedral, 130
St. Ignatius: lodging, 61; shopping, 63;
    sights, 58
St. Ignatius Mission, 58
St. Lawrence O'Toole Church, 148
St. Mary: lodging, 94; sights, 90, 93
St. Mary Lake and River, 90
St. Mary's Mission, 52
St. Paul's Episcopal Church (Fort Benton),
    120
St. Peter's Catholic Church (Wibaux),
    254–55
St. Richard's Catholic Church (Columbia
    Falls), 67
Salmon Lake, 60
Salmon Lake State Park, 65–66
Sapphire Gallery, 142
Scapegoat Wilderness Area, 134, 140
Scobey: lodging, 266; sights, 265–66
Seeley Lake (town): shopping, 64
Seeley Lake, 60
Selway-Bitterroot Wilderness Area, 56–57
Senior travelers, 34
Shawmut: sights, 237
Shelby: dining, 119; lodging, 118; sights,
    116; visitor information, 117
Sheridan: sights, 160
Sheridan County Museum, 266
Shiloh Rifle Manufacturing Co., 193
Showdown Ski Area, 122
Sidney: dining, 269; lodging, 269; sights,
    268
Silver Gate: sights, 197
Skiing. *See* Outdoor adventures *in area
    chapters*
Sluice Boxes State Park, 121, 123
Smith River State Park, 123
Smokejumper Training Center and Aerial
    Fire Depot, 45
Snakes, 15
Sodbuster Museum, 267
Soldier's Chapel, 173
Somers: dining, 62; shopping, 63

South central Montana, 169–206; calendar
    of events, 20–27; introduction, 169;
    maps, 171, 175; outdoor adventures,
    199–205; transportation, 205–206
Southeast Montana, 232–60; calendar of
    events, 20–27; introduction, 232–33;
    maps, 235, 239; outdoor adventures,
    257–59; transportation, 259–60
Southwest Montana, 129–68; calendar of
    events, 20–27; introduction, 129; maps,
    131, 135, 147; outdoor adventures,
    163–67; transportation, 168
Spa Hot Springs Motel, 122
Specimen Ridge, 211
Spokane Bar Mine, 133
Sqélix'w-Aqsmakni'k Cultural Center,
    58–59
Square Butte Natural Area, 121
Steam Railroad Museum, 161–62
Stevensville: sights, 52
Stevensville Historical Museum, 52
Sun River Game Range, 114
Swan Lake, 60
Swan Lake Road (Route 83), 60
Sweetgrass: sights, 117
Swiftcurrent Lake, 91
Sylvan Pass, 215

Tammany Castle, 53
Taxis. *See* Transportation *in area chapters*
Ten Lakes Scenic Area, 72
Tennis, 80, 125, 165, 202, 258
Terry: sights, 253
Terry Badlands, 253
Thompson Falls area, 74–75; camping, 75;
    dining, 75; lodging, 75; parks, 75; sights,
    74–75
Thompson Falls State Park, 75
Thompson-Hickman Memorial Museum,
    161
Three Forks area, 179–83; camping, 182,
    183; dining, 182; lodging, 181; parks,
    182–83; sights, 179–81
Tobacco Valley Historic Village, 72
Tongue River Reservoir State Park, 251
Towe Ford Museum, 143
Tower Junction. *See* Tower-Roosevelt area
Tower-Roosevelt area (Yellowstone): din-
    ing, 222; lodging, 220; sights, 211–12
Townsend: lodging, 136
Trail Creek Access Recreation Area,
    180
Trails. *See* Outdoor adventures *in area
    chapters*
Train travel. *See* Transportation *in area
    chapters*
Trout Creek: lodging, 75
Troy: dining, 73; sights, 72

Troy Museum, 72
Twin Bridges: dining, 162
UL Bend National Wildlife Refuge, 265
Ulm Pishkun State Park, 109, 113
United States High Altitude Sports Center, 148
University of Montana, 44–45
Upper Geyser Basin, 217
Upper Missouri National Wild and Scenic River, 120
Upper Musselshell Museum, 237
Upper Terrace Loop Drive (Yellowstone), 210

Valley County Pioneer Museum, 264
Vandalia: lodging, 266
Victor: dining, 55; shopping, 56; sights, 53
Victor Heritage Museum, 53
Victorian Village, 192–93
Virgelle: sights, 121
Virginia City: dining, 162; lodging, 162; nightlife, 162–63; shopping, 162; sights, 161; visitor information, 161
Visitor information, 27–28. See also Visitor information in area and town entries

Wahkpa Chug'n archaeology site, 118
Walkerville: sights, 148
War Horse National Wildlife Refuge, 267
Washoe Theater, 141
Waterton Inter-Nation Shoreline Cruises, 95
Waterton Lakes National Park area, 95–97; camping, 97; dining, 97; lodging, 96–97; parks, 97; sights, 95–96; visitor information, 95
Weather, 18–20, 208
Weeping Wall, 90
Welcome Creek Wilderness Area, 51
West Glacier: dining, 88; lodging, 86; sights, 86, 87; visitor information, 87
West Thumb. See Grant Village-West Thumb area
West Thumb Bay, 215
West Thumb Geyser Basin, 215–16
West Yellowstone Airport, 230
West Yellowstone area, 183–86; camping, 186; dining, 185; lodging, 184–85; nightlife, 186; parks, 186; shopping, 185–86; sights, 183–84; visitor information, 184

Western Gateways area (Glacier National Park), 85–86, 88; camping, 88; dining, 88; lodging, 86, 88; parks, 88; sights, 85–86
Western Heritage Center, 234
Western Hi-Line area, 116–19; camping, 119; dining, 119; lodging, 118–19; nightlife, 119; parks, 119; sights, 116–18
Western Montana College, 156
White Sulphur Springs (town): lodging, 122–23; sights, 122
Whitefish: dining, 68–69; lodging, 67–68; nightlife, 69–70; shopping, 69; sights, 66
Whitefish Lake, 66
Whitefish Lake State Park, 70–71
Whitewater rafting. See Rafting
Whoop-Up Trail, 117
Wibaux: sights, 254
Wildlife, 14–16, 33, 99
Winter sports, 40, 227. See also specific sports
Wisdom: dining, 155; sights, 154–55
Wise River: dining, 155; lodging, 155; sights, 154
Wolf Point: dining, 266; lodging, 266; sights, 265
Wolf Point Area Historical Society Museum, 265
Wolves, 14
Women, traveling alone, 33
Woodland Park, 70
World Museum of Mining, 146–47

Yellowstone Airport, 205
Yellowstone Art Center, 234
Yellowstone IMAX Theatre, 183
Yellowstone Institute, 212
Yellowstone Kelly Grave, 234
Yellowstone Lake area: dining, 222; lodging, 221; sights, 214–15; visitor information, 214
Yellowstone National Park area, 207–31; calendar of events, 20–27; camping, 223, 224; dining, 222; introduction, 207–208; lodging, 220–22; map, 209; outdoor adventures, 224–30; parks, 222–24; sights, 208–20; transportation, 230–31; weather, 208
Yellowstone River Trout Hatchery, 193
Yellowstone Wildlife Museum, 197
Yellowtail Dam, 246
Yesterday's Playthings, 143

ZooMontana, 236
Zortman: sights, 262, 264

Lodging Index

All Seasons Mine Co. Hotel & Casino, 198
Alpine Lodge, 173–74
Al's Westward Ho Motel, 185
Aspen Village Inn, 96

Bad Rock Country B&B, 68
Barrister Bed & Breakfast, 134
Bayshore Inn, 96
Best Western Colonial Inn, 136
Best Western Copper King Park Hotel, 150
Best Western GranTree Inn, 174
Best Western Hamilton Inn, 54
Best Western Heritage Inn, 109
Best Western Outlaw Inn, 67
Best Western Paradise Inn, 158
Best Western Ponderosa Inn, 238
Best Western War Bonnet Inn, 255
Bighorn Lodge, 75
Blue Spruce Lodge, 75
Bonanza Creek Country, 123
Broken Spur Motel, 181
Brownie's Grocery and AYH Hostel, 94
Buckboard Inn, 255
Burggraf's Countrylane B&B, 62

C-J Motel, 248–49
C. M. Russell Lodge, 194
Caboose Motel, 72
Canyon Lodge & Cabins, 220–21
Capri Motel, 150
Cattle King Motor Inn, 266
Colonial House, 46
Copper King Mansion, 148
Corral Motel, 238
Country Lane Bed & Breakfast, 114
Crandell Mountain Lodge, 96–97
Creekside Inn, 46

Deffy's Motel, 54
Double J Bed & Breakfast, 266

El-Cortez Motel, 97
El Toro Inn, 118–19
Elk Horn Hot Springs Lodge, 155

Fairmont Hot Springs Resort, 143
Fairweather Inn, 162
Finlen Hotel and Motor Inn, 150
Flathead Lake Lodge, 61
Fort at Lolo Hot Springs, 54

Fort Motel, 121
4B's Inn North, 46
4B's Inn South, 46

Gallatin Gateway Inn, 174
Glacier Gateway Inn, 118
Glacier Highland Motel, 86
Glacier Park Lodge, 93–94
Goldsmith's Inn, 46
Grant Village, 221
Great Falls Inn, 109
Great Northern Chalets, 86

Hensley 287 Motel, 114
Hibernation House, 68
Holiday Inn (Bozeman), 174
Holiday Inn Billings Plaza, 238
Holiday Inn Missoula-Parkside, 46
Huckleberry Hannah's, 72
Hungry Horse Motel, 86
Huntley Lodge at Big Sky, 174

Izaak Walton Inn, 88

Jacobson's Scenic View Cottages, 94
Jordan Motor Inn, 255–56
Josephine Bed & Breakfast, 238

Kalispell Grand Hotel, 67
Kendrick House Inn, 248
Kilmorey Lodge, 96
King's Carriage Inn, 136
Kootenai Country Inn B&B, 72
KwaTaqNuk Resort at Flathead Bay, 61

Lake Lodge and Cabins, 221
Lake McDonald Lodge, 91
Lake Yellowstone Hotel & Cabins, 221
Leeper's Motel, 136

Madison Hotel Youth Hostel, 184
Mammoth Hot Springs Hotel, 220
Mandorla Ranch Bed & Breakfast, 61
Many Glacier Hotel, 91
Metlen Hotel, 157
Middle Fork Motel, 86
Montana Mountain Lodge, 122
Mountain Holiday Motel, 67
Mountain Pine Motel, 94
Murray Hotel, 190

North Fork Hostel, 88
Northland Lodge, 97

O'Haire Manor Motel, 118
Old Faithful Inn, 221
Old Faithful Lodge and Cabins, 221
Old Faithful Snow Lodge & Cabins, 221–22

Park Plaza Hotel, 136
Pioneer Lodge, 121
Pollard Hotel, 197
Prince of Wales Hotel, 96

Radisson Northern Hotel, 238
Rainbow Valley Motel, 181
Richland Motor Inn, 269
Rimrock Inn, 238
Rising Sun Motor Inn, 92
Rock Creek Resort, 197
Roosevelt Lodge and Cabins, 220
Ruby's Reserve Street Inn, 46

Sacajawea Hostel, 174
Sacajawea Inn, 181
Sacred Ground, 248
Sagebrush Inn, 256
St. Mary Lodge and Resort, 94
Scharf's Motor Inn, 144
Sherman Motor Inn, 266
The Sanders—Helena's Bed & Breakfast, 134
Sovekammer Bed & Breakfast, 109
Spa Hot Springs Motel, 123
Stage Coach Inn, 185
Stillwater Inn, 67
The Summit Bed & Breakfast Inn, 143–44
Sundance Lodge, 155
Sundowner Motel, 157
Swan Hill Bed and Breakfast, 61
Swiftcurrent Motor Inn, 92
Switzer House Inn, 67

Timbers Motel, 61–62
TownHouse Inns of Havre, 118
Travelers Lodge, 185
Triple Crown Motor Inn, 109

Village Inn Motel, 92
Village Red Lion Motor Inn, 46
Virginia City Country Inn, 162
Voss Inn, 173

War Bonnet Inn, 150
War Bonnet Lodge, 94
Western Motel, 248
Westwood Motor Inn, 255
Wright Nite Inns Wagon Wheel Motel, 109–10

Yellowstone Village Motel, 191
Yodeler Motel, 197
Yogo Inn, 269

GUEST RANCHES
Bear Creek Guest Ranch, 94
Beartooth Ranch, 189
Boulder River Ranch, 194
C-B Cattle and Guest Ranch, 189
Diamond J Ranch, 189
G Bar M Ranch, 189
Grassy Mountain Ranch, 136
Hell Creek Guest Ranch, 269
Klicks' K Bar L Ranch, 115
Lakeview Guest Ranch, 158
Lone Mountain Ranch, 174–75
Lost Fork Ranch, 181
Mountain Sky Guest Ranch, 190
Nez Perce Ranch, 54–55
Schively Ranch, 248
Seven Lazy P Ranch, 114–15
Triple Creek Ranch, 55
West Fork Meadows Ranch, 55

LODGING SERVICES
Alberta Tourism Office, 96
Dude Ranchers' Association, 188
Flathead Convention & Visitors Association, 68
Glacier Park, Inc., Lodging, 91
TW Recreational Services, 220
Waterton Chamber of Commerce, 96

Dining Index

Alice's Restaurant, 185
Allentown Restaurant, 62
Alley Cat Grill, 48
Anna's Oven, 158
Avalon Café & Books, 47

Bacchus Pub, 175
Bad Bubba's BBQ, 55
Bale of Hay Saloon, 162
Banque Club (Fort Benton), 121
Banque Club (Hamilton), 55
Barclay II Supper Club & Lounge, 144
Bear Pit Dining Room, 222
Beck's Montana Cafe, 73
Bert & Ernie's Saloon and Eatery, 137
Bigfork Inn, 63
Black Angus Supper Club, 119
Black Dog Café, 47–48
Black Horse Inn, 56
Blue Anchor Restaurant, 162
The Boondocks, 73
Borrie's, 110
Boxcars, 119
Bridge Street Gallery & Wine Café, 63
Broken Arrow Casino & Steakhouse, 144
Bruno's Italian Specialties, 242
Buck's T-4, 176
Buffalo Lodge, 158
Bulldog Pub & Steakhouse, 68
Busy Bee, 242

Calamity Jane's Steakhouse, 191
Canyon Lodge Dining Room, 222
China Garden, 62
Community Food Co-op, 176
Continental Divide Restaurant, 182
Crosswinds Restaurant, 158
Custer's Last Root Beer Stand, 182

Eddie's Restaurant, 92
Eddie's Supper Club, 110
El Comedor, 110
Exchange Bar & Grill, 55

Fenders Restaurant & Lounge, 68
Fetty's Bar & Cafe, 155
Food For Thought, 47
4B's Restaurant, 119
Four Seasons Deli, 222
Fred's Mesquite Diner, 176

Gameroom Grill, 176
Girdle Mountain Summer House, 123
Glacier Grande Rio Grande Cafe, 68
Glacier Highland Motel Restaurant, 88
Glacier Village Restaurant, 94–95
Goat Lick Dining Room, 94
The Granary, 242
Grand Hotel, 194
Granny's Home Cooking, 75
Great Wall Restaurant, 242
The Grubstake, 56

The Hamilton, 55
Hearthstone Whole Grain Bakery & Café,
    176
Hole in the Wall, 256
Huckleberry Patch, 88

Jaker's Steak & Fish House, 239, 242
Jake's Restaurant, 110
Jersey Lilly Bar & Café, 242
Joan & Bill's Restaurant, 198
John Bozeman's Bistro, 176
Juliano's, 239

Kathy's Kitchen, 119
Khanthaly's Eggrolls, 242

Lake Yellowstone Hotel Dining Room,
    222
Lamp Post Dining Room, 97
Lazy Doe, 123
Lighterside Restaurant, 68
Lily Restaurant, 48
Log Cabin Family Restaurant, 115
Lonesome Dome, 75
Lost Horse Saloon & Eatery, 56
Louie's Olive Dining Room, 256
Lydia's Supper Club, 151

Mama Cassie's Italian Ristorante, 110
Mammoth Hotel Dining Room, 222
Merry Mixer Restaurant & Lounge, 249
Metals Banque Restaurant, 151
The Mine Shaft, 158
Montana Bar & Cafe, 249
Montana Brewing Company, 242
Montana Grill on Flathead Lake, 62
Montana Hanna's Trout Hole Restaurant,
    194

Morning Light, 110
Mustard Seed, 48

Old Nine Mile Inn, 95
Old West Dinner Cookout, 222
On Broadway, 137
Out to Lunch at Caras Park, 47
Outpost Deli, 115
Overland Express, 137

Pekin Noodle Parlor, 151
Pius' International Room, 198
The Place, 69
Pony Express, 222
Pork Chop John's, 151
Purple Cow, 249

Queen City Cafe, 136–37

Red Rooster Supper Club, 151
Rocky Mountain Pasta Company, 175
The Rose Room, 115
Rose's Cantina, 155
Rose's Tea Room, 144
Round Barn, 198
Rustler's Roost, 185

Sakelaris' Kitchen, 256
Sam's Supper Club, 266
Santorno's Italian Restaurant, 48
Schoolhouse Restaurant, 182
Serrano's, 95

17 Broadway: The Restaurant, 198
Seven-Up Ranch Supper Club, 137
Shake & Burger Hut, 249
Silver Basin Inn, 88
South 40, 269
Star Bakery, 162
Stavers Restaurant, 55
The Steakhouse, 222
Stockmen's Bar & Cafe, 266
Stonehouse Restaurant, 136
Swan River Café, 63
Sykes' Grocery, Market & Restaurant, 68

Terrace Grill, 222
Three Bear Restaurant, 185
3D International, 110
Tracy's Restaurant at Meadow Lake, 69
Twilite Dining & Lounge, 256

Uptown Café, 151

Valerie's Tea Room, 97

Walkers Grill, 239
White Knight Pub & Seafood, 73
Whole Famdamily, 269
Winchester Cafe, 191
Windbag Saloon, 137
Wise River Club, 155

Yellowstone Mine Restaurant, 191

Notes

HIDDEN GUIDES

Adventure travel or a relaxing vacation?—"Hidden" guidebooks are the only travel books in the business to provide detailed information on both. Aimed at environmentally aware travelers, our motto is "Adventure Travel Plus." These books combine details on unique hotels, restaurants and sightseeing with information on camping, sports and hiking for the outdoor enthusiast.

THE NEW KEY GUIDES

Based on the concept of ecotourism, The New Key Guides are dedicated to the preservation of Central America's rare and endangered species, architecture and archaeology. Filled with helpful tips, they give travelers everything they need to know about these exotic destinations.

ULTIMATE FAMILY GUIDES

These innovative guides present the best and most unique features of a family destination. Quality is the keynote. In addition to thoroughly covering each destination, they feature short articles and one-line "teasers" that are both fun and informative.

Order Form

Ulysses Press books are available at bookstores everywhere. If any of the following titles are unavailable at your local bookstore, ask the bookseller to order them. Or you can order them directly from Ulysses Press (P.O. Box 3440, Berkeley, CA 94703; 510-601-8301, 800-377-2542, fax: 510-601-8307).

HIDDEN GUIDEBOOKS

____ Hidden Arizona, $13.95

____ Hidden Boston and Cape Cod, $11.95

____ Hidden Carolinas, $16.95

____ Hidden Coast of California, $16.95

____ Hidden Colorado, $13.95

____ Hidden Florida, $16.95

____ Hidden Florida Keys and
Everglades, $9.95

____ Hidden Hawaii, $16.95

____ Hidden Idaho, $13.95

____ Hidden Maui, $12.95

____ Hidden Montana, $13.95

____ Hidden New England, $16.95

____ Hidden New Mexico, $13.95

____ Hidden Oregon, $13.95

____ Hidden Pacific Northwest, $16.95

____ Hidden Rockies, $16.95

____ Hidden San Francisco and
Northern California, $15.95

____ Hidden Southern California,
$16.95

____ Hidden Southwest, $16.95

____ Hidden Tahiti, $16.95

____ Hidden Wyoming, $13.95

THE NEW KEY GUIDEBOOKS

____ The New Key to Belize, $14.95

____ The New Key to Cancún and
the Yucatán, $14.95

____ The New Key to Costa Rica, $16.95

____ The New Key to Ecuador and
the Galápagos, $15.95

____ The New Key to Guatemala, $14.95

ULTIMATE FAMILY GUIDEBOOKS

____ Disneyland and Beyond, $12.95

____ Disney World and Beyond, $12.95

Mark the book(s) you're ordering and enter the total cost here ⇨ [   ]

California residents add 8% sales tax here ⇨ [   ]

Shipping, check box for your preferred method and enter cost here ⇨ [   ]

❑ BOOK RATE   **FREE! FREE! FREE!**

❑ PRIORITY MAIL $3.00 First book, $1.00/each additional book

❑ UPS 2-DAY AIR $7.00 First book, $1.00/each additional book

[   ]

Billing, enter total amount due here and check method of payment ⇨

❑ CHECK   ❑ MONEY ORDER

❑ VISA/MASTERCARD _____ EXP. DATE _____

NAME _____ PHONE _____

ADDRESS _____

_____

CITY _____ STATE _____ ZIP _____

MONEY-BACK GUARANTEE ON DIRECT ORDERS PLACED THROUGH ULYSSES PRESS.

ABOUT THE AUTHOR

JOHN GOTTBERG ANDERSON is a co-author of several other books for Ulysses Press, including *Hidden Pacific Northwest* and *Hidden Rockies*. Formerly chief editor of the Insight Travel Guide series and travel news editor and graphics editor for the *Los Angeles Times*, he has traveled and worked all over the world. He has written ten other books and co-authored nine more, and his credits in more than 50 magazines and newspapers include *Travel & Leisure* and *Islands*. He is presently a contributing editor for *International Living* magazine and the restaurant critic for the *Idaho Statesman* in Boise where he lives.

ABOUT THE ILLUSTRATOR

DOUG MCCARTHY is the co-owner of Graphic Detail, a specialty graphics company in Berkeley. A native New Yorker, he lives in the San Francisco Bay area with his family.